HTTP Programming Recipes for
C# Bots

HTTP Programming Recipes for C# Bots

by Jeff Heaton

Heaton Research, Inc.
St. Louis

HTTP Programming Recipes for C# Bots, First Edition

First printing

Publisher: Heaton Research, Inc

Author: Jeff Heaton

Editor: Mark Biss

Cover Art: Carrie Spear

ISBN's for all Editions:
0-9773206-7-7, Softcover
0-9773206-9-3, Adobe PDF e-book

SOFTWARE LICENSE AGREEMENT: TERMS AND CONDITIONS

The media and/or any online materials accompanying this book that are available now or in the future contain programs and/or text files (the "Software") to be used in connection with the book. Heaton Research, Inc. hereby grants to you a license to use and distribute software programs that make use of the compiled binary form of this book's source code. You may not redistribute the source code contained in this book, without the written permission of Heaton Research, Inc. Your purchase, acceptance, or use of the Software will constitute your acceptance of such terms.

The Software compilation is the property of Heaton Research, Inc. unless otherwise indicated and is protected by copyright to Heaton Research, Inc. or other copyright owner(s) as indicated in the media files (the "Owner(s)"). You are hereby granted a license to use and distribute the Software for your personal, noncommercial use only. You may not reproduce, sell, distribute, publish, circulate, or commercially exploit the Software, or any portion thereof, without the written consent of Heaton Research, Inc. and the specific copyright owner(s) of any component software included on this media.

In the event that the Software or components include specific license requirements or end-user agreements, statements of condition, disclaimers, limitations or warranties ("End-User License"), those End-User Licenses supersede the terms and conditions herein as to that particular Software component. Your purchase, acceptance, or use of the Software will constitute your acceptance of such End-User Licenses.

By purchase, use or acceptance of the Software you further agree to comply with all export laws and regulations of the United States as such laws and regulations may exist from time to time.

SOFTWARE SUPPORT

Components of the supplemental Software and any offers associated with them may be supported by the specific Owner(s) of that material but they are not supported by Heaton Research, Inc.. Information regarding any available support may be obtained from the Owner(s) using the information provided in the appropriate README files or listed elsewhere on the media.

Should the manufacturer(s) or other Owner(s) cease to offer support or decline to honor any offer, Heaton Research, Inc. bears no responsibility. This notice concerning support for the Software is provided for your information only. Heaton Research, Inc. is not the agent or principal of the Owner(s), and Heaton Research, Inc. is in no way responsible for providing any support for the Software, nor is it liable or responsible for any support provided, or not provided, by the Owner(s).

WARRANTY

Heaton Research, Inc. warrants the enclosed media to be free of physical defects for a period of ninety (90) days after purchase. The Software is not available from Heaton Research, Inc. in any other form or media than that enclosed herein or posted to www.heatonresearch. com. If you discover a defect in the media during this warranty period, you may obtain a replacement of identical format at no charge by sending the defective media, postage prepaid, with proof of purchase to:

```
Heaton Research, Inc.
Customer Support Department
1734 Clarkson Rd #107
Chesterfield, MO 63017-4976


Web: www.heatonresearch.com
E-Mail: support@heatonresearch.com
```

After the 90-day period, you can obtain replacement media of identical format by sending us the defective disk, proof of purchase, and a check or money order for $10, payable to Heaton Research, Inc..

DISCLAIMER

Heaton Research, Inc. makes no warranty or representation, either expressed or implied, with respect to the Software or its contents, quality, performance, merchantability, or fitness for a particular purpose. In no event will Heaton Research, Inc., its distributors, or dealers be liable to you or any other party for direct, indirect, special, incidental, consequential, or other damages arising out of the use of or inability to use the Software or its contents even if advised of the possibility of such damage. In the event that the Software includes an online update feature, Heaton Research, Inc. further disclaims any obligation to provide this feature for any specific duration other than the initial posting.

The exclusion of implied warranties is not permitted by some states. Therefore, the above exclusion may not apply to you. This warranty provides you with specific legal rights; there may be other rights that you may have that vary from state to state. The pricing of the book with the Software by Heaton Research, Inc. reflects the allocation of risk and limitations on liability contained in this agreement of Terms and Conditions.

SHAREWARE DISTRIBUTION

This Software may contain various programs that are distributed as shareware. Copyright laws apply to both shareware and ordinary commercial software, and the copyright Owner(s) retains all rights. If you try a shareware program and continue using it, you are expected to register it. Individual programs differ on details of trial periods, registration, and payment. Please observe the requirements stated in appropriate files.

*This book is dedicated to
my sister Carrie.*

Acknowledgments

There are several people who I would like to acknowledge. First, I would like to thank the many people who have given me suggestions and comments on the e-book form of this book over the years.

I would like to thank Mary McKinnis for editing the book. I would also like to thank Mary McKinnis for trying out the book examples and offering many helpful suggestions.

I would like to thank my sister Carrie Spear for layout and formatting suggestions. I would like to thank Jeffrey Noedel for suggestions on the book's cover and design.

Contents at a Glance

Contents

Table of Figures

Table of Listings

Table of Tables

INTRODUCTION

The .NET runtime provides a rich set of classes to allow for programmatic access to the web. Using these classes HTTP and HTTPS programs can be created that automate tasks performed by human users of the web. These programs are called bots. Chapters 1 and 2 introduce you to HTTP programming.

Chapter 1 of this book begins by examining the structure of HTTP requests. If you are to create programs that make use of the HTTP protocol it is important to understand the structure of the HTTP protocol. This chapter explains what packets are exchanged between web servers and web browsers, as well as the makeup of these packets.

Chapter 2 shows how to monitor the packets being transferred between a web server and web browser. Using a program, called a Network Analyzer, you can quickly see what HTTP packets are being exchanged. To create a successful bot, your bot must exchange the same packets with the web server that a user would. A Network Analyzer can help quickly create a bot by showing you

From Chapter 3 and beyond this book is structured as a set of recipes. You are provided with short concise programming examples for many common HTTP programming tasks. Most of the chapters are organized into two parts. The first part introduces the topic of the chapter. The second part is a collection of recipes. These recipes are meant to be starting points for your own programs that will require similar functionality.

Chapter 3 shows how to execute simple HTTP requests. A simple HTTP request is one that accesses only a single web page. All data that is needed will be on that page and no additional information must be passed to the web server.

Chapter 4 goes beyond simple requests and shows how to make use of other features of the HTTP protocol. HTTP server and client headers are introduced. Additionally, you will be shown how to access data from basic HTML files.

Chapter 5 shows how to use HTTPS. HTTPS is the more secure version of HTTP. Use of HTTPS is generally automatic in C#. However, you will be shown some of the HTTPS specific features that C# provides, and how to use them. You will also be introduced to HTTP authentication, which is a means by which the web server can prompt the user for an id and password.

Chapter 6 shows how to access data from a variety of HTML sources. An HTML parser is developed that will be used with most of the remaining recipes in this book. You are shown how to use this parser to extract data from forms, lists, tables and other structures. Recipes are provided that will serve as a good starting point for any of these HTML constructs.

Chapter 7 shows how to interact with HTML forms. HTML forms are very important to web sites that need to interact with the user. This chapter will show how to construct the appropriate response to an HTML form. You are shown how each of the control types of the form interacts with the web server.

Chapter 8 shows how to handle cookies and sessions. You will see that the web server can track who is logged on and maintain a session using either cookies or a URL variable. A useful class will be developed that will handle cookie processing in C#.

Chapter 9 explains the effects that JavaScript can have on a bot. JavaScript allows programs to be executed by the web browser. This can complicate matters for bots. The bot programmer must understand how JavaScript helps to shape the content of HTTP packets being produced by the browser. The bot must provide these same packets if it is to work properly.

Chapter 10 explains the effects that AJAX can have on a bot. AJAX is based on XML and JavaScript. It has many of the same effects on a bot program as JavaScript does. However, most AJAX web sites are designed to communicate with the web server using XML. This can make creating a bot for an AJAX website easier.

Chapter 11 introduces web services. Web services have replaced many of the functions previously performed by bots. Sites that make use of web services provide access to their data through XML. This makes it considerably easier to access their data than writing a traditional bot. Additionally, you can use web services in conjunction with regular bot programming. This produces a hybrid bot.

Chapter 12 shows how to create bots that make use of RSS feeds. RSS is an XML format that allows quick access to the newest content on a web site. Bots can be constructed to automatically access RSS information from a web site.

Chapter 13 introduces the Heaton Research Spider. The Heaton Research Spider is an open source implementation of a C# spider. There is also a Java version of the Heaton Research Spider. A spider is a program that is designed to access a large number of web pages. The spider does this by continuously visiting the links of web pages, and then pages found at those links. A web spider visits sites much as a biological spider crawls its web.

The remaining chapters of the chapters of this book do not include recipes. Chapters 14 and 15 explain how the Heaton Research Spider works. Chapter 16 explains how to create well behaved bots.

Chapter 14 explains the internals of the Heaton Research Spider. The Heaton Research Spider is open source. Because of this you can modify it to suit your needs. Chapter 14 discusses the internal structure of the Heaton Research Spider. By default the Heaton Research Spider uses computer memory to track the list of visited URLs. This chapter explains how this memory based URL tracking works. The next chapter explains how to use an SQL database instead of computer memory.

Chapter 15 explains how the Heaton Research Spider makes use of databases. The Heaton Research Spider can use databases to track the URLs that it has visited. This allows the spider to access a much larger volume of URLs than when using computer memory to track the URL list.

The book ends with Chapter 16 which discusses how to create "Well Behaved Bots". Bots are not welcome on all web sites. Some web sites publish files that outline how bots are to access their site. It is very important to respect the wishes of the web master when creating a bot.

CHAPTER 1: THE STRUCTURE OF HTTP REQUESTS

- Understanding the Structure of Surfing
- Using the HTTP Recipes Web Site
- Understanding HTTP Requests

This book shows how to create HTTP programs in C#. Though the code presented is targeted at C#, the examples could be translated to any of the other .Net languages, such as Visual Basic .Net. HTTP programming allows programs to be constructed that send and retrieve information from web sites in much the same way as a human user surfs the web. These programs are called bots. This book presents many useful recipes for commonly performed HTTP programming tasks. Using these recipes a wide array of bots can be constructed.

To create HTTP programs with C# an understanding of the structure of HTTP requests is required. This chapter introduces this structure. Understanding this structure allows the programmer to create programs that surf the web just as a user does.

The HTTP Recipes Examples Site

The C# bots created in this book are only half of the HTTP communication protocol. These bots must communicate with a web server. For example, a typical HTTP bot may access a popular online bookseller and obtain a price for a certain book. I could write an example bot for this book that accesses Amazon.com and obtains this price. However, there are several problems with this.

- Amazon may prohibit bot access of their site
- Amazon may update their site and break my bot

Both issues are important. If the examples in this book were all written to use real-world web sites, a major site redesign to any of these sites could leave many of the book examples nonfunctional. One minor change to one of these sites, and all related examples in the book would immediately become out of date.

Additionally, some sites do not allow access by bots. There are two main ways to stop bot access to a web site.

- Lawyers
- Technology

Some sites specify in their Terms of Service (TOS) agreement that their site may not be accessed programmatically with a bot. From a technical standpoint, they may do nothing to actually prevent bots from accessing their site. They just reserve the right to take legal action for accessing their site programmatically. If you have any questions about the legality of accessing a particular site, always contact a lawyer. Such information is beyond the scope of this book.

Because of these reasons, the book examples all make use of a special demonstration web site owned by Heaton Research. The web pages, used by the book's bots, are on special web site will never change. This special web site contains many pages and applications that simulate many of the real-world web sites that bots may be written for. This web site can be accessed at the following URL:

`http://www.httprecipes.com/`

If accessed with a browser, the recipe site appears as Figure 1.1.

Figure 1.1: The HTTP Recipes Web Site

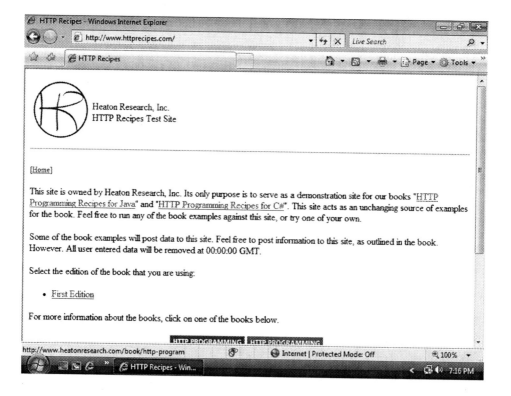

As can be seen from Figure 1.1, the first thing the web site presents the surfer with is the edition of this book. If future editions of this book are released, in the years to come, the examples on this site for a particular edition will not change. New areas will be added for new editions. Since this is the first edition of the book, choose the first edition.

The homepage for the first edition of this book is shown in Figure 1.2.

Figure 1.2: The Homepage for this Book

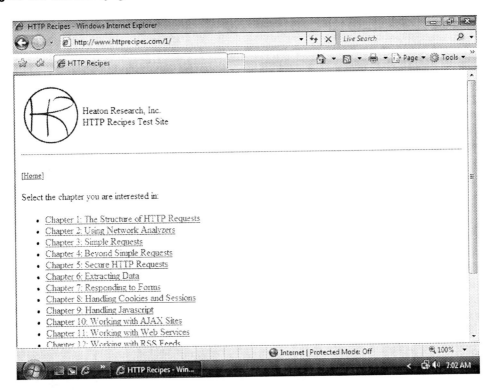

From this page links are provided to all of the chapters from this book. Some of the examples require access the site using a web browser. Other examples use bots to access this site. Some examples are are a combination of both.

The examples site will be put to use in the following sections.

The Structure of Surfing

As a user uses the web browser there is considerable network activity occurring to support the browsing experience. The Hyper Text Transport Protocol (HTTP) is what allows this to happen. HTTP specifies how web browsers and web servers manage the flurry of requests and responses that occur while a web user is surfing the web. Once it understood how web browsers and servers communicate, the built in HTTP classes provided by C#, can be used to obtain information from a web server programmatically.

If you already understand the structure of HTTP requests between web servers and web browsers, you may be able to skip this chapter and proceed directly to Chapter 2, "Analyzing Sites", or Chapter 3, "Simple HTTP Requests". Chapter 2 expands on Chapter 1 by showing how to use a "network analyzer" to examine, first hand, the information exchanged between a web server and web browser. A network analyzer can be very valuable when attempting to program a bot to access a very complex web site. However, if you are already familiar with using network analyzers, you may proceed directly to Chapter 3, which begins with C# HTTP programming.

The first thing to understand about web browsing is that it is made up of a series of HTTP requests and responses. The web browser sends a request to the server, and the server responds. This is a one sided communication. The opposite never occurs. The web server never requests something of the web browser.

For a typical surfing session, the HTTP protocol begins when the browser requests the first page from a web server. It continues as additional pages from that site are requested. To see how this works, the next section examines the requests that are sent between the web server and web browser.

Examining HTTP Requests

In this section the requests that pass between the web server and web browser are examined. The first step is to examine the HTTP requests for a typical web page. This page is covered in the next section. Understanding how a single page is transmitted is key to seeing how that page fits into a typical surfing session.

A Typical Web Page

A typical web page is displayed on the browser by placing text and images via requests. One of the first things to understand about HTTP requests is that at the heart of each request is a Uniform Resource Locater (URL). The URL tells the web server which file should be sent. The URL could point to an actual file, such as a Hyper Text Markup Language (HTML), or it could point to an image file, such as a GIF or JPEG.

URLs are what the web user types into a browser to access a web page. Chapter 3, "Simple HTTP Requests", explains what each part of the URL is for. For now, they simply identify a resource, somewhere on the Internet, that is being requested.

The "typical web page" that for this example is at the following URL:

`http://www.httprecipes.com/1/1/typical.php`

The actual contents of the "typical web page" are shown in Figure 1.3.

Figure 1.3: A Typical Web Page

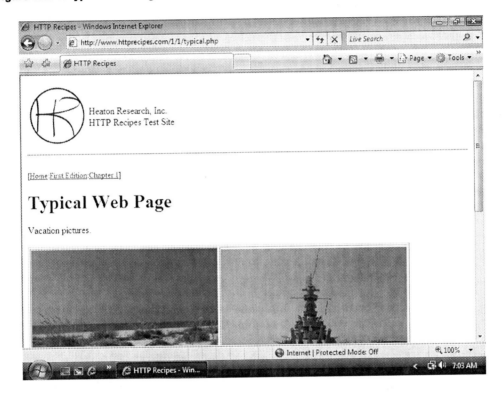

As can be seen in Figure 1.3, four pictures are displayed in the middle of the page. There are actually a total of five pictures, if the Heaton Research logo is counted. When a web page such as this is opened, the HTML, as well as all images must be downloaded.

The first HTTP request is always for the URL that was typed into the browser. This URL is usually an HTML page. The HTML page is a single HTTP request. The text of this HTML file is all that this HTTP request transfers.

It is important to note that only one physical file is transferred per HTTP request. The HTML page is downloaded and examined for other embedded files that are required to display the web page. Listing 1.1 shows the HTML of the "typical web page".

Listing 1.1: HTML for the Typical Web Page

```
<!DOCTYPE HTML PUBLIC "-//W3C//DTD HTML 4.01 Transitional//EN">

<HTML>
<HEAD>
      <TITLE>HTTP Recipes</TITLE>
      <meta http-equiv="Content-Type" content="text/html;
charset=UTF-8">
      <meta http-equiv="Cache-Control" content="no-cache">
</HEAD>

<BODY>

<table border="0"><tr><td>
<a href="http://www.httprecipes.com/"><img src="/images/logo.gif"
alt="Heaton Research Logo" border="0"></a>
</td><td valign="top">Heaton Research, Inc.<br>
HTTP Recipes Test Site
</td></tr>
</table>
<hr><p><small>[<a href="/">Home</a>:<a href="/1/">
First Edition</a>:<a href="/1/1/">Chaper 1</a>]</small></p>
<h1>Typical Web Page</h1>
<p>Vacation pictures.</p>
<table border=1>
<tr><td><img src="beach.jpg" height="240" width="320" alt="Beach">
</td><td><img src="ship.jpg" height="240" width="320"
alt="Battleship"></td></tr>
<tr><td><img src="birds.jpg" height="240" width="320" alt="Birds">
</td><td><img src="flower.jpg" height="240" width="320"
alt="Beach Flowers"></td></tr>
</table>
<hr>
<p>Copyright 2006 by <a href=
"http://www.heatonresearch.com/">Heaton Research, Inc.</a></p>
</BODY>
</HTML>
```

As can be seen from the above listing, there are a total of five **<img>** HTML tags. The following five tags are found:

- <img src="/images/logo.gif" alt="Heaton Research Logo" border="0">
- <img src="beach.jpg" height="240" width="320" alt="Beach">
- <img src="ship.jpg" height="240" width="320" alt="Battleship">
- <img src="birds.jpg" height="240" width="320" alt="Birds">
- <img src="flower.jpg" height="240" width="320" alt="Beach Flowers">

Once the HTML has been downloaded, it is scanned for `<img>` tags. These `<img>` tags cause other requests to be generated to download the images. The above tags are converted to the following five URL's:

- http://www.heatonresearch/images/logo.gif
- http://www.heatonresearch/1/1/beach.jpg
- http://www.heatonresearch/1/1/ship.jpg
- http://www.heatonresearch/1/1/birds.jpg
- http://www.heatonresearch/1/1/flower.jpg

As can be seen from the above list, the requests are given in fully qualified form. The URL for the file `beach.jpg` is given in the form `http://www.heatonresearch.com/1/1/beach.jpg`, not in the form "`beach.jpg`" as it is represented in the HTML file. Since the web server has no idea what page is currently being browsed, a web browser must fully qualify every request that is sent.

A Typical Surfing Session

Once the user is browsing the "typical web page," examined in the last section, they will not likely stay there long. The typical web user will "surf," and visit a large number of pages. The typical web page example contains five different pages that the user may choose to surf to. All of these pages are linked to with anchor tags `<a>`. The following anchor tags are found in Listing 1.1:

- <a href="http://www.httprecipes.com/">
- <a href="/">
- <a href="/1/">
- <a href="/1/1/">
- <a href="http://www.heatonresearch.com/">

Just as was done with the `<img>` tags, the above URLs must be converted into their fully qualified form. The above list, when converted into fully qualified form, gives the following five URL's:

- http://www.httprecipes.com/
- http://www.httprecipes.com/
- http://www.httprecipes.com/1/
- http://www.httprecipes.com/1/1/
- http://www.heatonresearch.com/

As can be seen, some of the `<a>` tags convert to the same target. For example, two of the tags open the URL `http://www.httprecipes.com/`.

When a user chooses one of the links, the URL is moved to the address line of the browser. The new URL is handled as if the user had specifically requested the page by typing the URL into the address line of the browser. This process repeats as the user selects more and more pages.

So far HTTP requests have only been discussed as abstract concepts. The actual make up of an HTTP request has not yet been discussed. This is covered in the next section where the structure of an HTTP request is examined.

HTTP Requests and Responses

In the last section HTTP requests generated during a typical surfing session were examined. Now these requests will be examined in detail. First, the different types of requests are discussed. There are a total of three standard HTTP requests that are commonly used:

- GET
- POST
- HEAD

The **GET** request is the most common request. Any time the user enters a URL into a web browser, a **GET** request is issued. Additionally, each hyperlink followed, or image downloaded is also a **GET** request.

The **POST** request is usually the response to an HTML form. Whenever a form is filled out and submitted, a **POST** request is being issued.

The **HEAD** request is rarely used. It allows only the HTTP headers to be requested. The actual contents of the "file" requested will not be sent. A web browser will not generate the **HEAD** request; however, some search engines make use of it to determine if a URL is still valid. Because the **HEAD** request is not generated by a web browser and is of little real use to a bot, this book will not discuss it further.

The response from the web server, to the **GET** and **POST** requests is the same. In both cases, the response is an HTML file, image, or some other form of data. What is returned depends on what the web server is programmed to return for the request it has received. The usual response to a **POST** is an HTML page that displays the result of the form. For example, the response to a **POST** from an order form might be a HTML page that contains the user's order number.

In the next few sections how the **GET** and **POST** requests work are explained in greater detail.

GET Requests

Choosing between **GET** and **POST** usually comes down to how much data must pass to the web site. **GET** allows only a limited amount of data to be passed to the web server. **POST** allows a nearly infinite amount of data to be passed to the web server. However, if you are writing an HTTP program to communicate with an existing web site, the choice is not yours. You must conform to what that site expects. Therefore, most HTTP applications will need to support a mix of **GET** and **POST** requests.

The **GET** request is good for when little, or no, additional information must be sent to the web server with a request. For example, the following URL, if sent with a **GET** request, will pass no data to the web server.

`http://www.httprecipes.com/1/test.php`

The above URL simply requests the `test.php` page and does not pass any arguments on to the page. However, several arguments may need to be passed. What if the bot needed to pass two arguments named "`first`" and "`last`"? To pass these two arguments the following URL would be used:

`http://www.httprecipes.com/1/test.php?first=Jeff&last=Heaton`

This would pass two arguments to the `test.php` page. As can be seen, passing arguments with a **GET** request requires them to be appended onto the URL. The question mark (?) indicates that the arguments have started. Each argument is the name of the argument, followed by an equal sign (=), followed by the value of the argument. Each argument is separated from the other arguments using an ampersand (&) symbol.

If there are a large number of arguments to pass, **GET** can be cumbersome. In such cases, the **POST** request should be considered. Of course, as previously stated, if using an existing web site, the bot must conform to what request type is already being used.

Figure 1.4 shows the results of the above URL.

Figure 1.4: Result of GET Request

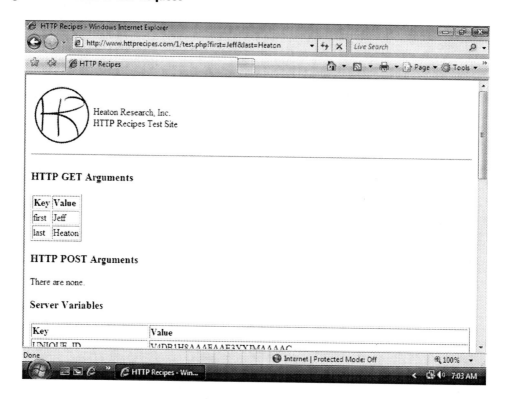

As can be seen, the two arguments showed up as URL arguments in the address bar.

POST Requests

GET request are limited by size. All arguments must fit on the URL. **POST** requests have no such limitation. This is possible because the data that sent with a **POST** request is transmitted separately from the URL.

To use an HTTP post, there will usually be an HTML page with a form. Figure 1.5 shows such a form.

Figure 1.5: An HTML Form

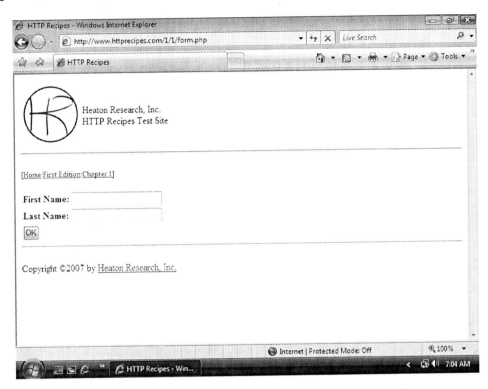

The arguments used by the form are specified in the HTML. Listing 1.2 shows the HTML that was used to produce Figure 1.5.

Listing 1.2: The HTML Form

```
<!DOCTYPE HTML PUBLIC "-//W3C//DTD HTML 4.01 Transitional//EN">

<HTML>
<HEAD>
     <TITLE>HTTP Recipes</TITLE>
     <meta http-equiv="Content-Type" content="text/html;
charset=UTF-8">
     <meta http-equiv="Cache-Control" content="no-cache">
</HEAD>

<BODY>

<table border="0"><tr><td>
<a href="http://www.httprecipes.com/">
<img src="/images/logo.gif" alt="Heaton Research Logo" bor-
der="0"></a>
```

```
</td><td valign="top">Heaton Research, Inc.<br>
HTTP Recipes Test Site
</td></tr>
</table>
<hr><p><small>[<a href="/">Home</a>:<a href="/1/">First Edition
</a>]</small></p>
<table border="0">
  <form method="post" action="/1/test.php">
  <tr><td><b>First Name:</b></td><td><input name="first"></td>
</tr>

  <tr><td><b>Last Name:</b></td><td><input name="last"></td></tr>
  <tr><td colspan="2"><input type="submit" value="OK"></td></tr>
  </form>
</table>

<hr>
<p>Copyright 2006 by <a href="http://www.heatonresearch.com/">
Heaton Research, Inc.</a></p>
</BODY>
</HTML>
```

As can be seen from the above form, there are two **<input>** tags that both accept text from the user. These tags are picked up as posted variables when the **POST** request is sent to the web server. The result of the POST request is shown in Figure 1.6.

Figure 1.6: Result of the POST Request

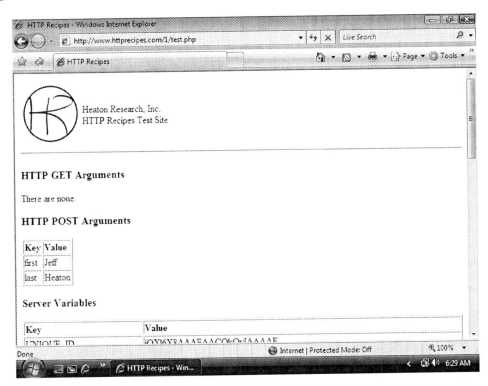

Notice how Figure 1.6 is different than Figure 1.5? The arguments are displayed as **POST** arguments, rather than HTTP **GET** arguments. Additionally, the request type is **POST**.

So far, only the data passed in HTTP requests and responses has been examined. There are also headers that contain useful information. The headers are examined in the next section.

HTTP Headers

HTTP headers are additional information that is transferred along with both HTTP requests and responses. HTTP requests and responses will return different headers. In the following sections both HTTP request and response headers are examined.

HTTP headers provide many important elements of the browsing experience. For example, HTTP headers allow browsers to know length and type of data they are displaying. They also allow pages to be secure and can prompt for user and password information. Some of the specific types of information that can be found in the HTTP headers are summarized here:

- User authentication
- Data type
- Data length
- Cookies to maintain state

This book covers each of these uses for headers. HTTP request headers will be examined first.

HTTP Request Headers

HTTP request headers are sent as part of the HTTP request. These headers tell the web server nearly everything about the request. The **GET** request is made up entirely of headers. The **POST** request contains an extra block of data, immediately after the headers that contain the posted arguments.

Listing 1.3 shows a typical HTTP request.

Listing 1.3: Typical Request Headers

```
GET /1/1/typical.php HTTP/1.1
Accept: image/gif, image/x-xbitmap, image/jpeg, image/pjpeg,
application/x-shockwave-flash, */*
Referer: http://www.httprecipes.com/1/1/
Accept-Language: en-us
UA-CPU: x86
Accept-Encoding: gzip, deflate
User-Agent: Mozilla/4.0 (compatible; MSIE 7.0; Windows NT 5.1;
.NET CLR 1.1.4322; .NET CLR 2.0.50727)
Host: www.httprecipes.com
Connection: Keep-Alive
```

There are really two parts to the headers: the first line and then the rest of the header lines. The first line, which begins with the request type, is the most important line in the header block, and it has a slightly different format than the other header lines. The request type can be **GET**, **POST**, **HEAD**, or one of the other less frequently used headers. Browsers will always use **GET** or **POST**. Following the request type is the file that is being requested. In the above request, the following URL is being requested:

```
http://www.httprecipes.com/1/1/typical.php
```

The above URL is not represented exactly as seen above in the request header. The "`Host`" header line in the header names the web server that contains the file. The request shows the remainder of the URL, which in this case is `/1/1/typical.php`. Finally, the third thing that the first line provides is the version of the HTTP protocol being used. As of the writing of this book there are only two versions currently in widespread use:

- HTTP/1.1
- HTTP/1.0

This book only deals with HTTP 1.1. Because this book is about writing programs to connect to web servers, it will be assumed that HTTP 1.1 is being used, which is what C# uses when the C# HTTP classes are used.

The lines after the first line make up the actual HTTP headers. Their format is colon delimited. The header name is to the left of the colon and the header value is to the right. It is valid to have two of the same header names in the same request. Two headers of the same name are used when cookies are specified. Cookies will be covered in Chapter 8, "Handling Sessions and Cookies."

The headers give a variety of information. Examining the headers shows type of browser being used as well as the operating system, as well as other information. In the headers listed above in Listing 1.3, the Internet Explorer 7 browser was being used on the Windows XP platform.

The headers finally terminate with a blank line. If the request had been a **POST**, any posted data would follow the blank line. Even when there is no posted data, as is the case with a **GET**, the blank line is still required.

A web server should respond to every HTTP request from a web browser. The web server's response is discussed in the next section.

HTTP Response Headers

When the web server responds to a HTTP request, HTTP response header lines are sent. The HTTP response headers look very similar to the HTTP request headers. Listing 1.4 shows the contents of typical HTTP response headers.

Listing 1.4: Typical Response Headers

```
HTTP/1.1 200 OK
Date: Sun, 02 Jul 2006 22:28:58 GMT
Server: Apache/2.0.40 (Red Hat Linux)
Last-Modified: Sat, 29 Jan 2005 04:13:19 GMT
ETag: "824319-509-c6d5c0"
Accept-Ranges: bytes
Content-Length: 1289
Connection: close
Content-Type: text/html
```

As can be seen from the above listing, at first glance, response headers look nearly the same as request headers. However, look at the first line.

Although the first line is space delimited as in the request, the information is different. The first line of HTTP response headers contains the HTTP version and status information about the response. The HTTP version is reported as 1.1, and the status Code, **200**, means "OK," no error. Also, this is where the famous error code **404** (page not found) comes from.

Error codes can be grouped according to the digit in their hundreds position:

- 1xx: Informational - Request received, continuing process
- 2xx: Success - The action was successfully received, understood, and accepted
- 3xx: Redirection - Further action must be taken in order to complete the request
- 4xx: Client Error - The request contains bad syntax or cannot be fulfilled
- 5xx: Server Error - The server failed to fulfill an apparently valid request

Immediately following the headers will be a blank line, just as was the case with HTTP requests. Following the blank line delimiter will be the data that was requested. It will be of the length specified in the **Content-Length** header. The **Content-Length** header in Listing 1.4 indicates a length of 1289 bytes. For a list of HTTP codes, refer to Appendix E, "HTTP Response Codes."

Recipes

In this chapter, the structure of HTTP requests and responses was examined. As shown in Listing 1.3 and 1.4, the structure of HTTP is not terribly complex. As a result, it is relatively easy to create a web server. This is what the two recipes in this chapter will deal with. The first Recipe, 1.1, will show how to create a really simple web server. Next, Recipe 1.2 will show how to extend the simple web server to use HTML and image files, just as a regular web server would.

The recipes in this chapter make use of C# sockets. Sockets are the lowest level that an application programmer will usually get to the Internet connection. The socket level allows a web server to be created. After this chapter, all C# recipes will make use of the C# HTTP classes. If desired, HTTP programming could be performed at the socket level; however, using the C# HTTP classes will get the needed functionality, without the complexity of dealing directly with sockets.

Recipe #1.1: A Simple Web Server

The first recipe is a "Hello World" program of sorts. Recipe 1.1 is a web server. Its purpose is to show how to serve web pages from your program. This very simple program only serves one web page. This page simply says "Hello World".

When this program is launched the port that web server will listen at must be specified. Normally web servers listen at port **80**. However, there may already be a web server running at port **80**. If this is the case a higher port number such as **8080** or **8081** should be used. Typing the following command in a command prompt window will start the web server.

```
Recipe1_1 8080
```

This will start the web server on port **8080**. If something already has that port in use then a **BindingException** error message will be shown, as seen in Listing 1.5. For more information on how to execute the recipes in this book refer to Appendix B, "Compiling and Executing Examples."

Listing 1.5: Port Already in Use

```
Unhandled Exception: System.Net.Sockets.SocketException: Only one
usage of each
socket address (protocol/network address/port)
is normally permitted
    at System.Net.Sockets.Socket.DoBind(EndPoint endPointSnapshot,
SocketAddresssocketAddress)
    at System.Net.Sockets.Socket.Bind(EndPoint localEP)
    at HeatonResearch.httprecipes.ch1.Recipe1_1.SimpleWebServer..
ctor(Int32 port) in C:\Documents and Settings\jeff\My Documents\
Visual Studio 2005\Projects\HTTPRecipes\Recipe1_1\SimpleWebServer.
cs:line 42
    at HeatonResearch.httprecipes.ch1.Recipe1_1.SimpleWebServer.
Main(String[] args) in C:\Documents and Settings\jeff\My Docu-
ments\Visual Studio 2005\Projects\HTTPRecipes\Recipe1_1\SimpleWeb-
Server.cs:line 137
```

If the web server is started properly, and no error occurs, there should be no output. The web server is now waiting for a connection. Connecting to the web server is easy. Use any web browser and access the following URL:

```
http://localhost:8080/
```

No matter what request is sent to this web server, it will produce a page that says Hello World. The output from Recipe 1.1 is shown in Figure 1.7.

Figure 1.7: Hello World

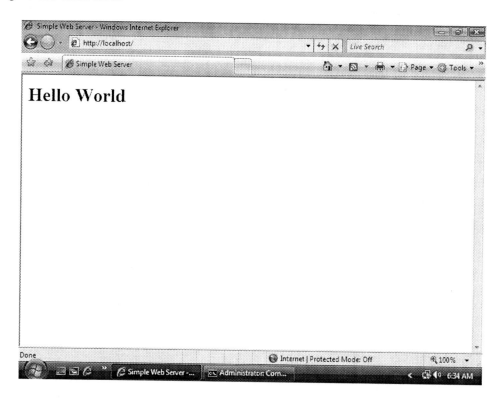

Now that the program has been demonstrated, it is time to take a look at what was necessary to implement this program. Recipe 1.1 is shown in Listing 1.6.

Listing 1.6: Simple Web Server (SimpleWebServer.cs)

```
using System;
using System.Net.Sockets;
using System.Net;
using System.Text;

namespace HeatonResearch.httprecipes.ch1.Recipe1_1
{
    class SimpleWebServer
    {
        /// <summary>
        /// The server socket that will listen for connections
        /// </summary>
        private Socket server;


        /// <summary>
```

```
/// Construct the web server to listen on the
/// specified port.
/// </summary>
/// <param name="port">The port to use for the
/// server.</param>
public SimpleWebServer(int port)
{
    server = new Socket(
        AddressFamily.InterNetwork,
        SocketType.Stream, ProtocolType.IP);
    server.Bind(new IPEndPoint(
        IPAddress.Loopback, port));
}


/// <summary>
/// The run method endlessly waits for connections.
/// As each connection is opened(from web browsers)
/// the connection is passed off to
/// handleClientSession.
/// </summary>
public void run()
{
    server.Listen(10);
    for(;;)
    {
        Socket socket = server.Accept();
        HandleClientSession(socket);
    }
}

/// <summary>
/// Read a string from the socket.
/// </summary>
/// <param name="socket">The socket to read from.
/// </param>
/// <returns>The string read.</returns>
private String SocketRead(Socket socket)
{
    StringBuilder result = new StringBuilder();
    byte []buffer = new byte[1];

    while( socket.Receive(buffer)>0 )
    {
        char ch = (char)buffer[0];
        if( ch=='\n')
            break;
```

```
                  if ( ch!='\r')
                        result.Append(ch);
        }

        return result.ToString();

    }

    /// <summary>
    /// Write a string to the socket, followed by a
    /// line break.
    /// </summary>
    /// <param name="socket">The socket to write to.
    /// </param>
    /// <param name="str">What to write to the socket.
    /// </param>
    private void SocketWrite(Socket socket,String str)
    {
        System.Text.ASCIIEncoding  encoding=
              new System.Text.ASCIIEncoding();
        socket.Send(encoding.GetBytes(str) );
        socket.Send(encoding.GetBytes("\r\n"));
    }

    /// <summary>
    ///  Handle a client session. This method displays
    ///  the incoming
    ///  HTTP request and responds with a
    ///  "Hello World" response.
    /// </summary>
    /// <param name="socket">The client socket.</param>
    private void HandleClientSession(Socket socket)
    {
        // read in the first line
        Console.WriteLine("**New Request**");
        String first = SocketRead(socket);
        Console.WriteLine(first);

        // read in headers and post data
        String line;
        do
        {
            line = SocketRead(socket);
            if(line!=null)
                  Console.WriteLine(line);
        } while (line!=null && line.Length>0 );
```

```
            // write the HTTP response
            SocketWrite(socket,"HTTP/1.1 200 OK");
            SocketWrite(socket,"");
            SocketWrite(socket,"<html>");
            SocketWrite(socket,"<head><title>
                Simple Web Server</title></head>");
            SocketWrite(socket,"<body>");
            SocketWrite(socket,"<h1>Hello World</h1>");
            SocketWrite(socket,"<//body>");
            SocketWrite(socket,"</html>");

            // close everything up
            socket.Close();
        }


        /// <summary>
        /// The main entry point for the application.
        /// </summary>
        [STAThread]
        static void Main(string[] args)
        {
            SimpleWebServer webServer =
                new SimpleWebServer(80);
            webServer.run();
        }
    }
}
```

C# supports two primary types of sockets: server sockets and client sockets. Both types are implemented through the **Socket** class. A socket becomes a server socket when the **Bind** method is called to bind the server socket to a specific port. This program begins by creating a server socket and binding it to the specified port. This is done with the following line of code in the **WebServer** constructor:

```
server = new Socket(AddressFamily.InterNetwork,SocketType.
Stream,ProtocolType.IP);
server.Bind(new IPEndPoint(IPAddress.Loopback,port));
```

Once the server connection has been opened, the program must wait for connections. This is done using the **Accept** function of the **Socket** object. This is done in the **Run** method. The **Run** method begins by entering an endless loop, as seen here:

```
for (;;)
{
```

This command causes the web server to wait endlessly for connections. The server does not include a mechanism for shutting itself down. To shut down the server simply, press **ctrl-c** or close the web server's window.

Next, the **Accept** function is called to accept a connection. If no connection is available, then the **Accept** function blocks (or waits), until a connection is available. Because of this, the **Accept** call is often put inside of a thread. This would allow the rest of the program to continue executing while the thread waits for a connection. However, for this simple example, everything will be done in a single thread.

```
Socket socket = server.Accept();
```

When a connection is made, a **Socket** object is returned. This object is passed onto the **HandleClientSession** method to fulfill the request.

```
HandleClientSession(socket);
```

The **HandleClientSession** method will handle all input and output to the socket with the functions **ReadSocket** and **WriteSocket**. These functions will be discussed later in this section. As was discussed earlier in the chapter, the first line of an HTTP request has a special format. Because of this, the first line is read separately. It is then printed out.

```
// read in the first line
Console.WriteLine("**New Request**");
String first = SocketRead(socket);
Console.WriteLine(first);
```

Once the first line has been read in, the headers can be read. The headers are read until a blank line is found. As was discussed earlier in this chapter, a blank line indicates the end of HTTP headers.

```
// read in headers and post data
String line;
do
{
  line = SocketRead(socket);
  if(line!=null)
    Console.WriteLine(line);
} while (line!=null && line.Length>0 );
```

Once the first blank line is hit, the program is done reading the HTTP headers. Because this server only supports **GET** requests, the program is also done reading the HTTP request. Now it is time to write the HTTP response. The following lines of code write a simple HTML message that says "Hello World" to the browser.

```
// write the HTTP response
SocketWrite(socket,"HTTP/1.1 200 OK");
SocketWrite(socket,"");
SocketWrite(socket,"<html>");
```

```
SocketWrite(socket,
  "<head><title>Simple Web Server</title></head>");
SocketWrite(socket,"<body>");
SocketWrite(socket,"<h1>Hello World</h1>");
SocketWrite(socket,"<//body>");
SocketWrite(socket,"</html>");
```

Now that the message has been written, it is time to close the streams. The following lines of code do this.

```
// close everything up
socket.Close();
```

The above recipe showed how to create a simple web server. In addition to this basic functionality, this recipe can be expanded to be a custom web server that will respond to different requests. For example, a web server could be constructed to give information about how a process is running or other status information collected by the computer.

Most web servers simply present files to the browser. However, Recipe 1.2 generated its response internally. This can be a very useful technique to display status information for your web server. The next recipe, Recipe 1.2, shows how to create a web server that will allow access to files.

Reading from the Socket

The **ReadSocket** function will read a single line of text from the socket. This line is delimited by a new-line character (\n). The **ReadSocket** function can be called to read each of the HTTP headers sent by the web browser.

To read from the socket use the **Receive** function. The **Receive** function will attempt to fill a buffer with data read from the socket. For the simple web server we will read the data one character at a time. If the character is a new-line character (\n) then the reading stops. If the character is not a carriage return, then it is appended to the current line.

```
StringBuilder result = new StringBuilder();
byte []buffer = new byte[1];

while( socket.Receive(buffer)>0 )
{
  char ch = (char)buffer[0];
  if( ch=='\n')
    break;
  if( ch!='\r')
    result.Append(ch);
}

return result.ToString();
```

Finally, the line that was built up in the **result** variable is returned as a **String**.

Writing to the Socket

To write a line of text to the socket the **WriteLine** method is used. This method uses the **ASCIIEncoding** class to properly encode the ASCII line into a binary form that can be transmitted with the socket.

```
System.Text.ASCIIEncoding  encoding=
      new System.Text.ASCIIEncoding();
socket.Send(encoding.GetBytes(str) );
socket.Send(encoding.GetBytes("\r\n"));
```

The specified line of text is written. After the line is written, the end of line carriage return and linefeed (\r\n) are written.

Recipe #1.2: File Based Web Server

This recipe shows how to create a very common sort of web server. This web sever exposes a directory tree to the Internet. This directory tree is called the "HTTP root", or "web root". Files are placed into this directory to be accessed by web browsers. A default file, named **index.html**, should be placed into this directory. This file is displayed when the user browses to the directory. The **index.html** file usually has links to the other files in that directory, and serves as a starting point.

This web server requires only two configuration arguments. Both of these are specified in the command line. The two parameters are:

- HTTP Port
- HTTP Root Directory

For example, to start the web server using port **8080** and the directory **c:\httproot** as the root directory, the following command is used.

```
Recipe1_2 8080 c:\httproot\
```

The web server featured in this recipe is an expanded version of the server featured in Recipe 1.1. Because of this the details will not be repeated that are the same between the two web servers; therefore, Recipe 1.1 should be reviewed for additional information. For more information on how to execute the recipes in this book refer to Appendix B, "Compiling and Executing Examples."

Now the construction of the web server will be examined. Listing 1.7 shows the source code necessary for the file based web server.

Listing 1.7: File Based Web Server (WebServer.cs)

```
using System;
using System.Net.Sockets;
```

```csharp
using System.Net;
using System.Text;
using System.IO;

namespace HeatonResearch.httprecipes.ch1.Recipe1_2
{
    class WebServer
    {
        /// <summary>
        /// The server socket that will listen for connections
        /// </summary>
        private Socket server;

        /// <summary>
        /// Used to convert strings to byte arrays.
        /// </summary>
        private System.Text.ASCIIEncoding  encoding=
            new System.Text.ASCIIEncoding();

        /// <summary>
        /// Where the HTML files are stored.
        /// </summary>
        private String httproot;

        /// <summary>
        /// Construct the web server to listen on the
        /// specified port.
        /// </summary>
        /// <param name="port">The port to use for the
        /// server.</param>
        public WebServer(int port,String httproot)
        {
            server = new Socket(
            AddressFamily.InterNetwork,SocketType.Stream,
                ProtocolType.IP);
            server.Bind(new IPEndPoint(
                IPAddress.Loopback,80));
            this.httproot = httproot;
        }

        /// <summary>
        /// The run method endlessly waits for connections
        ///   as each connection is opened(from web browsers)
        /// the connection is passed off to
        /// handleClientSession.
        /// </summary>
```

```
public void Run()
{
    server.Listen(10);
    for(;;)
    {
        Socket socket = server.Accept();
        HandleClientSession(socket);
    }
}

/// <summary>
/// Read a string from the socket.
/// </summary>
/// <param name="socket">The socket to read from.
/// </param>
/// <returns>The string read.</returns>
private String SocketRead(Socket socket)
{
    StringBuilder result = new StringBuilder();
    byte []buffer = new byte[1];

    while( socket.Receive(buffer)>0 )
    {
        char ch = (char)buffer[0];
        if( ch=='\n')
            break;
        if( ch!='\r')
            result.Append(ch);
    }

    return result.ToString();

}

/// <summary>
/// Write a string to the socket, followed by a
/// line break.
/// </summary>
/// <param name="socket">The socket to write to.
/// </param>
/// <param name="str">What to write to the socket.
/// </param>
private void SocketWrite(Socket socket,String str)
{
    socket.Send(encoding.GetBytes(str) );
    socket.Send(encoding.GetBytes("\r\n"));
```

```
}

/// <summary>
///  Handle a client session. This method displays
/// the incoming
///  HTTP request and responds with a
/// "Hello World" response.
/// </summary>
/// <param name="socket">The client socket.</param>
private void HandleClientSession(Socket socket)
{
     // read in the first line
     Console.WriteLine("**New Request**");
     String first = SocketRead(socket);
     Console.WriteLine(first);

     // read in headers and post data
     String line;
     do
     {
          line = SocketRead(socket);
          if(line!=null)
               Console.WriteLine(line);
     } while (line!=null && line.Length>0 );

     // write the HTTP response
     char []delim = {' '};
     String []tok = first.Split();
     String verb = tok[0];
     String path = tok[1];
     String version = tok[2];

     if ( String.Compare(verb,"GET",true)==0 )
          SendFile(socket, path);
     else
          Error(socket, 500, "Unsupported command");

     // close everything up
     socket.Close();
}
/// <summary>
/// Add a slash to the end of a path, if there is
/// not a slash there already.  This method adds
/// the correct type of slash, depending on the
/// operating system.
/// </summary>
```

```csharp
/// <param name="path">The path to add a slash to.
/// </param>
private void AddSlash(StringBuilder path)
{
    if (!path.ToString().EndsWith("\\"))
        path.Append("\\");
}

/// <summary>
/// Determine the correct "content type" based on
/// the file extension.
/// </summary>
/// <param name="path">The file being transfered.
/// </param>
/// <returns>The correct content type for this file.
/// </returns>
private String GetContent(String path)
{
    path = path.ToLower ();
    if (path.EndsWith(".jpg") ||
            path.EndsWith(".jpeg"))
            return "image/jpeg";
    else if (path.EndsWith(".gif"))
            return "image/gif";
    else if (path.EndsWith(".png"))
            return "image/png";
    else
            return "text/html";
}

/// <summary>
/// Transmit a HTTP response.  All responses are
/// handled by this method.
/// </summary>
/// <param name="socket">The socket to transmit to.
/// </param>
/// <param name="code">The response code, i.e. 404
/// for not found.</param>
/// <param name="message">The message, usually OK or
/// error message.</param>
/// <param name="body">The data to be transfered.
/// </param>
/// <param name="content">The content type.</param>
private void Transmit(
        Socket socket,
        int code,
```

```
        String message,

        byte []body,
        String content)
{
        StringBuilder headers = new StringBuilder();
        headers.Append("HTTP/1.1 ");
        headers.Append(code);
        headers.Append(' ');
        headers.Append(message);
        headers.Append("\n");
        headers.Append("Content-Length: "
                + body.Length + "\n");
        headers.Append(
        "Server: Heaton Research Example Server\n");
        headers.Append("Connection: close\n");
        headers.Append("Content-Type: " + content
                + "\n");
        headers.Append("\n");
        socket.Send(encoding.GetBytes(
                headers.ToString()));
        socket.Send(body);
}


/// <summary>
/// Display an error to the web browser.
/// </summary>
/// <param name="socket">The socket to display the
/// error to.</param>
/// <param name="code">The response code, i.e. 404
/// for not found.</param>
/// <param name="message">The error that occured.
/// </param>
private void Error(Socket socket, int code,
        String message)
{
        StringBuilder body = new StringBuilder();
        body.Append("<html><head><title>");
        body.Append(code + ":" + message);
        body.Append(
"</title></head><body><p>An error occurred.</p><h1>");
        body.Append(code);
        body.Append("</h1><p>");
        body.Append(message);
        body.Append("</p></body></html>");
        Transmit(   socket,
```

```
                              code,
                              message,
                              encoding.GetBytes(body.ToString()),
                              "text/html");
        }




        /// <summary>
        /// Send a disk file.  The path passed in is from
        /// the URL, this URL is translated into a local
        /// disk file, which is then transfered.
        /// </summary>
        /// <param name="socket">The socket to send to.
        /// </param>
        /// <param name="path">The file requested from
        /// the URL.</param>
        private void SendFile(Socket socket, String path)
        {
                char []delim = { '/' };



                // parse the file by /'s and build a local file
                String []tok = path.Split(delim);
                Console.WriteLine(path);
                StringBuilder physicalPath =
                        new StringBuilder(httproot);
                AddSlash(physicalPath);

                foreach(String e in tok)
                {
                        if (!e.Trim().Equals("\\") )
                        {
                                if (e.Equals("..") || e.Equals("."))
                                {
                                        Error(socket, 500,
                                                "Invalid request");
                                        return;
                                }
                                AddSlash(physicalPath);
                                physicalPath.Append(e);
                        }
                }
```

```
        // if there is no file specified, default
        // to index.html

        if (physicalPath.ToString().EndsWith("\\"))
        {
                physicalPath.Append("index.html");
        }

        String filename = physicalPath.ToString();
        // open the file and send it if it exists
        FileInfo file = new FileInfo(filename);
        if (file.Exists)
        {
                // send the file
                FileStream fis =
                        File.Open(filename,FileMode.Open);
                byte []buffer =
                        new byte[(int) file.Length];
                fis.Read(buffer,0,buffer.Length);
                fis.Close();
                this.Transmit(socket, 200, "OK",
                        buffer, GetContent(filename));
        }

                // file does not exist, so send file
                // not found
        else
        {
                this.Error(socket, 404, "File Not Found");
        }
}


/// <summary>
/// The main entry point for the application.
/// </summary>
[STAThread]
static void Main(string[] args)
{
        if (args.Length < 2)
        {
                Console.WriteLine(
        "Usage:\nRecipe1_2 [port] [http root path]");
        }
        else
        {
                int port;
```

```
                            try
                            {
                                    port = int.Parse(args[0]);
                                    WebServer server =
                                            new WebServer(port, args[1]);
                                    server.Run();
                            }
                            catch (ArgumentNullException)
                            {
                                    Console.WriteLine(
                                            "Invalid port number");
                            }
                            catch(FormatException)
                            {
                                    Console.WriteLine(
                                            "Invalid port number");
                            }
                            catch(OverflowException)
                            {
                                    Console.WriteLine(
                                            "Invalid port number");
                            }
                    }
            }
    }
}
```

The **Main** function, the constructor, and the **Run** method are all nearly the same as those in Recipe 1.1. The only difference is the support of the additional command line argument for the http root path. For more information on these three methods, review Recipe 1.1.

The **HandleClientSession** method begins the same as Recipe 1.1; however, once the connection is established, this recipe becomes more complex.

```
// write the HTTP response
char []delim = {' '};
String []tok = first.Split();
String verb = tok[0];
String path = tok[1];
String version = tok[2];

if ( String.Compare(verb,"GET",true)==0 )
  SendFile(socket, path);
else
  Error(socket, 500, "Unsupported command");
```

As can be seen above, the first line of the HTTP request is parsed. The first line of a HTTP request will be something like the following form.

```
GET /index.html HTTP/1.1
```

As previously discussed in this chapter, there are three parts of this line, separated by spaces. Using the **Split** function the string can be broken into the three parts. The verb is checked to see if it is a request other than **GET**. If the request is not a **GET** request, then an error is displayed. Otherwise, the path is sent onto the **SendFile** method.

The next few sections will discuss the major methods provided in this recipe.

The Send File Method

The **SendFile** method is used to send a file to the web browser. This consists of a two step process:

- Figure out the local path to the file
- Read in and transmit the file

An HTTP request will come in requesting a file path such as **/images/logo.gif**. This must be translated to a local path such as **c:\httproot\images\logo.gif**. This transformation is the first thing that the **SendFile** method does.

First the **Split** function is used to break up the path using slashes (/) as delimiters. This is done using the following lines of code.

```
// parse the file by /'s and build a local file
String []tok = path.Split(delim);
Console.WriteLine(path);
StringBuilder physicalPath = new StringBuilder(httproot);
AddSlash(physicalPath);
```

The **physicalPath** variable will hold the path to the file to be transferred. A slash is added, using the **AddSlash** function. The **physicalPath** is now ready to have subdirectories or files concatenated to it. The **SendFile** method will then parse the HTTP path and concatenate any sub directories followed by the file requested to the **physicalPath** variable. The following lines of code begin this loop:

```
foreach(String e in tok)
{
  if (!e.Trim().Equals("\\") )
  {
```

As the elements of the file are parsed, the program must look out for the previous directory code of "..". If ".." is allowed to be part of the path, a malicious user could use ".." to access the parent HTTP root directory. This would be a security risk. Therefore, if the string ".." is located inside of the URL, an error is displayed.

```
if (e.Equals("..") || e.Equals("."))
```

```
{
   Error(socket, 500, "Invalid request");
   return;
}
```

For each section, the sub directory, or file, is concatenated to the **physicalPath** variable. Additionally, a slash is added for each of the sub directory levels.

```
AddSlash(physicalPath);
physicalPath.Append(e);
```

Now, that the entire path has been parsed, it is time to check for a default file. If the path specified by the user is a directory only, the default file **index.html** needs to be specified as shown below:

```
// if there is no file specified, default
// to index.html

if (physicalPath.ToString().EndsWith("\\"))
{
   physicalPath.Append("index.html");
}

String filename = physicalPath.ToString();
```

Once the path is complete, there are really only two possibilities that will occur. Either the file will be transmitted to the user or a **404** error will be generated. The error code **404**, which is the most famous of HTTP error codes, means that the file was not found.

Next the file that is to be transmitted must be read. The following lines of code will read the file.

```
// open the file and send it if it exists
FileInfo file = new FileInfo(filename);
if (file.Exists)
{
   // send the file
   FileStream fis = File.Open(filename,FileMode.Open);
   byte []buffer = new byte[(int) file.Length];
   fis.Read(buffer,0,buffer.Length);
   fis.Close();
   this.Transmit(socket, 200, "OK", buffer, GetContent(filename));
}
```

As can be seen from the above lines of code, the file is read into an array of bytes. Once the file has been read, the **Transmit** method is called. The **Transmit** method actually transmits the data to the web browser.

If the file can not be found, an error is sent to the web browser.

```
// file does not exist, so send file not found
else
{
  this.Error(socket, 404, "File Not Found");
}
```

Notice the last parameter sent to the **Transmit** method. It is the content type. This tells the web browser what type of data the file contains. The next section explains how this is determined.

The Get Content Function

Since the **Transmit** method needs to know what type of data is being transferred, the **GetContent** function should be called to determine the content type. The content type will be a string such as **image/gif** for a GIF image or **text/html** for an HTML file. This type is determined by the file extension, as shown in the following lines of code:

```
path = path.ToLower ();
if (path.EndsWith(".jpg") || path.EndsWith(".jpeg"))
  return "image/jpeg";
else if (path.EndsWith(".gif"))
  return "image/gif";
else if (path.EndsWith(".png"))
  return "image/png";
else
  return "text/html";
```

The **GetContent** function can be called to quickly determine the content type based on the filename. Content types themselves will be discussed in greater detail in Chapter 4, "Using the HTTP Classes".

The Error Method

When an error occurs, the **Error** method is called. The **Error** method accepts three arguments:

- The output stream
- The error code
- The error message

The **Error** method works by constructing an HTML page that displays the error. This code can be seen here:

```
StringBuilder body = new StringBuilder();
body.Append("<html><head><title>");
body.Append(code + ":" + message);
body.Append("</title></head><body><p>An error occured.</p><h1>");
body.Append(code);
body.Append("</h1><p>");
```

```
body.Append(message);
body.Append("</p></body></html>");
```

This HTML page is then converted into an array of bytes. Next, this array of bytes, along with the **code** and **message**, is passed to the **Transmit** method. Finally, the **Transmit** method will send this data to the web browser.

```
Transmit(socket, code, message, encoding.GetBytes(body.To-
String()), "text/html");
```

The **Error** method is handy because it can be called from several different locations when an error occurs.

The Transmit Method

Both the **Error** and **SendFile** methods use the **Transmit** method to actually send the page to the web browser. This is very convenient because the **Transmit** method properly handles all of the HTTP headers, and thus saves both the **Error** and **SendFile** methods from both having to implement this functionality.

First, the HTTP headers are constructed. The HTTP headers are constructed into a **StringBuilder**, as seen here:

```
StringBuilder headers = new StringBuilder();
headers.Append("HTTP/1.1 ");
headers.Append(code);
headers.Append(' ');
headers.Append(message);
headers.Append("\n");
headers.Append("Content-Length: " + body.Length + "\n");
headers.Append("Server: Heaton Research Example Server\n");
headers.Append("Connection: close\n");
headers.Append("Content-Type: " + content + "\n");
headers.Append("\n");
```

Once the headers have been constructed, both the header and body can be transmitted. This is done using the following two commands.

```
socket.Send(encoding.GetBytes(headers.ToString()));
socket.Send(body);
```

As can be seen, Recipe 1.2 implements a very simple, yet functional, web server. This web server is far from being "industrial strength", but it would serve as a great starting point for any sort of application that would require a built-in web server.

Summary

This book is about how to write programs that browse the web, just as a human does. Such programs are called bots. To create bots, it is important to review how web browsing works at a technical level, to form a foundation for the rest of the book. In this chapter, the general structure of web browsing and HTTP requests were explored. The two recipes in this chapter were both web servers. The first web server did nothing more than display the text "Hello World" to any request; however, the second example implemented a full file based web server. Both of these recipes focused on socket programming and web servers. Socket programming uses the **Socket** class provided by C#. Although socket programming is touched on, most of this book will focus on creating applications that access web servers. These applications will mainly use the C# HTTP classes to access a web server, rather than direct sockets.

The next chapter will show how to use certain tools to examine the interaction between a web browser and server. These tools will be very helpful, when you create programs of your own to access web servers. They will allow the programmer to understand exactly what information the desired web server expects.

CHAPTER 2: EXAMINING HTTP TRAFFIC

- Using WireShark
- Using Network Analyzers for Debugging
- Analyzing Cookies
- Analyzing Forms

The goal of most bot programs is to access data that a web user could access with a web browser. The advantage is that a bot is an automated program and can access a large amount of data quickly. Creating bots can be challenging. If the data that is to be accessed is on a single public web page, the task is easy. However, usually a bot must navigate through a series of pages to find the data it needs.

Why would a bot need to navigate through several pages to access a piece of data? Perhaps the most common reason is that some web sites require a user to log into the web server before they are allowed to get to the data they would like to view. Your bank would surely require you to log into the bank web site, prior to viewing your bank balances. To access such a site, the bot must be able to send the web server the same data in exactly the same format as a regular browser session with a human user.

These more complex bots can be difficult to debug manually. Fortunately, by using a program called a "Network Analyzer", manual debugging is not necessary. Network analyzers are also frequently referred to as "Packet Sniffers".

Using a Network Analyzer

A network analyzer is a program that allows TCP/IP traffic between the web server and a web browser to be monitored. With a network analyzer, a typical web browser accessing the desired web server can be monitored. This shows exactly what information is transmitted.

The network analyzer is useful during all of the bot's development phases. Initially, the network analyzer can be used to analyze a typical session with the desired web server. This shows the HTTP requests and responses the bot must support. Once the bot is created, the network analyzer is used again during the debugging process and then to verify the final product.

Using a Network Analyzer to Design a Bot

The first step in designing a bot is to analyze the HTTP requests and responses that flow between the web browser and web server. The bot will need to emulate these requests in order to obtain the desired data from the web server.

Sometimes this flow of requests and responses are difficult to determine. Just viewing the source of the HTML pages and trying to understand what is going on can be a lengthy task. For sites that use techniques such as AJAX, the requests can become quite complex.

To analyze HTTP requests and properly design the bot, the network analyzer should be started and begin recording network traffic. This will be discussed later in this chapter. The web browser should then be launched and the web browser started. It is a good idea to clear the browser's cache at this point. The procedure for clearing the cache varies with each browser; this option is usually located under the Internet configuration. Cached files may cause some information to be hidden from the network analyzer.

Once the web browser is launched, the desired web site should be accessed. While on the desired web site, use the site as a regular user would. The objective while using the analyzer is to get to the data that the bot should access. Take as direct a path to the desired data as possible. The simpler the path, the easier it will be to emulate. As the web site is navigated, the network analyzer will record the progress. The analyzer will capture every request made by the web browser. In order to access this site, the bot must provide the same requests to the web server.

Using a Network Analyzer to Debug a Bot

Creating a bot for some sites can be tricky. For example, a site may use complex messages to communicate with the web server. If the bot does not exactly reproduce these requests, it will not function properly. If the bot is not functioning properly, then a network analyzer should be used to debug the bot.

The technique that I normally use is to run the network analyzer while my bot runs. The network analyzer can track the HTTP requests issued by the bot just as easily as it can track the requests issued by a real user on a web browser.

If the web server is not communicating properly with the bot, then one of the HTTP requests must be different than what a regular web browser would issue. The packets captured from the bot's session with the desired web site should then be compared to the packets captured from a regular browser session with the desired web site.

The next section will show how to use a Network Analyzer. There are many different Network Analyzers available. The one that will be used for this book is WireShark. WireShark is a free open source network analyzer that runs on a wide variety of operating systems.

Understanding WireShark

WireShark is one of the most popular network analyzers available. WireShark was once known by the name Ethereal, but due to copyright issues changed their name to WireShark. WireShark can be downloaded from the following web site:

`http://www.wireshark.org/`

WireShark supports a wide variety of operating systems. To use WireShark, choose the version for the operating system, then download and install that version.

Preparing the Browser

Most web browsers are configured to display a home page when the browser is first started. This home page will have an undesirable effect when attempting to analyze packets sent by the web browser. The homepage will cause a flurry of network packets to be sent when the web browser is first opened. This amounts to extra data being captured that has nothing to do with the web site being analyzed. To avoid this, set the web browser's home page to "blank". This can easily be done using the browser "Internet Options" menu in Internet Explorer, which is shown in Figure 2.1

Figure 2.1: Internet Explorer Options

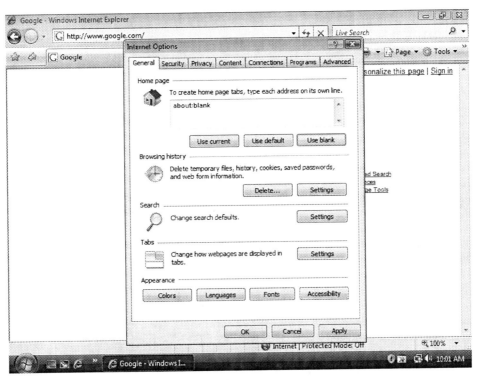

As seen in Figure 2.1, Internet Explorer can be configured to use a blank homepage by clicking the "Use Blank" button.

To set the home page to blank in Firefox use the "Preferences" menu. This located under the general tab and called "Use Blank Page".

Now that the browser is set up, WireShark can be started. When WireShark is started, it will appear similar to Figure 2.2

Figure 2.2: WireShark

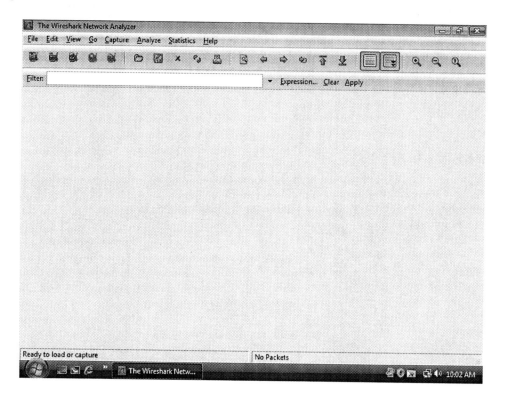

Now that WireShark has been started, it is time to use it to monitor HTTP traffic. This will be covered in the next sections.

Select an Interface

Before packets can be captured with WireShark, WireShark must be told what interface the packets should be captured from. This will most likely be the Ethernet card. However, if a dial-up modem connection is being used, then it should be specified as the interface. Select the "Interfaces..." option of the "Capture" menu. WireShark will now appear as the image in Figure 2.3.

Figure 2.3: Select an Interface

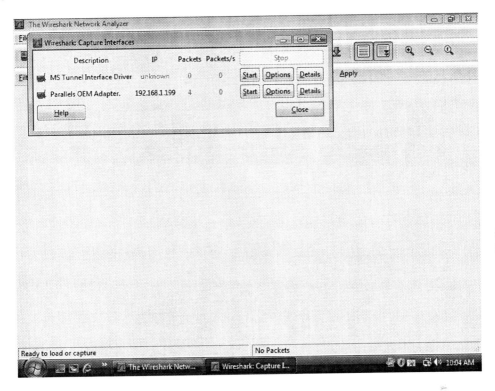

Once the correct interface is found, notice its "Capture" button next to the interface. As mentioned previously, the browser's home page should be set to blank and the browser's cache cleared. Once these steps have been preformed the "Capture" button can be pressed. This will begin the process of capturing packets.

Capturing Packets

Once the "Capture" button has been pressed, packet capture will begin. Capturing packets is the main task usually performed by a network analyzer. The term "capture" may be a bit misleading. The packets are left "as is" and are not taken out of the network stream. Rather the packets are "spied" upon.

These packets will contain the HTTP requests and responses being transferred between the web browser and the desired web server. While capturing packets, NetShark will appear as the image in Figure 2.4.

Figure 2.4: Capturing Packets

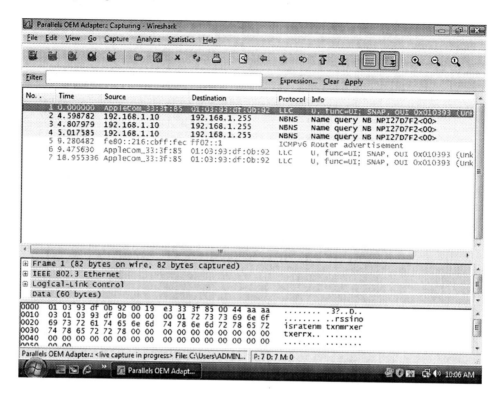

Now that packets are being captured the browser should be started. Proceed to the following URL:

http://www.httprecipes.com/

Once the web page has completely displayed, close the web browser. Now select Wire-Shark. WireShark will now appear as the image in Figure 2.5.

Figure 2.5: Captured Packets

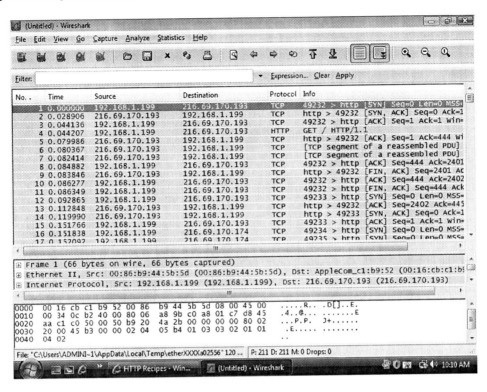

As can be seen from Figure 2.5 there are quite a few packets! Almost all of them are of no importance to creating a bot. Sift through the unimportant packets using a filter.

Filtering Packets

Look at Figure 2.5. Notice the "Protocol" column? This column contains a few packets of the type HTTP. These are the packets that are of interest. We will filter out all other packets. To create a filter, click on the "Expression…" button. This will display the image in Figure 2.6.

Figure 2.6: Filter Options

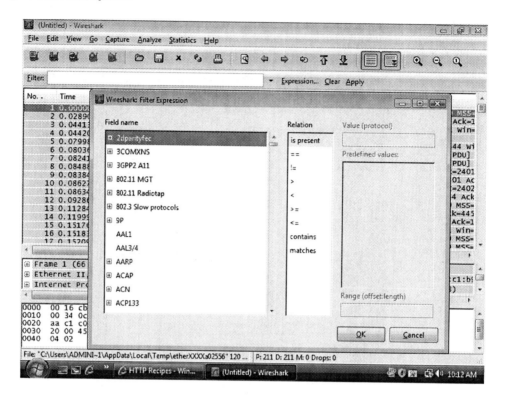

From this window choose HTTP for the "Field Name" list, and "is present" from the "Relation" list. Once these two are chosen, click "OK". This will return you to the packet list screen, seen in Figure 2.5.

At this point all of the packets are still visible. This is because no filtering has yet taken place. To use the filter, click the "Apply" button near the "Expression" button that was clicked to create the filter. Once the filter is applied, there will be considerably fewer packets. Figure 2.7 shows the filtered packet list.

Figure 2.7: Filtered to Only HTTP Packets

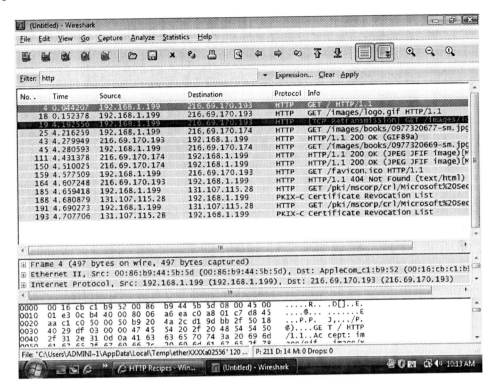

Examining a HTTP Request

We will now examine an HTTP request in greater detail. Click on the first row, as seen in Figure 2.7. The middle pane should be resized to be larger so that the HTTP headers can be seen. This will result in Figure 2.8 appearing.

Figure 2.8: The Parts of an HTTP Request Packet

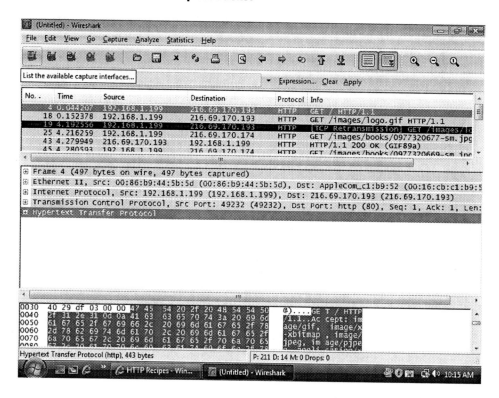

As can seen in Figure 2.8 the packet is broken into the following sections:

- Frame 9
- Ethernet II
- Internet Protocol (IP)
- Transmission Control Protocol (TCP)
- Hypertext Transfer Protocol (HTTP)

Of these, the only one that is important is the HTTP part of the packet. Clicking the plus (+) next to this section will expand it. After expanding, the HTTP part of the packet is seen as in Figure 2.9.

Figure 2.9: An HTTP Request

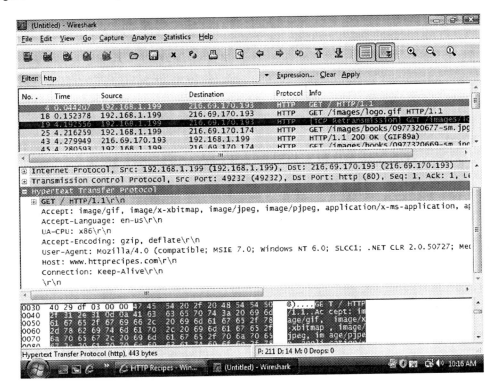

The HTTP headers for this **GET** request can be seen in Figure 2.9. As the book progresses, many of these HTTP headers will be explained. For example, consider the **User-Agent** header. This tells the web server what sort of browser is being used. For this example, Internet Explorer was used.

Examining an HTTP Response.

HTTP responses can also be examined using WireShark. Figure 2.10 shows the response packet from the logo GIF file.

Figure 2.10: An HTTP Response

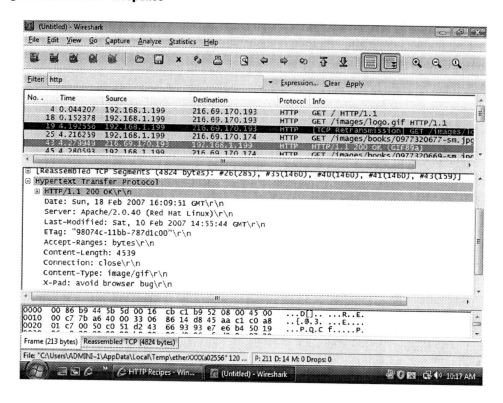

As seen in Figure 2.10 there are a different set of headers that come back from the server. For example there is a header named **Server**, which tells what version of a web server I am running the HTTP Recipes site from. As seen in Figure 2.10, the HTTP recipes site is running Apache 2.0.

Reassembled PDU

Sometimes the packet will not arrive in one piece. Instead, the packet arrives as several Protocol Data Units (PDU). WireShark will try to reassemble these units back into a single packet. Such a packet is called a reassembled PDU. This packet can be seen on the second row of Figure 2.5. Selecting the reassembled PDU produces Figure 2.11.

Figure 2.11: A Reassembled PDU

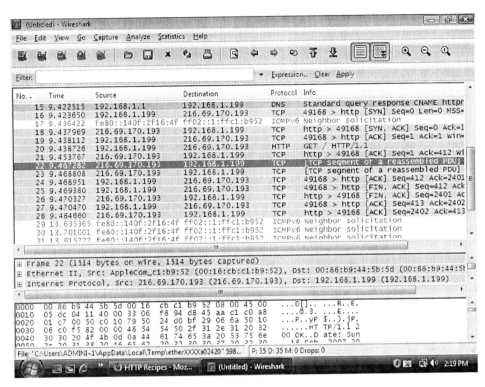

When working with a reassembled PDU, the display will not be as nice as a regular packet. The headers of the response are in the bottom pane of Figure 2.11.

Recipes

This chapter includes two recipes. These two recipes demonstrate how to examine two very important request items for bots:

- Cookies
- Forms

Cookies and forms are used by many websites. This book has an entire chapter devoted to each. Chapter 7, "Responding to Forms" discusses HTML forms. Chapter 8, "Handling Sessions and Cookies" discusses cookies. For now how to examine cookies in a request will be explained.

Recipe #2.1: Examining Cookies

Cookies are used to maintain a state in a web server. A web server can attach a cookie to a response so that it can identify that browser when the web server sees another request from this web browser. Cookies will be discussed in much greater detail in Chapter 8, "Handling Sessions and Cookies". For now we will simply examine a cookie in the network analyzer.

To see cookies in action, visit a web site that makes use of cookies. The following page, on the HTTP Recipes site, uses cookies:

```
http://www.httprecipes.com/1/2/cookies.php
```

The contents of this page are shown in Figure 2.12.

Figure 2.12: Ready to Create a Cookie

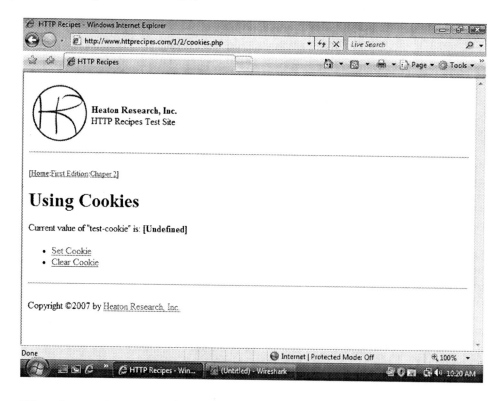

When the page is first accessed, there will be no cookie, so the cookie will show the value of "Undefined". When the "Set Cookie" button is clicked, the cookie's value can be set to any value.

Cookies always have a name. This cookie is named test-cookie. Remember this name! It will allow you to locate the correct packet in the network monitor.

Before clicking anything, start WireShark. If the cookie was already set, ensure you click "Clear Cookie" before continuing. Begin capturing packets and return to the web browser. Once back at the web browser, select "Set Cookie". Enter a value for the cookie, such as "Hello", and you will be taken back to the page shown in Figure 2.12. However, this time, the value previously set to the cookie to should be displayed.

Select WireShark and stop capturing packets. Filter to just HTTP packets in WireShark and look for the HTTP response just after the **POST 1/2/cookies-set.php** request. Figure 2.13 shows this.

Figure 2.13: Cookie as Part of a HTTP Response

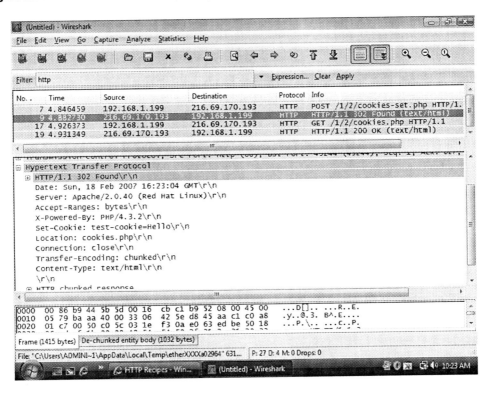

Notice the cookie? It is created by the **Set-Cookie** HTTP tag. Once the server has set a cookie, the browser must echo this cookie with each request. Look at the next request, which is **GET /1/2/cookies.php**. This request can be seen in Figure 2.14.

Figure 2.14: Cookie as Part of a HTTP Request

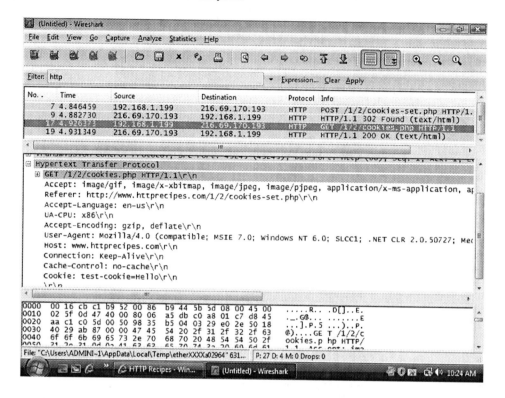

Notice the **Cookie** header in the request above. This will be sent by the web browser now that the server has requested it. This tag now allows the server to identify this particular web browser.

Tracking cookie usage can be very important when writing a bot. Using a network analyzer can assist in seeing how a web server is making use of cookies.

Recipe #2.2: Examining Forms

Forms are another key element of most web sites. Using the network analyzer, it can quickly be determined how a web server makes use of forms. Forms will be covered in much greater detail in Chapter 7. For now, capturing forms with a network analyzer will be covered.

To demonstrate HTML forms, the following URL from the HTTP Recipes site will be used:

```
http://www.httprecipes.com/1/2/forms.php
```

Figure 2.15 shows the contents of this URL.

Figure 2.15: An HTML Form

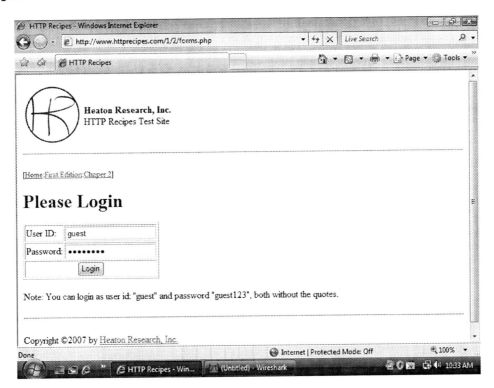

This form allows a user name and password to be entered. Turn on packet capturing in WireShark to see what happens when this form is submitted. Fill in the correct user name and password and click the "Login" button. This should allow a login to the web site.

Once logged in, stop capturing packets. Examine the HTTP request, labeled **POST /1/2/forms2.php**, this will reveal Figure 2.16.

Figure 2.16: An HTTP Form Request

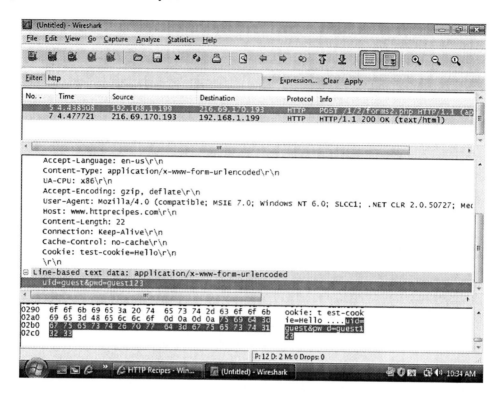

As seen in the above figure, the form data is communicated in the following line:

```
uid=guest&pwd=guest123
```

This is the format in which a web browser sends form data back to the web server. When a bot is created to respond to forms, data must be sent in this format.

Summary

In this chapter, network analyzers were demonstrated. A network analyzer shows exactly what data is being exchanged between a web server and a web browser. There are many different network analyzers to choose from. The network analyzer that will be used in book is WireShark. WireShark was formerly known as Ethereal.

Cookies allow a web browser to maintain a state. Values can be attached to a web browser, which the web browser will return with each request. Chapter 8 will cover cookies in much greater detail. Using a network analyzer, it can be quickly determined how a web server uses cookies.

Forms allow a web browser to receive input from the user. Forms are a very important part of most web sites. Chapter 7, "Responding to Forms" discusses forms in much greater detail. Using a network analyzer, it can quickly be determined how a web server is making use of HTML forms.

Now that HTTP packets have been covered, it is time to begin writing HTTP applications. The next chapter will show how to create HTTP programs, or bots, that can perform simple requests of web sites.

CHAPTER 3: SIMPLE REQUESTS

- Using the URL Class
- Downloading a Page
- Downloading an Image
- Parsing Data

The HTTP protocol is used to exchange information between an HTTP server and an HTTP client. Usually the HTTP client is a user with a web browser; however, this is not always the case. Sometimes, the HTTP client is a bot, which is a program using the web. C# provides many classes that allow C# programs to use web pages. In this chapter, these classes will be introduced.

The concept of a web page is very important to the HTTP transfer process. Information that you would like to access, using HTTP, will be on a specific web page. The web browsing experience is based on many different web pages. For example, every time a link is clicked, the browser usually moves to a new web page. Likewise, the information you would like to access, using HTTP programming, is on such a page.

Each of these pages has a unique address, which is used to identify that page. This address is the Uniform Resource Locater (URL). The quickest way to find the URL of your "page of interest", is to navigate directly to that page with a web browser. The web browser's address line will show the address of the desired page.

As seen in Figure 3.1, the browser is currently at the URL address of `http://www.httprecipes.com/1/3/time.php`. If you want to collect data from this web page, you would use this URL.

Figure 3.1: The Address of a Web Page

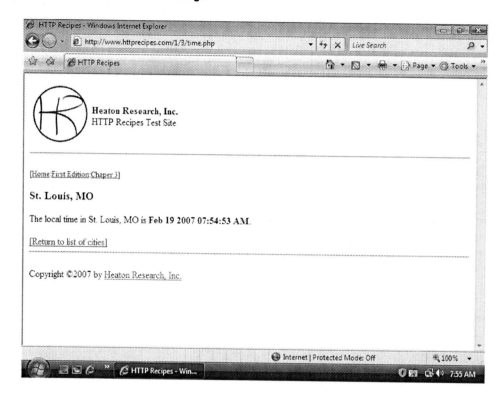

Constructing URLs

C# expresses URLs using the **Uri** class. A URI, or Uniform Resource Identifier, is a superset to which URLs belong. The HTTP protocol uses URLs; however C# expresses URLs as **Uri** objects. This can be a bit confusing. For the purposes of HTTP, the terms URI and URL can mostly be used interchangeably. The book will use both terms. The book will use the term URI when referring to the C# **Uri** class. The book will use the term URL when referring to the textual URLs found on web sites. The C# **URI** class is written as Uri, with the "r" and "i" lowercase. Whereas the concept URL is written in all uppercase.

The **Uri** class allows the program to take a simple text string, such as **http://www.httprecipes.com/**, and transform it into a **Uri** object that C# can deal with. The following code segment demonstrates this.

```
try
{
  Uri u = new Uri("http://www.httprecipes.com/");
} catch (UriFormatException e)
{
  Console.WriteLine( e.ToString() );
}
```

As you can see, a **Uri** object can be constructed simply by passing a **String**, containing the desired URL, to the constructor of the **Uri** class. You should also notice that a **catch** block is used. This is because the **UriFormatException** exception can be thrown. The **UriFormatException** will be thrown if an invalid URL is provided.

For example, the following would throw the **UriFormatException**.

```
try
{
  Uri u = new Uri("http;//www.httprecipes.com/");
} catch (UriFormatException e)
{
    Console.WriteLine( e.ToString() );
}
```

The **UriFormatException** would be thrown because the specified "http" protocol ends with a semicolon instead of a colon.

What is a URL?

In the last section I showed you how to construct a **Uri** object. I also explained that a **UriFormatException** would be thrown if an invalid URL is specified. To understand what an invalid URL is, you should first understand the format of a good URL. URLs follow the following format:

```
Scheme://Host/Path?Query
```

As seen above, the URL is made up of the following four components:

- Scheme
- Host
- Path
- Query

In the next sections, each of these components will be discussed. We will start with the scheme.

URL Scheme

The scheme is the protocol that will be used to transfer data. This book will explain the "http" and "https" schemes. Many of the more common schemes are listed in Table 3.1.

Table 3.1: Common HTML Schemes

Scheme	Name
http	HTTP resources
https	HTTP over SSL
ftp	File Transfer Protocol
mailto	E-mail address
ldap	Lightweight Directory Access Protocol lookups
file	Resources available on the local computer or over a local file sharing network
news	Usenet newsgroups
gopher	The Gopher protocol
telnet	The TELNET protocol
data	URL scheme for inserting small pieces of content in place

Following the URL scheme, the URL's host is specified. The URL host will be explained in the next section.

URL Host

The host specifies to which server the HTTP request is to be directed. There are several different formats in which the URL host can be represented. First, it can be in the typical domain form, such as:

```
www.httprecipes.com
```

Second, it can be expressed as an IP address, such as:

```
127.0.0.1
```

Finally, it can be expressed as a symbol that is resolved in the "**hosts**" file on the computer, such as:

```
localhost
```

Following the URL host is the URL path and query. The URL path and query will be discussed in the next section.

URL Path and Query

The path specifies which file to retrieve, or which script to run on the server. The "query" specifies parameters to be passed to the URL. The query immediately follows the path delimited by a question mark. The following URL specifies only a path:

`http://www.httprecipes.com/1/1/cities.php`

The above URL specifies a path of "`/1/1/cities.php`".

Parameters can be passed using the query portion of the URL. The following URL demonstrates this concept.

`http://www.httprecipes.com/1/1/city.php?city=2`

The above URL passes one parameter using the query string. A parameter named "city" is passed to the query string. The parameter "city" has the value of "2". It is also possible to pass multiple parameters. If you are passing multiple parameters, separate them with the ampersand symbol (&). The following URL makes use of the ampersand to pass in two parameters. These parameters are named "city" and "zip code".

`http://www.httprecipes.com/1/1/city.php?city=2&zipcode=63017`

So far the URLs we have examined all contain standard ASCII (American Standard Code for Information Interchange) letters and numbers. In the next section, you will learn how to encode special characters into the URL.

Encoding Special Characters into a URL

URLs can contain a wide variety of characters; however, there are only certain characters that you can put directly into a URL. For example, you cannot put a space into a URL. If you wanted to pass the value "John Smith" to the variable "name", do not construct a URL such as:

`http://www.httprecipes.com/1/test.php?name=John Smith`

The above URL is invalid because spaces are not allowed in a URL. To put a space into a URL, write the URL as:

`http://www.httprecipes.com/1/test.php?name=John%20Smith`

The above URL contains the characters "%20" instead of a space. This is because a space is ASCII code 32. The decimal number "32" is "20" in hexadecimal.

However, the space character is special. There is a second way that it can be represented. Spaces can be represented with the plus (+) character. Therefore, it is valid to represent the above URL as:

```
http://www.httprecipes.com/1/test.php?name=John+Smith
```

This means the only way to represent a "+" symbol in a URL is to use the hexadecimal ASCII code "%2B". Now that you understand how to construct a URL, it is time to see how to use them. This will be covered in the next section.

Reading from URLs

C# allows you to read data from URLs. This forms the basis of HTTP programming in C#. In this chapter you will learn how to construct simple requests from web sites. What is a simple request? A simple request is a request where you only request data from a URL. It can get much more complex than that. As you progress through the book you will learn more complex HTTP programming topics such as:

- HTTPS
- Posting Data
- Cookies
- Authentication
- Content Types

For now, we will focus on getting data from a URL and leave the more complex operations for later. You need to conduct three basic steps to read data from a URL. A summary of these steps is:

- Create a **Uri** Object
- Open a stream
- Read data from the stream

We will begin by examining the C# **Uri** class.

The Uri Class

C# provides a class to hold URLs. Even though a URL is actually a string, it is convenient to have the **Uri** class. The **Uri** class has several advantages over strings. There are methods to:

- Determine if the **Uri** is valid
- Extract information, such as host or schema
- Open a connection to the Uri

To create a **Uri** object, simply pass the string URL string to the constructor of the **Uri** class, as follows:

```
Uri url = new Uri("http://www.httprecipes.com");
```

This will create a new **Uri** object that is ready to be used. However, it can throw a checked exception, named **UriFormatException**. As mentioned previously, to handle the exception, use the following code.

```
try
{
  Uri url = new Uri("http://www.httprecipes.com");
}
catch(UriFormatException e)
{
  Console.WriteLine("This Uri is not valid.");
}
```

The **UriFormatException** will be thrown if the URI is invalid. For example, a URL such as the following would throw the exception:

http:////www.httprecipes.com/

The above URL would throw the exception, because the URL has four slashes (////), which is not valid. It is important to remember that the **Uri** class only checks to see if the URL is valid. It does NOT check to see if the URL exists on the Internet. Existence of the URL will not be verified until a connection is made. The next section discusses how to open a connection.

Opening the Stream

C# uses streams to access files and perform other I/O operations. When you access the URI, you will be given a **Stream**. This **Stream** is used to download the contents of the URL. The **Uri** class makes it easy to open a stream for the URL.

To open a stream, you must first obtain a **WebRequest** object. This object can be obtained by calling the **Create** function of the **HttpWebRequest** class. The **Create** function accepts a URI to specify which page will be downloaded.

From the **WebRequest** object you can obtain an **HttpWebResponse** object. The **HttpWebResponse** object allows you to obtain a stream by calling **GetResponseStream**. The following code shows how this is done.

```
try
{
  WebRequest http = HttpWebRequest.Create(url);
  HttpWebResponse response = (HttpWebResponse)http.GetResponse();
  Stream stream = response.GetResponseStream();
}
catch(UriFormatException e)
```

```
{
  Console.WriteLine("Invalid URL");
}
catch(IOException e)
{
  Console.WriteLine("Could not connect to URL");
}
```

As you can see, the above code is similar to the code from the last section. However, an additional line follows the **Uri** declaration. This line calls the **GetResponseStream** function, and receives a **Stream** object. You will see what to do with this object in the next section.

The above code also has to deal with an additional exception. The **IOException** can be thrown by the **GetResponseStream** function, so it is necessary to catch the exception. Remember from the previous section that the constructor of the **Uri** class does not check to see if a URI actually exists. The URI is checked at this point. If the URI does not exist or if there is any trouble connecting to the web server that holds that URI, then an **IOException** will be thrown.

Now that you have constructed the **Uri** object and opened a connection, you are ready to download the data from that URI.

Downloading the Contents

Downloading the contents of a web page uses the same procedure you would use to read data from any input stream. If you want to read the entire contents of the URI you should use a **StreamReader**. The **StreamReader** class provides the **ReadToEnd** function that will until the end of the stream has been reached.

```
Uri uri = new Uri("http://www.httprecipes.com");
WebRequest http = HttpWebRequest.Create(uri);
HttpWebResponse response = (HttpWebResponse)http.GetResponse();
StreamReader stream =
  new StreamReader(response.GetResponseStream(),
  System.Text.Encoding.ASCII   );

String result = stream.ReadToEnd();
Console.WriteLine( result );

response.Close();
stream.Close();
return result;
```

As you can see, the above code continues what we have already seen. Just as in the previous code segments, the **Uri** object is first created. Next a stream is opened to the URL. Finally, the entire contents of the URI are read to a string.

Recipes

This chapter illustrated how to use some of the basic HTTP functionality built into C#. You have seen how you can use the **Uri** class to open a stream to a web page. You also saw how to read the contents of the web page into a string. The recipes for this chapter will build on this.

There are five recipes for this chapter. These recipes provide you with reusable code that demonstrates the basic HTTP programming learned in this chapter. These recipes demonstrate the following functionalities:

- Download the contents of a web page
- Extract data from a web page
- Pass parameters to a web page
- Parse time and date information

We will begin with recipe 3.1, which demonstrates how to download the contents of a web page.

Recipe #3.1: Downloading the Contents of a Web Page

This recipe is the culmination of the example code quoted up to this point, in this chapter. Recipe 3.1 accesses a URL and downloads the contents into string that is then displayed.

This is shown in Listing 3.1.

Listing 3.1: Download a Web Page (GetPage.cs)

```
using System;
using System.Net;
using System.IO;

namespace Recipe3_1
{
    class GetPage
    {
        /// <summary>
        /// This method downloads the specified URL into a C#
        /// String. This is a very simple method, that you can
        /// reused anytime you need to quickly grab all
        /// data from a specific URL.
        /// </summary>
        /// <param name="url">The URL to download.</param>
        /// <returns>The contents of the URL that was
        /// downloaded.</returns>
        public String DownloadPage(Uri url)
        {
            WebRequest http = HttpWebRequest.Create(url);
```

```csharp
            HttpWebResponse response =
                    (HttpWebResponse)http.GetResponse();
            StreamReader stream = new StreamReader(
                    response.GetResponseStream(),
                    System.Text.Encoding.ASCII   );

            String result = stream.ReadToEnd();

            response.Close();
            stream.Close();
            return result;
        }

        /// <summary>
        /// Run the example.
        /// </summary>
        /// <param name="page">The page to download.</param>
        public void Go(String page)
        {
            Uri u = new Uri(page);
            String str = DownloadPage(u);
            Console.WriteLine(str);
        }

        /// <summary>
        /// The main entry point for the application.
        /// </summary>
        [STAThread]
        static void Main(string[] args)
        {
            GetPage module = new GetPage();
            String page;
            if (args.Length == 0)
                    page =
            "http://www.httprecipes.com/1/3/time.php";
            else
                    page = args[0];
            module.Go(page);
        }
    }
}
```

The above example can be run in two ways. If you run the example without any parameters (by simply typing "Recipe3_1"), it will download from the following URL, which is hardcoded in the recipe:

`http://www.httprecipes.com/1/3/time.php`

If you run the program with arguments it will download the specified URL. For example, to download the contents of the homepage of the recipes site use the following command:

`Recipe3_1 http://www.httprecipes.com/1/3/time.php`

The contents of **http://www.httprecipes.com** will now be displayed to the console, instead of **http://www.httprecipes.com/1/3/time.php**. For more information on how to execute the recipes in this book refer to Appendix B, "Compiling and Executing Examples."

This recipe provides one very useful function. The **DownloadPage** function, shown here:

`public String DownloadPage(Uri url)`

This function accepts a **Uri**, and downloads the contents of that web page. The contents are returned as a string. The implementation of the **DownloadPage** function is simple, and follows the code already discussed in this chapter.

This recipe can be applied to any real-world site that contains data on a single page for which you wish to download the HTML.

Once you have the web page downloaded into a string, you may be wondering what you can do with the data. As you will see from the next recipe, you can extract information from that page.

Recipe #3.2: Extract Simple Information from a Web Page

If you need to extract simple information from a web page, this recipe serves as a good foundation for more complex programs. This recipe downloads the contents of a web page and extracts a piece of information from that page. For many tasks, this recipe is all that is needed. This is particularly so, if you can get to the data directly from a URL and do not need to log in, or pass through any intermediary pages.

This recipe will download the current time for the city of St. Louis, MO. To do this it will use the following URL:

`http://www.httprecipes.com/1/3/time.php`

The above URL is one of the examples on the HTTP recipes web site. The contents of this page are shown in Listing 3.2. The piece of data that we would like to extract from Figure 3.2 is the current date and time. Figure 3.2 shows exactly what the web page looks like to a user.

Figure 3.2: The Current Time

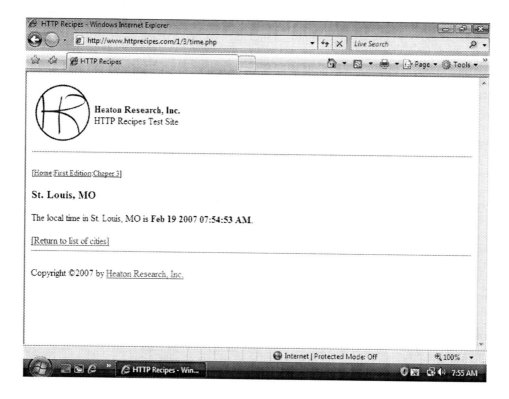

To know how to extract this date and time, we need to see what this page looks like to the computer. To do this, we must examine the HTML source. While viewing the above URL in a web browser, select "View Source". This shows Listing 3.2.

Listing 3.2: HTML Source for the Current Time

```
<!DOCTYPE HTML PUBLIC "-//W3C//DTD HTML 4.01 Transitional//EN">

<HTML>
<HEAD>
     <TITLE>HTTP Recipes</TITLE>
     <meta http-equiv="Content-Type" content="text/html;
charset=UTF-8">
     <meta http-equiv="Cache-Control" content="no-cache">
</HEAD>
```

```
<BODY>

<table border="0"><tr><td>
<a href="http://www.httprecipes.com/">
<img src="/images/logo.gif" alt="Heaton Research Logo" bor-
der="0"></a>
</td><td valign="top">Heaton Research, Inc.<br>
HTTP Recipes Test Site
</td></tr>
</table>
<hr><p><small>[<a href="/">Home</a>:<a href="/1/">
First Edition</a>
:<a href="/1/3/">Chaper 3</a>]</small></p>


<h3>St. Louis, MO</h3>
The local time in St. Louis, MO is <b>Jun 27 2006 05:58:38 PM</b>.

<br><br><a href="cities.php">[Return to list of cities]</a><br>

<hr>
<p>Copyright 2006 by <a href="http://www.heatonresearch.com/">
Heaton Research, Inc.</a></p>
</BODY>
</HTML>
```

Look at the above listing and see if you can find the time and date for St. Louis. Did you find it? It is the line about two-thirds of the way down that starts with the text "The local time in St. Louis, MO is". To extract this data we need to look at the two HTML tags that enclose it. For this web page, the time and date are enclosed in the **** and **** tags.

The following example, shown in Listing 3.3, will download this data, and extract the date and time information.

Listing 3.3: Get the Time in St. Louis (GetTime.cs)

```csharp
using System;
using System.Net;
using System.IO;

namespace Recipe3_2
{
    class GetTime
    {
        /// <summary>
        /// This method is very useful for grabbing
```

```csharp
/// information from a HTML page.
/// </summary>
/// <param name="str">The string to parse.</param>
/// <param name="token1">The text, or tag,
/// that comes before the desired text</param>
/// <param name="token2">The text, or tag, that
/// comes after the desired text</param>
/// <param name="count">Which occurrence of
/// token1 to use, 1 for the first</param>
/// <returns>The contents of the URL that was
/// downloaded.</returns>
public String Extract(String str,
  String token1, String token2, int count)
{
    int location1, location2;

    location1 = location2 = 0;
    do
    {
        location1 = str.IndexOf(token1,
            location1+1);

        if (location1 == -1)
            return null;

        count--;
    } while (count > 0);

    location2 = str.IndexOf(token2, location1 + 1);
    if (location2 == -1)
        return null;

    location1+=token1.Length;
    return str.Substring(location1,
        location2-location1 );
}

/// <summary>
/// This method downloads the specified URL into a C#
/// String. This is a very simple method, that you can
/// reused anytime you need to quickly grab all
/// data from a specific URL.
/// </summary>
/// <param name="url">The URL to download.</param>
/// <returns>The contents of the URL that was
/// downloaded.</returns>
```

```
public String DownloadPage(Uri url)
{
      WebRequest http = HttpWebRequest.Create(url);
      HttpWebResponse response =
            (HttpWebResponse)http.GetResponse();
      StreamReader stream = new
            StreamReader(
            response.GetResponseStream(),
            System.Text.Encoding.ASCII    );

      String result = stream.ReadToEnd();

      response.Close();
      stream.Close();
      return result;
}

/// <summary>
/// Run the example.
/// </summary>
public void Go()
{
      Uri u =
new Uri("http://www.httprecipes.com/1/3/time.php");
      String str = DownloadPage(u);

      Console.WriteLine(Extract(str, "<b>",
            "</b>", 1));
}



/// <summary>
/// The main entry point for the application.
/// </summary>
[STAThread]
static void Main(string[] args)
{
      GetTime module = new GetTime();
      module.Go();
}
   }
}
```

The main portion of this program is contained in a method named **Go**. The following three lines do the main work performed by the **Go** method.

```
Uri u = new Uri("http://www.httprecipes.com/1/3/time.php");
```

```
String str = DownloadPage(u);

Console.WriteLine(Extract(str, "<b>", "</b>", 1));
```

First, a **Uri** object is constructed with the URL that we are to download from. This **Uri** object is then passed to the **DownloadPage** function.

Using the **DownloadPage** function from the last recipe, we can download the above HTML into a string. Now that the above data is in a string, you may ask - what is the easiest way to extract the date and time? Any C# string parsing method can do this. However, this recipe provides one very useful function, **Extract** to do this. The contents of the **Extract** function are shown here:

```
int location1, location2;

location1 = location2 = 0;
do
{
  location1 = str.IndexOf(token1, location1+1);

  if (location1 == -1)
    return null;

  count--;
} while (count > 0);

location2 = str.IndexOf(token2, location1 + 1);
if (location2 == -1)
  return null;

location1+=token1.Length;
return str.Substring(location1, location2-location1 );
```

As you can see from above, the **Extract** function is passed a string to parse, including the beginning and ending tags. The **Extract** function will then scan the specified string, and find the beginning tag. In this case, the beginning tag is **<b>**. Once the beginning tag is found, the **Extract** function will return all text found until the ending tag is found.

It is important to note that the beginning and ending text need not be HTML tags. You can use any beginning and ending text you wish with the **Extract** function.

You might also notice that the **Extract** function accepts a number as its last parameter. In this case, the number passed was one. This number specifies which instance of the beginning text to locate. In this example there was only one **<b>** to find. What if there were several? Passing in a two for the last parameter would have located the text at the second instance of the **<b>** tag.

The **Extract** function is not part of C#. It is a useful function that I developed to help with string parsing. The extract function returns some text that is bounded by two token strings. Now, let's take a look at how it works.

The **Extract** function begins by declaring two **int** variables. Additionally the parameters **token1** and **token2** are passed in. The parameter **token1** holds the text, which is usually an HTML tag at the beginning of the desired text. The parameter **token2** holds the text, which is usually an HTML tag at the end of the desired text.

```
int location1, location2;

location1 = location2 = 0;
```

These two variables will hold the location of the beginning and ending text. To begin, set both to zero. Next, the function will begin looking for instances of **token1**. This is done with a **do/while** loop.

```
do
{
  location1 = str.IndexOf(token1, location1+1);

  if (location1 == -1)
    return null;
```

As you can see **location1** is set to the location of **token1**. The search begins at **location1**. Since **location1** begins with the value of zero, this search also begins at the beginning of the string. If no instance of **token1** is found, the **null** is returned to let the caller know that the string could not be extracted.

Each time an instance of **token1** is found, the variable **count** is decreased by one. This is shown here:

```
  count--;
} while (count > 0);
```

Once the final instance of **token1** has been found, it is time to locate the ending token. This is done with the following lines of code:

```
location2 = str.IndexOf(token2, location1 + 1);
if (location2 == -1)
  return null;

location1+=token1.Length;
return str.Substring(location1, location2-location1 );
```

The above code locates **token2** using **IndexOf**. If the second token is not found, then **null** is returned to indicate an error. Otherwise **Substring** is called to return the text between the two tokens. It is important to remember to add the length of **token1** to **location1**. If you do not add this to **location1**, you will extract **token1** along with the desired text.

This recipe can be applied to any real-world site that contains data on a single page that you wish to extract. Although this recipe extracted information from the web page, it did not do anything with it. The next recipe will process the downloaded data.

Recipe #3.3: Parsing Dates and Times

This recipe shows how to extract data from several pages. It also shows how to parse date and time information. This recipe will download the date and time for several US cities. It will extract this data from the following URL:

http://www.httprecipes.com/1/3/cities.php

Figure 3.3 shows this web page.

Figure 3.3: Cities for which to Display Time

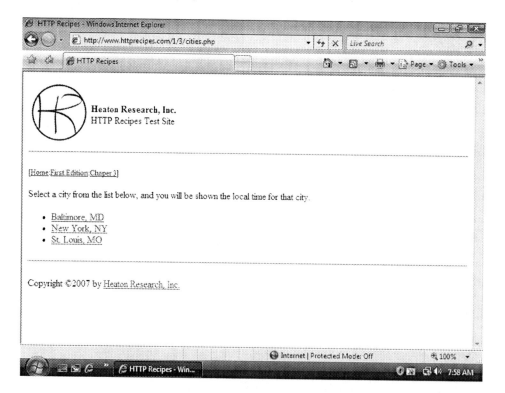

As you can see from the above list, there are three USA cities for which you may choose to find the time. To find the time for each city, click on the link and view that city's page. This means a total of four pages to access - first the city list page, then a page for each of the three cities.

The following recipe will access the city list page, obtain the URL for each city, and then obtain the time for that city. Now, let's examine Listing 3.4 - the HTML that makes up the city list page.

Listing 3.4: The HTML for the Cities List

```
<!DOCTYPE HTML PUBLIC "-//W3C//DTD HTML 4.01 Transitional//EN">

<HTML>
<HEAD>
     <TITLE>HTTP Recipes</TITLE>
     <meta http-equiv="Content-Type" content="text/html;
charset=UTF-8">
     <meta http-equiv="Cache-Control" content="no-cache">
</HEAD>

<BODY>

<table border="0"><tr><td>
<a href="http://www.httprecipes.com/">
<img src="/images/logo.gif" alt="Heaton Research Logo" bor-
der="0"></a>
</td><td valign="top">Heaton Research, Inc.<br>
HTTP Recipes Test Site
</td></tr>
</table>
<hr><p><small>[<a href="/">Home</a>:<a href="/1/">First Edition
</a>:
<a href="/1/3/">Chaper 3</a>]</small></p>

<p>Select a city from the list below, and you will be
shown the local time for that city.<br>
<ul>
<li><a href="city.php?city=2">Baltimore, MD</a>
<li><a href="city.php?city=3">New York, NY</a>
<li><a href="city.php?city=1">St. Louis, MO</a></ul>

<hr>
<p>Copyright 2006 by <a href="http://www.heatonresearch.com/">
Heaton Research, Inc.</a></p>
</BODY>
</HTML>
```

Can you find the cities in the above HTML? Find the **<li>** tags and you will find the cities. Each of these city lines link to the **city.php** page. For example, to display Baltimore's time, access the following URL:

http://www.httprecipes.com/1/3/city.php?city=2

This recipe will access the city list page to obtain a list of cities. That list will then be used to build a second list that will contain the times for each of those cities. See Recipe 3.3 in Listing 3.5.

Listing 3.5: Get the Time for Select Cities (GetCityTime.cs)

```csharp
using System;
using System.IO;
using System.Net;

namespace Recipe3_3
{
    class GetCityTime
    {

        /// <summary>
        /// This method is very useful for grabbing
        /// information from a
        /// HTML page.
        /// </summary>
        /// <param name="str">The string to parse.</param>
        /// <param name="token1">The text, or tag, that
        /// comes before the desired text</param>
        /// <param name="token2">The text, or tag, that
        /// comes after the desired text</param>
        /// <param name="count">Which occurrence of token1
        /// to use, 1 for the first</param>
        /// <returns>The contents of the URL that was
        /// downloaded.</returns>
        public String Extract(String str, String token1,
              String token2, int count)
        {
            int location1, location2;

            location1 = location2 = 0;
            do
            {
                location1 = str.IndexOf(
                    token1, location1+1);

                if (location1 == -1)
```

```
                return null;

            count--;
      } while (count > 0);

      location2 = str.IndexOf(token2, location1 + 1);
      if (location2 == -1)
            return null;

      location1+=token1.Length;
      return str.Substring(location1,
            location2-location1 );
}


/// <summary>
/// This method downloads the specified URL into a C#
/// String. This is a very simple method, that you can
/// reused anytime you need to quickly grab all
/// data from a specific URL.
/// </summary>
/// <param name="url">The URL to download.</param>
/// <returns>The contents of the URL that was
/// downloaded.</returns>
public String DownloadPage(Uri url)
{
      WebRequest http = HttpWebRequest.Create(url);
      HttpWebResponse response =
            (HttpWebResponse)http.GetResponse();
      StreamReader stream =
            new StreamReader(
                  response.GetResponseStream(),
                  System.Text.Encoding.ASCII   );

      String result = stream.ReadToEnd();

      response.Close();
      stream.Close();
      return result;
}

/**
 * Run the example.
 */
public DateTime getCityTime(int city)
{
      Uri u = new Uri(
```

```csharp
            "http://www.httprecipes.com/1/3/city.php?city="
                + city);
        String str = DownloadPage(u);

        DateTime date = DateTime.Parse(
            Extract(str, "<b>", "</b>", 1));
        return date;
    }


    /// <summary>
    /// Run the example.
    /// </summary>
    public void Go()
    {
        Uri u =
new Uri("http://www.httprecipes.com/1/3/cities.php");
        String str = DownloadPage(u);
        int count = 1;
        bool done = false;

        while (!done)
        {
            String line = Extract(
                str, "<li>", "</a>", count);

            if (line != null)
            {
                String dl = Extract(
                    line, "=", "\"", 2);
                int cityNum = int.Parse(dl);
                int i = line.IndexOf(">");
                String cityName = line.Substring(
                    i + 1);
                DateTime cityTime =
                    getCityTime(cityNum);
                String time =
                    cityTime.ToShortTimeString();
                Console.WriteLine(count
+ " " + cityName + "\t" + time);
            }
            else
                done = true;
            count++;
        }
    }
```

```
/// <summary>
/// The main entry point for the application.
/// </summary>
[STAThread]
static void Main(string[] args)
{
        GetCityTime module = new GetCityTime();
        module.Go();
}
    }
}
```

This recipe uses the same **Extract** and **DownloadPage** as the previous examples. However, the main **Go** method is different. We will begin by examining the **Go** method to see how the list of cities is downloaded.

First, a **Uri** object is constructed for the city list URL, and the entire contents are downloaded.

```
Uri u = new Uri("http://www.httprecipes.com/1/3/cities.php");
String str = DownloadPage(u);
```

After the entire contents of the city list page have been downloaded, we must parse through the HTML and find each of the cities. To begin, a **count** variable is created, which holds the current city number. Secondly, a **done** variable is created and initialized to **false**. This is demonstrated in the following lines of code:

```
int count = 1;
bool done = false;

while (!done)
{
  String line = Extract(str, "<li>", "</a>", count);
```

To extract each city, the beginning and ending tokens to search between must be identified. If you examine Listing 3.4, you will see that each city is on a line between the tokens **<li>** and **</a>**.

```
<li><a href="city.php?city=2">Baltimore, MD</a>
```

Calling the **Extract** function with these two tokens will return Baltimore as follows:

```
<a href="city.php?city=2">Baltimore, MD
```

The above value will be copied into the **line** variable that is then parsed.

```
if (line != null)
{
  String dl = Extract(line, "=", "\"", 2);
  int cityNum = int.Parse(dl);
  int i = line.IndexOf(">");
  String cityName = line.Substring(i + 1);
  DateTime cityTime = getCityTime(cityNum);
```

Next, we will parse out the city number by extracting what is between the **=** and the quote character. Given the line extracted (shown above), the extract function should return a "2" for Baltimore. Finally, we parse the city and state by searching for a **>** symbol. Extracting everything to the right of the **>** symbol will give us "Baltimore, MD." We now have the city's number, as well as its name and state.

We now can pass the city's number into the **GetCityTime** function. The **GetCityTime** function performs the same operation as the last recipe; that is, it will access the **Uri** for the city for which we are seeking the time. The time will be returned as a string. For more information about how the **GetCityTime** function works, review Recipe 3.2.

Now that we have the city time, we will format and display it, as shown below:

```
  String time = cityTime.ToShortTimeString();
  Console.WriteLine(count + " " + cityName + "\t" + time);
}
else
  done = true;
count++;
}
```

Notice in the above code, that in this program, the time is formatted to exclude the date. This allows us to display each of the cities, and the current time, without displaying the date.

This recipe can be revised and applied to any real-world site containing a list that leads to multiple other pages from which you wish to extract data.

Recipe #3.4: Downloading a Binary File

The last two recipes for this chapter demonstrate how to download data from a web site directly to a disk file. The first recipe will download to a binary file; the second will show how to download to a text file. A binary file download makes an exact copy of what was at the URL. The binary download is best used with a non-text resource, such as an image, sound or application file. Text files must be treated differently and will be discussed in detail in Recipe 3.5.

To demonstrate downloading to a binary file, this recipe will download an image from the HTTP recipes site. This image can be seen on the web page at the following URL:

`http://www.httprecipes.com/1/3/sea.php`

The contents of this page are shown in Figure 3.4.

Figure 3.4: An Image to Download

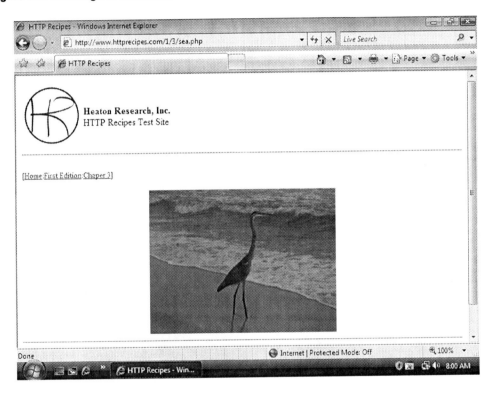

If you examine the HTML source for this page you will find that the actual image is located at the following URL:

`http://www.httprecipes.com/1/3/sea.jpg`

Now let's examine how to download an image by downloading a binary file. The example recipe, Recipe 3.4, is shown below in Listing 3.6.

Listing 3.6: Download a Binary File (DownloadBinary.cs)

```
using System;
using System.IO;
using System.Net;

namespace Recipe3_4
{
    class DownloadBinary
    {
        /// <summary>
        /// Used to convert strings to byte arrays.
        /// </summary>
        private System.Text.UTF8Encoding
            encoding=new System.Text.UTF8Encoding();

        /// <summary>
        /// This method downloads the specified URL into a C#
        /// String. This is a very simple method, that you can
        /// reused anytime you need to quickly grab all data
        /// from a specific URL.
        /// </summary>
        /// <param name="url">The URL to download.</param>
        /// <returns>The contents of the URL that was
        /// downloaded.</returns>
        public void DownloadBinaryFile(Uri url,
            String filename)
        {
            byte []buffer = new byte[4096];
            FileStream os = new FileStream(
                filename,FileMode.Create);
            WebRequest http = HttpWebRequest.Create(url);
            HttpWebResponse response =
                (HttpWebResponse)http.GetResponse();
            Stream stream = response.GetResponseStream();

            int count = 0;
            do
            {
                count = stream.Read(buffer,0,
                    buffer.Length);
                if(count>0)
                    os.Write(buffer,0,count);
            } while(count>0);

            response.Close();
            stream.Close();
```

```
                os.Close();
        }




    /// <summary>
    /// The main entry point for the program.
    /// </summary>
    /// <param name="args">Program arguments.</param>
        static void Main(string[] args)
        {
                if (args.Length != 2)
                {
                        DownloadBinary d = new DownloadBinary();
                        d.DownloadBinaryFile(new Uri(
"http://www.httprecipes.com/1/3/sea.jpg"), "./sea2.jpg");
                }
                else
                {
                        DownloadBinary d = new DownloadBinary();
                        d.DownloadBinaryFile(new Uri(args[0]),
                            args[1]);
                }
        }
    }
}
```

This recipe is very similar to Recipe 3.1. However, in this recipe, you must specify a URL and a file to save that URL to. For example, to download the Heaton Research logo, use the following command:

```
Recipe3_4 http://www.httprecipes.com/images/logo.gif ./logo.gif
```

The above arguments would download the image shown above to a file named **logo.jpg**. For more information on how to execute the recipes in this book refer to Appendix B, "Compiling and Executing Examples."

As mentioned, this recipe is very similar to Recipe 3.1. It uses the same **DownloadPage** function as Recipe 3.1; however, an extra method is added named **SaveBinaryPage**. This method is shown here.

```
public void DownloadBinaryFile(Uri url,String filename)
```

As you can see, this method accepts a **filename** and a **page**. The specified page content will be saved to the local file specified by **filename**. The variable, **page,** contains the contents of the page, as returned by the **DownloadPage** function.

To save a binary file, the data must be read in blocks, and then written to a file. First a buffer, size 4,096, is created to hold the blocks of data.

```
byte []buffer = new byte[4096];
```

Next a file is opened to store the binary file to.

```
FileStream os = new FileStream(filename,FileMode.Create);
```

A web connection is opened to download the URL from.

```
WebRequest http = HttpWebRequest.Create(url);
HttpWebResponse response = (HttpWebResponse)http.GetResponse();
Stream stream = response.GetResponseStream();
```

A **do/while** loop is used to read each of the blocks and then write them to the file. Once a zero-sized block is read, there is no more data to download.

```
int count = 0;
do
{
  count = stream.Read(buffer,0,buffer.Length);
  if(count>0)
    os.Write(buffer,0,count);
} while(count>0);

response.Close();
stream.Close();
os.Close();
```

Finally, the stream and file are closed. This recipe could be applied to any real-world site where you need to download images, or other binary files to disk.

In this recipe, you learned how to download a binary file. Binary files are exact copies of what is downloaded from the URL. In the next recipe you will see how to download a text file.

Recipe #3.5: Downloading a Text File

This recipe will download a web page to a text file. But why is a text file treated differently to a binary file? They are treated differently because different operating systems end lines differently. Table 3.2 summarizes how the different operating systems store text file line breaks.

Table 3.2: How Operating Systems End Lines

Operating System	ASCII Codes	C#
UNIX	#10	"\n"
Windows	#13 #10	"\r\n"
Mac OSX	#10	"\n"
Mac Classic	#13	"\r"

To download a text file properly, the program must make sure that the line breaks are compatible with the operating system. C# currently runs primarily on the Windows platform. However, projects such as Mono will continue to expand C#'s reach. Because of this, it is important to handle text files properly for the operating system your bot is running on. Listing 3.7 shows how this is done.

Listing 3.7: Download a Text File (DownloadText.cs)

```
using System;
using System.IO;
using System.Net;

namespace Recipe3_5
{
    class DownloadText
    {
        /// <summary>
        /// Download the specified text page.
        /// </summary>
        /// <param name="page">The URL to download from.
        /// </param>
        /// <param name="filename">The local file to
        /// save to.</param>
        public void DownloadTextFile(String page,
            String filename)
        {
            Uri u = new Uri(page);
            FileStream os =
                new FileStream(filename,FileMode.Create);
            HttpWebRequest http =
                (HttpWebRequest)HttpWebRequest.Create(u);
            HttpWebResponse response =
                (HttpWebResponse)http.GetResponse();
            StreamReader reader = new StreamReader(
response.GetResponseStream(),System.Text.Encoding.ASCII   );
            StreamWriter writer = new StreamWriter(os,
                System.Text.Encoding.ASCII   );
```

```
                http.AllowAutoRedirect = false;
                    String line;
                    do
                    {
                            line = reader.ReadLine();
                            if( line!=null )
                                    writer.WriteLine(line);

                    } while(line!=null);

                    reader.Close();
                    writer.Close();
                    os.Close();
            }


            /// <summary>
            /// The main entry point for the application.
            /// </summary>
            [STAThread]
            static void Main(string[] args)
            {
                    if (args.Length != 2)
                    {
                            DownloadText d = new DownloadText();
                            d.DownloadTextFile(
"http://www.httprecipes.com/1/3/text.php", "./text.html");
                    }
                    else
                    {
                            DownloadText d = new DownloadText();
                            d.DownloadTextFile(args[0], args[1]);
                    }
            }
        }
    }
}
```

It is easy to use this recipe. For example, to download the main page of the HTTP recipes site, use the following command:

```
Recipe3_5 http://www.httprecipes.com/ ./contents.txt
```

The above arguments would download the contents of the main page of the HTTP recipes site to the file named **contents.txt**. For more information on how to execute the recipes in this book refer to Appendix B, "Compiling and Executing Examples."

This recipe works differently than Recipe 3.4, in that the text file is not first loaded to a string. Rather, the text file is read from the input stream as it is written to the output stream. One method, **DownloadText**, accepts an input stream and an output stream. The input stream should be from the URL, and the output stream should be to a disk file. This method is shown here:

```
private void downloadText(InputStream is, OutputStream os) throws
IOException
{
```

The first thing that the **DownloadText** method must do is create a **Uri** object to hold the page that is to be downloaded.

```
Uri u = new Uri(page);
```

Next a file is opened to hold the text file.

```
FileStream os = new FileStream(filename,FileMode.Create);
```

A stream is acquired for the desired page.

```
WebRequest http = HttpWebRequest.Create(u);
HttpWebResponse response = (HttpWebResponse)http.GetResponse();
```

The **StreamReader** class allows a stream to be read as text. When the **StreamReader** class is used C# will handle using the correct end of line characters.

```
StreamReader reader = new StreamReader(response.GetResponseStream(
),System.Text.Encoding.ASCII   );
```

The **StreamWriter** class allows a stream to be written as text. When the **StreamWriter** class is used, C# will write the correct end of line characters.

```
StreamWriter writer = new StreamWriter(os,System.Text.Encoding.
ASCII   );
```

To download the file, the URL is read line-by-line. As each line is read, it is written to the **StreamWriter**.

```
String line;
do
{
  line = reader.ReadLine();
  if( line!=null )
    writer.WriteLine(line);
} while(line!=null);
```

Finally all of the streams are closed.

```
reader.Close();
writer.Close();
os.Close();
```

The algorithm is useful because it allows you to convert incoming text to exactly how the operating system would like it to be represented.

Summary

In this chapter you learned how to perform basic HTTP operations with C#. You learned how to access a URL and download the contents of that URL.

C# contains a **Uri** class. This class allows you to open connections to a URI. You can obtain a stream to the URI. Once you have a **Stream**, you can read from the URI essentially the same as if you were reading from a file.

It was explained that downloading to a binary file means making an exact copy of the incoming data and is preferred when downloading images, audio and other binary data. Downloading a text file requires you to translate the incoming line breaks to the correct format for your operating system.

In this chapter you learned how to use the **Uri** and **Stream** classes to access web pages. This is fine for simple requests; however, for more complex requests you will need to use the **WebRequest** and **WebResponse** classes. This topic will be introduced in the next chapter.

CHAPTER 4: BEYOND SIMPLE REQUESTS

- The WebRequest Class
- The WebResponse Class
- Reading HTTP Response Headers
- Setting HTTP Request Headers
- Managing HTTP Timeouts

The connection between a bot and a web server is very important. In the previous chapters this link was established using either a **Socket** object or through a Stream. In summary, the two ways to open a connection to a web server are via:

- Socket, or
- WebRequest and WebResponse

In the previous chapter you saw how to open a stream to a URL. Review the following commands.

```
HttpWebRequest http = (HttpWebRequest)HttpWebRequest.Create(url);
HttpWebResponse response = (HttpWebResponse)http.GetResponse();
Stream stream = response.GetResponseStream();
```

In the previous chapter we used the stream to read data from URL. You will also notice that there are two other objects created in addition to the stream. The additional objects created are a **WebRequest** and an **HttpWebResponse**. These objects allow you to perform additional operations on the HTTP connection, other than simply reading from it. These operations include:

- Reading data from the URL
- Posting data to the URL
- Setting client headers
- Reading server headers
- Setting socket parameters

In the next several two sections the **HttpWebRequest** and **HttpWebResponse** will be examined.

Using HttpWebRequest

The **HttpWebRequest** class is a child class of the **WebRequest** class. For HTTP connections you can use either class. However, some of the HTTP options are only available with the **HttpWebRequest**. Therefore, most of the examples in this book use the **HttpWebRequest** class.

One of the main options available through the **HttpWebRequest** class is the ability to set request headers. Request headers are sent by the web browser to the web server to provide additional information to the web server. These headers are commonly used for the following purposes:

- Identifying the type of web browser
- Transmitting any cookies
- Facilitating HTTP authentication

There are other things that can be accomplished with HTTP request headers; however, these are the most common. HTTP authentication will be explained in Chapter 5, "Secure HTTP Requests," and cookies will be explained in Chapter 8, "Handling Sessions and Cookies". Setting the type of browser will be covered later in this section.

Setting HTTP Request Headers

The **Headers** property of the **HttpWebRequest** class provides several functions and methods that can be used to access HTTP request headers. These functions and methods are shown in Table 4.1.

Table 4.1: HTTP Request Header Methods and Functions

Method or Function Name	Purpose
Set (String key, String value)	Set the header to the specified value. If a header named that already exists, it is overwritten.
Add (String key, String value)	Adds the specified header. If there is already a header named this, then a second is created.
Keys	Returns a list of all HTTP headers.

Usually the only method from the above list that you will use will be the **Set** method. The others are useful when you need to query what values have already been set. If there is already a header with the specified name, Set will overwrite it. **Add** can be used to add more than one of the same request headers with the same name. Usually, you do not want to do this. Adding more than one header of the same name is useful when dealing with cookies - which are discussed in Chapter 8, "Handling Sessions and Cookies".

Identifying the Browser Type

One of the HTTP request headers identifies the browser type that the user is using. Many web sites take this header into account. For example, some web sites are only designed to work with certain versions of Microsoft Internet Explorer. To make use of such sites, you need to change how **HttpWebRequest** reports the browser type.

The browser type can be determined from the **user-agent** HTTP request header. You can easily set the value of this, or any, HTTP request header using the **set** method of the Headers collection. For example, to identify the bot as a browser of type "My Bot", use the following command:

```
http.Headers.Set("user-agent", "My Bot");
```

The **user-agent** header is often used to identify the bot. For example, each of the major search engines use spiders to find pages for their search engines. These search engine companies use **user-agent** headers to identify them as a search engine spider, and not a human user.

When you write a bot of your own, you have some decisions to make with the **user-agent** header. You can either identify the bot, as seen above, or you can emulate one of the common browsers. If a web site requires a version of Internet Explorer, you will have to emulate Internet Explorer.

Table 4.2 shows the header used by most major browsers to identify them. As you can see, this header also communicates what operating system the user is running as well.

Table 4.2: Identities of Several Major Browsers

Browser	User-Agent Header
FireFox 1.5	Mozilla/5.0(PC) (Windows; U; Windows NT 5.1; en-US; rv:1.8.0.4) Gecko/20060508 Firefox/1.5.0.4
Internet Explorer 6.0	Mozilla/4.0(PC) (compatible; MSIE 6.0; Windows NT 5.1; SV1; .NET CLR 1.1.4322)
Safari v2 (Mac)	Mozilla/5.0 (Macintosh; U; PPC Mac OS X; en) AppleWebKit/418.8 (KHTML, like Gecko) Safari/419.3
Firefox v1.5 (Mac)	Mozilla/5.0 (Macintosh; U; PPC Mac OS X Mach-O; en-US; rv:1.8.0.4) Gecko/20060508 Firefox/1.5.0.4
Internet Explorer 5.1 (Mac)	Mozilla/4.0 (compatible; MSIE 5.14; Mac_PowerPC)
Java(PC/Mac)	Java/1.5.0_06
C#	By default no user-agent is provided.

You will also notice from the above list, I have C# and Java listed as browsers. This is what C# or Java will report to a web site, if you do not override the **user-agent**. It is usually better to override this value with something else. C# provides no user agent by default.

Using HttpWebResponse

The HttpWebResponse. The server headers contain many useful pieces of information. Server headers are commonly used for:

- Determining the type of data at a URL
- Determining the cookies in use
- Determining the web server software in use
- Determining the size of the content at this URL

For the bots that you create, you will most commonly use server headers to determine the type of data at a URL and to support cookies.

Reading Server Headers

The **HttpWebResponse** class is a child class of the **WebResponse** class. For HTTP connections you can use either class. However, some of the HTTP options are only available with the **HttpWebResponse**. As a result, most of the examples in this book make use of the **HttpWebResponse** class.

Once you retrieve the contents of a URL back from the server, there are headers available to the program. The web server provided this second set of headers. The **Headers** property of the **HttpWebResponse** class provides access to these headers. In the next section you will see how to access the headers.

MIME Types

One very important HTTP response header is the content type. The **content-type** header tells the web browser what type of data the URL is attached to. For example, to determine the type of content at a URL, you would use the following line of code:

```
Console.WriteLine(response.Headers["Content-Type"]);
```

This type of information is called a Multipurpose Internet Mail Extension (MIME). The "Mail" in MIME is largely historical. MIME types were originally developed for email attachments, long before there was a World Wide Web (WWW). However, they are now applied to many different Internet applications, such as web browsers and servers.

A MIME type consists of two identifiers separated by a slash (/). For example, **text/html** is a mime type that identifies a resource as an HTML document. The first part of the type, in this case **text**, identifies the family of the type. The second identifies the exact type, within that family. Plain text files are also part of the **text** family, and have the type **text/plain**. Some of the common MIME types are summarized in Table 4.3.

Table 4.3: MIME Families

MIME Family	Purpose
application	Application, or raw binary data
audio	Sounds and music
example	Used only for example types
image	Image
message	Mail messages
model	Compound type document
multipart	Another compound type documents
text	Text formats
video	Video formats

There are many different MIME types under each of these families. However, there is only a handful that you will commonly see. Table 4.4 summarizes these.

Table 4.4: Common MIME Types

MIME Type	Purpose
image/gif	GIF image files
image/jpeg	JPEG image files
image/png	PNG image files
image/tiff	TIFF image files
text/html	HTML text files
text/plain	Unformatted text files

Often, the program will only need to look at the family. For example, if you wanted to download `text` and binary files differently, you would simply look at the family part of the MIME type. If it is determined that `text` is the family, you may download the URL as a text file. Any other family would require downloading the information as a binary file. The difference between a binary file and a text file is that binary files are copied exactly to the hard drive, whereas text file's line endings are reformatted properly for the resident operating system.

Calling Sequence

As you have seen in this chapter, a variety of operations can be performed on the **HttpWebRequest** and **HttpWebResponse** classes. You can set request headers, read response headers, **POST** data and read response data. Please note, however, that these operations must follow a very specific order. For example, you can't set a request header, after you are already reading the response. If you are reading the web server's reply, the request has already been sent. Therefore, all request information must be set before you begin working with the response. The general order that you should follow is:

- Step 1: Obtain a **HttpWebRequest** object.
- Step 2: Set any HTTP request headers.
- Step 3: POST data, if this is a POST request.
- Step 4: Obtain a **HttpWebResponse** object.
- Step 4: Read HTTP response headers.
- Step 5: Read HTTP response data.

If you ever face a bug where it seems the request headers are being ignored, check to see if you are not already calling a method related to the response before setting the header. All headers must be set before the request is sent.

Other Useful Options

In addition to headers, there are that the **HttpWebRequest** and **HttpWebResponse** classes provide other useful options. Although there are a number of options in the **HttpWebRequest** and **HttpWebResponse** classes, most are used only for very rare or obscure situations. In this section we will examine the two most commonly used options in these classes. The two most frequently used are "timeouts" and "redirect following". The next two sections will cover these options.

Timeout

While connecting to a URL C# will only wait a specified number of seconds. One timeout value is provided to the **HttpWebRequest** class. The two timeouts that can occur are:

- Timeout while connecting to the web host.
- Timeout while transferring data with the web host.

To control the timeout you should use the **Timeout** property of the **HttpWebRequest** object. This would be done as follows:

```
Request.Timeout = 1000;
```

The above code would set the timeout to 1000 milliseconds, or one second.

Redirect Following

One very handy feature in HTTP is "redirect following". Many web sites make use of the HTTP redirect internally, so you will most likely encounter redirects when writing a bot. The HTTP redirect allows the server to redirect the web browser to a new URL.

To see an HTTP redirect in action, enter the following URL into your web browser. You would expect the browser to take you to the URL you entered.

`http://www.httprecipes.com/1/4/redirect.php`

However, you do not end up on the above URL. You actually end up at the root of the "Recipe Site" at the following URL:

`http://www.httprecipes.com/`

This was due to an HTTP redirect. By default, the **HttpWebRequest** class will follow all such redirects automatically and often. You do not need to even be concerned with them. Web browsers will always follow redirects automatically. However, if you would like to handle the redirects yourself, you can disable auto following. The following line of code would do this:

```
request.AllowAutoRedirect = false;
```

If you disable redirection following, you may manually follow the redirects by looking at the **location** response header.

Recipes

This chapter includes four recipes. These four recipes will demonstrate the following:

- Scanning a URL for headers
- Searching a range of IP addresses for web sites
- Downloading a binary or text file
- Monitoring a site to see that it stays up

These recipes will introduce you to some of the things that can be done with the **HttpWebRequest and HttpWebResponse classes**.

Recipe #4.1: Scan URL

Sometimes it is helpful to examine the headers for a particular URL. Recipe 4.1 shows how to use the **HttpWebResponse** class to access the headers for a particular URL. This program is shown in Listing 4.1.

Listing 4.1: Scan a URL for HTTP Response Headers (ScanURL.cs)

```csharp
using System;
using System.IO;
using System.Net;

namespace Recipe4_1
{
    class ScanURL
    {
        /// <summary>
        /// Scan the URL and display headers.
        /// </summary>
        /// <param name="u">The URL to scan.</param>
        public void Scan(String u)
        {
            Uri url = new Uri(u);
            WebRequest http = HttpWebRequest.Create(url);
            WebResponse response = http.GetResponse();

            int count = 0;
            String key, value;

            for(count=0;count<
                    response.Headers.Keys.Count;count++)
            {
                key = response.Headers.Keys[count];
                value = response.Headers[key];

                if (value != null)
                {
                    if (key == null)
                        Console.WriteLine(value);
                    else
                        Console.WriteLine(
                                key + ": " + value);
                }
            }
        }

        /// <summary>
        /// The main entry point for the application.
        /// </summary>
        [STAThread]
        static void Main(string[] args)
        {
```

```
        if (args.Length != 1)
        {
    Console.WriteLine(
            "Usage: Recipe4_1 [URL to Scan]");
        }
        else
        {
            ScanURL d = new ScanURL();
            d.Scan(args[0]);
        }
    }


    }
}
```

This program is designed to accept one parameter, which is the URL that you would like to scan. For example, to scan the web site **http://www.httprecipes.com/** you would use the following command.

```
Recipe4_1 http://www.httprecipes.com/
```

Issuing the above command would cause the program to access the web site and then display all HTTP server headers that were returned.

All of the work performed by this program is done inside the **Scan** method. The first thing that the scan method does is to create a new **Uri** object that is used to create an **HttpWebRequest** object from there. The following lines of code do this.

```
Uri url = new Uri(u);
WebRequest http = HttpWebRequest.Create(url);
WebResponse response = http.GetResponse();
```

Once the connection has been established, a few local variables are created to keep track of the headers being displayed. The **key** variable will hold the name of each header found. The **value** variable will hold the value of that header. The **count** variable keeps a count of the header we are on.

```
int count = 0;
String key, value;
```

Next, a **for** loop will be used to loop through each of the headers.

```
for(count=0;count<response.Headers.Keys.Count;count++)
{
  key = response.Headers.Keys[count];
  value = response.Headers[key];
```

The headers are read in one by one and displayed.

```
if (value != null)
{
  if (key == null)
    Console.WriteLine(value);
  else
    Console.WriteLine(key + ": " + value);
```

This process will continue until all headers have been displayed.

Recipe #4.2: Scan for Sites

You can also use the C# HTTP classes to determine if there is an active web server at a specific URL. Recipe 4.2 shows how to loop through a series of IP addresses to find any web servers. To use this program, you must specify an IP address prefix. An example of this would be **192.168.1**. Specifying this prefix would visit 256 IP addresses. It would visit from **192.168.1.0** to **192.168.1.255**.

This next recipe shows how to decrease the timeout for connection. Because almost all of the IP addresses do not have web servers, it takes a while for this example to run. This is because by default, C# will wait several minutes to connect to a web server.

Because of this the connection timeout is taken down to only a few seconds. For a more thorough scan the timeout can be increased. Listing 4.2 shows the site scanner:

Listing 4.2: Scan for Web Sites (ScanSites.cs)

```csharp
using System;
using System.Net;
using System.IO;
using System.Collections.Generic;

namespace Recipe4_2
{
    class ScanSites
    {
        /// <summary>
        /// This method is very useful for grabbing
        /// information from a HTML page.  It extracts
        /// text from between two tokens, the
        /// tokens need not be case sensitive.
        /// </summary>
        /// <param name="str">The string to extract from.
        /// </param>
        /// <param name="token1">The text, or tag, that
        /// comes before the desired text</param>
        /// <param name="token2">The text, or tag, that
        /// comes after the desired text</param>
```

```csharp
/// <param name="count">Which occurrence of token1
/// to use, 1 for the first</param>
/// <returns></returns>
public String ExtractNoCase(String str,
      String token1, String token2,
      int count)
{
      int location1, location2;

      // convert everything to lower case
      String searchStr = str.ToLower();
      token1 = token1.ToLower();
      token2 = token2.ToLower();

      // now search
      location1 = location2 = 0;
      do
      {
            location1 =
            searchStr.IndexOf(token1, location1 + 1);

            if (location1 == -1)
                  return null;

            count--;
      } while (count > 0);

      // return the result from the original
      // string that has mixed case
      location1 += token1.Length;
      location2 = str.IndexOf(token2, location1 + 1);
      if (location2 == -1)
            return null;

      return str.Substring(location1,
            location2-location1 );
}

/// <summary>
/// This method downloads the specified URL into a C#
/// String. This is a very simple method, that you can
/// reused anytime you need to quickly grab all
/// data from a specific URL.
/// </summary>
/// <param name="url">The URL to download.</param>
/// <param name="timeout">The amount of time to
```

```csharp
/// wait before aborting.</param>
/// <returns>The contents of the URL that was
/// downloaded.</returns>
public String DownloadPage(Uri url,int timeout)
{
try
{
    WebRequest http = HttpWebRequest.Create(url);
    http.Timeout = timeout;
    HttpWebResponse response =
       (HttpWebResponse)http.GetResponse();
    StreamReader stream = new StreamReader(
response.GetResponseStream(), System.Text.Encoding.ASCII);

    String result = stream.ReadToEnd();

    response.Close();
    stream.Close();
    return result;
}
catch (Exception)
{
    return null;
}
}

/// <summary>
/// Scan the specified IP address and return the
/// title of the webpage found there, or null if
/// no connection can be made.
/// </summary>
/// <param name="ip">The IP address to scan.</param>
/// <returns>The title of the webpage, or null
/// if no website.</returns>
private String scanIP(String ip)
{
String title = null;

    Console.WriteLine("Scanning: " + ip);
    String page = DownloadPage(
        new Uri("http://" + ip), 1000);
if (page != null)
{
    title = ExtractNoCase(page, "<title>",
        "</title>", 0);
    if (title == null)
```

```csharp
            title = "[Untitled site]";
    }

        return title;
    }



    /// <summary>
    /// Scan a range of 256 IP addressed.  Provide
    /// the prefix of the IP address, without the
    /// final fourth.  For example "192.168.1".
    /// </summary>
    /// <param name="ip">The IP address prefix
    /// (i.e. 192.168.1)</param>
public void scan(String ip)
{
    if (!ip.EndsWith("."))
    {
        ip += ".";
    }

    // Create a list to hold sites found.
    List<String> list = new List<String>();

    // Scan through IP addresses ending in 0 - 255.
    for (int i = 1; i < 255; i++)
    {
        String address = ip + i;
        String title = scanIP(address);
        if (title != null)
            list.Add(address + ":" + title);
    }

    // Now display the list of sites found.
    Console.WriteLine();
    Console.WriteLine("Sites found:");
    if (list.Count > 0)
    {
        foreach (String site in list)
        {
            Console.WriteLine(site);
        }
    }
    else
    {
        Console.WriteLine("No sites found");
    }
```

```
            }

            /// <summary>
            /// The main entry point for the application.
            /// </summary>
            [STAThread]
            static void Main(string[] args)
            {
            if (args.Length != 1)
            {
                Console.WriteLine(
"Usage: Recipe4_2 [IP prefix, i.e. 192.168.1]");
            }
            else
            {
                ScanSites d = new ScanSites();
                d.scan(args[0]);
            }
            }
        }
}
```

To run this program, you must specify the IP prefix. For example, to scan the IP prefix **192.168.1**, use the following command:

```
Recipe4_2 192.168.1
```

You may find more sites on your home network than you knew existed. For example, I found that my laser printer has a web site. Logging into my printer's built in web site shows me how much toner is still available. You can see the results of my scan in Figure 4.1.

Figure 4.1: Scan for Sites

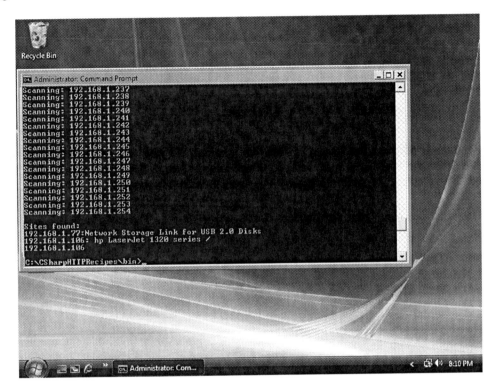

First the IP prefix is checked to see if it ends with a period ".". If it does not end this way, then a period is appended. This is because we need the IP prefix in the form:

```
192.168.1.
```

not

```
192.168.1
```

We will be appending a count from 0 to 255 to the end, so the trailing period is completely necessary.

```
if (!ip.EndsWith("."))
{
   ip += ".";
}
```

Next, an array is created to hold a list of the sites that are located. The sites located are not displayed until the end of the scan.

```
// Create a list to hold sites found.
List<String> list = new List<String>();
```

Now we are ready to scan. A **for** loop is used to count from 0 to 255.

```
// Scan through IP addresses ending in 0 - 255.
for (int i = 1; i < 255; i++)
{
  String address = ip + i;
  String title = scanIP(address);
  if (title != null)
    list.Add(address + ":" + title);
}
```

For each IP address, the **ScanIP** function is called. If a valid site exists at that address, the title (from the HTML) is returned. If no valid site is found, then the value **null** is returned. The **ScanIP** function is covered in detail later in this section.

Once the loop completes, we display what sites were found. The code to do this is shown below:

```
// Now display the list of sites found.
Console.WriteLine();
Console.WriteLine("Sites found:");
if (list.Count > 0)
{
  foreach (String site in list)
  {
    Console.WriteLine(site);
  }
}
```

The user is informed if there are no sites to display.

```
else
{
  Console.WriteLine("No sites found");
}
```

As you saw above, for each IP address, the **ScanIP** method was called. I will now show you how the **ScanIP** function is constructed.

The **ScanIP** function begins by displaying the IP address that is currently being scanned. The **DownloadPage** method is called to retrieve the HTML at the URL formed from the IP address. The following lines of code do this.

```
String title = null;

Console.WriteLine("Scanning: " + ip);
String page = DownloadPage(new Uri("http://" + ip), 1000);
```

If the **DownloadPage** function returns **null**, then the page could not be downloaded. If the page was downloaded, then look for the title and record it. If the page failed to download, there is nothing to record.

```
if (page != null)
{
  title = ExtractNoCase(page, "<title>", "</title>", 0);
  if (title == null)
    title = "[Untitled site]";
}
return title;
```

The **DownloadPage** function is the one we created in Chapter 3; however, you will notice an additional parameter. The second parameter specifies a 1,000-millisecond timeout. If a connection is not made in one second, (1,000 milliseconds), the connection will abort and throw an exception.

The **ExtractNoCase** function is called to extract the text between the **<title>** and **</title>** tags. The **ExtractNoCase** is a special version of the extract function introduced in Chapter 3. The **ExtractNoCase** version of extract does not care about the case of the tags. For example, **<title>** and **<Title>** would be considered the same. If no title is found, then the site is listed as an "Untitled Site".

This recipe makes use of the **ExtractNoCase** which is a new version of **DownloadPage**. Both of these functions can be seen in Listing 4.2. They are both slight modifications of the functions introduced in Chapter 3, "Simple HTTP Requests". For more information on these functions, see Chapter 3.

Recipe #4.3: Download Binary or Text

Downloading a file from a URL is a common task for a bot. However, different procedures must be followed depending on the type of file being downloaded. If the file is binary, such as an image, then an exact copy of the file must be made on the local computer. If the file is text, then the line breaks must be properly formatted for the current operating system.

Chapter 3 introduced two recipes for downloading files from a URL. One version downloads a text file; the other downloads a binary file. As you saw earlier in this chapter, the **content-type** header tells what type of file will be downloaded. Recipe 4.3 contains a more sophisticated URL downloader, than that in Chapter 3. It first determines the type of file and then downloads it in the appropriate way. Listing 4.3 shows this new URL downloader.

Listing 4.3: Download Text or Binary (DownloadURL.cs)

```
using System;
using System.Collections.Generic;
using System.Text;
using System.IO;
```

```csharp
using System.Net;

namespace Recipe4_3
{
    class DownloadURL
    {
        /// <summary>
        /// Download the specified text page.
        /// </summary>
        /// <param name="response">The HttpWebResponse to
        /// download from.</param>
        /// <param name="filename">The local file to save to.
        /// </param>
        public void DownloadBinaryFile(
            HttpWebResponse response, String filename)
        {
            byte[] buffer = new byte[4096];
            FileStream os = new FileStream(filename,
                    FileMode.Create);
            Stream stream = response.GetResponseStream();

            int count = 0;
            do
            {
                count = stream.Read(buffer, 0, buffer.Length);
                if (count > 0)
                    os.Write(buffer, 0, count);
            } while (count > 0);

            response.Close();
            stream.Close();
            os.Close();
        }

        /// <summary>
        /// Download the specified text page.
        /// </summary>
        /// <param name="response">The HttpWebResponse to
        /// download from.</param>
        /// <param name="filename">The local file to save to.
        /// </param>
        public void DownloadTextFile(
            HttpWebResponse response, String filename)
        {
            byte[] buffer = new byte[4096];
            FileStream os = new FileStream(filename,
```

```
        FileMode.Create);
    StreamReader reader = new StreamReader(
            response.GetResponseStream(),
            System.Text.Encoding.ASCII);
    StreamWriter writer = new StreamWriter(os,
            System.Text.Encoding.ASCII);

    String line;
    do
    {
        line = reader.ReadLine();
        if (line != null)
            writer.WriteLine(line);

    } while (line != null);

    reader.Close();
    writer.Close();
    os.Close();
}


/// <summary>
/// Download either a text or binary file from a URL.
/// The URL's headers will be scanned to determine the
/// type of tile.
/// </summary>
/// <param name="remoteURL">The URL to download from.
/// </param>
/// <param name="localFile">The local file to save to.
/// </param>
public void Download(Uri remoteURL, String localFile)
{
    WebRequest http = HttpWebRequest.Create(remoteURL);
    HttpWebResponse response =
            (HttpWebResponse)http.GetResponse();

    String type =
    response.Headers["Content-Type"].ToLower().Trim();
    if (type.StartsWith("text"))
        DownloadTextFile(response, localFile);
    else
        DownloadBinaryFile(response, localFile);

}
```

```
/// <summary>
/// The main entry point for the program.
/// </summary>
/// <param name="args">Program arguments.</param>
static void Main(string[] args)
{
    if (args.Length != 2)
    {
        Console.WriteLine(
    "Usage: Recipe4_3 [URL to Download] [Output File]");
    }
    else
    {
        DownloadURL d = new DownloadURL();
        d.Download(new Uri(args[0]), args[1]);
    }
}


    }
}
```

To run this program you must specify the URL to download and the local file. For example, to download the contents of **http://www.httprecipes.com** to the file **local.html**, use the following command:

```
Recipe4_3 http://www.httprecipes.com/ local.html
```

This program makes use of the following two methods that were first introduced in Chapter 3.

- DownloadText
- DownloadBinary

These two methods are exactly the same as the ones used in Chapter 3; therefore, they will not be discussed again here. If you would like more information about these two functions, refer to Chapter 3.

The example presented here connects to the specified URL and determines the type of that URL. Once the type is determined, the URL is downloaded by calling the appropriate download method, either **DownloadText** or **DownloadBinary**.

```
WebRequest http = HttpWebRequest.Create(remoteURL);
HttpWebResponse response = (HttpWebResponse)http.GetResponse();
```

Next, the **content-type** header is checked to determine what type of file it is. If it starts with "text", then the file is in the "text family", and it will be downloaded as a text file. Otherwise, the file is downloaded as a binary file.

```
String type = response.Headers["Content-Type"].ToLower().Trim();

if (type.StartsWith("text"))
  DownloadTextFile(response, localFile);
else
  DownloadBinaryFile(response, localFile);
```

Next, the **content-type** header is checked to determine the type of file. If it starts with "text", then the file is in the "text family" and it will be downloaded as a text file. Otherwise, the file is downloaded as a binary file.

This recipe can be used anywhere you need to download the contents of a URL. It frees the programmer from having to determine the type of file downloaded.

Recipe #4.4: Site Monitor

Bots are great at performing repetitive tasks. Probably one of the most repetitive tasks known, is checking to see if a web server is still up. If a person were to perform this task, they would sit at a computer with a stopwatch. Every minute, the user would click the refresh button on the browser, and make sure that the web site still loaded.

Recipe 4.4 will show how to accomplish this same task, using a bot. This program will attempt to connect to a web server every minute. As soon as the web server stops responding, the program displays a message alerting the user that the web server is down. This program is shown in Listing 4.4.

Listing 4.4: Monitor Site (MonitorSite.cs)

```
using System;
using System.Collections.Generic;
using System.Text;
using System.Net;
using System.IO;
using System.Threading;

namespace Recipe4_4
{
    class MonitorSite
    {
        /// <summary>
        /// Scan a URL every minute to make sure it is still up.
        /// </summary>
        /// <param name="url">The URL to monitor.</param>
        public void Monitor(Uri url)
        {
            while (true)
            {
```

```
                    Console.WriteLine("Checking " + url +
                      " at " + (new DateTime()));

                    // Try to connect.
                    try
                    {
                        WebRequest http = HttpWebRequest.Create(url);
                        HttpWebResponse response =
(HttpWebResponse)http.GetResponse();
                        Console.WriteLine("The site is up.");
                    }
                    catch (IOException)
                    {
                        Console.WriteLine("The site is down!!!");
                    }
                    Thread.Sleep(60000);
                }
            }

        /// <summary>
        /// Download either a text or binary file from a URL.
        /// The URL's headers will be scanned to determine the
        /// type of tile.
        /// </summary>
        /// <param name="remoteURL">The URL to download from.
        /// </param>
        /// <param name="localFile">The local file to save to.
        /// </param>
        static void Main(string[] args)
        {
            if (args.Length != 1)
            {
                Console.WriteLine(
                  "Usage: Recipe4_4 [URL to Monitor]");
            }
            else
            {
                MonitorSite d = new MonitorSite();
                d.Monitor(new Uri(args[0]));
            }
        }

    }
}
```

To run this program, you must specify which URL to monitor. For example, to monitor the web site at **http://www.httprecipes.com,** use the following command:

```
Recipe4_4 http://www.httprecipes.com/
```

The program begins by entering an endless loop. (Because of this, in order to exit this program, you must press **ctrl-c** or close its window.)

```
while (true)
{
  Console.WriteLine("Checking " + url + " at " +
    (new DateTime()));
```

The program then attempts to connect to the web server by creating a **WebRequest** object that corresponds to the specified **Uri** class.

```
try
{
  WebRequest http = HttpWebRequest.Create(url);
  HttpWebResponse response = (HttpWebResponse)http.GetResponse();
```

If the site responds, then a message is displayed to indicate that the site is still up. If an exception is thrown, it is reported that the site is down.

```
  Console.WriteLine("The site is up.");
}
catch (IOException)
{
  Console.WriteLine("The site is down!!!");
}

  Console.WriteLine("The site is up.");
} catch (IOException e1)
{
  Console.WriteLine("The site is down!!!");
}
```

The program will now wait for a minute before checking again. To do this, the **Sleep** method of the **Thread** class is called.

```
Thread.Sleep(60000);
```

This program is a very simple web site monitoring utility. A more "industrial strength" version would perform some additional operations, such as:

- E-Mailing on failure
- Paging on failure
- Tracking multiple sites

As it is written, this recipe implements only the basic functionality.

Summary

This chapter showed how to use the **HttpWebRequest** and **HttpWebResponse** classes. These classes add much more functionality than was provided by using only a **Stream**, as was done in Chapter 3.

Using the **HttpWebRequest** and **HttpWebResponse** classes allows access to both the HTTP request and response headers. Accessing these headers provides you with useful information about the HTTP transaction. These headers give such information as the type of document, the web server being used, the web browser being used and other important information. The **HttpWebRequest** and **HttpWebResponse** classes also allow you to specify timeouts.

This chapter presented four recipes. The first recipe showed how to scan a site and view the headers. The second recipe showed how to scan a range of IP addresses for web sites. The third recipe will download either a text or binary file. The fourth recipe will monitor a web site to make sure it does not go down.

So far, we have only made use of the HTTP protocol. The HTTP protocol is not secure, because it does not encrypt data being transmitted. For non-sensitive information this is fine. However, when you must pass sensitive information, the HTTPS protocol is usually used. The next chapter will discuss the HTTPS protocol.

CHAPTER 5: SECURE HTTP REQUESTS

- HTTP Security
- Using HTTPS
- Using HTTP Authentication

The HTTP protocol, as it was originally designed, is completely unencrypted. Everything transmitted by the HTTP protocol is transmitted in plain text. There is no way for a web server to be sure who is requesting data. Likewise, there is no way for a web browser to be sure what web server it is requesting data from. This presents a security risk because a third party could intercept packets that are being exchanged between your browser and the web server. If these packets are encrypted then it is less of a problem if they are intercepted.

Several mechanisms were added to HTTP to create security. Many web sites use HTTP's secure mechanisms. If your bot program is to access data on a site using the secure mechanisms of HTTP, you will need to know how to support them.

Two primary mechanisms provide HTTP with security. These two mechanisms, which will be discussed in this chapter, are:

- HTTPS, and
- HTTP Authentication

This chapter will show you how to support both secure mechanisms of HTTP in your C# programs.

Using HTTPS in C#

HTTPS is implemented as a protocol just like HTTP. Whereas an HTTP URL starts with "http", an HTTPS protocol starts with "https". For example, the following URL specifies a secure page on the HTTP recipe site:

```
https://www.httprecipes.com/1/5/https.php
```

It is important to understand that a URL starting with "https" is not just a secure version of the same URL beginning with an "http". Consider the following URL:

```
http://www.httprecipes.com/1/5/https.php
```

The two URLs you see in this section are exactly the same, except that one is HTTP and the other HTTPS. You might think that entering the second URL would take you to an unencrypted version of the **https.php** page. It does not. If you enter the second URL into a web browser, you will get a page not found, or the 404, error.

This is because the file **https.php** does not exist on the "HTTP Recipes" Site's unencrypted server. This is the important distinction. There are two web servers running at **www.httprecipes.com**. There is an unencrypted HTTP server running at port 80. There is also an encrypted HTTPS server running at port 443. These two servers do not share the same set of HTML files. In the case of the HTTP Recipes site, Chapter 5 is hosted on the HTTPS server, and the rest of the chapters on the HTTP server.

Hypertext Transfer Protocol Secure (HTTPS) uses sockets just like HTTP. However, it uses a special socket called a secure socket. Secure sockets are implemented using the Secure Socket Layer (SSL). SSL, which is supported by C#, provides two very important security mechanisms, which are listed here.

- Encrypted packets, and
- Server verification

Web servers commonly use both of these mechanisms. These two mechanisms will be discussed in the next two sections.

Understanding Encrypted Packets

The aspect that most users associate with HTTPS, is data encryption. When you use an HTTPS site, you normally see a small "lock symbol" near the bottom of your browser. Once you see the lock, you know that your data is being encrypted, and you are using a secure site.

Data encryption is very important. When you enter a credit card number into a web site, you want to be sure that only that web site gains access to your credit card number. Because TCP/IP traffic can travel through a number of different hosts before it finally reaches your intended web server, you do not want a malicious user intercepting your credit card number somewhere between you and the web server.

By encrypting the packets being exchanged between you and the web server, the problem of your packets getting intercepted is decreased. If someone does intercept your packet, it will be encrypted.

Understanding Server Verification

Encryption is not the only benefit provided by HTTPS. Server verification is another important benefit. Consider what happens when you access the following URL:

```
https://www.httprecipes.com/1/5/https.php
```

The web browser takes apart the URL and finds the hostname. In this case, the host name is `www.httprecipes.com`. This is a domain name, which the web browser then looks up in a Domain Name System (DNS) server. As at the writing of this book, the IP address for `www.httprecipes.com` is `216.69.170.193`. But how do you know that the IP address `216.69.170.193` is really the HTTP Recipes site? IP addresses sometimes change when the web master switches hosting companies, or for other reasons. Someone could have hijacked the `www.httprecipes.com` DNS entry and pointed it to a malicious web server running on a different IP address.

HTTPS solves this problem. Part of the SSL protocol, upon which HTTPS is based, verifies that the IP address returned by DNS is the actual address of the site. Every website that uses HTTPS must be issued with a SSL certificate. Usually these certificates are issued by Verisign (`http://www.verisign.com`). When a web server is granted a certificate, the company that issues the certificate verifies that the IP address to which the certificate is issued, matches the domain name.

When you access `https://www.httprecipes.com`, your web browser looks up the returned IP address of `216.69.170.193` with the company that issued the HTTP Recipes site your SSL certificate. If these IP addresses do not match, then your browser will warn you.

Most certificate issuers provide "seals" that web masters can place on their web sites to show that their identity has been verified. Figure 5.1 shows the seal on the HTTP Recipes site:

Figure 5.1: HTTPS Verification Seal

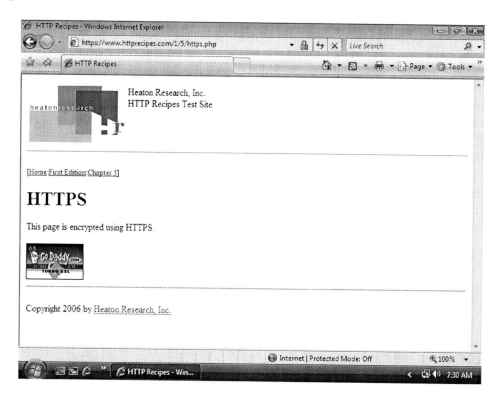

You can click the site's seal and be taken to the certificate issuer's web site. This will display the certificate. The SSL certificate for HTTP Recipes can be seen in Figure 5.2.

Figure 5.2: The HTTP Recipes Certificate

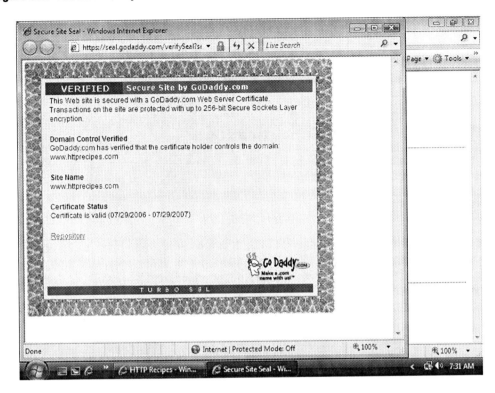

Now that you understand what HTTPS is and how it is used, the next section will show you how to write C# programs that use HTTPS.

Using HTTPS in C#

C# provides methods that make it simple to connect to an HTTPS website. The following code would open a **Stream** to an HTTPS server:

```
try
{
  Uri uri = new Uri("https://www.httprecipes.com/1/5/https.php");

  WebRequest http = HttpWebRequest.Create(url);
  HttpWebResponse response = (HttpWebResponse)http.GetResponse();
  Stream stream = response.GetResponseStream();
}
catch(UriFormatException e)
{
  Console.WriteLine("Invalid URL");
}
catch(IOException e)
```

```
{
  Console.WriteLine("Could not connect to URL");
}
```

Does something seem familiar about this code? It is exactly the same code that was introduced in Chapter 4 with the https URL, now used to access an HTTP URL. C# supports HTTPS transparently. Simply pass an "https" based URL to any of the codes used in this book and HTTPS will be supported.

Understanding HTTP Authentication

As you saw earlier in this chapter, HTTPS allows you to determine that the web server you are connecting to is what it claims to be. HTTP authentication provides the other side of this verification. HTTP authentication allows the server to determine that the web user is who they say that they are.

HTTP authentication is not tied to HTTPS. It can be used with either HTTP or HTTPS. To access a page protected by HTTP authentication, a web user must enter both a user id and password. If a username and password are not provided, or if it is incorrect, the user will receive an HTTP error.

Most websites do not use HTTP authentication; instead, many websites use their own authentication. This works by displaying a form to the user and prompting for identifying information, usually an id and password.

HTTP Authentication in Action

You have probably seen sites that make use of HTTP authentication. Sites that use HTTP authentication popup a window that prompts you for a user id and password. HTTP authentication always pops up a second window. If you are being prompted for a user id and password on the actual webpage, then the site is performing its own authentication. To see HTTP authentication in action, visit the following URL:

`https://www.httprecipes.com/1/5/auth.php`

This URL will display the page show in Figure 5.3.

Figure 5.3: Ready to Enter a Protected Area

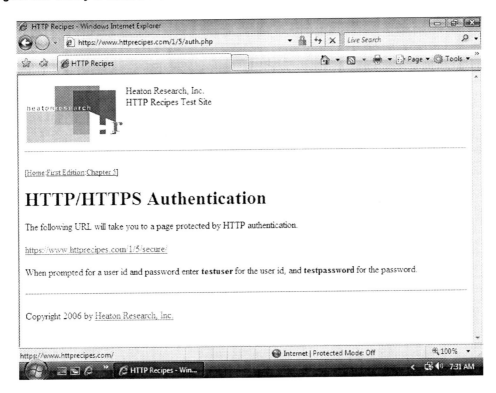

Click the URL displayed on the page, and you will be taken to the secure area. Note the user id and password prompts displayed on the page. When you enter the secure area you will see a popup that prompts you for your user id and password. This page is shown in Figure 5.4.

Figure 5.4: Enter your ID and Password

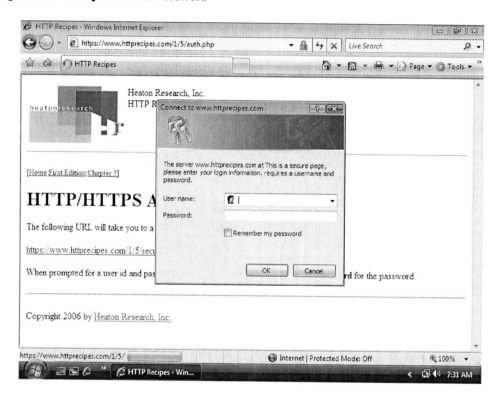

If you enter the correct user id and password you will be taken to the secure area. If you enter an invalid user id and password, you will be prompted several more times. Eventually, the browser will take you to an error page if you fail to enter the correct user id and password. For this site, the correct user id is "testuser" and the password is "testpassword".

Supporting HTTP Authentication in C#

Most websites use their own authentication and do not rely on HTTP authentication. Chapter 7, "Accessing Forms", will show how to access sites that make use of their own authentication. However, if the site that you would like to access makes use of HTTP authentication, then you must support that as well.

The C# HTTP classes provide support HTTP authentication. To make use of HTTP authentication, you will have to add a special HTTP class called **NetworkCredential**. This class allows you to specify a user id and password to login.

```
NetworkCredential networkCredential = new NetworkCredential("user
id","password");
WebRequest http = HttpWebRequest.Create(remoteURL);
http.PreAuthenticate = true;
http.Credentials = networkCredential;
```

Recipe 5.2 demonstrates adding this header, and using HTTP authentication.

Recipes

This chapter includes two recipes. These two recipes will demonstrate the following:

- Determining if a URL uses HTTPS, and
- Using HTTP authentication

The first recipe will introduce you to some of the things that can be done with the **HttpWebRequest** class. The second recipe shows how to access a site that uses HTTP authentication.

Recipe #5.1

This recipe is a fairly simple example of using the **HttpWebRequest** class. This example simply checks a URL connection to see if it is HTTPS or not. I use this code when I need to be sure that a connection is being made over a secure link. Unless you care about examining HTTPS certificate chains and cipher suites directly, this is probably the only use you will have for the **HttpWebRequest** object.

This program is fairly short, so it is implemented entirely in the **main** method. This HTTPS checker program is shown below in Listing 5.1.

Listing 5.1: Is a Connection HTTPS (IsHTTPS.cs)

```
using System;
using System.Collections.Generic;
using System.Text;
using System.IO;
using System.Net;

namespace Recipe5_1
{
    class Program
    {
        /// <summary>
        /// The main entry point for the program.
        /// </summary>
        /// <param name="args">Program arguments.</param>
        static void Main(string[] args)
        {
            String strURL = "";

            // obtain a URL to use
            if (args.Length < 1)
            {
                strURL = "https://www.httprecipes.com/1/5/";
```

```
        }
        else
        {
            strURL = args[0];
        }

        Uri url = new Uri(strURL);
        WebRequest http = HttpWebRequest.Create(url);
        http.PreAuthenticate = true;
        HttpWebResponse response =
                (HttpWebResponse)http.GetResponse();

        Console.WriteLine(response.ToString());

        if (String.Compare(url.Scheme,"https",true)==0 )
        {
            Console.WriteLine("Successful HTTPS connection");
        }
        else
        {
            Console.WriteLine("Successful HTTP connection");
        }
    }
  }
}
```

This program can be passed a URL to access on the command line; or, if no URL is provided, the program will default to the following URL:

https://www.httprecipes.com/1/5/secure/

You can also specify a URL. For example, to run this recipe with the URL of **http://www.httprecipes.com/**, use the following command:

```
IsHTTPS http://www.httprecipes.com
```

This program begins by obtaining a URL. The URL is either provided from the command line, or defaults to a page on the HTTP Recipes site. The following lines of code do this.

```
Uri url = new Uri(strURL);
WebRequest http = HttpWebRequest.Create(url);
http.PreAuthenticate = true;
HttpWebResponse response = (HttpWebResponse)http.GetResponse();
```

At this point a connection will either have been made or an exception thrown. We can now check to see if this is an HTTPS connection or not.

```
Console.WriteLine(response.ToString());
```

```
if (String.Compare(url.Scheme,"https",true)==0 )
{
  Console.WriteLine("Successful HTTPS connection");
}
else
{
  Console.WriteLine("Successful HTTP connection");
}
```

This recipe will be rarely used; however, it demonstrates one practical purpose of using HTTPS directly.

Recipe #5.2

The next recipe is very useful if you need to retrieve data from a site that requires HTTP authentication. First, the code downloads the contents of a URL and then saves it to a local file. This recipe can be used either in whole or in part.

Used in its entirety, this recipe provides a method, named **Download**. This method requires the URL to download the local file to save to, and the user id and password. The **Download** method will then download the contents. If the user id or password is invalid, an exception will be thrown.

If your application doesn't call for downloading directly to a file, you could use part of this recipe. Perhaps your application needs only to parse data at an HTTP authenticated site. If this is the case, use the code in the **Download** method that sets up the **NetworkCredential**.

I have used this recipe in both ways for several bots that required HTTP authenticated access. The program is shown in Listing 5.2.

Listing 5.2: Download Authenticated URL (AuthDownloadURL.cs)

```
using System;
using System.Collections.Generic;
using System.Text;
using System.Net;
using System.IO;

namespace Recipe5_2
{
    class AuthDownloadURL
    {
        /// <summary>
        /// Download the specified binary page.
        /// </summary>
```

```csharp
/// <param name="response">The HttpWebResponse to
/// download from.</param>
/// <param name="filename">The local file to save to.
/// </param>
public void DownloadBinaryFile(HttpWebResponse response,
    String filename)
{
    byte[] buffer = new byte[4096];
    FileStream os = new FileStream(filename,
        FileMode.Create);
    Stream stream = response.GetResponseStream();

    int count = 0;
    do
    {
        count = stream.Read(buffer, 0, buffer.Length);
        if (count > 0)
            os.Write(buffer, 0, count);
    } while (count > 0);

    response.Close();
    stream.Close();
    os.Close();
}

/// <summary>
/// Download the specified text page.
/// </summary>
/// <param name="response">The HttpWebResponse to
/// download from.</param>
/// <param name="filename">The local file to save to.
/// </param>
public void DownloadTextFile(HttpWebResponse response,
    String filename)
{
    byte[] buffer = new byte[4096];
    FileStream os = new FileStream(filename,
        FileMode.Create);
    StreamReader reader = new StreamReader(
        response.GetResponseStream(),
        System.Text.Encoding.ASCII);
    StreamWriter writer =
        new StreamWriter(os,
            System.Text.Encoding.ASCII);

    String line;
```

```csharp
    do
    {
        line = reader.ReadLine();
        if (line != null)
            writer.WriteLine(line);

    } while (line != null);

    reader.Close();
    writer.Close();
    os.Close();
}


/// <summary>
/// Download either a text or binary file from a URL.
/// The URL's headers will be scanned to determine the
/// type of tile.  The user id and password are
/// authenticated.
/// </summary>
/// <param name="remoteURL">The URL to download from.
/// </param>
/// <param name="localFile">The local file to save to.
/// </param>
/// <param name="uid">The user id to use.</param>
/// <param name="pwd">The password to use.</param>
public void Download(Uri remoteURL,
    String localFile,String uid,String pwd)
{

    NetworkCredential networkCredential =
            new NetworkCredential(uid, pwd);
    WebRequest http = HttpWebRequest.Create(remoteURL);
    http.PreAuthenticate = true;
    http.Credentials = networkCredential;
    HttpWebResponse response =
            (HttpWebResponse)http.GetResponse();

    String type =
response.Headers["Content-Type"].ToLower().Trim();
        if (type.StartsWith("text"))
            DownloadTextFile(response, localFile);
        else
            DownloadBinaryFile(response, localFile);


}
```

```
/// <summary>
/// The main entry point for the program.
/// </summary>
/// <param name="args">Program arguments.</param>
static void Main(string[] args)
{
    AuthDownloadURL d = new AuthDownloadURL();
    if (args.Length != 4)
    {
        d.Download(
          new Uri(
          "https://www.httprecipes.com/1/5/secure/"),
            "test.html",
            "testuser",
            "testpassword");
    }
    else
    {

        d.Download(new Uri(args[0]),
          args[1], args[2], args[3]);
    }
  }
 }
}
```

This program can be passed a URL, local filename, user id and password on the command line. If no parameters are provided, the program will default to the following URL:

`https://www.httprecipes.com/1/5/secure/`

The program will also default to a local file of **test.html**, a user id of **testuser**, and a password of **testpassword**.

You can also specify a URL. For example, to run this recipe with the URL of **http://www.httprecipes.com/**, a local file of **index.html**, a user id of **user** and a password of **password**, use the following command:

`Recipe5_2 http://www.httprecipes.com ./index.html user password`

This recipe is very similar to Recipe 4.3, except that it can download from an HTTP authenticated site as well as a regular site. Only the new code relating to HTTP authentication will be discussed here. If you would like to review how this recipe actually downloads a binary or text file, refer to Recipe 4.3. The downloading code is the same in both recipes.

To access an HTTP authenticated site, the program uses the **NetworkCredential** class. This **Download** method begins by creating a **NetworkCredential** object and using it to connect to the web site.

```
NetworkCredential networkCredential = new NetworkCredential(uid,
pwd);
WebRequest http = HttpWebRequest.Create(remoteURL);
http.PreAuthenticate = true;
http.Credentials = networkCredential;
HttpWebResponse response = (HttpWebResponse)http.GetResponse();
```

From this point forward this recipe is the same as Recipe 4.3. The **Content-Type** header is checked to see if this is a text or binary file. If this is a text file, then it is downloaded with **DownloadTextFile**. If this is a binary file, then it is downloaded with **DownloadBinaryFile**.

```
String type = response.Headers["Content-Type"].ToLower().Trim();
if (type.StartsWith("text"))
  DownloadTextFile(response, localFile);
else
  DownloadBinaryFile(response, localFile);
```

This recipe can be used as a starting point for any operation requiring HTTP authentication. It does not matter to this recipe if HTTPS is used or not. This recipe supports either HTTP or HTTPS.

Summary

This chapter showed you how to use HTTP security mechanisms. HTTP has two built-in security mechanisms. Firstly, HTTP supports encryption through HTTPS. Secondly, HTTP provides authentication, which requires users to identify themselves.

HTTP encryption is supported through HTTPS. Any website that you access that makes use of HTTPS will begin with the prefix **https://**. HTTPS encrypts the data so that it cannot be intercepted. Support for HTTPS is built into C#. You are only required to use an HTTPS URL where you would normally use an HTTP URL. HTTPS encryption prevents a third party from examining packets being exchanged between your browser and the web server.

HTTP authentication allows the web server to prompt the user for a user id and password. The web server then can determine the identity of the user accessing it. Most web sites do not use HTTP authentication, rather they use their own HTML forms to authenticate. However, some sites make use of HTTP authentication, and to access these sites with a bot, you will have to support HTTP authentication.

C# contains support for HTTP authentication. To use HTTP authentication with C# a **NetworkCredential** object must be constructed. This object will then be used to connect to the site.

This chapter provided two recipes. The first determines if a URL is using HTTPS. The second recipe downloads data from an HTTP authenticated site.

Up to this point, the chapters have shown you how to access data. In the next chapter we will begin to learn what to do with HTTP data once you have retrieved it. Chapter 6 will show how to parse HTML and extract data from forms, lists, tables and other HTML constructs.

CHAPTER 6: EXTRACTING DATA

- Parsing HTML
- Extracting from forms
- Extracting lists, images and hyperlinks
- Extracting data form multiple pages

The previous chapters explained how to extract simple data items from web pages. This chapter will expand on this. This chapter focuses on how to extract more complex data structures from HTML messages. Of course, HTML is not the only format from which to extract. Later chapters will discuss non-HTML formats, such as XML.

This chapter will present several recipes for extracting data from a variety of different HTML forms, such as:

- Extracting data spread across many HTML pages
- Extracting images
- Extracting hyperlinks
- Extracting data from HTML forms
- Extracting data from HTML lists
- Extracting data from HTML tables

Extracting data from these types of HTML structures is more complex than the simple data extracted in previous chapters. To extract this data we require an HTML parser. There are three options for obtaining an HTML parser.

- Using the HTML parser built into C#
- Using a third-party HTML parser
- Writing your own HTML parser

C# includes a full-featured HTML parser; this is done using the browser control. I've used this parser for a number of projects; however, it has some limitations. It requires everything to be passed through the Internet Explorer control. This consumes a large amount of unneeded memory. Using this additional memory can be a problem when using a large number of threads; such is the case when a spider is created.

Besides the C# HTML parser, there are also several third-party HTML parsers available. However, it is really not too complex to create a simple lightweight HTML parser. The idea of this book is to present small examples of HTTP programming you can implement into your own programs. In this way, we will create our own HTML parser.

Implementing an HTML parser is not complex. The HTML parser presented in this chapter is implemented in three classes. Before getting to the recipes for this chapter, we will first examine the HTML parser. This HTML parser will later be used by all of the recipes in this chapter. If you are not interested in how to implement an HTML parser, you can easily skip to the recipes section of this chapter.

Peekable Stream

To properly parse any data, let alone HTML, it is very convenient to have a peekable stream. A peekable stream is a regular C# **Stream**, except that you can peek several characters ahead, before actually reading these characters. First, we will examine why it is so convenient to use **PeekableInputStream**.

Consider parsing the following line of HTML:

```
<b>Hello World</b>
```

The first thing we would like to know is whether we parsing an HTML tag or HTML text. Using the **PeekableInputStream**, we can look at the first character and determine if we are starting with a tag or text. Once we know that we are parsing text, we can begin reading the actual text characters.

The **PeekableInputStream** class is also very useful for HTML comments. Consider the following HTML comment:

```
<!--HTML Comment-->
```

To determine if something is an HTML comment, look at the first four characters of the tag. Using the **PeekableInputStream** we can examine the next four characters and see if we are about to read a comment.

Using PeekableInputStream

Using the **PeekableInputStream** is simple. The usage of **PeekableInputStream** closely follows the usage of the C# class **Stream**. First, you must already have a **Stream**. You will then attach the **PeekableInputStream** to the existing **Stream**. The following code demonstrates this:

```
FileStream fstream = new FileStream(filename, FileMode.Open);
PeekableInputStream peek = new PeekableInputStream(fstream);
```

Now that you have created the **PeekableInputStream**, we can read from it just like a normal **Stream**.

```
int i = peek.Read();
```

However, we can now peek as well.

```
int i = peek.Peek();
```

It is important to note that **peek** and read return an **int** rather than a **byte** or a **char**. This allows **Peek** and **rRad** to both return **-1** when the end has been reached.

The above code will peek at the next byte to be read by the underlying **Stream**. The next time you call the **Read** function, you will get the same byte that was returned by the peek. Multiple calls to the **Peek** function will always return the same byte, because you are only peeking at the byte, not reading it and advancing into the stream.

It is also possible to peek several bytes into the future by passing a parameter to the **Peek** function. The following code would **Peek** three bytes into the stream, and return the third byte to be read.

```
int i = peek.Peek(2);
```

Remember, the **Peek** function is zero based, so passing the number two, returns the third byte.

Implementing Peekable Stream

In the last section you saw how to use the **PeekableInputStream** class. This section will show you how to implement the **PeekableInputStream**. The **PeekableInputStream** class is shown in Listing 6.1.

Listing 6.1: The Peekable Stream (PeekableInputStream.cs)

```
using System;
using System.Collections.Generic;
using System.Text;
using System.IO;

namespace HeatonResearch.Spider.HTML
{
    /// <summary>
    /// PeekableInputStream: This class allows a stream to be
    /// read like normal.  However, the ability to peek is added.
    /// The calling method can peek as far as is needed.  This is
    /// used by the ParseHTML class.
    /// </summary>
    public class PeekableInputStream:Stream
    {
        /// <summary>
        /// The underlying stream.
        /// </summary>
        private Stream stream;

        /// <summary>
        /// Bytes that have been peeked at.
        /// </summary>
```

```csharp
private byte[] peekBytes;

/// <summary>
/// How many bytes have been peeked at.
/// </summary>
private int peekLength;

/// <summary>
/// Construct a peekable input stream based on the
/// specified stream.
/// </summary>
/// <param name="stream">The underlying stream.</param>
public PeekableInputStream(Stream stream)
{
    this.stream = stream;
    this.peekBytes = new byte[10];
    this.peekLength = 0;
}

/// <summary>
/// Specifies that the stream can read.
/// </summary>
public override bool CanRead
{
    get { return true; }
}

/// <summary>
/// Specifies that the stream cannot write.
/// </summary>
public override bool CanWrite
{
    get { return false; }
}

/// <summary>
/// Specifies that the stream cannot seek.
/// </summary>
public override bool CanSeek
{
    get { return false; }
}

/// <summary>
/// Specifies that the stream cannot determine its length.
/// </summary>
```

```csharp
public override long Length
{
    get { throw new NotSupportedException(); }
}

/// <summary>
/// Specifies that the stream cannot determine its
/// position.
/// </summary>
public override long Position
{
    get
    {
        throw new NotSupportedException();
    }
    set
    {
        throw new NotSupportedException();
    }
}

/// <summary>
/// Not supported.
/// </summary>
public override void Flush()
{
    // writing is not supported, so nothing to do here
}

/// <summary>
/// Not supported.
/// </summary>
/// <param name="value">The length.</param>
public override void SetLength(long value)
{
    throw new NotSupportedException();
}

/// <summary>
/// Not supported.
/// </summary>
/// <param name="offset"></param>
/// <param name="origin"></param>
/// <returns></returns>
public override long Seek(long offset, SeekOrigin origin)
{
```

```
            throw new NotSupportedException();
        }

        /// <summary>
        /// Read bytes from the stream.
        /// </summary>
        /// <param name="buffer">The buffer to read the
        /// bytes into.</param>
        /// <param name="offset">The offset to begin storing
        /// the bytes at.</param>
        /// <param name="count">How many bytes to read.</param>
        /// <returns>The number of bytes read.</returns>
        public override int Read(byte[] buffer, int offset,
            int count)
        {
            if (this.peekLength == 0)
            {
                return stream.Read(buffer,offset,count);
            }

            for (int i = 0; i < count; i++)
            {
                buffer[offset + i] = Pop();
            }
            return count;
        }

        /// <summary>
        /// Not supported.
        /// </summary>
        /// <param name="buffer"></param>
        /// <param name="offset"></param>
        /// <param name="count"></param>
        public override void Write(byte[] buffer, int offset,
            int count)
        {
            throw new NotSupportedException();
        }

        /// <summary>
        /// Read a single byte.
        /// </summary>
        /// <returns>The byte read, or -1 for end of stream.
        /// </returns>
        public int Read()
        {
```

```
    byte[] b = new byte[1];
    int count = Read(b, 0, 1);
    if (count < 1)
        return -1;
    else
        return b[0];
}


/// <summary>
/// Peek ahead the specified depth.
/// </summary>
/// <param name="depth">How far to peek ahead.</param>
/// <returns>The byte read.</returns>
public int Peek(int depth)
{
    // does the size of the peek buffer need to
    // be extended?
    if (this.peekBytes.Length <= depth)
    {
        byte[] temp = new byte[depth + 10];
        for (int i = 0; i < this.peekBytes.Length; i++)
        {
            temp[i] = this.peekBytes[i];
        }
        this.peekBytes = temp;
    }

    // does more data need to be read?
    if (depth >= this.peekLength)
    {
        int offset = this.peekLength;
        int length = (depth - this.peekLength) + 1;
        int lengthRead = this.stream.Read(
          this.peekBytes, offset, length);

        if (lengthRead <1)
        {
            return -1;
        }

        this.peekLength = depth + 1;
    }

    return this.peekBytes[depth];
}
```

```
        private byte Pop()
        {
            byte result = this.peekBytes[0];
            this.peekLength--;
            for (int i = 0; i < this.peekLength; i++)
            {
                this.peekBytes[i] = this.peekBytes[i + 1];
            }

            return result;
        }
    }
}
```

The **PeekableInputStream** class makes use of three **private** variables to hold its current state. These three variables are shown here.

```
private Stream stream;
private byte[] peekBytes;
private int peekLength;
```

The first variable, **stream** holds the underlying **Stream**. The second variable, **peekBytes**, holds the bytes that have been "peeked" at from the file, yet have not been actually read by a call to the read function of the **PeekableInputStream** class. The third variable, **peekLength**, tracks how much of the **peekBytes** variable array contains actual data.

The **Read** function must be implemented, because the **PeekableInputStream** class is derived from the **Stream** class. This function begins by checking the **peekLength** variable. If no bytes have been peeked, then the **Read** function can simply call the **Read** function for the underlying **Stream**.

```
if (this.peekLength == 0)
{
  return stream.Read(buffer,offset,count);
}
```

If there is data in the **peekBytes** buffer, the **Pop** function is called to fill the buffer with the requested number of bytes.

```
for (int i = 0; i < count; i++)
{
  buffer[offset + i] = pop();
}
return count;
```

Of course, this function relies on the **Pop** function, which returns the topmost byte from the data that has already been peeked. The **peekLength** variable is decreased by one to reflect the byte just read.

```
byte result = this.peekBytes[0];
this.peekLength--;
```

Next the **Pop** function moves the other **peekByte** entries one to the left.

```
for (int i = 0; i < this.peekLength; i++)
{
  this.peekBytes[i] = this.peekBytes[i + 1];
}


return result;
```

The **Pop** function is used internally by the **PeekableInputStream**, and cannot be called directly. It is important never to call the Pop function when **peekLength** is zero.

Parsing HTML

The **ParseHTML** class does HTML parsing. This class is used by all of the recipes in this chapter. Additionally, many recipes through the remainder of the book will use the **ParseHTML** class. I will begin by showing you how to use this class. In a later section, I will show you an example of a **ParseHTML** class implementation.

Using ParseHTML

It is very easy to use the **ParseHTML** class. Simply declare a new object, and call the parsing functions. The following code fragment demonstrates some of the **ParseHTML** class's functionality:

```
WebRequest http = HttpWebRequest.Create(url);
HttpWebResponse response = (HttpWebResponse)http.GetResponse();
Stream istream = response.GetResponseStream();
ParseHTML parse = new ParseHTML(istream);

int ch;

while ((ch = parse.Read()) != -1)
{
  if (ch == 0)
  {
    HTMLTag tag = parse.Tag;
    Console.WriteLine("Read HTML tag: " + tag);
  }
  else
  {
    Console.WriteLine("Read HTML text character: " + ((char)ch) );
  }
}
```

As you can see from the above code, a **Stream** is acquired from a URL. This **Stream** is used to construct a **ParseHTML** object. The **ParseHTML** class can parse HTML from any **Stream** object.

Next, the code enters a loop calling **parse.Read()**. Once **parse.Read()** returns a negative one value, there is nothing more to parse, and the program ends. If **parse.Read()** returns a zero, an HTML tag was encountered. You may then call **parse.Tag** property to determine which tag was encountered.

If neither a negative one nor zero is returned, then a regular character has been found in the HTML. This process continues until a negative one is encountered indicating End Of File (EOF).

Implementing ParseHTML

In this section we will examine how the **ParseHTML** class is implemented. The **ParseHTML** class makes use of the **PeekableInputStream** class, which was discussed in one of this chapter's previous sections. The **ParseHTML** class is shown in Listing 6.2.

Listing 6.2: Parsing HTML (ParseHTML.cs)

```csharp
using System;
using System.Collections.Generic;
using System.Text;
using System.IO;

namespace HeatonResearch.Spider.HTML
{
    /// <summary>
    /// This class implements an HTML parser.  This parser is used
    /// by the Heaton Research spider, but it can also be used
    /// as a stand alone HTML parser.
    /// </summary>
    public class ParseHTML
    {
        /// <summary>
        /// A mapping of certain HTML encoded
        /// values(i.e.  )
        /// to their actual character values.
        /// </summary>
        private static Dictionary<String, char> charMap;

        /// <summary>
        /// The stream that we are parsing from
        /// </summary>
        private PeekableInputStream source;
```

```csharp
/// <summary>
/// The HTML tag just parsed.
/// </summary>
private HTMLTag tag;

/// <summary>
/// The current HTML tag. Access this property if the read
/// function returns 0.
/// </summary>
public HTMLTag Tag
{
    get
    {
        return tag;
    }
    set
    {
        tag = value;
    }
}

/// <summary>
/// Is there an end tag we are "locked into", such as
/// a comment tag, script tag or similar.
/// </summary>
private String lockedEndTag;


/// <summary>
/// Construct the HTML parser based in the
/// specified stream.
/// </summary>
/// <param name="istream">The stream that will
/// be parsed.</param>
public ParseHTML(Stream istream)
{
    this.source = new PeekableInputStream(istream);
    Tag = new HTMLTag();

    if (charMap == null)
    {
        charMap = new Dictionary<String, char>();
        charMap.Add("nbsp", ' ');
        charMap.Add("lt", '<');
        charMap.Add("gt", '>');
```

```
                charMap.Add("amp", '&');
                charMap.Add("quot", '\"');
                charMap.Add("bull", (char)149);
                charMap.Add("trade", (char)129);
            }
        }

        /// <summary>
        /// Read a single character from the HTML source,
        /// if this function returns zero(0) then you should
        /// call getTag to see what tag was found. Otherwise
        /// the value returned is simply the next character
        /// found.
        /// </summary>
        /// <returns>The character read, or zero if there is
        /// an HTML tag. If zero is returned, then call getTag
        /// to get the next tag.</returns>
        virtual public int Read()
        {
            // handle locked end tag
            if (this.lockedEndTag != null)
            {
                if (PeekEndTag(this.lockedEndTag))
                {
                    this.lockedEndTag = null;
                }
                else
                {
                    return this.source.Read();
                }
            }

            // look for next tag
            if (this.source.Peek(0) == '<')
            {
                ParseTag();
                if (!this.Tag.Ending
                    && (String.Compare(this.Tag.Name, "script",
 true) == 0
 || String.Compare(this.Tag.Name, "style", true) == 0))
                {
                    this.lockedEndTag = this.Tag.Name.ToLower();
                }
                return 0;
            }
            else if (this.source.Peek(0) == '&')
```

```
        {
            return ParseSpecialCharacter();
        }
        else
        {
            return (this.source.Read());
        }
    }

/// <summary>
/// Represent as a string.  Read all text and ignore tags.
/// </summary>
/// <returns></returns>
public override String ToString()
{

    StringBuilder result = new StringBuilder();

    int ch = 0;
    StringBuilder text = new StringBuilder();
    do
    {
        ch = Read();
        if (ch == 0)
        {
            if (text.Length > 0)
            {
                text.Length = 0;
            }
        }
        else if (ch != -1)
        {
            text.Append((char)ch);
        }
    } while (ch != -1);
    if (text.Length > 0)
    {
    }
    return result.ToString();

}

/// <summary>
/// Parse any special characters(i.e.  ).
/// </summary>
/// <returns>The character that was parsed.</returns>
```

```csharp
private char ParseSpecialCharacter()
{
    char result = (char)this.source.Read();
    int advanceBy = 0;

    // is there a special character?
    if (result == '&')
    {
        int ch = 0;
        StringBuilder buffer = new StringBuilder();

        // Loop through and read special character.
        do
        {
            ch = this.source.Peek(advanceBy++);
            if ((ch != '&') && (ch != ';')
                && !char.IsWhiteSpace((char)ch))
            {
                buffer.Append((char)ch);
            }

        } while ((ch != ';') && (ch != -1)
                && !char.IsWhiteSpace((char)ch));

        String b = buffer.ToString().Trim().ToLower();

        // did we find a special character?
        if (b.Length > 0)
        {
            if (b[0] == '#')
            {
                try
                {
                    result =
                        (char)int.Parse(b.Substring(1));
                }
                catch (FormatException)
                {
                    advanceBy = 0;
                }
            }
            else
            {
                if (charMap.ContainsKey(b))
                {
                    result = charMap[b];
```

```
                }
                else
                {
                    advanceBy = 0;
                }
            }
        }
        else
        {
            advanceBy = 0;
        }
    }

    while (advanceBy > 0)
    {
        Read();
        advanceBy--;
    }

    return result;
}

/// <summary>
/// See if the next few characters are an end tag.
/// </summary>
/// <param name="name">The end tag we are looking for.
/// </param>
/// <returns></returns>
private bool PeekEndTag(String name)
{
    int i = 0;

    // pass any whitespace
    while ((this.source.Peek(i) != -1)
        && char.IsWhiteSpace((char)this.source.Peek(i)))
    {
        i++;
    }

    // is a tag beginning
    if (this.source.Peek(i) != '<')
    {
        return false;
    }
    else
    {
```

```
            i++;
        }

        // pass any whitespace
        while ((this.source.Peek(i) != -1)
            && char.IsWhiteSpace((char)this.source.Peek(i)))
        {
            i++;
        }

        // is it an end tag
        if (this.source.Peek(i) != '/')
        {
            return false;
        }
        else
        {
            i++;
        }

        // pass any whitespace
        while ((this.source.Peek(i) != -1)
            && char.IsWhiteSpace((char)this.source.Peek(i)))
        {
            i++;
        }

        // does the name match
        for (int j = 0; j < name.Length; j++)
        {
            if (char.ToLower((char)this.source.Peek(i))
              != char
              .ToLower((char)name[j]))
            {
                return false;
            }
            i++;
        }

    return true;
}

/// <summary>
/// Remove any whitespace characters that are next in
/// the InputStream.
/// </summary>
```

```
protected void EatWhitespace()
{
    while (char.IsWhiteSpace((char)this.source.Peek(0)))
    {
        this.source.Read();
    }
}



/// <summary>
/// Parse an attribute name, if one is present.
/// </summary>
/// <returns>The attribute name parsed.</returns>
protected String ParseAttributeName()
{
    EatWhitespace();

    if ("\"\'".IndexOf((char)this.source.Peek(0)) == -1)
    {
        StringBuilder buffer = new StringBuilder();
        while (!char.IsWhiteSpace(
          (char)this.source.Peek(0))
            && (this.source.Peek(0) != '=') &&
              (this.source.Peek(0) != '>')
            && (this.source.Peek(0) != -1))
        {
            int ch = ParseSpecialCharacter();
            buffer.Append((char)ch);
        }
        return buffer.ToString();
    }
    else
    {
        return (ParseString());
    }
}



/// <summary>
/// Called to parse a double or single quote string.
/// </summary>
/// <returns>The string parsed.</returns>
protected String ParseString()
{
    StringBuilder result = new StringBuilder();
    EatWhitespace();
```

```
        if ("\"\'".IndexOf((char)this.source.Peek(0)) != -1)
        {
            int delim = this.source.Read();
            while ((this.source.Peek(0) != delim) &&
              (this.source.Peek(0) != -1))
            {
                if (result.Length > 1000)
                {
                    break;
                }
                int ch = ParseSpecialCharacter();
                if ((ch == 13) || (ch == 10))
                {
                    continue;
                }
                result.Append((char)ch);
            }
            if ("\"\'".IndexOf((char)this.source.Peek(0))
              != -1)
            {
                this.source.Read();
            }
        }
        else
        {
            while (!char.IsWhiteSpace(
              (char)this.source.Peek(0))
                && (this.source.Peek(0) != -1) &&
                    (this.source.Peek(0) != '>'))
            {
                result.Append(ParseSpecialCharacter());
            }
        }

        return result.ToString();
}


/// <summary>
/// Called when a tag is detected. This method will
/// parse the tag.
/// </summary>
protected void ParseTag()
{
    this.Tag.Clear();
    StringBuilder tagName = new StringBuilder();
```

```
this.source.Read();

// Is it a comment?
if ((this.source.Peek(0) == '!') &&
    (this.source.Peek(1) == '-')
  && (this.source.Peek(2) == '-'))
{
    while (this.source.Peek(0) != -1)
    {
        if ((this.source.Peek(0) == '-') &&
            (this.source.Peek(1) == '-')
            && (this.source.Peek(2) == '>'))
        {
            break;
        }
        if (this.source.Peek(0) != '\r')
        {
            tagName.Append((char)this.source.Peek(0));
        }
        this.source.Read();
    }
    tagName.Append("--");
    this.source.Read();
    this.source.Read();
    this.source.Read();
    return;
}

// Find the tag name
while (this.source.Peek(0) != -1)
{
    if (char.IsWhiteSpace((char)this.source.Peek(0))
        || (this.source.Peek(0) == '>'))
    {
        break;
    }
    tagName.Append((char)this.source.Read());
}

EatWhitespace();
this.Tag.Name = tagName.ToString();

// Get the attributes.

while ((this.source.Peek(0) != '>')
```

```
                      && (this.source.Peek(0) != -1))
            {
                String attributeName = ParseAttributeName();
                String attributeValue = null;

                if (attributeName.Equals("/"))
                {
                    EatWhitespace();
                    if (this.source.Peek(0) == '>')
                    {
                        this.Tag.Ending = true;
                        break;
                    }
                }

                // is there a value?
                EatWhitespace();
                if (this.source.Peek(0) == '=')
                {
                    this.source.Read();
                    attributeValue = ParseString();
                }

                this.Tag.SetAttribute(attributeName,
                  attributeValue);
            }
            this.source.Read();
        }


    }
}
```

The **ParseHTML** class makes use of three variables to track HTML parsing. These variables are shown here.

```
private PeekableInputStream source;
private HTMLTag tag;
private static Dictionary<String, char> charMap;
```

As you can see, all three variables are private. The **source** variable holds the **PeekableInputStream** that is being parsed. The **tag** variable holds the last HTML tag found by the parser. The **charMap** variable holds a mapping between HTML encoded characters, such as ** **, and their character code.

We will now examine each of the major **ParseHTML** functions.

The Constructor

The **ParseHTML** class's constructor has two responsibilities. The first is to create a new **PeekableInputStream** object based on the **Stream** that was passed in as an argument. The second is to initialize the **charMap** variable, if it has not already been initialized.

```
this.source = new PeekableInputStream(istream);
Tag = new HTMLTag();

if (charMap == null)
{
  charMap = new Dictionary<String, char>();
  charMap.Add("nbsp", ' ');
  charMap.Add("lt", '<');
  charMap.Add("gt", '>');
  charMap.Add("amp", '&');
  charMap.Add("quot", '\"');
  charMap.Add("bull", (char)149);
  charMap.Add("trade", (char)129);
}
```

In HTML encoding, there are two ways to store several of the more common characters. For example, the double quote character can be stored by its ASCII character value as **"** or as **"**. The ASCII character codes are easy to parse. Simply extract their numeric values and use that character code. For encodings such as **"** a lookup table is used.

As you can see from the above code, each of the special characters is loaded into a **Map**, which will allow the **ParseSpecialCharacter** method to quickly access them. This method will be discussed in greater detail later in this chapter.

Removing White Space with EatWhiteSpace

HTML documents generally have quite a bit of extra white space. This white space has nothing to do with the display, and is useless to the computer. However, the white space makes the HTML source code easier for a human to read. White space consists of the extra spaces, carriage returns and tabs placed in an HTML document.

The **Peek** function of the **PeekableInputStream** is very handy for eliminating white space. By peeking ahead and seeing if the next character is white space or not, you can decide if you need to remove it.

```
while (char.IsWhiteSpace((char)this.source.Peek(0)))
{
  this.source.Read();
}
```

As you can see from the above code, white space characters are read, and then removed, one by one, until **Peek** finds a non-white space character.

Parse a String with ParseString

Strings often occur inside HTML documents, particularly when used with HTML attributes. For example, consider the following HTML tags, all of which have the same meaning.

```
<img src="/images/logo.gif">
<img src='/images/logo.gif'>
<img src=/images/logo.gif>
```

The fist line is the most common. It uses double quotes to delineate the string value. The second uses single quotes. Though not the preferred method, the third does not use any delimiter at all. All three methods are common in HTML, so the **ParseHTML** class uses a function, named **ParseString** which handles all three.

First, the **ParseString** method creates a **StringBuilder** to hold the parsed string. Next, the **ParseString** method checks to see if there is a leading delimiter, which could be either a single or double quote.

```
StringBuilder result = new StringBuilder();
EatWhitespace();
if ("\"\'".IndexOf((char)this.source.Peek(0)) != -1)
{
```

While reading in the delimited string, the **ParseSpecialCharacter** function converts any special HTML characters encountered. This continues until we reach the end of the string, or the end of the file.

```
int delim = this.source.Read();
while ((this.source.Peek(0) != delim) && (this.source.Peek(0) !=
-1))
{
  if (result.Length > 1000)
  {
    break;
  }
  int ch = ParseSpecialCharacter();
  if ((ch == 13) || (ch == 10))
  {
    continue;
  }
result.Append((char)ch);
}
```

While the function is looping, and reading bytes, a few checks are performed. First, a sanity check is performed to make sure that the **result** has not grown to more than 1,000 bytes. This prevents invalid HTML from passing on massive attribute values. Secondly carriage return (character code 13) and line feed (character code 10) are both ignored. These two characters really do not have meaning as part of an HTML attribute.

After the loop completes, look for the ending delimiter and read it in if present. If the end of the file was found first, the ending delimiter might not be present. Of course it is bad HTML, if the end of file was found before the ending delimiter. But the parser must support bad HTML, because there is plenty of bad HTML on the Internet.

```
if ("\"\'".IndexOf((char)this.source.Peek(0)) != -1)
{
  this.source.Read();
}
```

If a leading delimiter is not found, then the string is parsed up to the first white space character.

```
else
{
  while (!char.IsWhiteSpace((char)this.source.Peek(0))
    && (this.source.Peek(0) != -1)
      && (this.source.Peek(0) != '>'))
  {
    result.Append(ParseSpecialCharacter());
  }
}
```

Because there is no delimiter, the only choice is to parse until the first white space character. This means that the string can contain no embedded white space characters.

```
return result.ToString();
```

Finally, the parsed string is returned.

Parse a Tag with ParseTag

The **ParseTag** method is called whenever an HTML tag is encountered. This method will parse the tag, as well as any HTML attributes of the tag. The **ParseTag** method first creates a **StringBuilder** object to hold the tag name, as well as a new **HTMLTag** object that will hold the tag and attributes. A call to the **Read** function moves past the opening less-than symbol for the tag.

```
this.Tag.Clear();
StringBuilder tagName = new StringBuilder();

this.source.Read();
```

Next, the **ParseTag** method checks to see if this tag is an HTML comment; in which case, the tag will be ignored. HTML comments begin with the **<!--** symbols.

```
// Is it a comment?
if ((this.source.Peek(0) == '!') && (this.source.Peek(1) == '-')
  && (this.source.Peek(2) == '-'))
{
```

If the tag is an HTML comment, enter a **while** loop to read the rest of the comment.

```
while (this.source.Peek(0) != -1)
{
  if ((this.source.Peek(0) == '-') && (this.source.Peek(1) == '-')
    && (this.source.Peek(2) == '>'))
  {
    break;
  }
  if (this.source.Peek(0) != '\r')
  {
      tagName.Append((char)this.source.Peek(0));
  }
this.source.Read();
}
```

Once the end of the end of the comment tag has been found, append the last characters of the comment and return.

```
  tagName.Append("--");
  source.Read();
  source.Read();
  source.Read();
  return;
}
```

If the tag is not a comment, then we must extract the name of the tag. If a tag has no attributes, then a "greater than sign" (>) symbol will be found, which will end the tag. If the tag has attributes, a white space character follows the tag name, followed by the attributes. To begin, enter a while loop that looks for the first non-white space character, or a tag ending "greater than sign" (>) symbol.

```
tagName.Append("--");
this.source.Read();
this.source.Read();
this.source.Read();
return;
}

// Find the tag name
while (this.source.Peek(0) != -1)
```

```
{
  if (char.IsWhiteSpace((char)this.source.Peek(0))
     || (this.source.Peek(0) == '>'))
  {
    break;
  }
  tagName.Append((char)this.source.Read());
}
```

Now, prepare to read the attributes, if there are any. First, remove any white space, and record the tag name.

```
EatWhitespace();
this.Tag.Name = tagName.ToString();
```

Next, enter a **while** loop to read all the attributes. If there are no attributes, this loop will end immediately, as it finds a tag ending "greater than sign" (>) symbol.

If an attribute is found, call the **ParseAttributeName** function to read the name of the attribute. The **ParseAttributeName** function will be explained in the next section.

```
// Get the attributes.

while ((this.source.Peek(0) != '>')
       && (this.source.Peek(0) != -1))
{
  String attributeName = ParseAttributeName();
  String attributeValue = null;
```

Some HTML tags have an ending tag built in. For example, the tag **
** has both a beginning and ending tag in one. If such a tag is found then the **Ending** property is set. The following lines of code handle this.

```
if (attributeName.Equals("/"))
{
  EatWhitespace();
  if (this.source.Peek(0) == '>')
  {
    this.Tag.Ending = true;
    break;
  }
}
```

Once the attribute name has been read, check to see if there is an attribute value. If an attribute value is present, the next character will be an equal sign. If an equal sign is found, read the following attribute value.

```
// is there a value?
EatWhitespace();
if (this.source.Peek(0) == '=')
{
  this.source.Read();
  attributeValue = ParseString();
}
```

Once the attribute has been read, set the attribute value. If there is no attribute value, set the attribute variable to null.

```
  this.Tag.SetAttribute(attributeName, attributeValue);
}
this.source.Read();
```

Once the tag name, and all attributes have been read, call **source.Read()** to read beyond the ending "greater than sign" (>) sign.

Parse an Attribute Name with ParseAttributeName

The **ParseAttributeName** function is called to parse the name of an attribute. This function begins by checking whether there is a single or double quote around the attribute name. For example, consider the following tag:

```
<!DOCTYPE HTML PUBLIC "-//W3C//DTD HTML 4.01 Transitional//EN">
```

The above tag contains two, name-only attributes: **HTML** and **PUBLIC**. Additionally, it contains a third double quote-delineated attribute.

The **ParseAttributeName** function uses the **Peek** function to determine if the attribute name is enclosed in either single or double quotes. If the name is not quoted, then a **StringBuilder** object is created to hold the attribute name.

```
EatWhitespace();

if ("\"\'".IndexOf((char)this.source.Peek(0)) == -1)
{
  StringBuilder buffer = new StringBuilder();
```

If the attribute name is not delineated, read the attribute name until either an equal sign or a tag ending "greater than sign" (>) is encountered. This will indicate the end of the attribute name. Either the attribute's value or the next attribute will follow.

```
while (!char.IsWhiteSpace((char)this.source.Peek(0))
   && (this.source.Peek(0) != '=') && (this.source.Peek(0) != '>')
   && (this.source.Peek(0) != -1))
```

```
{
    int ch = ParseSpecialCharacter();
    buffer.Append((char)ch);
}
return buffer.ToString();
```

If the attribute name is quoted, simply call **PrseString**.

```
} else
{
    return (ParseString());
}
```

Finally, return the result, the attribute name.

Parse Special Characters with ParseSpecialCharacter

Certain characters must be encoded when included in HTML documents. This is to prevent the HTML parser from confusing a naturally occurring less than or greater than sign with the beginning or end of an HTML tag. Characters such as the "greater than sign" (>) symbol are encoded as **>**. Additionally, you may choose to encode ASCII codes as well. For example, ASCII character 34 could be encoded as **"**.

The **ParseSpecialCharacter** function handles these character encodings. This function begins by reading the first character and seeing if it is an ampersand (&). If the first character is an ampersand, a **StringBuilder** object is setup to hold the rest of the character encoding.

```
char result = (char)this.source.Read();
int advanceBy = 0;

// is there a special character?
if (result == '&')
{
    int ch = 0;
    StringBuilder buffer = new StringBuilder();
```

Next, a loop is started that will read the rest of the character encoding up to the semicolon; which terminates all character encoding sequences.

```
// Loop through and read special character.
do
{
    ch = this.source.Peek(advanceBy++);
    if ((ch != '&') && (ch != ';') && !char.IsWhiteSpace((char)ch))
    {
        buffer.Append((char)ch);
    }
} while ((ch != ';') && (ch != -1) && !char.
```

```
IsWhiteSpace((char)ch));
```

If a beginning tag "less than sign" (<) character is found, then the character encoding is invalid, so we just return an ampersand. This is the best we can do with regards to decoding the character. The **do/while** loop continues until a semicolon is found, or we reach the end of the file.

```
if (ch == '<')
  return '&';
} while (ch != ';' && (ch != -1));
```

The entire character encoding is now loaded into the variable named **buffer**. The first thing to confirm is whether or not the first character is a pound sign (#). If the first character is a pound sign, this is ASCII encoding. We then should parse the number immediately following the pound sign and return that as the encoded character.

```
String b = buffer.ToString().Trim().ToLower();
```

If a special character encoding was found, we will need to parse it.

```
// did we find a special character?
if (b.Length > 0)
{
```

If the special encoding begins with a pound sign (#) then it is an ASCII character. If this is the case, the number is parsed and converted into the correct character.

```
  if (b[0] == '#')
  {
    try
    {
      result = (char)int.Parse(b.Substring(1));
    }
    catch (FormatException)
    {
      advanceBy = 0;
    }
  }
  else
  {
```

If the special character does not start with a pound sign, it is likely to be a symbolic special character, such as the **"** character, or similar. If this is the case, the parser then attempts to look the symbol up in the **charMap**.

```
    if (charMap.ContainsKey(b))
    {
      result = charMap[b];
    }
    else
```

```
    {
       advanceBy = 0;
    }
  }
}
```

Finally, if no special character was found, the parser does not advance any characters and the character sequence that we thought was a special character will be parsed normally.

```
else
{
  advanceBy = 0;
}
```

Now that the special character is processed, read past the number of bytes that were in the special character encoding.

```
while (advanceBy > 0)
{
  Read();
  advanceBy--;
}

return result;
```

Finally, the character that was obtained is returned.

Reading Characters

The **ParseHTML** class contains a function, named **Read** that is called to read the next character from an HTML file. The function will return zero if an HTML tag is encountered. Additionally, it will decode any special HTML characters.

The **Read** function begins by checking that the parser locked to a specific end tag. If the parser is locked to an end tag, this means that the parser will not attempt to parse anything further until that exact end tag is found. An example of this is the **<script>** tag. Once an opening **<script>** tag is found, nothing inside the **<script>** tag should be treated as HTML. The parser will not attempt any further parsing until an ending **</script>** tag is found.

```
// handle locked end tag
if (this.lockedEndTag != null)
{
  if (PeekEndTag(this.lockedEndTag))
  {
    this.lockedEndTag = null;
  }
  else
  {
```

```
      return this.source.Read();
   }
}
```

Next, the **Read** function looks for a "less than sign" (<). The "less than sign" (<) signals the beginning of an HTML tag. If a less-than sign is found, then the **ParseTag** method is called, and a zero is returned. Calling the **Tag** property from the **ParseHTML** object will access the tag, which was just parsed by the **ParseTag** method.

```
// look for next tag
if (this.source.Peek(0) == '<')
{
  ParseTag();
  if (!this.Tag.Ending
    && (String.Compare(this.Tag.Name, "script", true) == 0 ||
String.Compare(this.Tag.Name, "style", true) == 0))
  {
    this.lockedEndTag = this.Tag.Name.ToLower();
  }
return 0;
```

If a beginning tag of either **<script>** or **<style>** is found, the parser is locked to the end tag for the tag just found. If an ampersand is found, a special character will follow. Calling **ParseSpecialCharacter** will handle the special HTML character.

```
}
else if (this.source.Peek(0) == '&')
{
  return ParseSpecialCharacter();
}
```

If neither a tag nor a special character is found, a character is simply read from the underlying stream.

```
else
{
  return (this.source.Read());
}
```

The character just read is returned to the calling method or function.

Encapsulating HTML Tags

When access the **Tag** property of the HTML parse class, you are given an **HTMLTag** object. This object completely encapsulates the HTML tag that was just parsed. The **HTMLTag** class is shown in Listing 6.3.

Listing 6.3: HTML Tags (HTMLTag.cs)

```
using System;
using System.Collections.Generic;
using System.Text;

namespace HeatonResearch.Spider.HTML
{

    /// <summary>
    /// HTMLTag: This class holds a single HTML tag. This class
    /// subclasses the AttributeList class. This allows the
    /// HTMLTag class to hold a collection of attributes, just as
    /// an actual HTML tag does.
    /// </summary>
    public class HTMLTag
    {
        private String name;
        private bool ending;

        /// <summary>
        /// The name of the tag.
        /// </summary>
        public String Name
        {
            get
            {
                return name;
            }
            set
            {
                name = value;
            }
        }

        /// <summary>
        /// Is this tag both a beginning and an
        /// ending tag.
        /// </summary>
        public Boolean Ending
        {
            get
            {
                return ending;
            }
            set
            {
```

```
                    ending = value;
                }
            }

        /// <summary>
        /// The attributes of this tag.
        /// </summary>
        private Dictionary<String, String> attributes = new
    Dictionary<String, String>();

        /// <summary>
        /// Clear out this tag.
        /// </summary>
        public void Clear()
        {
            this.attributes.Clear();
            this.Name = "";
            this.Ending = false;
        }

        /// <summary>
        /// Access the individual attributes by name.
        /// </summary>
        public String this[string key]
        {
            get
            {
                if( attributes.ContainsKey(key.ToLower()) )
                    return this.attributes[key.ToLower()];
                else
                    return null;
            }
            set
            {
                this.attributes.Add(key.ToLower(), value);
            }
        }

        /// <summary>
        /// Convert this tag back into string form, with the
        /// beginning &lt; and ending &gt;.
        /// </summary>
        /// <returns>The attribute value that was found.</returns>
        public override String ToString()
        {
            StringBuilder buffer = new StringBuilder("<");
```

```
            buffer.Append(this.Name);

            foreach (String key in attributes.Keys)
            {
                String value = this.attributes[key];
                buffer.Append(' ');

                if (value == null)
                {
                    buffer.Append("\"");
                    buffer.Append(key);
                    buffer.Append("\"");
                }
                else
                {
                    buffer.Append(key);
                    buffer.Append("=\"");
                    buffer.Append(value);
                    buffer.Append("\"");
                }
            }

            if (this.Ending)
            {
                buffer.Append('/');
            }
            buffer.Append(">");
            return buffer.ToString();
        }

        /// <summary>
        /// Set the specified attribute.
        /// </summary>
        /// <param name="key">The attribute name.</param>
        /// <param name="value">The attribute value.</param>
        public void SetAttribute(String key, String value)
        {
            attributes.Remove(key.ToLower());
            attributes.Add(key.ToLower(), value);
        }
    }
}
```

The HTML tag class contains two properties, which are used to hold the HTML tag.

- attributes
- name

The **attributes** variable contains a map, which holds all of the name value pairs that make up the HTML attributes. The **name** attribute contains a **String** that holds the name of the HTML tag.

Most of the code in Listing 6.3 is contained in the **ToString** function. The **ToString** function is responsible for converting this **HTMLTag** object back into a textual HTML tag.

The first action performed by the **ToString** function is to create a **StringBuilder** to hold the textual tag, as it is created. The **StringBuilder** object begins with a less-than character followed by the tag name.

```
StringBuilder buffer = new StringBuilder("<");
buffer.Append(this.Name);
```

Next, a loop is entered to display each of the attributes. The attribute's value is read into a **String** object, named **value**. A leading space is placed in front of each attribute. This makes the attribute easier to read.

```
foreach (String key in attributes.Keys)
{
  String value = this.attributes[key];
  buffer.Append(' ');
```

If a value is not present, display the **key**, which is the name of the attribute. The key will be stored enclosed in quotes.

```
  if (value == null)
  {
    buffer.Append("\"");
    buffer.Append(key);
    buffer.Append("\"");
```

If a value is present, display the key followed by an equals sign, followed by the value. The value will be enclosed in quotes.

```
  }
  else
  {
    buffer.Append(key);
    buffer.Append("=\"");
    buffer.Append(value);
    buffer.Append("\"");
  }
}
```

```
  } else
  {
    buffer.Append(key);
    buffer.Append("=\"");
```

```
    buffer.Append(value);
    buffer.Append("\"");
  }
}
```

If the tag is both a beginning and ending tag, for example **
**, then the ending slash must be displayed.

```
if (this.Ending)
{
  buffer.Append('/');
}
```

After all the attributes have been displayed, a trailing "greater than sign" (>) sign is appended to the **StringBuilder** object. This ends the tag.

```
buffer.Append(">");
return buffer.ToString();
```

Once the loop is completed, the **StringBuilder** object is converted to a **String**, by calling its **ToString** method. This **String** is returned.

Recipes

This chapter includes seven recipes. These recipes explain how to extract data from a variety of different HTML page types. Specifically, the recipes show:

- Extracting data from a choice list
- Extracting data from a HTML list
- Extracting data from a table
- Extracting data from hyperlinks
- Extracting images from an HTML page
- Extracting data from HTML sub-pages
- Extracting data from HTML partial-pages

All of the recipes in this chapter will make use of the HTML parsing classes described in the first part of this chapter. We will begin with the first recipe, which shows how to extract data from a choice list.

Recipe #6.1: Extracting Data from a Choice List

Many websites contains choice lists. These choice lists, which are usually part of a form, allow you to pick one option from a scrolling list of many different options. This recipe will extract data from the choice list, at the following URL.

http://www.httprecipes.com/1/6/form.php

You can see this choice list in Figure 6.1.

Figure 6.1: An HTML Choice List

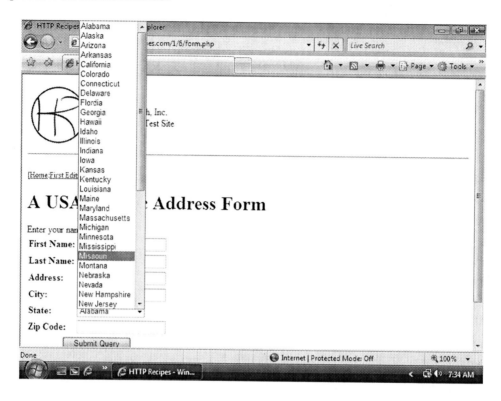

As you can see, there is a listing of all fifty US states. This recipe will show how to extract these states, and their abbreviations. The recipe is shown in Listing 6.4.

Listing 6.4: Parse a Choice List (ParseChoiceList.cs)

```
using System;
using System.Collections.Generic;
using System.Text;
using System.IO;
using System.Net;
using HeatonResearch.Spider.HTML;


namespace Recipe6_1
{
    class ParseChoiceList
    {
        /// <summary>
        /// Called for each option item that is found.
        /// </summary>
        /// <param name="name">The name of the option item.
        /// </param>
```

```
/// <param name="value">The value of the option item.
/// </param>
private void ProcessOption(String name, String value)
{
    StringBuilder result = new StringBuilder();
    result.Append('\"');
    result.Append(name);
    result.Append("\",\"");
    result.Append(value);
    result.Append('\"');
    Console.WriteLine(result.ToString());
}


/// <summary>
/// Advance to the specified HTML tag.
/// </summary>
/// <param name="parse">The HTML parse object to use.
/// </param>
/// <param name="tag">The HTML tag.</param>
/// <param name="count">How many tags like this to find.
/// </param>
/// <returns>True if found, false otherwise.</returns>
private bool Advance(ParseHTML parse,
  String tag, int count)
{
    int ch;
    while ((ch = parse.Read()) != -1)
    {
        if (ch == 0)
        {
            if (String.Compare(parse.Tag.Name, tag,true)
                == 0)
            {
                count--;
                if (count <= 0)
                    return true;
            }
        }
    }
    return false;
}


/// <summary>
/// Process the specified URL and extract the
/// option list there.
/// </summary>
```

```csharp
/// <param name="url">The URL to process.</param>
/// <param name="optionList">Which option list to
/// process, zero for first.</param>
public void Process(Uri url, int optionList)
{
    String value = "";
    WebRequest http = HttpWebRequest.Create(url);
    HttpWebResponse response =
            (HttpWebResponse)http.GetResponse();
    Stream istream = response.GetResponseStream();
    ParseHTML parse = new ParseHTML(istream);
    StringBuilder buffer = new StringBuilder();

    Advance(parse, "select", optionList);

    int ch;
    while ((ch = parse.Read()) != -1)
    {
        if (ch == 0)
        {
            HTMLTag tag = parse.Tag;
            if (String.Compare(tag.Name, "option") == 0)
            {
                value = tag["value"];
                buffer.Length = 0;
            }
            else if (String.Compare(tag.Name, "/option")
                        == 0)
            {
                ProcessOption(buffer.ToString(), value);
            }
            else if (String.Compare(tag.Name, "/choice")
                        == 0)
            {
                break;
            }
        }
        else
        {
            buffer.Append((char)ch);
        }
    }
}

/// <summary>
/// The main method.
```

```
/// </summary>
/// <param name="args">Not used.</param>
static void Main(string[] args)
{
    Uri u = new Uri(
            "http://www.httprecipes.com/1/6/form.php");
    ParseChoiceList parse = new ParseChoiceList();
    parse.Process(u, 1);
}
}
}
```

If you examine the HTML source code that makes up the states choice list, you will see:

```
<select name="state">
  <option value="AL">Alabama</option>
  <option value="AK">Alaska</option>
  <option value="AZ">Arizona</option>
  <option value="AR">Arkansas</option>
  <option value="CA">California</option>
  <option value="CO">Colorado</option>
  <option value="CT">Connecticut</option>
  <option value="DE">Delaware</option>
...
  <option value="WV">West Virginia</option>
  <option value="WI">Wisconsin</option>
  <option value="WY">Wyoming</option>
</select>
```

In the next section, you will see how to parse these **<option>** tags into a comma delimited list of states and abbreviations.

Parsing the Choice List

To parse the choice list, it is necessary to extract the state abbreviation, as well as the state name. The **Process** method is used to process the list. This method begins by defining several variables that will be needed to parse the choice list. A **Stream** is opened for the URL being parsed, and a new **ParseHTML** object is constructed.

```
String value = "";
Stream is = url.openStream();
ParseHTML parse = new ParseHTML(is);
StringBuilder buffer = new StringBuilder();
```

There may be more than one choice list on the page being parsed. Each choice list is surrounded by a beginning **<select>** tag, and an ending **</select>** tag. If there is more than one choice list, then we must advance to the correct one. This is accomplished by the **Advance** function.

The **Advance** function has three parameters. The first is the parse object being used to parse the HTML. This object will be advanced to the correct location. The second parameter is the name of the tag to which we are advancing. In this case, we are advancing to a **<select>** tag. Finally, the third parameter tells the **Advance** function which instance of the second parameter to look for. Zero specifies the first instance; one specifies the second instance, and so on.

```
Advance(parse, "select", optionList);
```

Once we have advanced to the correct choice list location, it is time to begin looking for **<option>** tags. We begin with a while loop that reads data from the **Parse** object. As soon as the **Read** function returns a zero, we know that we have found an HTML tag.

```
int ch;
while ((ch = parse.Read()) != -1)
{
  if (ch == 0)
  {
    HTMLTag tag = parse.Tag;
```

First, we check to see if it is an opening **<option>** tag. If it is, then we read the **value** attribute. This attribute will hold the abbreviation for that state.

```
    if (String.Compare(tag.Name, "option") == 0)
    {
      value = tag["value"];
      buffer.Length = 0;
```

Next, we check to see if the tag encountered is an ending **</option>** tag. If it is, then we have found one state. The **ProcessOption** method is called to display that state as part of the comma separated list, which is the output from this recipe.

```
    else if (String.Compare(tag.Name, "/option") == 0)
    {
      ProcessOption(buffer.ToString(), value);
    }
```

If an ending **</choice>** tag is found, then the list has ended, and we are done.

```
    else if (String.Compare(tag.Name, "/choice") == 0)
    {
      break;
    }
```

If it was a character that we found, and not a tag, then append it to the buffer. The buffer will hold the state names that are between the **<option>** and **</option>** tags.

```
    else
    {
      buffer.Append((char)ch);
    }
```

```
     }
}
```

Once the loop completes, all fifty states will have been extracted.

Implementing the Advance Function

Our **Advance** function requires three arguments: the first is the object being parsed, the second is the name of the tag we are looking for, and the third is the encounter of the tag we are stopping on minus one. As previously mentioned, the **Advance** function advances through several instances of a tag, looking for the one specified. To do this, the **Advance** function enters a while loop that will continue until the end of the file is reached.

```
int ch;
while ((ch = parse.Read()) != -1)
{
```

For each HTML tag encountered, compare the tag name to the tag we are looking for.

```
  if (ch == 0)
  {
    if (String.Compare(parse.Tag.Name, tag,true) == 0)
    {
```

If the tag name matches, decrease the **count** variable. If the **count** has reached zero, then we have advanced to the correct location and we are finished advancing.

```
      count--;
      if (count <= 0)
        return true;
    }
  }
}
```

If we fail to find the tag, return false.

```
return false;
```

Several other recipes in this chapter use the **Advance** function.

Recipe #6.2: Extracting Data from an HTML List

Many websites contains lists of data. This recipe will extract data from an HTML list, at the following URL.

`http://www.httprecipes.com/1/6/list.php`

You can see this choice list in Figure 6.2.

Figure 6.2: An HTML List

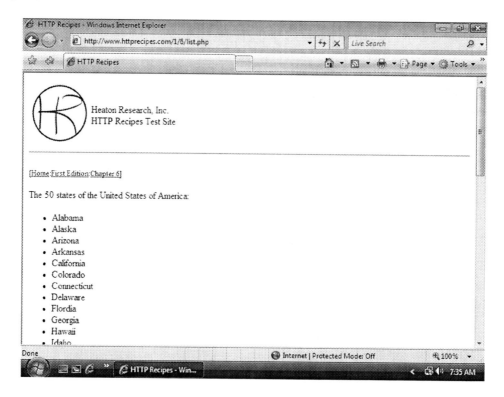

As you can see, there is a listing of all fifty US states. This recipe will show how to extract these states. The recipe is shown in Listing 6.5.

Listing 6.5: Parse an HTML List (ParseList.cs)

```
using System;
using System.Collections.Generic;
using System.Text;
using System.Net;
using System.IO;
using HeatonResearch.Spider.HTML;

namespace Recipe6_2
{
    class ParseList
    {
        /// <summary>
        /// Handle each list item, as it is found.
        /// </summary>
        /// <param name="item">The list item that was
            just found.</param>
```

```
private void ProcessItem(String item)
{
    Console.WriteLine(item);
}

/// <summary>
/// Advance to the specified HTML tag.
/// </summary>
/// <param name="parse">The HTML parse object to use.
/// </param>
/// <param name="tag">The HTML tag.</param>
/// <param name="count">How many tags like this to find.
/// </param>
/// <returns>True if found, false otherwise.</returns>
private bool Advance(ParseHTML parse, String tag,
    int count)
{
    int ch;
    while ((ch = parse.Read()) != -1)
    {
        if (ch == 0)
        {
            if (String.Compare(parse.Tag.Name, tag,true)
                == 0)
            {
                count--;
                if (count <= 0)
                    return true;
            }
        }
    }
    return false;
}

/// <summary>
/// Called to extract a list from the specified URL.
/// </summary>
/// <param name="url">The URL to extract the list
/// from.</param>
/// <param name="listType">What type of list, specify
/// its beginning tag (i.e. <UL>)</param>
/// <param name="optionList">Which list to search,
/// zero for first.</param>
public void Process(Uri url, String listType,
    int optionList)
public void Process(Uri url, String listType,
```

```
    int optionList)
{

    String listTypeEnd = listType + "/";
    WebRequest http = HttpWebRequest.Create(url);
    HttpWebResponse response =
            (HttpWebResponse)http.GetResponse();
    Stream istream = response.GetResponseStream();
    ParseHTML parse = new ParseHTML(istream);
    StringBuilder buffer = new StringBuilder();
    bool capture = false;

    Advance(parse, listType, optionList);

    int ch;
    while ((ch = parse.Read()) != -1)
    {
        if (ch == 0)
        {
            HTMLTag tag = parse.Tag;
            if (String.Compare(tag.Name, "li", true) == 0)
            {
                if (buffer.Length > 0)
                    ProcessItem(buffer.ToString());
                buffer.Length = 0;
                capture = true;
            }
            else if (String.Compare(tag.Name, "/li", true)
                == 0)
            {
                Console.WriteLine(buffer.ToString());
                ProcessItem(buffer.ToString());
                buffer.Length = 0;
                capture = false;
            }
            else if (String.Compare(tag.Name, listTypeEnd,
                true) == 0)
            {
                break;
            }
        }
        else
        {
            if (capture)
                buffer.Append((char)ch);
        }
    }
```

```
        }

    static void Main(string[] args)
    {
        Uri u = new Uri(
            "http://www.httprecipes.com/1/6/list.php");
        ParseList parse = new ParseList();
        parse.Process(u, "ul", 1);
    }
  }
}
```

The **Process** method of the **ParseList** class extracts the data from the list. This method begins by creating the variables needed to parse the list. HTML has various list types (such as **<ul>**, **<ol>** and other list tags). Therefore, the type of list must be passed in. Also, the variable **listTypeEnd** is created to contain the ending tag. For example, an **<ol>** list would end with an **</ol>** tag. The **capture** variable tracks whether we are capturing the "non-tag" text or not. This variable will be enabled when we reach an **<li>** tag, which means we need to start capturing the text of the current item.

```
String listTypeEnd = listType + "/";
WebRequest http = HttpWebRequest.Create(url);
HttpWebResponse response = (HttpWebResponse)http.GetResponse();
Stream istream = response.GetResponseStream();
ParseHTML parse = new ParseHTML(istream);
StringBuilder buffer = new StringBuilder();
bool capture = false;
```

The **Advance** method takes us to the correct list in the HTML page. The Advance method is discussed in Recipe 6.1.

```
Advance(parse, listType, optionList);
```

Next, we begin reading the HTML tags. This continues until the end of the file is reached.

```
int ch;
while ((ch = parse.Read()) != -1)
{
  if (ch == 0)
  {
    HTMLTag tag = parse.Tag;
```

If an **<li>** tag is encountered, then we clear the buffer and begin capturing. If there was data already in the buffer, then we record that item, as it will be one of the fifty states.

```
if (String.Compare(tag.Name, "li", true) == 0)
{
  if (buffer.Length > 0)
    ProcessItem(buffer.ToString());
```

```
buffer.Length = 0;
capture = true;
```

If we find an ending `</li>` tag, then we clear the buffer and prepare for the next tag. However, often, the ending `</li>` tag is not used: as a result this recipe does not require the ending `</li>` tag. To fully support the possibility of not having an ending `</li>` tag, first we must check to see if there is already a tag in the buffer when we reach the next `<li>` tag.

```
}
else if (String.Compare(tag.Name, "/li", true) == 0)
{
  Console.WriteLine(buffer.ToString());
  ProcessItem(buffer.ToString());
  buffer.Length = 0;
  capture = false;
}
```

If we find the ending tag type, then we have finished.

```
else if (String.Compare(tag.Name, listTypeEnd, true) == 0)
{
  break;
}
```

If we found a regular character - not an HTML tag - add it to the buffer, if we are currently capturing characters.

```
}
else
{
  if (capture)
    buffer.Append((char)ch);
}
```

When the loop is complete, we will have parsed all fifty states from the HTML list.

Recipe #6.3: Extracting Data from a Table

Many websites contain tables. These tables allow each website to arrange data by rows and columns. This recipe extracts data from the table at the following URL:

`http://www.httprecipes.com/1/6/table.php`

You can see this table in Figure 6.3.

Figure 6.3: An HTML Table

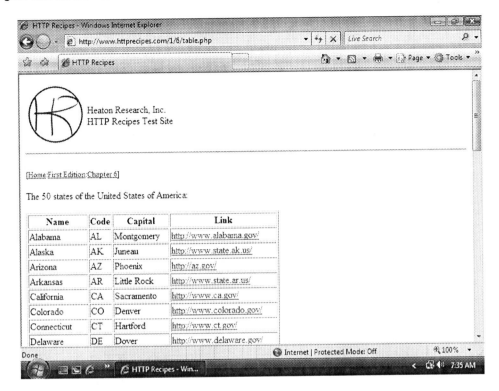

As you can see, there is a table of all fifty US states, along with capital cities and official links. This recipe will show how to extract these states and their data. The recipe is shown in Listing 6.6.

Listing 6.6: Parse a Table (ParseTable.cs)

```
using System;
using System.Collections.Generic;
using System.Text;
using System.Net;
using System.IO;
using HeatonResearch.Spider.HTML;


namespace Recipe6_3
{
    class ParseTable
    {
        /// <summary>
        /// Advance to the specified HTML tag.
        /// </summary>
```

```
/// <param name="parse">The HTML parse object to use.
/// </param>
/// <param name="tag">The HTML tag.</param>
/// <param name="count">How many tags like this to find.
/// </param>
/// <returns>True if found, false otherwise.</returns>
private bool Advance(ParseHTML parse, String tag,
    int count)
{
    int ch;
    while ((ch = parse.Read()) != -1)
    {
        if (ch == 0)
        {
            if (String.Compare(parse.Tag.Name, tag,true)
                == 0)
            {
                count--;
                if (count <= 0)
                    return true;
            }
        }
    }
    return false;
}


/// <summary>
/// This method is called once for each table row located,
/// it contains a list of all columns in that row.  The
/// method provided simply prints the columns to the
/// console.
/// </summary>
/// <param name="list">Columns that were found on
/// this row.</param>
private void ProcessTableRow(List<String> list)
{
    StringBuilder result = new StringBuilder();
    foreach (String item in list)
    {
        if (result.Length > 0)
            result.Append(",");
        result.Append('\"');
        result.Append(item);
        result.Append('\"');

    }
```

```
    Console.WriteLine(result.ToString());
}

/// <summary>
/// Called to parse a table.  The table number at
/// the specified URL will be parsed.
/// </summary>
/// <param name="url">The URL of the HTML page that
/// contains the table.</param>
/// <param name="tableNum">The table number to parse,
/// zero for the first.</param>
public void Process(Uri url, int tableNum)
{
    WebRequest http = HttpWebRequest.Create(url);
    HttpWebResponse response =
      (HttpWebResponse)http.GetResponse();
    Stream istream = response.GetResponseStream();
    ParseHTML parse = new ParseHTML(istream);
    StringBuilder buffer = new StringBuilder();
    List<String> list = new List<String>();
    bool capture = false;

    Advance(parse, "table", tableNum);

    int ch;
    while ((ch = parse.Read()) != -1)
    {
        if (ch == 0)
        {
            HTMLTag tag = parse.Tag;
            if (String.Compare(tag.Name, "tr", true) == 0)
            {
                list.Clear();
                capture = false;
                buffer.Length = 0;
            }
            else if (String.Compare(tag.Name, "/tr", true)
                == 0)
            {
                if (list.Count > 0)
                {
                    ProcessTableRow(list);
                    list.Clear();
                }
            }
            else if (String.Compare(tag.Name, "td", true)
```

```
                                    == 0)
                    {
                        if (buffer.Length > 0)
                            list.Add(buffer.ToString());
                        buffer.Length = 0;
                        capture = true;
                    }
                    else if (String.Compare(tag.Name, "/td", true)
                        == 0)
                    {
                        list.Add(buffer.ToString());
                        buffer.Length = 0;
                        capture = false;
                    }
                    else if (String.Compare(tag.Name, "/table",
                        true) == 0)
                    {
                        break;
                    }
                }
                else
                {
                    if (capture)
                        buffer.Append((char)ch);
                }
            }
        }
    }


    static void Main(string[] args)
    {
        Uri u = new Uri(
            "http://www.httprecipes.com/1/6/table.php");
        ParseTable parse = new ParseTable();
        parse.Process(u, 2);
    }
  }
}
```

An HTML table is contained between the tags <table> and </table>. The table consists of a series of rows which are contained between the <tr> and </tr> tags. Each table row contains several columns, each of which is contained between the <td> and </td> tags. Additionally, some tables have header columns contained between <th> and </th> tags.

The HTML for the states table is shown below:

```
<table border="1">
<tr>
  <th>Name</th>
  <th>Code</th>
  <th>Capital</th>
  <th>Link</th>
</tr>
<tr>
  <td>Alabama</td>
  <td>AL</td>
  <td>Montgomery</td>
  <td>
    <a href="http://www.alabama.gov/">http://www.alabama.gov/
    </a></td>
</tr>
<tr>
  <td>Alaska</td>
  <td>AK</td>
  <td>Juneau</td>
  <td>
    <a href="http://www.state.ak.us/">http://www.state.ak.us/
    </a></td>
</tr>
...
<tr>
  <td>Wyoming</td>
  <td>WY</td>
  <td>Cheyenne</td>
  <td><a href="http://wyoming.gov/">http://wyoming.gov/</a></td>
</tr>
</table>
```

The data we will parse is located between the **<td>** and **</td>** tags. However, the other tags tell us to which row the data belongs.

Parsing the Table

The table is parsed by the **Process** method of the **ParseTable** class. This method begins by opening a **Stream** to the URL that contains the table. A **ParseHTML** object is created to parse this **Stream**. A variable named **buffer** is created to hold the data for each table cell. A variable named **list** is created to hold each column of data for a given row. A variable named **capture** tracks whether we are capturing HTML text into the buffer variable or not. Capturing will occur when we are between **<td>** and **</td>** tags.

```
Stream istream = response.GetResponseStream();
ParseHTML parse = new ParseHTML(istream);
StringBuilder buffer = new StringBuilder();
```

```
List<String> list = new List<String>();
bool capture = false;
```

The Advance method will take us to the correct table in the HTML page. The **Advance** method is discussed in Recipe 6.1.

```
Advance(parse, "table", tableNum);
```

Next, we begin reading the HTML tags. We continue until the end of the file is reached.

```
int ch;
while ((ch = parse.Read()) != -1)
{
  if (ch == 0)
  {
    HTMLTag tag = parse.Tag;
```

When a **<tr>** tag is located, a new table row has begun. This means that we must clear out the last table row.

```
    if (String.Compare(tag.Name, "tr", true) == 0)
    {
      list.Clear();
      capture = false;
      buffer.Length = 0;
    }
```

When a **</tr>** tag is located, a table row has ended. If any columns have been recorded, call **ProcessTableRow** to process the row just ended.

```
    else if (String.Compare(tag.Name, "/tr", true) == 0)
    {
      if (list.Count > 0)
      {
        ProcessTableRow(list);
        list.Clear();
      }
    }
```

When a **<td>** tag is located, a table column is about to begin. If any data was already being captured for a column, record it to the list. Set the variable named **capture** to **true** so that the text following the **<td>** tag will be captured.

```
    else if (String.Compare(tag.Name, "td", true) == 0)
    {
      if (buffer.Length > 0)
        list.Add(buffer.ToString());
      buffer.Length = 0;
      capture = true;
    }
```

When a `</td>` tag is located, a column has just ended. This column should be recorded to the variable **list** and capturing should stop.

```
else if (String.Compare(tag.Name, "/td", true) == 0)
{
  list.Add(buffer.ToString());
  buffer.Length = 0;
  capture = false;
}
```

When a `</table>` tag is located, the table has ended. Parsing is now finished.

```
else if (String.Compare(tag.Name, "/table", true) == 0)
{
  break;
}
```

If we are capturing characters and we find a regular character (not an HTML tag), then add it to the buffer.

```
else
{
  if (capture)
    buffer.Append((char)ch);
}
}
```

The loop will continue until all cells of the table have been processed.

Parsing a Table Row

For each row of recorded data, the **ProcessRow** method is called. This method prints the data in a comma delimited format. The first step by the **ProcessRow** method is the creation of a **StringBuilder**. The code then iterates over the columns sent to it in the **list** variable.

```
StringBuilder result = new StringBuilder();
foreach (String item in list)
{
```

Add each column recorded to the **StringBuilder**. Ensure each column is enclosed in quotes.

```
if (result.Length > 0)
  result.Append(",");
result.Append('\"');
result.Append(item);
result.Append('\"');
}
```

Finally, display the complete row.

```
Console.WriteLine(result.ToString());
```

This method is called for all rows in the table.

Recipe #6.4: Extracting Data from Hyperlinks

Hyperlinks are very common on web sites. Hyperlinks hold the web site together. This recipe will extract the hyperlinks from the following URL:

http://www.httprecipes.com/1/6/link.php

You can see the hyperlinks in Figure 6.4.

Figure 6.4: Hyperlinks

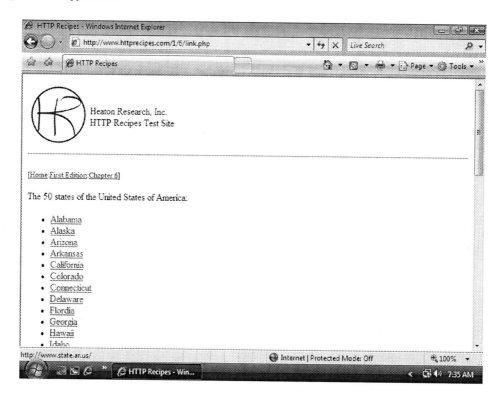

As you can see, there is a listing of all fifty US states. This recipe shows how to extract these states, and their links. The recipe is shown in Listing 6.7.

Listing 6.7: Parse Hyperlinks (ExtractLinks.cs)

```
using System;
using System.Collections.Generic;
using System.Text;
using System.Net;
using System.IO;
using HeatonResearch.Spider.HTML;

namespace Recipe6_4
{
    class ExtractLinks
    {
        private void ProcessOption(String name, String value)
        {
            StringBuilder result = new StringBuilder();
            result.Append('\"');
            result.Append(name);
            result.Append("\",\"");
            result.Append(value);
            result.Append('\"');
            Console.WriteLine(result.ToString());
        }

        /// <summary>
        /// Process the specified URL.
        /// </summary>
        /// <param name="url">The URL to process.</param>
        /// <param name="optionList">Whcih option list
        /// to process.</param>
        public void Process(Uri url, int optionList)
        {
            String value = "";
            WebRequest http = HttpWebRequest.Create(url);
            HttpWebResponse response =
                    (HttpWebResponse)http.GetResponse();
            Stream istream = response.GetResponseStream();
            ParseHTML parse = new ParseHTML(istream);
            StringBuilder buffer = new StringBuilder();

            int ch;
            while ((ch = parse.Read()) != -1)
            {
                if (ch == 0)
                {
                    HTMLTag tag = parse.Tag;
                    if (String.Compare(tag.Name, "a", true) == 0)
```

```
                        {
                            value = tag["href"];
                            Uri u = new Uri(url, value.ToString());
                            value = u.ToString();
                            buffer.Length = 0;
                        }
                        else if (String.Compare(tag.Name, "/a", true)
                            == 0)
                        {
                            ProcessOption(buffer.ToString(), value);
                        }
                    }
                    else
                    {
                        buffer.Append((char)ch);
                    }
                }
            }

        static void Main(string[] args)
        {
            Uri u = new Uri(
                "http://www.httprecipes.com/1/6/link.php");
            ExtractLinks parse = new ExtractLinks();
            parse.Process(u, 1);
        }
    }
}
```

The **Process** method of **ExtractLinks** is used to process the hyperlinks. The method begins by creating a few variables required to process the links. This method begins by opening a **Stream** to the URL containing the hyperlinks. A **ParseHTML** object is created to parse this **Stream**. A variable named **buffer** is created to hold the data for each link.

```
String value = "";
WebRequest http = HttpWebRequest.Create(url);
HttpWebResponse response = (HttpWebResponse)http.GetResponse();
Stream istream = response.GetResponseStream();
ParseHTML parse = new ParseHTML(istream);
StringBuilder buffer = new StringBuilder();
```

The method loops across every tag and text character in the HTML file.

```
int ch;
while ((ch = parse.Read()) != -1)
{
```

When an HTML tag is found, it is checked to see if it is an **<a>** (anchor) tag. If the tag is an anchor, then the **href** attribute is saved to the **value** variable. Additionally, the buffer variable is cleared.

```
if (ch == 0)
{
  HTMLTag tag = parse.Tag;
  if (String.Compare(tag.Name, "a", true) == 0)
  {
    value = tag["href"];
    Uri u = new Uri(url, value.ToString());
    value = u.ToString();
    buffer.Length = 0;
```

When the **</a>** tag is found, the tag's text and **href** value are both displayed.

```
  }
  else if (String.Compare(tag.Name, "/a", true) == 0)
  {
    ProcessOption(buffer.ToString(), value);
  }
```

If we find a regular character (not an HTML tag) it is added to the buffer.

```
  else
  {
    buffer.Append((char)ch);
  }
}
```

This loop continues until all links in the file have been processed.

Recipe #6.5: Extracting Images from HTML

Images are very common on web sites. This recipe extracts all images from the following URL.

```
http://www.httprecipes.com/1/6/image.php
```

You can see this images in Figure 6.5.

Figure 6.5: HTML Images

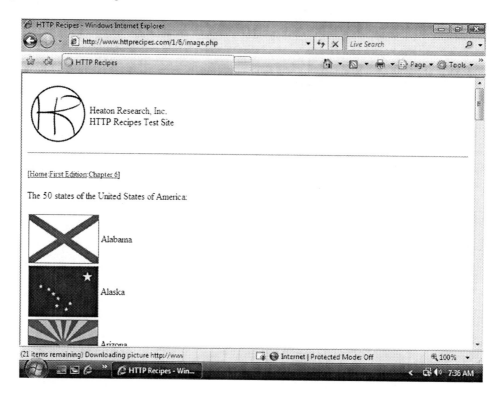

You have probably noted that there are images of the flags for all fifty US states. This recipe shows how to extract these images and can be viewed in Listing 6.8.

Listing 6.8: Extracting Images from HTML (ExtractImages.cs)

```
using System;
using System.Collections.Generic;
using System.Text;
using System.Net;
using System.IO;
using HeatonResearch.Spider.HTML;


namespace Recipe6_5
{
    class ExtractImages
    {
        /// <summary>
        /// Download the specified text page.
        /// </summary>
        /// <param name="response">The HttpWebResponse to
        /// download from.</param>
```

```
/// <param name="filename">The local file to save to.
/// </param>
public void DownloadBinaryFile(
    HttpWebResponse response, String filename)
{
    byte[] buffer = new byte[4096];
    FileStream os = new FileStream(filename,
        FileMode.Create);
    Stream stream = response.GetResponseStream();

    int count = 0;
    do
    {
        count = stream.Read(buffer, 0, buffer.Length);
        if (count > 0)
            os.Write(buffer, 0, count);
    } while (count > 0);

    response.Close();
    stream.Close();
    os.Close();
}

/// <summary>
/// Extract just the filename from a URL.
/// </summary>
/// <param name="u">The URL to extract from.</param>
/// <returns>The filename.</returns>
private String ExtractFile(Uri u)
{
    String str = u.PathAndQuery;

    // strip off path information
    int i = str.LastIndexOf('/');
    if (i != -1)
        str = str.Substring(i + 1);
    return str;
}

/// <summary>
/// Process the specified URL and download the images.
/// </summary>
/// <param name="url">The URL to process.</param>
/// <param name="saveTo">A directory to save the
/// images to.</param>
public void Process(Uri url, String saveTo)
```

```
        {
            WebRequest http = HttpWebRequest.Create(url);
            HttpWebResponse response =
                    (HttpWebResponse)http.GetResponse();
            Stream istream = response.GetResponseStream();
            ParseHTML parse = new ParseHTML(istream);

            int ch;
            while ((ch = parse.Read()) != -1)
            {
                if (ch == 0)
                {
                    HTMLTag tag = parse.Tag;
                    if (String.Compare(tag.Name, "img", true)
                        == 0)
                    {
                        String src = tag["src"];
                        Uri u = new Uri(url, src);
                        String filename = ExtractFile(u);
                        String saveFile =
                                Path.Combine(saveTo, filename);
                        WebRequest http2 =
                                HttpWebRequest.Create(u);
                        HttpWebResponse response2 =
                        (HttpWebResponse)http2.GetResponse();
                        this.DownloadBinaryFile(response2,
                                saveFile);
                        response2.Close();
                    }
                }
            }
        }

        static void Main(string[] args)
        {
            Uri u = new Uri(
                    "http://www.httprecipes.com/1/6/image.php");
            ExtractImages parse = new ExtractImages();
            parse.Process(u, ".");
        }
    }
}
```

HTML images are stored in the **<img>** tag. This tag contains an attribute, named **src** that contains the URL for the image to be displayed. A typical HTML image tag looks like this:

```
<img src="/images/logo.gif" width="320" height="200"
alt="Company Logo">
```

The only attribute that this recipe will be concerned with is the **src** attribute. The other tags are optional and they may, or may not, be present.

Extracting Images

This method loops across every tag and text character in the HTML file.

```
WebRequest http = HttpWebRequest.Create(url);
HttpWebResponse response = (HttpWebResponse)http.GetResponse();
Stream istream = response.GetResponseStream();
ParseHTML parse = new ParseHTML(istream);
```

When an HTML tag is found, it is checked to see if it is an **<img>** tag. If the tag is an image, then the **src** attribute is analyzed to determine the path to the image.

```
int ch;
while ((ch = parse.Read()) != -1)
{
  if (ch == 0)
  {
    HTMLTag tag = parse.Tag;
    if (String.Compare(tag.Name, "img", true) == 0)
    {
      String src = tag["src"];
```

To download the image, we need to obtain the fully qualified URL. For example, if the **<img>** tag's **src** attribute contains the value **/images/logo.gif**, we need **http://www.heatonresearch.com/images/logo.gif**. To obtain this URL, use the **Uri** class as follows:

```
Uri u = new Uri(url, src);
```

Next, extract the filename from the URL and append the filename to the local path to which the file is being saved. Then, the **DownloadBinaryPage** method will download the image. This method was explained in Chapter 3.

```
        String filename = ExtractFile(u);
        String saveFile = Path.Combine(saveTo, filename);
        WebRequest http2 = HttpWebRequest.Create(u);
        HttpWebResponse response2 =
                (HttpWebResponse)http2.GetResponse();

        this.DownloadBinaryFile(response2, saveFile);
        response2.Close();
    }
  }
}
```

This method looks across all images on the page.

Extracting a Filename

The **ExtractFile** function is used to get the filename portion of a URL. Consider the following URL:

```
http://www.heatonresearch.com/images/logo.gif
```

The filename portion is **logo.gif**. To extract this part of the URL, the path of the URL is first converted to a string.

```
String str = u.PathAndQuery;
```

This string is then searched for the last slash (/) character. Everything to the right of the slash is treated as the filename.

```
// strip off path information
int i = str.LastIndexOf('/');
if (i != -1)
   str = str.Substring(i + 1);
return str;
```

This method is used to strip the filename from each image, so that the image can be saved to a local path with the same filename.

Recipe #6.6: Extracting from Sub-Pages

So far, all of the data that has been extracted has been from a single HTML page. Often you will want to aggregate data spread across many pages. The last two recipes in this chapter demonstrate how to do this. This recipe shows how to download data from a list of linked pages. The list is contained here:

```
http://www.httprecipes.com/1/6/subpage.php
```

You can see this list of linked pages in Figure 6.6.

Figure 6.6: A List of Subpages

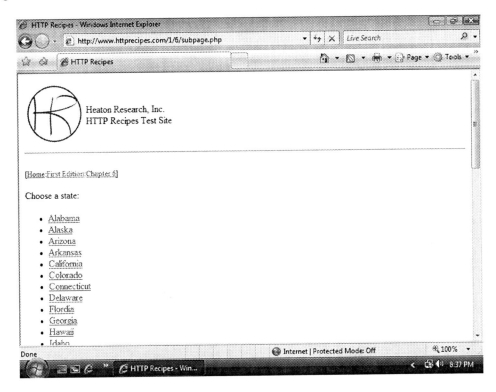

Each state on the list is hyperlinked to a sub-page. For example, the Missouri item links to the following URL:

```
http://www.httprecipes.com/1/6/subpage2.php?state=MO
```

This sub-page is shown below in Figure 6.7.

Figure 6.7: The Missouri Sub-Page

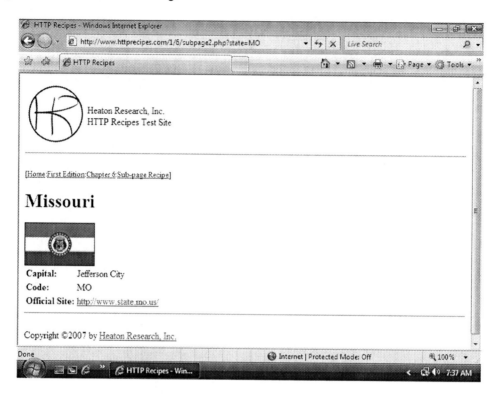

The data that we would like to gather is located on the sub-page. However, to find each sub-page, the list on the main page must be processed. This recipe shows how to extract data from all of the sub-pages. The recipe is shown in Listing 6.9.

Listing 6.9: Parse HTML Sub-Pages (ExtractSubPage.cs)

```csharp
using System;
using System.Collections.Generic;
using System.Text;
using System.Net;
using System.IO;
using HeatonResearch.Spider.HTML;

namespace Recipe6_6
{
    class ExtractSubPage
    {

        /// <summary>
        /// This method downloads the specified URL into a C#
        /// String. This is a very simple method, that you can
```

```
/// reused anytime you need to quickly grab all data from
/// a specific URL.
/// </summary>
/// <param name="url">The URL to download.</param>
/// <returns>The contents of the URL that was
/// downloaded.</returns>
public String DownloadPage(Uri url)
{
    WebRequest http = HttpWebRequest.Create(url);
    HttpWebResponse response =
            (HttpWebResponse)http.GetResponse();
    StreamReader stream = new
            StreamReader(response.GetResponseStream(),
            System.Text.Encoding.ASCII);

    String result = stream.ReadToEnd();

    response.Close();
    stream.Close();
    return result;
}


/// <summary>
/// This method is very useful for grabbing
/// information from an HTML page.  It extracts text
/// from between two tokens, the tokens need not be
/// case sensitive.
/// </summary>
/// <param name="str">The string to extract from.</param>
/// <param name="token1">The text, or tag, that comes
/// before the desired text</param>
/// <param name="token2">The text, or tag, that comes
/// after the desired text</param>
/// <param name="count">Which occurrence of token1 to
/// use, 1 for the first</param>
/// <returns></returns>
public String ExtractNoCase(String str, String token1,
    String token2,
    int count)
{
    int location1, location2;

    // convert everything to lower case
    String searchStr = str.ToLower();
    token1 = token1.ToLower();
    token2 = token2.ToLower();
```

```csharp
        // now search
        location1 = location2 = 0;
        do
        {
            location1 = searchStr.IndexOf(token1,
              location1 + 1);

            if (location1 == -1)
                return null;

            count--;
        } while (count > 0);

        // return the result from the original string
        // that has mixed
        // case
        location1 += token1.Length;
        location2 = str.IndexOf(token2, location1 + 1);
        if (location2 == -1)
            return null;

        return str.Substring(location1, location2 -
            location1);
    }

    /// <summary>
    /// Process each subpage. The subpages are where the
    /// data actually is.
    /// </summary>
    /// <param name="u">The URL of the subpage.</param>
    private void ProcessSubPage(Uri u)
    {
        String str = DownloadPage(u);
        String code = ExtractNoCase(str,
            "Code:<b></td><td>", "</td>", 0);
        if (code != null)
        {
            String capital = ExtractNoCase(str,
              "Capital:<b></td><td>", "</td>", 0);
            String name = ExtractNoCase(str, "<h1>",
              "</h1>", 0);
            String flag = ExtractNoCase(str,
              "<img src=\"", "\" border=\"1\">", 2);
            String site = ExtractNoCase(str,
              "Official Site:<b></td><td><a href=\"",
```

```
            "\"", 0);

        Uri flagURL = new Uri(u, flag);

        StringBuilder buffer = new StringBuilder();
        buffer.Append("\"");
        buffer.Append(code);
        buffer.Append("\",\"");
        buffer.Append(name);
        buffer.Append("\",\"");
        buffer.Append(capital);
        buffer.Append("\",\"");
        buffer.Append(flagURL.ToString());
        buffer.Append("\",\"");
        buffer.Append(site);
        buffer.Append("\"");
        Console.WriteLine(buffer.ToString());
    }
}


/// <summary>
/// Process the specified URL and extract data from
/// all of the subpages
/// that this page links to.
/// </summary>
/// <param name="url">The URL to process.</param>
public void Process(Uri url)
{
    String value = "";
    WebRequest http = HttpWebRequest.Create(url);
    HttpWebResponse response =
            (HttpWebResponse)http.GetResponse();
    Stream istream = response.GetResponseStream();
    ParseHTML parse = new ParseHTML(istream);

    int ch;
    while ((ch = parse.Read()) != -1)
    {
        if (ch == 0)
        {
            HTMLTag tag = parse.Tag;
            if (String.Compare(tag.Name, "a", true) == 0)
            {
                value = tag["href"];
                Uri u = new Uri(url, value.ToString());
                value = u.ToString();
```

```
                        ProcessSubPage(u);
                    }
                }
            }
        }

        static void Main(string[] args)
        {
            Uri u = new Uri(
                "http://www.httprecipes.com/1/6/subpage.php");
            ExtractSubPage parse = new ExtractSubPage();
            parse.Process(u);
        }
    }
}
```

This recipe performs two tasks. First, a list of the sub-pages must be obtained from the main page. Secondly, each sub-page must be loaded, and its data extracted.

Obtaining the List of Sub-Pages

The **Process** method of the **ExtractSubPage** class obtains a list of all sub-pages and passes each sub-page to the **ProcessSubPage** method. This method begins by opening a **Stream** to the URL containing the table. A **ParseHTML** object is created to parse this **Stream**.

```
String value = "";
WebRequest http = HttpWebRequest.Create(url);
HttpWebResponse response = (HttpWebResponse)http.GetResponse();
Stream istream = response.GetResponseStream();
ParseHTML parse = new ParseHTML(istream);
```

The method loops across every tag and text character in the HTML file.

```
int ch;
while ((ch = parse.Read()) != -1)
{
  if (ch == 0)
  {
    HTMLTag tag = parse.Tag;
    if (String.Compare(tag.Name, "a", true) == 0)
    {
```

When an **<a>** tag is located, its **href** attribute is examined.

```
    value = tag["href"];
```

A new **Uri** object is created from the parent URL and the **href** value. This provides the fully qualified URL for the sub-page.

```
    Uri u = new Uri(url, value.ToString());
```

The **ProcessSubPage** method is then called for each sub-page.

```
    value = u.ToString();
    ProcessSubPage(u);
  }
 }
}
```

This method will loop through all sub-pages and call **ProcessSubPage** for each.

Extracting from the Sub-Pages

Extracting data from the sub-pages is not very different to any of the other data extraction examples. The **ProcessSubPage** method begins by downloading the HTML page. Next, the **ProcessSubPage** method tries to locate the postal code.

```
String str = DownloadPage(u);
            String code = ExtractNoCase(str, "Code:<b></td><td>",
"</td>", 0);
```

If no postal code is located, we know there is no US state information on this page. There are several extra links on the parent page that do not point to state sub-pages. This allows these pages to be quickly discarded.

The state's postal code is located by searching for the key text **Code:<b></td><td>**, which occurs just before the postal code in the HTML file. You will also notice that we use a new function, named **ExtractNoCase**. The **ExtractNoCase** function is very similar to the **Extract** method introduced in Chapter 3. However, **ExtractNoCase** does not require that the beginning and ending text strings match the case exactly on the HTML page.

```
if (code != null)
{
```

Next we extract the state's capital, name, flag and official site.

```
  String capital = ExtractNoCase(str,
      "Capital:<b></td><td>", "</td>", 0);
  String name = ExtractNoCase(str, "<h1>", "</h1>", 0);
  String flag = ExtractNoCase(str, "<img src=\"", "\"
      border=\"1\">", 2);
  String site = ExtractNoCase(str, "Official Site:<b></td>
      <td><a href=\"", "\"", 0);
```

The flag is a URL, so we use the **Uri** class to obtain a fully qualified URL to the state flag.

```
  Uri flagURL = new Uri(u, flag);
```

Next store the state's information to a **StringBuilder** as a comma delineated line.

```
StringBuilder buffer = new StringBuilder();
buffer.Append("\"");
buffer.Append(code);
buffer.Append("\",\"");
buffer.Append(name);
buffer.Append("\",\"");
buffer.Append(capital);
buffer.Append("\",\"");
buffer.Append(flagURL.ToString());
buffer.Append("\",\"");
buffer.Append(site);
buffer.Append("\"");
Console.WriteLine(buffer.ToString());
}
```

This method will be called for every sub-page on the system.

Recipe #6.7: Extracting from Partial-Pages

Many web sites use partial pages. A partial page occurs when you are presented with a list of data. However, you do not see all of your data at once. You are also given options to move forwards and backwards through a large list of data. Search engine results are a perfect example of this. You can see an example here:

http://www.httprecipes.com/1/6/partial.php

You can see this list in Figure 6.8.

Figure 6.8: A Partial HTML Page

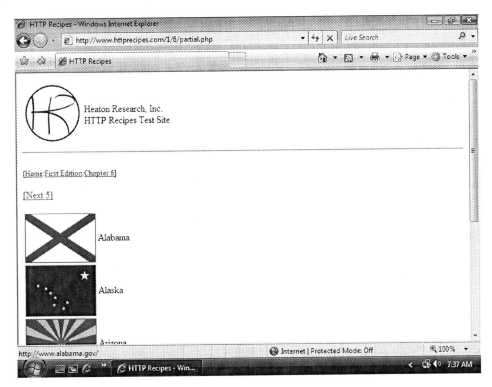

You can see that the states' images are shown five at a time. This recipe processes all of the "next page" links until all pages have been downloaded. The recipe is shown in Listing 6.10.

Listing 6.10: Parse HTML Partial-Pages (ExtractPartial.cs)

```csharp
using System;
using System.Collections.Generic;
using System.Text;
using System.Net;
using System.IO;
using HeatonResearch.Spider.HTML;

namespace Recipe6_7
{
    class ExtractPartial
    {
        /// <summary>
        /// This method downloads the specified URL into a C#
        /// String. This is a very simple method, that you can
        /// reused anytime you need to quickly grab all data from
```

```
/// a specific URL.
/// </summary>
/// <param name="url">The URL to download.</param>
/// <returns>The contents of the URL that was
/// downloaded.</returns>
public String DownloadPage(Uri url)
{
    WebRequest http = HttpWebRequest.Create(url);
    HttpWebResponse response =
      (HttpWebResponse)http.GetResponse();
    StreamReader stream = new StreamReader(
          response.GetResponseStream(),
          System.Text.Encoding.ASCII);

    String result = stream.ReadToEnd();

    response.Close();
    stream.Close();
    return result;
}


/// <summary>
/// This method is very useful for grabbing
/// information from a HTML page.  It extracts text
/// from between two tokens, the tokens need not be
/// case sensitive.
/// </summary>
/// <param name="str">The string to extract from.</param>
/// <param name="token1">The text, or tag, that
/// comes before the desired text</param>
/// <param name="token2">The text, or tag, that comes
/// after the desired text</param>
/// <param name="count">Which occurrence of token1 to
/// use, 1 for the first</param>
/// <returns></returns>
public String ExtractNoCase(String str, String token1,
    String token2,
    int count)
{
    int location1, location2;

    // convert everything to lower case
    String searchStr = str.ToLower();
    token1 = token1.ToLower();
    token2 = token2.ToLower();
```

```csharp
    // now search
    location1 = location2 = 0;
    do
    {
        location1 = searchStr.IndexOf(token1, location1
            + 1);

        if (location1 == -1)
            return null;

        count--;
    } while (count > 0);

    // return the result from the original string that
    // has mixed case
    location1 += token1.Length;
    location2 = str.IndexOf(token2, location1 + 1);
    if (location2 == -1)
        return null;

    return str.Substring(location1, location2 -
            location1);
}


/// <summary>
/// Called to process each individual item found.
/// </summary>
/// <param name="officialSite">The official site for
/// this state.</param>
/// <param name="flag">The flag for this state.</param>
private void ProcessItem(Uri officialSite, Uri flag)
{
    StringBuilder result = new StringBuilder();
    result.Append("\"");
    result.Append(officialSite.ToString());
    result.Append("\",\"");
    result.Append(flag.ToString());
    result.Append("\"");
    Console.WriteLine(result.ToString());
}


/// <summary>
/// Called to process each partial page.
/// </summary>
```

```csharp
/// <param name="url">The URL of the partial page.</param>
/// <returns>Returns the next partial page, or null
/// if no more.</returns>
public Uri Process(Uri url)
{
    Uri result = null;
    StringBuilder buffer = new StringBuilder();
    String value = "";
    String src = "";

    WebRequest http = HttpWebRequest.Create(url);
    HttpWebResponse response =
            (HttpWebResponse)http.GetResponse();
    Stream istream = response.GetResponseStream();
    ParseHTML parse = new ParseHTML(istream);
    bool first = true;

    int ch;
    while ((ch = parse.Read()) != -1)
    {
        if (ch == 0)
        {
            HTMLTag tag = parse.Tag;
            if (String.Compare(tag.Name, "a", true) == 0)
            {
                buffer.Length = 0;
                value = tag["href"];
                Uri u = new Uri(url, value.ToString());
                value = u.ToString();
                src = null;
            }
            else if (String.Compare(tag.Name, "img", true)
                == 0)
            {
                src = tag["src"];
            }
            else if (String.Compare(tag.Name, "/a", true)
                == 0)
            {
                if (String.Compare(buffer.ToString(),
                        "[Next 5]", true) == 0)
                {
                    result = new Uri(url, value);
                }
                else if (src != null)
                {
```

```
                    if (!first)
                    {
                        Uri urlOfficial =
                            new Uri(url, value);
                        Uri urlFlag = new Uri(url, src);
                        ProcessItem(urlOfficial, urlFlag);
                    }
                    else
                        first = false;
                }
            }
        }
        else
        {
            buffer.Append((char)ch);
        }
    }

    return result;
}


/// <summary>
/// Called to download the state information from
/// several partial pages.
/// Each page displays only 5 of the 50 states, so it
/// is necessary to link each partial page together.
/// This method calls "process" which will process
/// each of the partial pages, until there is no
/// more data.
/// </summary>
public void Process()
{
    Uri url = new Uri(
        "http://www.httprecipes.com/1/6/partial.php");
    do
    {
        url = Process(url);
    } while (url != null);

}


static void Main(string[] args)
{
    ExtractPartial parse = new ExtractPartial();
    parse.Process();
}
```

```
    }
}
```

This recipe works by downloading the first page, then following the "next page" links until the end is reached.

Processing the First Page

The **Process** method of the **ExtractPartial** class is used to access the first page and download subsequent pages. It is important to note that there are two **Process** methods in the **ExtractPartial**. The **Process** method used to start downloading is the **Process** method. This method accepts no parameters and begins by obtaining a URL to the first page.

```
Uri url = new Uri("http://www.httprecipes.com/1/6/partial.php");
do
{
  url = Process(url);
} while (url != null);
```

The URL is passed to the process method that accepts a URL. This process method returns the URL to the next page. This process continues until all pages have been downloaded.

Processing Individual Pages

The overloaded **process** method that accepts a URL is called for each partial-page it finds. The method begins by creating some variables that will be needed to process the page. The **result** variable holds the next partial-page or **null** if there is no next page. The **buffer** variable holds non-tag text encountered. The **value** variable holds the **href** attribute for **<a>** tags found. The **src** variable holds the **src** attribute for **<img>** tags encountered.

```
Uri result = null;
StringBuilder buffer = new StringBuilder();
String value = "";
String src = "";
```

This method begins by opening a **Stream** to the URL that contains the table. A **ParseHTML** object is created to parse this **Stream**. The method then loops over all of the text and tags in the HTML file.

```
WebRequest http = HttpWebRequest.Create(url);
HttpWebResponse response = (HttpWebResponse)http.GetResponse();
Stream istream = response.GetResponseStream();
ParseHTML parse = new ParseHTML(istream);
bool first = true;

int ch;
```

```
while ((ch = parse.Read()) != -1)
{
  if (ch == 0)
  {
    HTMLTag tag = parse.Tag;
    if (String.Compare(tag.Name, "a", true) == 0)
    {
```

When an **<a>** tag is encountered, the URL of the image is recorded.

```
      buffer.Length = 0;
      value = tag["href"];
      Uri u = new Uri(url, value.ToString());
      value = u.ToString();
      src = null;
    }
```

If an **<img>** tag is encountered, the **src** attribute is recorded.

```
else if (String.Compare(tag.Name, "img", true) == 0)
{
  src = tag["src"];
}
```

When an ending **</a>** tag is found, check the text of the link. If the text of the link was "[Next 5]" then the link to the next page has been found.

```
else if (String.Compare(tag.Name, "/a", true) == 0)
{
  if (String.Compare(buffer.ToString(), "[Next 5]", true) == 0)
  {
    result = new Uri(url, value);
  }
}
```

If the link to the next page has been found, record it so we can return it when this method is completed.

```
        result = new URL(url, value);
      } else if (src != null)
      {
```

If this is not the first link on the page, display the link and flag "URL found". We do not process the first link on the page because it is not related to a state. It is the link to the homepage.

```
        if (!first)
        {
          Uri urlOfficial = new Uri(url, value);
          Uri urlFlag = new Uri(url, src);
          ProcessItem(urlOfficial, urlFlag);
```

```
              }
         else
           first = false;
         }
      }
   }
```

If a tag was not found, add the text to the buffer.

```
else
{
   buffer.Append((char)ch);
}
```

Finally, return the next page, if it was found.

```
return result;
```

This method will continue function the next page until it has reached the end of all 50 states.

Summary

This chapter showed you how to extract data from HTML. Most of the data that a bot would like to access will be in HTML form. Previous chapters showed how to extract data from simple HTML constructs. This chapter expanded on that considerably.

The chapter began by showing you how to create an HTML parser. This HTML parser is fairly short in length, but it can handle any HTML file, even if not properly formatted. The HTML parser built into C# might face problems with improperly formatted HTML. Unfortunately, there is quite an amount of improperly formatted HTML on the web.

HTML pages come in a variety of formats. This chapter included seven recipes to show you how to extract data from many of these formats. You were shown how to extract hyperlinks, images, forms, and from multiple pages.

So far, the recipes in this book have mainly downloaded data from a web server. There has not been much interactivity with the web server. In the next chapter you will see how a bot can send form data to a web server. This allows the bot to interact with the web server just like a human using a form.

CHAPTER 7: RESPONDING TO FORMS

- Understanding Forms
- Responding to a Form with HTTP GET
- Responding to a Form with HTTP POST
- Sending Files with HTTP Upload

Most web sites use forms. Forms allow web sites to gather information from a user. Because forms are very important to websites, it is also very important that an HTTP programmer knows how to use C# to interact with forms.

This chapter explains how to work with the forms you will encounter on web sites. You will see how to work with basic forms that include text, buttons and other controls. You will also be shown how to use multipart forms. These forms allow the user to upload files to the web server.

I will begin with reviewing how to construct forms.

Understanding HTML Forms

HTML forms are contained in HTML documents. The HTML form occurs between the beginning `<form>` and ending `</form>` elements. Inside the form, various `<input>` and other elements allow different controls to be used with the form.

To see a form in action, load the following URL in a browser. This shows most of the controls that can be added to a form.

```
http://www.httprecipes.com/1/7/input.php
```

This form contains various controls and shows what HTML forms are capable of. You can see this form in Figure 7.1.

Figure 7.1: A HTML form

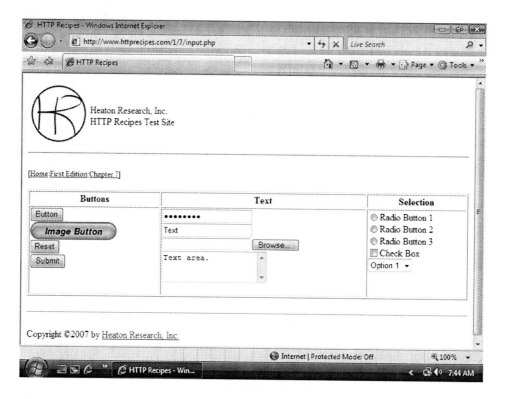

To write a C# program that can respond to a form, you must examine forms in HTML. In this section, we will examine each of the HTML tags that make up a form. If you are already familiar with form HTML code, you may go to the next section.

Form Tag

The actual **<form>** tag contains two useful pieces of information. First, the **<form>** tag tells you if the form request should be an HTTP **GET** or an HTTP **POST** request. Both these request types are handled differently. Second, the **<form>** tag tells you to which URL the HTTP request should be sent. Consider the following **<form>** tag:

```
<form method="get" action="/process.php">
```

The **method** attribute of this tag tells us that this will be an HTTP **GET** request. The **action** attribute of this tag tells us that the request will go to **/process.php**. A POST **<form>** element looks very similar:

```
<form method="post" action="/process.php">
```

The main difference between the two is that the second tag specifies that this request uses the HTTP **POST**, and not the HTTP **GET**.

Some `<form>` elements do not contain an `action` attribute. If this is the case, then the request will be sent back to the same page that contains the form. For example, the following `<form>` tag specifies to post back to the page that contains the form.

```
<form method="post">
```

This is a very common practice. Often, the page that contains the `<form>` is also capable of processing the data that returns from the form.

`<input>` Tags

Most form elements are expressed as `<input>` tags. The input tag contains a `type` property that tells what type of `<input>` tag this is. Table 7.1 summarizes the different `<input>` tag types.

Table 7.1: Common <input> Tag Types

Tag Type	Purpose
button	Buttons are used to perform JavaScript actions.
checkbox	Checkboxes allow the form to capture true/false data.
file	The file type allows files to be uploaded with a multipart form.
hidden	Hidden controls hold a value, but cannot be seen or interacted with.
image	Images are like buttons, except their appearance is governed by the image.
password	Password fields work just like text fields, except you cannot see what is typed.
radio	Radio buttons allow a multi-choice input.
reset	The reset button does not send data to the web server. It allows you to reset all of the form's controls to their default values.
submit	The submit button submits the form's data to the web server.
text	Text fields allow the user to enter single-line text information.

In the next few sections, each of the controls that can be placed on a form will be explored.

Form Buttons

There are several types of form buttons that web servers can use. The HTML necessary to create each of these button types is shown here.

```
<input type="button" name="button" value="Button">
<input type="image" name="image" value="Image" src="/images/but-
```

```
ton.png">
<input type="reset" name="reset" value="Reset">
<input type="submit" name="submit" value="Submit">
```

The most commonly used are the **image** button and the **submit** button. The **image** button allows you to create a button that looks like any image that you choose. The regular **submit** button looks like an ordinary button. Both of these button types will submit the form.

The **reset** button type does not send any data back to the web server. Rather, the **reset** button simply resets all of the form data back to their default values. Reset buttons are not seen on web forms nearly as often as they used to be.

The **button type** attribute is used with JavaScript. JavaScript can be difficult to create a bot for. JavaScript will be covered in Chapter 9.

The **name** attribute of the buttons specifies the name of the button. The name is not displayed to the user. However, the **name** attribute is very important, because it gives the web server a name to identify the button.

The **value** attribute specifies the text of the button that is displayed to the user. Additionally, the **value** attribute is returned, along with the name to allow the web server to further identify the button. For example, consider the following buttons:

```
<input type="submit" name="action" value="Button1">
<input type="submit" name="action" value="Button2">
```

If the user were to click "Button 1", the following data would be returned to the web server:

```
action=Button1
```

This is how data is always returned to the web server, as name-value pairs. This allows you to have more than one button with the same name. For example, the above two buttons are both named **action**. If the user were to click Button2, the following would be returned to the web server.

```
action=Button2
```

This is called a name-value pair. All data returned from HTML forms will be returned as name-value pairs.

Text Controls

There are several types of form text controls that web servers can use. The HTML necessary to create each of these control types is shown here.

```
<input type="password" name="password" value="Password">
<input type="text" name="text" value="Text">
```

```
<input type="file" name="file" value="File">
<textarea rows="3" cols="20" name="textarea">Text area.</textarea>
<input type="hidden" name="hidden" value="Hidden">
```

The **text** control displays a rectangular field for the user to enter text. The **password** control works the same way; however, the user is not allowed to see what is entered. The **hidden** control is simply a name-value pair sent directly to the web server. The user cannot see or change a **hidden** control.

The **file** control allows a file to be uploaded. The **file** control works quite differently from any of the other control types. It requires the form to be posted in a multi-part format. HTTP file uploads will be discussed later in this chapter.

Text controls are also sent to the server as a name-value pair. For example, consider the following text control.

```
<input type="text" name="userid">
```

If you entered the user id of "Jeff", the following would be sent to the web server.

```
userid=jeff
```

Even the **password** control is transmitted this way. Passwords from web sites are transmitted in a clear-text format. Of course, the best way to secure the password is to use HTTPS so that everything is encrypted.

Selection Controls

There are several types of form selection lists that web servers can use. The HTML necessary to create each of these control types is shown here.

```
<input type="radio" name="radio" value="1">Radio Button 1<br>
<input type="radio" name="radio" value="2">Radio Button 2<br>
<input type="radio" name="radio" value="3">Radio Button 3<br>
```

The above controls are **radio** buttons. Only one **radio** button can be selected at a time. Radio buttons are good for a multi-choice type of question and work just like every other control type, in that they return a name-value pair. For example, if the second **radio** control from the above list was selected, the following name-value pair would be returned to the server:

```
radio=radio2
```

The **checkbox** control works the same way, except that any number of check boxes can be selected.

```
<input type="checkbox" name="checkbox" value="Check Box">Check
Box<br>
```

A `choice` control works just like a radio button, except it takes less space on the page. The user selects from a drop-list of values.

```
<select name="choice">
  <option value="1">Option 1</option>
  <option value="2">Option 2</option>
  <option value="3">Option 3</option>
</select>
```

The drop-list returns data as a name-value pair, just like any other control. For example, if you choose "Option 2" from the above list, the following name-value pair would be returned:

```
choice=2
```

As you can see, to a bot, all controls are handled the same. The controls may look different to the user, but for a bot, they are all just name-value pairs.

POST or GET

In the previous section we mentioned two different ways of responding to a form: the HTTP **POST** and the HTTP **GET**. Both of these methods are commonly used by web servers and will be utilized by your programs. As an HTTP programmer you will not pick whether to use **POST** or **GET**; rather, you must use the protocol your target web server uses. The next two sections will discuss HTTP **POST** and HTTP **GET**.

Using HTTP GET

HTTP **GET** is the easiest way to respond to a form. It works in a similar way to HTTP **POST**, whereby a series of name-value pairs is transmitted; however, the amount of data you can transmit is limited. Most browsers allow the URL to be only a certain length. The length varies with the browser; however, the maximum URL length of most browsers is around 2,000 characters. Also, because all form data is visible on the browser's URL line, it is very easy for the user to tamper with the data sent.

There is no way to tell if a form is **GET** or **POST** by examining it on the screen. To make this determination, you must examine the HTML source code. A form that makes use of HTTP **GET** ,will have a **<form>** tag similar to the following:

```
<form action="somepage.php" method="GET">
```

As you recall from the last section, the data from an HTTP form is a series of name-value pairs. Consider a form that has two text fields, one named **first** and the other named **last**. If the user entered "Jeff" for the first field and "Heaton" for the second field, the two name-value pairs would be:

```
first=Jeff
last=Heaton
```

However, when two fields are transmitted, using either **GET** or **POST**, the name-value pairs are concatenated and separated by an ampersand (&). The two fields above would be encoded as:

```
first=Jeff&last=Heaton
```

In the case of an HTTP **GET**, the name-value pairs are concatenated onto the URL. The `<form>` tag above is set to send its data to a page named **somepage.php**. Thus, to send the fields first and last to **somepage.php**, the following URL would be used:

```
http://www.httprecipes.com/1/test.php?first=Jeff&last=Heaton
```

As you can see, the parameters are concatenated directly onto the end of the URL. A question mark (?) separates the parameters from the rest of the URL.

To see this in action, visit the following URL:

http://www.httprecipes.com/1/7/get.php

When you enter a state and click "Search" you will see Figure 7.2.

Figure 7.2: Using a HTTP GET based form

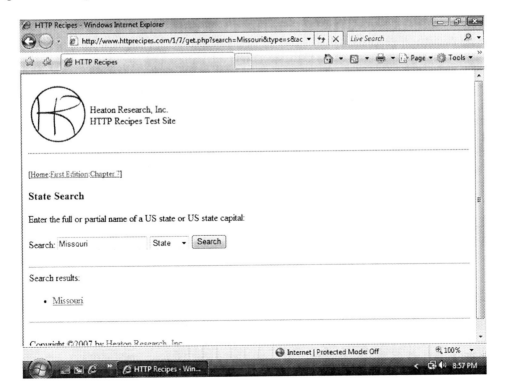

If you examine the browser URL line in Figure 7.2, you will see that the form name-value pairs have been concatenated to the URL.

Using HTTP POST

HTTP **POST** is slightly more complex than HTTP **GET**. It works in a similar way to HTTP **GET**, in that a series of name-value pairs is transmitted; however, you are not limited by the amount of data you can transmit. A form that makes use of HTTP **POST** will have a **<form>** tag similar to the following:

```
<form action="somepage.php" method="POST">
```

When data is transmitted using HTTP **POST**, the data is sent as part of the request packet, but it is not visible from the URL. To see how HTTP **POST** data is sent, consider the following URL:

http://www.httprecipes.com/1/7/post.php

When you enter a search string and click "Send", the following packet is sent to the web server:

```
POST /1/7/post.php HTTP/1.
Accept: image/gif, image/x-xbitmap, image/jpeg, image/pjpeg, ap-
plication/x-shockwave-flash, */*
Referer: http://www.httprecipes.com/1/7/post.php
Accept-Language: en-us
Content-Type: application/x-www-form-urlencoded
Accept-Encoding: gzip, deflate
User-Agent: Mozilla/4.0 (compatible; MSIE 6.0; Windows NT 5.1;
SV1; .NET CLR 1.1.4322; .NET CLR 2.0.50727)
Host: www.httprecipes.com
Content-Length: 36
Connection: Keep-Alive
Cache-Control: no-cache

search=Missouri&type=s&action=Search
```

As you can see from the above data, the form data is transmitted right after the HTTP headers. Later in this chapter you will be shown how you can quickly generate this data for posts of your own.

Multipart POST

In addition to the regular post discussed in the last section, there is also a multipart post. Most forms you will encounter are not multipart posts. The only time you will encounter a multipart post is when the form allows you to upload a file. You can easily tell a multipart post by the format of the **<form>** tag:

```
<form enctype="multipart/form-data" action="uploader.php"
method="POST">
```

You can easily identify a multipart form by the **enctype** attribute of the **<form>** element. If the **enctype** is **multipart/form-data**, you are dealing with a multipart form.

A multipart **POST** has a much different format than a regular post. In addition to the regular form elements, a multipart post allows files to be sent. There is an example of a multipart form at the following URL:

http://www.httprecipes.com/1/7/upload.php

You can also see the form in Figure 7.3.

Figure 7.3: A Multipart Form

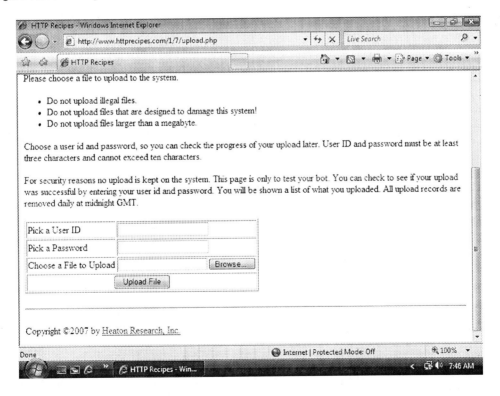

You can easily find the field that allows you to upload a file. The "Browse" button next to the file upload field allows you to navigate through your file system and locate a file to upload.

If you upload using the above form, the following request will be sent to the server:

```
POST /1/7/uploader.php HTTP/1.1
Accept: image/gif, image/x-xbitmap, image/jpeg, image/pjpeg,
application/x-shockwave-flash, */*
Referer: http://www.httprecipes.com/1/7/upload.php
Accept-Language: en-us
Content-Type: multipart/form-data; boundary=--------------------
-----7d63cf13501b4
Accept-Encoding: gzip, deflate
User-Agent: Mozilla/4.0 (compatible; MSIE 6.0; Windows NT 5.1;
SV1; .NET CLR 1.1.4322; .NET CLR 2.0.50727)
Host: www.httprecipes.com
Content-Length: 571
Connection: Keep-Alive
Cache-Control: no-cache


---------------------------7d63cf13501b4
Content-Disposition: form-data; name="uid"

jeff
---------------------------7d63cf13501b4
Content-Disposition: form-data; name="pwd"

1234
---------------------------7d63cf13501b4
Content-Disposition: form-data; name="MAX_FILE_SIZE"

1000000
---------------------------7d63cf13501b4
Content-Disposition: form-data; name="uploadedfile"; filename="C:\
Documents and Settings\jeff\Desktop\myfile.txt"
Content-Type: text/plain

This is the contents of myfile.txt.
---------------------------7d63cf13501b4--
```

One of the first things you should notice is the boundary. The boundary is specified in the **Content-Type** header. For this example, the boundary is:

```
---------------------------7d63cf13501b4
```

The boundary is used to separate each of the parts. There is one part for each control on the HTML form. The first two fields, named **uid** and **pwd** contain the user's id and password. These two fields have the values of "jeff" and "1234" respectively. The next field is a hidden field, named **MAX_FILE_SIZE**, which specified the maximum file size that this form will accept. In this case, it is a megabyte.

The final field, named **uploadedfile**, contains the file being uploaded. The raw binary image of the file is inserted here. For this example, I uploaded a very simple file that contains the text, "This is the contents of myfile.txt". You can see this string in the above form request.

As you can see there are a number of important considerations when responding to a form. In the next section, we will examine a class that can be used to quickly build both multipart and regular responses.

Processing Forms

All of the recipes in this chapter use a simple class named **FormUtility**. This class allows you to quickly create form responses for both regular and multipart form responses. The **FormUtility** class is shown in Listing 7.1.

Listing 7.1: Form Utility (FormUtility.cs)

```
using System;
using System.Collections.Generic;
using System.Text;
using System.IO;
using System.Web;

namespace HeatonResearch.Spider.HTML
{
    /// <summary>
    /// FormUtility: This class is used to construct responses to
    /// HTML forms. The class supports both standard HTML forms,
    /// as well as multipart forms.
    /// </summary>
    public class FormUtility
    {
        /// <summary>
        /// A random number generator.
        /// </summary>
        private static Random random = new Random();

        /// <summary>
        /// Used to convert strings into bytes.
        /// </summary>
        System.Text.ASCIIEncoding encoding =
            new System.Text.ASCIIEncoding();

        /// <summary>
        /// Generate a boundary for a multipart form.
        /// </summary>
        /// <returns>The boundary.</returns>
```

```csharp
public static String getBoundary()
{
    return "---------------------------" + RandomString()
+ RandomString()
        + RandomString();
}

/// <summary>
/// The boundary used for a multipart post. This field is
/// null if this is not a multipart form and has a value
/// if this is a multipart form.
/// </summary>
private String boundary;

/// <summary>
/// The stream to output the encoded form to.
/// </summary>
private Stream os;

/// <summary>
/// Keep track of if we're on the first form element.
/// </summary>
private bool first;

/// <summary>
/// Encode the specified string. This encodes all special
/// characters.
/// </summary>
/// <param name="str">The string to encode.</param>
/// <returns>The encoded string.</returns>
private static String Encode(String str)
{
    return HttpUtility.HtmlEncode(str);
}

/// <summary>
/// Generate a random string, of a specified length. This
/// is used to generate the multipart boundary.
/// </summary>
/// <returns>A random string.</returns>
protected static String RandomString()
{
    return "" + random.NextDouble();
}

/// <summary>
```

```
/// Prepare to access either a regular, or
/// multipart, form.
/// </summary>
/// <param name="os">The stream to output to.</param>
/// <param name="boundary">The boundary to be used,
/// or null if this is
/// not a multipart form.</param>
public FormUtility(Stream os, String boundary)
{
    this.os = os;
    this.boundary = boundary;
    this.first = true;
}


/// <summary>
/// Add a file to a multipart form.  Default mime type to
/// application/octet-stream.
/// </summary>
/// <param name="name">The field name.</param>
/// <param name="file">The file to attach.</param>
public void AddFile(String name, String file)
{
    AddFile(name, file, "application/octet-stream");
}


/// <summary>
/// Add a file to a multipart form.
/// </summary>
/// <param name="name">The field name.</param>
/// <param name="file">he file to attach.</param>
/// <param name="type">The mime type</param>
public void AddFile(String name, String file, String type)
{
    if (this.boundary != null)
    {
        Boundary();
        WriteName(name);
        Write("; filename=\"");
        Write(file);
        Write("\"");
        Newline();
        Write("Content-Type: ");

        Writeln(type);
        Newline();
```

```csharp
            byte[] buf = new byte[8192];
            int nread;

            Stream istream = new FileStream(file,
              FileMode.Open);
            while ((nread = istream.Read(buf, 0,
              buf.Length)) > 0)
            {
                this.os.Write(buf, 0, nread);
            }

            Newline();
        }
    }

    /// <summary>
    /// Add a regular text field to either a regular or
    /// multipart form.
    /// </summary>
    /// <param name="name">The name of the field.</param>
    /// <param name="value">The value of the field.</param>
    public void Add(String name, String value)
    {
        if (this.boundary != null)
        {
            Boundary();
            WriteName(name);
            Newline();
            Newline();
            Writeln(value);
        }
        else
        {
            if (!this.first)
            {
                Write("&");
            }
            Write(Encode(name));
            Write("=");
            Write(Encode(value));
        }
        this.first = false;
    }

    /// <summary>
    /// Complete the building of the form.
```

```
/// </summary>
public void Complete()
{
    if (this.boundary != null)
    {
        Boundary();
        Writeln("--");
        this.os.Flush();
    }
}

/// <summary>
/// Generate a multipart form boundary.
/// </summary>
private void Boundary()
{
    Write("--");
    Write(this.boundary);
}

/// <summary>
/// Create a new line by displaying a carriage return and
/// linefeed.
/// </summary>
private void Newline()
{
    Write("\r\n");
}

/// <summary>
/// Write the specified string, without a carriage return
/// and line feed.
/// </summary>
/// <param name="str">The string to write.</param>
private void Write(String str)
{

    byte[] buffer = encoding.GetBytes(str);
    this.os.Write(buffer, 0, buffer.Length);
}

/// <summary>
/// Write the name element for a multipart post.
/// </summary>
/// <param name="name">The name of the field.</param>
private void WriteName(String name)
```

```
        {
            Newline();
            Write("Content-Disposition: form-data; name=\"");
            Write(name);
            Write("\"");
        }

        /// <summary>
        /// Write a string, with a carriage return and linefeed.
        /// </summary>
        /// <param name="str">The string to write.</param>
        protected void Writeln(String str)
        {
            Write(str);
            Newline();
        }
    }
}
```

The next few sections demonstrate how the **FormUtility** class was constructed. If you are only interested in using the **FormUtility** class, and not how it works internally, you may go to the recipes.

There are three main features of the **FormUtility** class:

- Add a name-value pair
- Add a file
- Parse a query string

The next three sections will show how each of these features are implemented.

Add a Name-Value Pair

Adding a name-value pair is a very common operation performed for a form. Every form control results in a name-value pair. Adding a name-value pair is accomplished by calling the **Add** method.

The format for a name-value pair is very different when posting using a multipart form compared to a regular form. Therefore, the first thing that the **Add** method does is to determine if this is a multipart response. If the boundary variable is not **null**, then this is a multipart request.

```
if (this.boundary != null)
{
```

Next, the boundary and name are written.

```
  Boundary();
  WriteName(name);
  Newline();
  Newline();
  Writeln(value);
}
```

If the boundary variable was **null**, meaning this is not a multipart response, we must check to see if this is the first name-value pair. If it is not the first name-value pair, then an ampersand should be appended.

```
else
{
  if (!this.first)
  {
    Write("&");
  }
```

Next, we encode both the name and value. The name and value are written, separated by an equals sign.

```
  Write(Encode(name));
  Write("=");
  Write(Encode(value));
}
```

Now that we have completed the first name-value pair, we can set the **first** variable to false.

```
This.first = false;
```

The name-value pair has now been completed. The **Add** method can be called again to add another name-value pair.

Add a File

Name-value pairs are not the only data with which you may respond to a form. If this is a multipart response, then you can also respond with files. There is an overloaded version of the **Add** method that accepts a "File" object.

First, the **Add** method makes sure that this is a multipart response. If this is a multipart response, then the boundary variable will not be **null**. If you call the file version of **Add** on a non-multipart response, the method call will be ignored.

```
if (this.boundary != null)
{
```

First, a boundary line is written. Next, the field name is written followed by the filename. To see how this line looks when written out, refer to the section earlier in this chapter on the multipart **POST**.

```
Boundary();
WriteName(name);
Write("; filename=\"");
Write(file);
Write("\"");
Newline();
Write("Content-Type: ");

Writeln(type);
Newline();
```

After the name line has been written, the **Content-Type** should be written. This value is passed to the **Add** method. Once the content type has been written, it is time to write the file. The file is transferred byte-by-byte - no transformation takes place. First, several variables are set up to transfer the file. A buffer is then created to hold blocks of data. The variable **nread** tracks the amount of data being read.

```
byte[] buf = new byte[8192];
int nread;
```

Once the buffer is established, the file is opened and copied to the output stream.

```
Stream istream = new FileStream(file, FileMode.Open);
while ((nread = istream.Read(buf, 0, buf.Length)) > 0)
{
   this.os.Write(buf, 0, nread);
}
```

Once the file has been written, add a blank line.

```
Newline();
}
```

These two overloaded versions of the **Add** method allow you to add both files and regular fields.

Recipes

This chapter includes three recipes. These recipes demonstrate how to process various HTML forms. Specifically, you will see how to process each of the following form operations:

- Send an HTTP **GET** form response
- Send an HTTP **POST** form response
- Send a file with a multipart form

All of the recipes in this chapter use the form processing class described in the first part of this chapter. We will begin with the first recipe, which shows you how to process an HTTP **GET**.

Recipe #7.1: Using HTTP GET Forms

The first recipe shows how to access a web site and search. The form allows the user to search the US states and capitals. You can see this page at the following URL:

`http://www.httprecipes.com/1/7/get.php`

This page displays a simple form that allows the user to enter a search string and choose if they are searching states or capitals. You can see this recipe in Listing 7.2.

Listing 7.2: Using HTTP GET (FormGet.cs)

```
using System;
using System.Collections.Generic;
using System.Text;
using System.Net;
using System.IO;
using HeatonResearch.Spider.HTML;

namespace Recipe7_1
{
    class FormGET
    {
        /// <summary>
        /// Advance to the specified HTML tag.
        /// </summary>
        /// <param name="parse">The HTML parse object to use.
        /// </param>
        /// <param name="tag">The HTML tag.</param>
        /// <param name="count">How many tags like this to find.
        /// </param>
        /// <returns>True if found, false otherwise.</returns>
        private bool Advance(ParseHTML parse, String tag,
            int count)
        {
            int ch;
            while ((ch = parse.Read()) != -1)
            {
                if (ch == 0)
                {
                    if (String.Compare(parse.Tag.Name, tag, true)
                        == 0)
                    {
                        count--;
                        if (count <= 0)
                            return true;
                    }
                }
```

```
            }
        }
        return false;
}

/// <summary>
/// Handle each list item, as it is found.
/// </summary>
/// <param name="item">The item to be processed.</param>
private void ProcessItem(String item)
{
    Console.WriteLine(item.Trim());
}

/// <summary>
/// Access the website and perform a search for
/// either states or capitals.
/// </summary>
/// <param name="search">A search string.</param>
/// <param name="type">What to search
/// for(s=state, c=capital)</param>
public void Process(String search, String type)
{
    String listType = "ul";
    String listTypeEnd = "/ul";
    StringBuilder buffer = new StringBuilder();
    bool capture = false;

    // Build the URL.
    MemoryStream mstream = new MemoryStream();
    FormUtility form = new FormUtility(mstream, null);
    form.Add("search", search);
    form.Add("type", type);
    form.Add("action", "Search");
    form.Complete();

    System.Text.ASCIIEncoding enc =
        new System.Text.ASCIIEncoding();

    String str = enc.GetString(mstream.GetBuffer());
    String surl =
        "http://www.httprecipes.com/1/7/get.php?" + str;
    Uri url = new Uri(surl);
    WebRequest http = HttpWebRequest.Create(url);
    HttpWebResponse response =
        (HttpWebResponse)http.GetResponse();
```

```
Stream istream = response.GetResponseStream();
ParseHTML parse = new ParseHTML(istream);

// Parse from the URL.

Advance(parse, listType, 0);

int ch;
while ((ch = parse.Read()) != -1)
{
    if (ch == 0)
    {
        HTMLTag tag = parse.Tag;
        if (String.Compare(tag.Name, "li", true) == 0)
        {
            if (buffer.Length > 0)
                ProcessItem(buffer.ToString());
            buffer.Length = 0;
            capture = true;
        }
        else if (String.Compare(
            tag.Name, "/li", true) == 0)
        {
            ProcessItem(buffer.ToString());
            buffer.Length = 0;
            capture = false;
        }
        else if (String.Compare(tag.Name,
            listTypeEnd, true) == 0)
        {
            ProcessItem(buffer.ToString());
            break;
        }
    }
    else
    {
        if (capture)
            buffer.Append((char)ch);
    }
}


static void Main(string[] args)
{
    FormGET parse = new FormGET();
```

```
              parse.Process("Mi", "s");
        }
    }
}
```

The **Process** method of this recipe performs most of the work of submitting the form and processing the response. Two parameters are passed to the process method: the first is the search string to use and the second indicates whether we will be doing a state search or a capital search.

The **Process** method begins by setting up several variables that will be needed. The states or capitals returned from the search will be in an HTML list. So the starting and ending tags, which in this case are **<ul>** and **</ul>** are stored in the variables **listType** and **listTypeEnd**. Additionally, a **StringBuilder**, named **buffer** is created to hold the HTML text as it is encountered. The **bool** capture variable indicates if text is being captured to the **StringBuilder**.

```
String listType = "ul";
String listTypeEnd = "/ul";
StringBuilder buffer = new StringBuilder();
bool capture = false;
```

The **FormUtility** class is designed to output to a **Stream**. For an HTTP **POST** response, this is fine. However, since this is an HTTP **GET** request, the form data must be encoded into the URL. To do this, we create a **MemoryStream**. This stream allows the **FormUtility** to output the form data to a **Stream**, and once it's done we can obtain the formatted name-value pairs.

The three calls to the add method below set up the different required name-value pairs for the form.

```
// Build the URL.
MemoryStream mstream = new MemoryStream();
FormUtility form = new FormUtility(mstream, null);
form.Add("search", search);
form.Add("type", type);
form.Add("action", "Search");
form.Complete();
```

Next, the URL must be constructed. The URL is constructed by concatenating the output from the **MemoryStream** to the base URL. The URL can then be opened and downloaded. A **ParseHTML** object is then created to parse the HTML.

```
System.Text.ASCIIEncoding enc = new System.Text.ASCIIEncoding();

String str = enc.GetString(mstream.GetBuffer());
String surl = "http://www.httprecipes.com/1/7/get.php?" + str;
Uri url = new Uri(surl);
```

```
WebRequest http = HttpWebRequest.Create(url);
HttpWebResponse response = (HttpWebResponse)http.GetResponse();
Stream istream = response.GetResponseStream();
ParseHTML parse = new ParseHTML(istream);
```

With the **ParseHTML** object set up, we can advance to the beginning of the HTML list. The **Advance** method is covered in Chapter 6.

```
Advance(parse, listType, 0);
```

Now, the HTML will be parsed. Begin looping through, reading each character. When an HTML tag is located, examine it to determine what it is.

```
int ch;
while ((ch = parse.Read()) != -1)
{
  if (ch == 0)
  {
    HTMLTag tag = parse.Tag;
```

If the tag is an **<li>** tag, then we have found one of the result items. If there was already data in the buffer, then process it as a valid state or capital.

```
    HTMLTag tag = parse.Tag;
    if (String.Compare(tag.Name, "li", true) == 0)
    {
      if (buffer.Length > 0)
        ProcessItem(buffer.ToString());
      buffer.Length = 0;
      capture = true;
    }
```

Many web sites do not include ending **</li>** items. However, if they are present, stop capturing text. Process any text already captured as a valid state or capital.

```
    else if (String.Compare(tag.Name, "/li", true) == 0)
    {
      ProcessItem(buffer.ToString());
      buffer.Length = 0;
      capture = false;
    }
```

If the end of the list has been found, stop processing states and capitals.

```
    else if (String.Compare(tag.Name, listTypeEnd, true) == 0)
    {
      ProcessItem(buffer.ToString());
      break;
    }
  }
}
```

If you found a regular character and not a tag, append it to the **StringBuilder**.

```
else
{
  if (capture)
    buffer.Append((char)ch);
}
```

This recipe shows how to access data through an HTTP **GET**. Many web sites make use of HTTP **GET**. In fact, most search engines use HTTP **GET** from their main page.

Recipe #7.2: Using HTTP POST Forms

The second recipe shows how to access an HTTP **POST** form. The form allows the user to search the US states and capitals in the same way as Recipe 7.1. You can see this page at the following URL:

http://www.httprecipes.com/1/7/post.php

This page displays a simple form that allows the user to enter a search string and select if it is searching states or capitals. You can see this recipe in Listing 7.3.

Listing 7.3: Using HTTP POST (FormPOST.cs)

```
using System;
using System.Collections.Generic;
using System.Text;
using System.Net;
using System.IO;
using HeatonResearch.Spider.HTML;

namespace Recipe7_2
{
    class FormPOST
    {

        /// <summary>
        /// Advance to the specified HTML tag.
        /// </summary>
        /// <param name="parse">The HTML parse object
        /// to use.</param>
        /// <param name="tag">The HTML tag.</param>
        /// <param name="count">How many tags like this to
        /// find.</param>
        /// <returns>True if found, false otherwise.</returns>
        private bool Advance(ParseHTML parse, String tag,
            int count)
        {
```

```
    int ch;
    while ((ch = parse.Read()) != -1)
    {
        if (ch == 0)
        {
            if (String.Compare(parse.Tag.Name, tag,
                true) == 0)
            {
                count--;
                if (count <= 0)
                    return true;
            }
        }
    }
    return false;
}

/// <summary>
/// Handle each list item, as it is found.
/// </summary>
/// <param name="item">The item to display.</param>
private void ProcessItem(String item)
{
    Console.WriteLine(item.Trim());
}




/// <summary>
/// Access the website and perform a search for
/// either states or capitals.
/// </summary>
/// <param name="search">A search string.</param>
/// <param name="type">What to search for(s=state,
/// c=capital)</param>
public void Process(String search, String type)
{
    String listType = "ul";
    String listTypeEnd = "/ul";
    StringBuilder buffer = new StringBuilder();
    bool capture = false;

    // Build the URL and POST.
    Uri url = new Uri(
        "http://www.httprecipes.com/1/7/post.php");
    WebRequest http = HttpWebRequest.Create(url);
```

```csharp
http.Timeout = 30000;
http.ContentType =
      "application/x-www-form-urlencoded";
http.Method = "POST";
Stream ostream = http.GetRequestStream();

FormUtility form = new FormUtility(ostream, null);
form.Add("search", search);
form.Add("type", type);
form.Add("action", "Search");
form.Complete();
ostream.Close();

// read the results
HttpWebResponse response =
      (HttpWebResponse)http.GetResponse();
Stream istream = response.GetResponseStream();

ParseHTML parse = new ParseHTML(istream);

// parse from the URL

Advance(parse, listType, 0);

int ch;
while ((ch = parse.Read()) != -1)
{
    if (ch == 0)
    {
        HTMLTag tag = parse.Tag;
        if (String.Compare(tag.Name, "li", true) == 0)
        {
            if (buffer.Length > 0)
                ProcessItem(buffer.ToString());
            buffer.Length = 0;
            capture = true;
        }
        else if (
         String.Compare(tag.Name, "/li", true) == 0)
        {
            ProcessItem(buffer.ToString());
            buffer.Length = 0;
            capture = false;
        }
        else if (String.Compare(tag.Name,
                  listTypeEnd, true) == 0)
```

```
                        {
                            ProcessItem(buffer.ToString());
                            break;
                        }
                    }
                    else
                    {
                        if (capture)
                            buffer.Append((char)ch);
                    }
                }
            }


        static void Main(string[] args)
        {
            FormPOST parse = new FormPOST();
            parse.Process("Mi", "s");
        }
    }
}
```

This recipe is very similar to Recipe 7.1. The only difference is that this recipe uses HTTP **POST** and the previous recipe uses HTTP **GET**. We will only explain how to change to HTTP **POST**. For information on how this recipe parses the results, refer to Recipe 7.1.

The **Process** method for the recipe begins by building a URL object for the target page.

```
// Build the URL and POST.
Uri url = new Uri("http://www.httprecipes.com/1/7/post.php");
```

Next, a **WebRequest** is opened.

```
WebRequest http = HttpWebRequest.Create(url);
http.Timeout = 30000;
http.ContentType = "application/x-www-form-urlencoded";
http.Method = "POST";
Stream ostream = http.GetRequestStream();
```

The **Stream** object is passed to the **FormUtility** constructor. The form data is output to that stream.

```
FormUtility form = new FormUtility(ostream, null);
form.Add("search", search);
form.Add("type", type);
form.Add("action", "Search");
form.Complete();
ostream.Close();
```

Once all of the data has been sent for the form, a call to the **Complete** method finishes the transaction. Next, the resulting HTML will be parsed. Parsing the resulting HTML is handled exactly as in Recipe 7.1.

Recipe #7.3: Using Multipart Forms to Upload

The third recipe shows how to upload a file to a form, using HTTP upload. The form allows the user to upload a file to the HTTP recipes website. You can see this page at the following URL:

`http://www.httprecipes.com/1/7/uploadmenu.php`

From this page you have two options:

- upload a file
- check the status of a previous upload

Begin by uploading a file. When you upload a file, you should supply a user id and password. Later, this will allow you to check the status of the upload using the second option. For security reasons, files that you upload are deleted immediately. However, their size and type are recorded under your user name and password. This allows you to confirm whether your upload was successful.

This recipe must be provided with a user ID, password and the file you want to upload. The following command is an example of how to launch the recipe.

`Recipe7_3 userid password c:\myfile.txt`

Once you have uploaded your file, check the status of the file upload. You can do this by selecting the "Check the status of a previous upload" option on the previously mentioned URL. After you enter your user ID and password you will see a page similar to Figure 7.4.

Figure 7.4: A Successful Upload

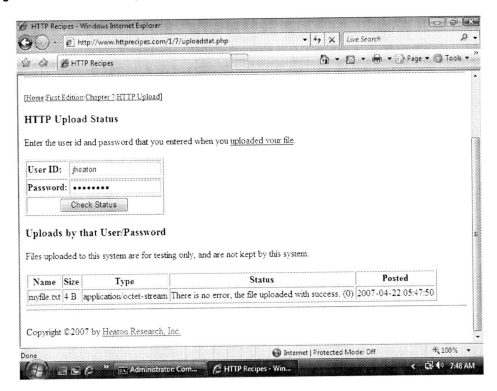

We will now examine how to implement this recipe. You can see this recipe in Listing 7.4.

Listing 7.4: Using Multipart Forms to Upload (FormUpload.cs)

```
using System;
using System.Collections.Generic;
using System.Text;
using System.Net;
using System.IO;
using HeatonResearch.Spider.HTML;

namespace Recipe7_3
{
    class FormUpload
    {
        /// <summary>
        /// Upload a file.
        /// </summary>
        /// <param name="uid">The user id for the form.</param>
        /// <param name="pwd">The password for the form.</param>
```

```csharp
/// <param name="file">The file to upload.</param>
public void Upload(String uid, String pwd, String file)
{
    // Get the boundary used for the multipart upload.
    String boundary = FormUtility.getBoundary();

    Uri url = new Uri(
        "http://www.httprecipes.com/1/7/uploader.php");
    WebRequest http = HttpWebRequest.Create(url);
    http.Timeout = 30000;
    // specify that we will use a multipart form
    http.ContentType = "multipart/form-data; boundary="
        + boundary;
    http.Method = "POST";
    Stream ostream = http.GetRequestStream();

    // Construct a form.
    FormUtility form = new FormUtility(ostream, boundary);
    form.Add("uid", uid);
    form.Add("pwd", pwd);
    form.AddFile("uploadedfile", file);
    form.Complete();
    ostream.Close();

    // Perform the upload.
    WebResponse response = http.GetResponse();
    Stream istream = response.GetResponseStream();
    istream.Close();
}

static void Main(string[] args)
{
    String uid = "";
    String pwd = "";
    String filename = "";

    if (args.Length < 3)
    {
        Console.WriteLine("Usage:");
        Console.WriteLine(
    "Recipe7_3 [User ID] [Password] [File to upload]");
    }
    else
    {
        uid = args[0];
        pwd = args[1];
```

```
                filename = args[2];

                FormUpload upload = new FormUpload();
                upload.Upload(uid, pwd, filename);
            }
        }
    }
}
```

Most of the work done by this recipe is done inside the **FormUtility** class. If you would like to review how any of the methods and functions in this recipe work, review "Multipart Post", an earlier section in this chapter.

This recipe starts by creating a boundary. A boundary is a random string of characters used to separate the different parts of the multipart response.

```
// Get the boundary used for the multipart upload.
String boundary = FormUtility.getBoundary();
```

A connection is opened to the URL that will receive the multipart response.

```
Uri url = new Uri("http://www.httprecipes.com/1/7/uploader.php");
WebRequest http = HttpWebRequest.Create(url);
http.Timeout = 30000;
```

Because this is going to be an HTTP **POST**, we set the "do output" option to "true". We also construct the **Content-Type** header to specify that this will be a multipart response. The boundary is specified inside of the **Content-Type** header.

```
// specify that we will use a multipart form
http.ContentType = "multipart/form-data; boundary=" + boundary;
http.Method = "POST";
```

A **Stream** object is obtained and we construct a new **FormUtility** object. Notice that a boundary is specified on the constructor to the **FormUtility** object. This tells the **FormUtility** object that this is going to be a multipart response. Additionally, the user ID and password are added to the form. The names "uid" and "pwd" are the names of the **<input>** tags that the user would normally enter their user ID and password into.

```
Stream ostream = http.GetRequestStream();
// Construct a form.
FormUtility form = new FormUtility(ostream, boundary);
form.Add("uid", uid);
form.Add("pwd", pwd);
```

Next, the file is added to the form. This version of the **Add** method of the **FormUtility** class takes care of everything necessary to transmit the file. Finally, the **Complete** method is called to complete building the form.

```
form.AddFile("uploadedfile", file);
```

```
form.Complete();
ostream.Close();
```

Next, the **Stream** is obtained and the request is transmitted. The **Stream** object is immediately closed; the response from the upload page is irrelevant.

```
// Perform the upload.
WebResponse response = http.GetResponse();
Stream istream = response.GetResponseStream();
istream.Close();
```

This recipe can be adapted to any case where you need to upload a file. The **FormUtility** class, used by this recipe, is a short utility class introduced earlier in this chapter.

Summary

Forms are a very common part of many web sites. Most bot programs are required to deal with forms. Forms can be transmitted to the web server in three ways: HTTP **GET**, HTTP **POST** and multipart **POST**.

A form can be sent back to the web server using the HTTP **GET** method. HTTP **GET** places all of the name-value pairs from the form's data onto the URL. When a web site uses HTTP **GET** for a form, the user can see all of their input on the URL line of the browser.

A form can also be returned to the web server using the HTTP **POST** method. HTTP **POST** sends the data as part of the HTTP packet, and it is not visible to the user. Because the data does not all need to fit onto a URL, much larger amounts of data can be sent with HTTP **POST**.

Finally, a form can also be sent as a multipart **POST**. A multipart **POST** is useful when you need to return a file to the web server. Multipart forms are used by many websites when a file needs to be uploaded. Though this is by far the least used of the form response types, you will need to make use of it if your bot needs to upload a file.

So far, all of the bots presented have been stateless; that is, the bot can simply jump to the page and retrieve the data. Very often a web server will require you to create a session before you can access any data. Creating a session is usually as easy as logging onto the system. Chapter 8 will show you how to login to websites and handle sessions.

CHAPTER 8: HANDLING SESSIONS AND COOKIES

- Understanding Sessions
- Using URL Variables to Maintain Sessions
- Using Cookies to Maintain Sessions

State management is a very important concept for many web sites. If a website is to allow a user to log into the system, and present pages customized to that user, state management is required. State management allows the web server to remember things from one page request to the next.

Consider the example of a user logging onto a system. Once the user has logged onto the system, the system must remember who is logged on. This is called state. Rather than sending web pages blindly, the web server now knows who the pages are going to. This allows the web server to customize these pages for each user, or perhaps block access to the pages depending on the user.

To access a site such as this requires extra programming consideration. The program must first login to the website and establish state. To support such a site, a program must be designed to implement state in the way that the target web site expects. There are several ways that web sites implement state; however, most sites fall into one of two categories:

- state through URL variables
- state through cookies

Both methods are very common. This chapter will cover both methods and provide a recipe for each.

URL Variables for State

A very simple way to maintain state is to use the URL line. By placing a variable on the URL that always holds the current state, you can identify who is logged on. It is considered a bad idea to merely place the user name on the URL line. So you will not likely see a URL like this:

```
http://www.httprecipes.com/menu.php?user=joe
```

This would be terribly insecure. A user would simply have to change the URL line and they could instantly become any user they liked. Usually a session number will be used instead. Consider the following URL.

```
http://www.httprecipes.com/1/8/cookieless.php
```

This URL presents a login page, as seen in Figure 8.1.

Figure 8.1: A Login Page

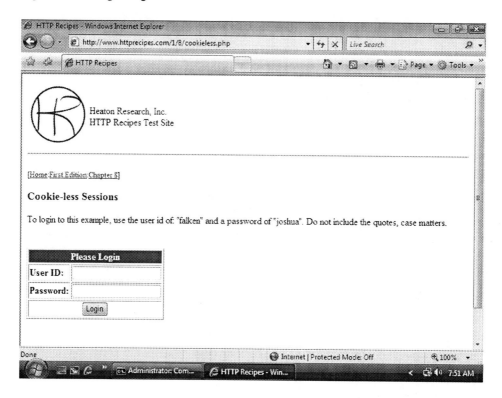

To login to the system, enter the user id of "falken" and the password of "joshua". You will then be taken to the search page. This search page is only available from inside the web site. You must login to access this page. However, notice the URL. It is now much longer, and will be similar to:

http://www.httprecipes.com/1/8/menunc.php?session=9pwoditnygyyvot9
7k2jexx8oakelnvz

This URL specifies a session. A session is usually only a row in the web server's database that links a session string, as seen above, to a user. The only way to imitate another user is to try and pick the session number for another user who is currently logged into the system. This will usually not work either, because the web server usually also stores the IP address associated with a session. As a result, if another user tries to hijack a session, the IP addresses will be different, and the attack will be thwarted.

There is nothing special about the session id that you see above. There are no hidden meanings behind the stream of letters and numbers that you see. The session id was randomly created to serve as a unique identifier.

A session is assigned after a successful user login. The session will remain with that user until they log off the system. If the user does not log off the system, their session will usually expire in some preset time. Having their session expire is not a problem to the user, they are simply asked to re-login to the system.

You have likely already seen session timeouts while using the web. Consider when you log into a web server to check your mail, and then leave the window open overnight. When you try to use the window again in the morning, you will likely be told that you session has "timed out". This is because of the amount of time that has elapsed and the web server deleted your session.

When a website uses sessions through the URL, the session variable must be passed to every page on the website. You will always see the session id at the top of the page. If you remove the session part of the URL, or modify it slightly, the site will immediately take you back to the login page. You cannot use the site without a valid session id.

One limitation of using the URL to maintain state is that the session id must be placed on every link generated by the site. Because of this, even if one page removes the session id, the session will be lost. Additionally, if the user temporarily closes the browser, and returns to the site, the state is also lost. If the user types in the session id as part of the URL when they attempt to re-access the site, the state would not be lost; however, this is not likely to be the case.

Cookies for State

A session id on the URL line is not the only way to maintain state. Cookies can also be used to maintain state. Cookies are different from using the URL to maintain state, because cookies are invisible to the user. Cookies are stored as part of the request and response headers. Cookies are nothing more than name value pairs. Cookies exist within a specified domain and no two cookies in the same domain can have the same name.

To see cookies in action visit the following URL:

```
http://www.httprecipes.com/1/8/cookie.php
```

When you access this page, you will see a form that allows you to login. To use this form, you should login with the user ID of "falken" and the password of "joshua". Once you are logged in, a cookie will be established with your browser. You will not be able to see this cookie. The cookie is contained inside the headers of both the request and the response. To see how the cookie is created, we must examine the response that the server sends back when you login to the site. You can see this response here:

```
HTTP/1.1 302 Found
Date: Thu, 31 Aug 2006 23:39:07 GMT
Server: Apache/2.0.40 (Red Hat Linux)
Accept-Ranges: bytes
X-Powered-By: PHP/4.3.2
Set-Cookie: hri-cookie=42252vvf5x4d5d69xq1ub653ltnh9xo7
Location: menuc.php
Content-Length: 0
Connection: close
Content-Type: text/html
```

Notice the cookie? When the server wants to create a cookie, the server returns the **Set-Cookie** header. This specifies that the cookie named **hri-cookie** has the value **42252vvf5x4d5d69xq1ub653ltnh9xo7**.

This tells the browser to always include this cookie in future requests. For example, if you were to perform a search while logged in, your HTTP POST request would look like this:

```
POST /1/8/menuc.php HTTP/1.1
Accept: image/gif, image/x-xbitmap, image/jpeg, image/pjpeg,
application/x-shockwave-flash, */*
Referer: http://www.httprecipes.com/1/8/menuc.php
Accept-Language: en-us
Content-Type: application/x-www-form-urlencoded
Accept-Encoding: gzip, deflate
User-Agent: Mozilla/4.0 (compatible; MSIE 6.0; Windows NT 5.1;
SV1; .NET CLR 1.1.4322; .NET CLR 2.0.50727)
Host: www.httprecipes.com
Content-Length: 32
Connection: Keep-Alive
Cache-Control: no-cache
Cookie: hri-cookie=42252vvf5x4d5d69xq1ub653ltnh9xo7

search=Miss&type=s&action=Search
```

As you can see, the browser is now sending the cookie back as a request header. When the server requests a cookie, the **Set-Cookie** header is used; when the browser sends this cookie back, the **Cookie** header is used.

The C# HTTP classes include full support for cookies. Recipe 8.2 will demonstrate how to use cookies with C#.

Recipes

This chapter includes two recipes. These recipes demonstrate how to process a variety of different HTTP sessions. Specifically, you will see how to process each of the following session types:

- Cookie-less session
- Cookie-based session

We will begin with the first recipe, which shows how to process a session without the use of cookies.

Recipe #8.1: A Cookie-less Session

This recipe shows how to manage a session using only the URL. No cookies are used to maintain state. This recipe shows how to login to a simple system and perform a basic search. This recipe will access the following URL:

`http://www.httprecipes.com/1/8/cookieless.php`

This recipe must go through several steps to get the data requested. First, it must login to the system and obtain a session. Next, it must submit the search. Finally, it must parse the results of the search. These steps are summarized in Table 8.1.

Table 8.1: Extracting from Cookieless Session

Step	Function
Step 1.	Post login information to http://www.httprecipes.com/1/8/cookieless.php
Step 2:	Extract session id from http://www.httprecipes.com/1/8/menunc. php?session=[Session id]
Step 3.	Be redirected to Post search to http://www.httprecipes.com/1/8/menunc. php?session=[Session id]
Step 4.	Parse search results.

This recipe is shown in Listing 8.1.

Listing 8.1: Cookieless Session (Cookieless.cs)

```
using System;
using System.Collections.Generic;
using System.Collections.Specialized;
using System.Text;
using System.Net;
using System.IO;
```

```csharp
using System.Web;
using HeatonResearch.Spider.HTML;

namespace Recipe8_1
{
    class Cookieless
    {

        /// <summary>
        /// Advance to the specified HTML tag.
        /// </summary>
        /// <param name="parse">The HTML parse object to use.
        /// </param>
        /// <param name="tag">The HTML tag.</param>
        /// <param name="count">How many tags like this to find.
        /// </param>
        /// <returns>True if found, false otherwise.</returns>
        private bool Advance(ParseHTML parse, String tag,
          int count)
        {
            int ch;
            while ((ch = parse.Read()) != -1)
            {
                if (ch == 0)
                {
                    if (String.Compare(parse.Tag.Name,
                        tag, true) == 0)
                    {
                        count--;
                        if (count <= 0)
                            return true;
                    }
                }
            }
            return false;
        }


        /// <summary>
        /// This method is called to log into the system
        /// and return a session id.  Once you have the
        /// session ID you can call the search function to
        /// perform searches.
        /// </summary>
        /// <param name="uid">The user id to use for login.
```

```
/// </param>
/// <param name="pwd">The password to use for login.
/// </param>
/// <returns>The session id if login was successful,
/// null if it was not.</returns>
private String Login(String uid, String pwd)
{
    Uri url = new Uri(
      "http://www.httprecipes.com/1/8/cookieless.php");
    WebRequest http = HttpWebRequest.Create(url);
    http.Timeout = 30000;
    http.ContentType =
          "application/x-www-form-urlencoded";
    http.Method = "POST";
    Stream ostream = http.GetRequestStream();

    FormUtility form = new FormUtility(ostream, null);
    form.Add("uid", uid);
    form.Add("pwd", pwd);
    form.Add("action", "Login");
    form.Complete();
    ostream.Close();
    WebResponse response = http.GetResponse();
    response.GetResponseStream();

    String query = response.ResponseUri.Query;
    if (query != null)
    {
        NameValueCollection c =
          HttpUtility.ParseQueryString(query);

        return c.Get("session");
    }
    else
        return null;
}

/// <summary>
/// Use the session to search for the specified
/// state or capital.  The search
/// method can be called multiple times per login.
/// </summary>
/// <param name="session">The session to use.</param>
/// <param name="search">The search string to use.</param>
/// <param name="type">What to search for
/// (s=state,c=capital).</param>
```

```csharp
/// <returns>A list of states or capitals.</returns>
public List<String> Search(String session,
    String search, String type)
{
    String listType = "ul";
    String listTypeEnd = "/ul";
    StringBuilder buffer = new StringBuilder();
    bool capture = false;
    List<String> result = new List<String>();

    // Build the URL.
    MemoryStream mstream = new MemoryStream();
    FormUtility form = new FormUtility(mstream, null);
    form.Add("search", search);
    form.Add("type", type);
    form.Add("action", "Search");
    form.Complete();

    Uri url = new Uri(
      "http://www.httprecipes.com/1/8/menunc.php?session="
        + session);
    WebRequest http = HttpWebRequest.Create(url);
    http.Timeout = 30000;
    http.ContentType =
          "application/x-www-form-urlencoded";
    http.Method = "POST";
    Stream ostream = http.GetRequestStream();

    // Perform the post.
    byte[] b = mstream.GetBuffer();
    ostream.Write(b, 0, b.Length);
    ostream.Close();

    // Read the results.
    WebResponse response = http.GetResponse();
    Stream istream = response.GetResponseStream();

    ParseHTML parse = new ParseHTML(istream);

    // Parse from the URL.
    Advance(parse, listType, 0);

    int ch;
    while ((ch = parse.Read()) != -1)
    {
        if (ch == 0)
```

```
            {
                HTMLTag tag = parse.Tag;
                if (String.Compare(tag.Name, "li", true) == 0)
                {
                    if (buffer.Length > 0)
                        result.Add(buffer.ToString());
                    buffer.Length = 0;
                    capture = true;
                }
                else if (String.Compare(tag.Name, "/li", true)
                     == 0)
                {
                    result.Add(buffer.ToString());
                    buffer.Length = 0;
                    capture = false;
                }
                else if (String.Compare(tag.Name, listTypeEnd,
                     true) == 0)
                {
                    result.Add(buffer.ToString());
                    break;
                }
            }
            else
            {
                if (capture)
                    buffer.Append((char)ch);
            }
        }

    return result;
}

/// <summary>
/// Called to login to the site and download a list
/// of states or capitals.
/// </summary>
/// <param name="uid">The user id to use for login.
/// </param>
/// <param name="pwd">The password to use for login.
/// </param>
/// <param name="search">The search string to use.</param>
/// <param name="type">What to search
/// for(s=state,c=capital).</param>
public void Process(String uid, String pwd,
    String search, String type)
```

```
        {
            String session = Login(uid, pwd);
            if (session != null)
            {
                List<String> list = Search(session, search, type);
                foreach (String item in list)
                {
                    Console.WriteLine(item);
                }
            }
            else
            {
                Console.WriteLine("Error logging in.");
            }
        }

        static void Main(string[] args)
        {
            Cookieless cookieless = new Cookieless();
            cookieless.Process("falken", "joshua", "Mi", "s");
        }
    }
}
```

Three primary methods are used in this recipe. The first, named **Process**, manages the bot's progress and calls the other two methods. The second, named **Login**, logs the user into the system. The third, called **Search**, is called by the process method to perform the search.

The Process Method

The **Process** method is called by the **Main** method. The **Process** method is passed four parameters. The parameter **uid** specifies the user id, **pwd** specifies the password, **Search** specifies what to search for and **type** specifies the type of search. Two search types are supported: a search type of "s" for states or "c" for capitals.

The **Process** method begins by calling the **Login** method. If the **Login** method was successful, then a session id is returned. This session id will be necessary to perform the search, because the web site requires that you be logged in to perform the search.

```
String session = Login(uid, pwd);
if (session != null)
{
```

If a session id was returned, then the **Search** function is called. The **Search** function returns a list of states that matched the search.

```
  List<String> list = Search(session, search, type);
  foreach (String item in list)
  {
    Console.WriteLine(item);
  }
}
```

If **null** was returned as the session id, then the login failed. In this case, either the user id or password (or both) were likely incorrect.

```
else
{
  Console.WriteLine("Error logging in.");
}
```

The **Process** method makes use of both the **Login** function and the **Search** function. The next two sections will describe how these functions work.

Logging In

The **login** method is responsible for logging the user into the system and returning a session id. This method begins by posting the user id and password to the web site. To do this, a URL object is constructed to post to the login form.

```
Uri url = new Uri("http://www.httprecipes.com/1/8/cookieless.
php");
WebRequest http = HttpWebRequest.Create(url);
http.Timeout = 30000;
http.ContentType = "application/x-www-form-urlencoded";
http.Method = "POST";
```

Next, an output **Stream** is obtained to post the data to. This **Stream** is passed to the constructor of the **FormUtility** class. Then the user id, password and login button are all added to the form. Since submit buttons can also send data to the form, it is important to designate that the Login button is used here.

```
Stream ostream = http.GetRequestStream();

FormUtility form = new FormUtility(ostream, null);
form.Add("uid", uid);
form.Add("pwd", pwd);
form.Add("action", "Login");
form.Complete();
ostream.Close();
```

The response **Stream** is not needed because we do not need to read any data from the form. We will get the session id from whatever page the login form redirects us to.

```
WebResponse response = http.GetResponse();
response.GetResponseStream();

String query = response.ResponseUri.Query;
```

If there is no query string on the URL, then the login failed, and we should return **null**. Otherwise, we call the **ParseQueryString** method of the **HttpUtility** class to extract the **session** attribute from the URL. The **Session** attribute contains the session id. The **HttpUtility** class is provided by C#.

```
if (query != null)
{
  NameValueCollection c = HttpUtility.ParseQueryString(query);

  return c.Get("session");
}
else
  return null;
```

Once the session id has been obtained, the **Search** function can be called.

Performing the Search

The **Search** method submits the search form and reads the results from that search. The session id must be attached to the URL to which it is posted.

The **search** method begins by setting up several variables that will be needed. The states or capitals returned from the search will be in an HTML list. The starting and ending tags, which in this case are **<ul>** and **</ul>**, are stored in the variables **listType** and **listTypeEnd**. Additionally, a **StringBuilder**, named **buffer** is created to hold the HTML text as it is encountered. The **bool** capture variable indicates if text is currently being captured to the **StringBuilder**.

```
String listType = "ul";
String listTypeEnd = "/ul";
StringBuilder buffer = new StringBuilder();
bool capture = false;
List<String> result = new List<String>();
```

The **FormUtility** class is designed to output to a **Stream**. For an HTTP POST response, this will be fine. The three calls to the add method below setup the different required name-value pairs for the form.

```
// Build the URL.
MemoryStream mstream = new MemoryStream();
FormUtility form = new FormUtility(mstream, null);
form.Add("search", search);
form.Add("type", type);
form.Add("action", "Search");
```

```
form.Complete();
```

A **Uri** object is created for the form's location plus the session ID. The rest of this procedure is similar to the list parsing example from recipes 7.1 and 7.2 in Chapter 7.

```
Uri url = new Uri("http://www.httprecipes.com/1/8/menunc.
php?session="
                    + session);
WebRequest http = HttpWebRequest.Create(url);
http.Timeout = 30000;
http.ContentType = "application/x-www-form-urlencoded";
http.Method = "POST";
Stream ostream = http.GetRequestStream();
```

The output from the **FormUtility** object is posted to the form. A **ParseHTML** object is setup to parse the search results.

```
// Perform the post.
byte[] b = mstream.GetBuffer();
ostream.Write(b, 0, b.Length);
ostream.Close();


// Read the results.
WebResponse response = http.GetResponse();
Stream istream = response.GetResponseStream();


ParseHTML parse = new ParseHTML(istream);
```

Now the HTML will be parsed. Begin by looping through, reading each character. When an HTML tag is located, examine that HTML tag to see what it is.

```
// Parse from the URL.
Advance(parse, listType, 0);

int ch;
while ((ch = parse.Read()) != -1)
{
  if (ch == 0)
  {
    HTMLTag tag = parse.Tag;
```

If the tag is an **<li>** tag, then we have found one of the result items. If there was already data in the buffer, then process it as a valid state or capital.

```
    if (String.Compare(tag.Name, "li", true) == 0)
    {
      if (buffer.Length > 0)
        result.Add(buffer.ToString());
      buffer.Length = 0;
      capture = true;
```

```
   }
```

Many web sites do not include ending **</li>** items; however, if they are present, then stop capturing text. Process any already captured text as a valid state or capital.

```
else if (String.Compare(tag.Name, "/li", true) == 0)
{
  result.Add(buffer.ToString());
  buffer.Length = 0;
  capture = false;
}
```

If we have reached the end of the list, then there is no more data to parse.

```
else if (String.Compare(tag.Name, listTypeEnd, true) == 0)
{
  result.Add(buffer.ToString());
  break;
}
```

If we are between an **<li>** and **</li>** tag, then we should be capturing text – since this is a list item and our data is contained in the list items.

```
else
{
  if (capture)
    buffer.Append((char)ch);
}
```

```
return result;
```

Finally, the list of states is returned.

Recipe #8.2: A Cookie Based Session

This recipe shows how to manage a session using cookies. Cookies are used to maintain state. This recipe shows how to login to a simple system and perform a basic search, which is the same as Recipe 8.1, except cookies are used. This recipe will access the following URL:

http://www.httprecipes.com/1/8/cookie.php

This recipe must go through several steps to get the data requested. First, it must login to the system and obtain a session. Next, it must submit the search. Finally, it must parse the results of the search. These steps are summarized in Table 8.2.

Table 8.2: Extracting from Cookie Based Session

Step	Function
Step 1.	Post login information to http://www.httprecipes.com/1/8/cookieless.php
Step 2:	Extract session id from the headers returned, look for the Set-Cookie header.
Step 3.	Be redirected to post search to http://www.httprecipes.com/1/8/menu.php use the cookie
Step 4.	Parse search results

This recipe is shown in Listing 8.2.

Listing 8.2: Cookie-Based Session (UseCookie.cs)

```
using System;
using System.Collections.Generic;
using System.Text;
using System.Net;
using System.IO;
using HeatonResearch.Spider.HTML;

namespace Recipe8_2
{
    class UseCookie
    {
        /// <summary>
        /// Holds the cookies used to keep the session.
        /// </summary>
        private CookieContainer cookies = new CookieContainer();

        /// <summary>
        /// Advance to the specified HTML tag.
        /// </summary>
        /// <param name="parse">The HTML parse object to use.
        /// </param>
        /// <param name="tag">The HTML tag.</param>
        /// <param name="count">How many tags like this to find.
        /// </param>
        /// <returns>True if found, false otherwise.</returns>
        private bool Advance(ParseHTML parse, String tag,
            int count)
        {
            int ch;
            while ((ch = parse.Read()) != -1)
            {
```

```
            if (ch == 0)
            {
                if (String.Compare(parse.Tag.Name, tag, true)
                    == 0)
                {
                    count--;
                    if (count <= 0)
                        return true;
                }
            }
        }
        return false;
    }


    /// <summary>
    /// This method is called to log into the system and
    /// establish the cookie.  Once the cookie is
    /// established, you can call the search function to
    /// perform searches.
    /// </summary>
    /// <param name="uid">The user id to use for
    /// login.</param>
    /// <param name="pwd">The password to use for
    /// login.</param>
    /// <returns>True if the login was successful.</returns>
    private bool Login(String uid, String pwd)
    {
        Uri url = new Uri(
            "http://www.httprecipes.com/1/8/cookie.php");
        HttpWebRequest http =
            (HttpWebRequest)HttpWebRequest.Create(url);
        http.CookieContainer = cookies;
        http.Timeout = 30000;
        http.ContentType =
            "application/x-www-form-urlencoded";
        http.Method = "POST";
        Stream ostream = http.GetRequestStream();

        FormUtility form = new FormUtility(ostream, null);
        form.Add("uid", uid);
        form.Add("pwd", pwd);
        form.Add("action", "Login");
        form.Complete();
        ostream.Close();

        HttpWebResponse response =
```

```csharp
    (HttpWebResponse)http.GetResponse();

    foreach (Cookie cookie in cookies.GetCookies(url))
    {
        if( String.Compare(cookie.Name,
                "hri-cookie",true)==0)
            return true;
    }
    return false;
}


/// <summary>
/// Use the cookie to search for the specified
/// state or capital.  The search
/// method can be called multiple times per login.
/// </summary>
/// <param name="search">The search string to use.</param>
/// <param name="type">What to search
/// for(s=state,c=capital).</param>
/// <returns>A list of states or capitals.</returns>
public List<String> Search(String search, String type)
{
    String listType = "ul";
    String listTypeEnd = "/ul";
    StringBuilder buffer = new StringBuilder();
    bool capture = false;
    List<String> result = new List<String>();

    // build the request
    Uri url =
    new Uri("http://www.httprecipes.com/1/8/menuc.php");


    HttpWebRequest http =
            (HttpWebRequest)HttpWebRequest.Create(url);
    http.CookieContainer = cookies;
    http.Timeout = 30000;
    http.ContentType =
            "application/x-www-form-urlencoded";
    http.Method = "POST";

    Stream ostream = http.GetRequestStream();

    // perform the post
    FormUtility form = new FormUtility(ostream, null);
    form.Add("search", search);
```

```csharp
form.Add("type", type);
form.Add("action", "Search");
form.Complete();
ostream.Close();

// read the results
WebResponse response = http.GetResponse();
Stream istream = response.GetResponseStream();
ParseHTML parse = new ParseHTML(istream);

// parse from the URL

Advance(parse, listType, 0);

int ch;
while ((ch = parse.Read()) != -1)
{
    if (ch == 0)
    {
        HTMLTag tag = parse.Tag;
        if (String.Compare(tag.Name, "li", true) == 0)
        {
            if (buffer.Length > 0)
                result.Add(buffer.ToString());
            buffer.Length = 0;
            capture = true;
        }
        else if (String.Compare(tag.Name, "/li", true)
            == 0)
        {
            result.Add(buffer.ToString());
            buffer.Length = 0;
            capture = false;
        }
        else if (String.Compare(tag.Name, listTypeEnd,
            true) == 0)
        {
            result.Add(buffer.ToString());
            break;
        }
    }
    else
    {
        if (capture)
            buffer.Append((char)ch);
    }
```

```
            }

        return result;
    }


    /// <summary>
    /// Called to login to the site and download a
    /// list of states or capitals.
    /// </summary>
    /// <param name="uid">The user id to use for
    /// login.</param>
    /// <param name="pwd">The password to use for
    /// login.</param>
    /// <param name="search">The search string to use.</param>
    /// <param name="type">What to search
    /// for(s=state,c=capital).</param>
    public void Process(String uid, String pwd,
        String search, String type)
    {
        if (Login(uid, pwd))
        {
            List<String> list = Search(search, type);
            foreach (String item in list)
            {
                Console.WriteLine(item);
            }
        }
        else
        {
            Console.WriteLine("Error logging in.");
        }
    }

    static void Main(string[] args)
    {
        UseCookie cookie = new UseCookie();
        cookie.Process("falken", "joshua", "Mi", "s");
    }
  }
}
```

The **Login** function for Recipe 8.2 is very similar to Recipe 8.1; however, cookies are used to maintain state. This recipe uses C#'s built in cookie handling to process the cookies.

The **login** method begins by creating a **Uri** object that will be used to perform the POST.

```
Uri url = new Uri("http://www.httprecipes.com/1/8/cookie.php");
HttpWebRequest http = (HttpWebRequest)HttpWebRequest.Create(url);
```

C# provides built-in support for cookies if you set the **CookieContainer** property of the **HttpWebRequest** object. When the **CookieContainer** property is set, C# will automatically track all cookies issued by the web site.

```
http.CookieContainer = cookies;
http.Timeout = 30000;
http.ContentType = "application/x-www-form-urlencoded";
http.Method = "POST";
Stream ostream = http.GetRequestStream();
```

Next, the form must be posted. The user id and password are sent, along with the "Log-in" button.

```
FormUtility form = new FormUtility(ostream, null);
form.Add("uid", uid);
form.Add("pwd", pwd);
form.Add("action", "Login");
form.Complete();
ostream.Close();
```

The response **Stream** is not needed because we do not need to read any data from the form. We will get the session id from the cookie attached to the response. The session id is stored in a cookie named **hri-cookie**. This cookie will automatically be applied when the search is performed.

```
HttpWebResponse response = (HttpWebResponse)http.GetResponse();

foreach (Cookie cookie in cookies.GetCookies(url))
{
  if( String.Compare(cookie.Name,"hri-cookie",true)==0)
    return true;
}
return false;
```

When the response from the server was received, C# automatically copied all of the cookies to the cookie container. These cookies will also be automatically transmitted on the next request.

Summary

Sessions are a very important concept in HTTP programming. You cannot access data from many websites until you have logged on. Logging onto a website establishes a session. To work with such websites, your bot must support sessions. There are two ways that web sites commonly support sessions: in the URL variables and in cookies.

Both methods work by causing the web browser to keep returning a session id to the web server. This session id is a unique number that identifies this one user from the others. The session id is usually stored in the database and maps the logged in user's session to the identity of the user.

The first method that web sites commonly use to support sessions is the URL line. You can easily attach a session id to a website's URL line. This session id must be passed to any page that the user will enter on the website.

The other common method to support sessions is to place the session id into a cookie. By setting a cookie, the web server can easily identify who has sent the request. The web browser will automatically set the cookie for future requests to the server. If the web server requires cookies, your bot must send these cookies.

So far, the recipes we have examined have not used client side scripting. In the next two chapters, you will be introduced to methods whereby your bot can handle client side scripting. Chapter 9 will show how to handle embedded Javascript on a web site. Chapter 10 will show how to use AJAX, which is a specialized Javascript method that combines XML.

CHAPTER 9: USING JAVASCRIPT

- What JavaScript means to Bots
- Processing Automatic Choice Lists
- Supporting JavaScript Includes
- Processing JavaScript Forms

Many web sites use JavaScript. JavaScript is a language that allows you to embed Java-like instructions into a web site. This allows a user's web browsing experience to be much more interactive. However, JavaScript also makes creating a bot, for a JavaScript enabled web site, much more complex.

When a bot encounters JavaScript, the bot will not automatically execute the JavaScript, as a regular browser would do. Rather, the bot programmer must examine the JavaScript first and understand which HTTP requests your bot must send to emulate the browser. This chapter will show you some techniques handling JavaScript.

Understanding JavaScript

Though JavaScript is similar to Java, there are many important differences. It is a common misunderstanding that Java and JavaScript are the same thing. This is not the case. The following are some of the important differences between Java and JavaScript:

- Java uses types, such as `int`
- JavaScript is typeless, everything is an object
- Java was developed by Sun Microsystems
- JavaScript was developed by NetScape, based on Java

JavaScript occurs between a beginning **`<script>`** and ending **`</script>`** tags. For example, the following code fragment defines a JavaScript function.

```
<script type="text/javascript">
function formValidate(form){

if( form.interest.value.length==0 )
      alert("You must enter an interest rate.");
else if( form.principle.value.length==0 )
      alert("You must enter a principle.");
else if( form.term.value.length==0 )
      alert("You must enter a term.");
else
      form.submit();
}
```

```
</script>
```

As you can see, the format for JavaScript is slightly different than Java. For example, the function declaration starts with the keyword **function**. Additionally, none of the variables have a type declaration.

You will find this **<script>** declaration mixed in with regular HTML on web sites. Some older browsers could not process JavaScript properly. These older browsers would simply display the JavaScript code to the end user. To prevent this from happening, HTML comments were often inserted around the JavaScript code.

Though every major browser supports JavaScript, you will still often see JavaScript code enclosed in HTML comments. For example, the above function could also be expressed as follows, using HTML comments:

```
<script type="text/javascript">
<!--
function formValidate(form){

if( form.interest.value.length==0 )
      alert("You must enter an interest rate.");
else if( form.principle.value.length==0 )
      alert("You must enter a principle.");
else if( form.term.value.length==0 )
      alert("You must enter a term.");
else
      form.submit();
}

//-->
</script>
```

In addition to directly inserting JavaScript code into HTML, JavaScript also supports an "include". Using a JavaScript include statement allows JavaScript, from an external file, to be included in the HTML document. This allows you to group commonly used functions into an "include file" that can be accessed from many different HTML documents. The following line of code demonstrates a JavaScript include:

```
<script type="text/javascript" src="include.js"></script>
```

Include files normally ending with a **.js** file extension.

Common JavaScript Techniques

JavaScript can be used to add a wide array of features to a web site. However, there are certain features that are very commonly used by many web sites that use JavaScript. Some of the most common JavaScript enabled features, used by web sites, include:

- Automatic Choice Lists
- JavaScript Includes
- JavaScript Forms
- AJAX

Of course, there are many additional JavaScript features and techniques. However, learning to handle these common techniques will enable you to understand and implement bots to handle other techniques as well.

From a bot's perspective, JavaScript does very little. A bot does not need to execute the JavaScript to work properly. The web browsing experience is only a series of HTTP requests and response packets. You must understand how the JavaScript influences the HTTP request packets, or simply use a packet sniffer to examine them. So long as your bot sends the same HTTP request packets as a browser does, your bot will function correctly.

We will now examine each of the common JavaScript techniques.

Working with Automatic Choice Lists

Choice lists are very common on web sites. A choice list is a drop-down list that allows the user to select from several options. Choice lists are often part of HTML forms. However, you may have also seen automatic choice lists. Automatic choice lists are usually not part of an HTML form. They will appear by themselves, or with an HTML button next to them.

Automatic choice lists are usually used for site navigation. When you select one of the options on the automatic choice list you will be taken immediately to a new page on the web site. To see an example of an automatic choice list, visit the URL:

```
http://www.httprecipes.com/1/9/article.php
```

You can see the automatic choice list in Figure 9.1.

Figure 9.1: An Automatic Choice List

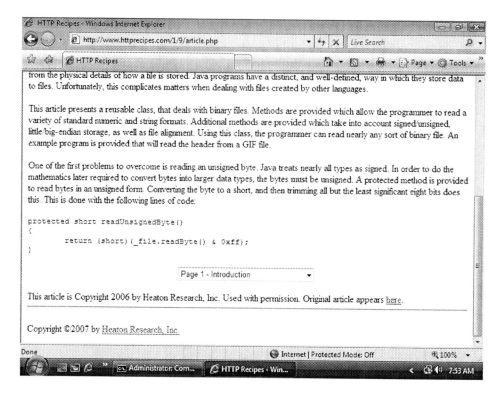

If you examine the HTML for this choice list, you will see that it is implemented with a regular **<select>** tag. However, the **<select>** tag does not directly operate with a form. You can see this HTML code here:

```
<center><select onchange="menuLink(this)">
<option SELECTED VALUE="/1/9/article.php?id=1">
Page 1 - Introduction</option>
<option  VALUE="/1/9/article.php?id=2">
Page 2 - Using the BinaryFile Class</option>
<option  VALUE="/1/9/article.php?id=3">
Page 3 - String Datatypes</option>
<option  VALUE="/1/9/article.php?id=4">
Page 4 - Numeric Datatypes</option>
<option  VALUE="/1/9/article.php?id=5">
Page 5 - Alignment</option>
<option  VALUE="/1/9/article.php?id=6">
Page 6 - Reading a GIF Header</option>
<option  VALUE="/1/9/article.php?id=7">
Page 7 - Summary</option>
</select></center>
```

As you can see from the above code, the **<select>** tag contains an **onchange** attribute. This attribute tells the browser to execute the **menuLink** function when the value of the choice list changes. Each of the **<option>** tags contains a link to the page that the user is requesting.

Using this information, the **menuLink** function can navigate to the correct page. The **menuLink** function is contained inside a beginning **<script>** and ending **</script>** tag. View this code here:

```
<script type="text/javascript">
function isValidUrl( url )
{
  return !(typeof(url)=="undefined" || url==null || url==""
  || url.toLowerCase()=="none" || url.toLowerCase()=="null" ||
url=="-1");
}

function openPopup( url, width, height, name, left, top )
{
  if (isValidUrl(url))
    window.open(url, ((name&&name!="")?name:"popup"),
      ((width&&width!="")?"width="+width+",":"")+
      ((height&&height!="")?"height="+height+",":"")+
      "status=no,toolbar=no,menubar=no,location=no,scrollbars=yes,
resizable=yes"
      +((left&&left!="")?",left="+left:"")+((top&&top!="")?",top="
+top:""));
}

function menuLink( menu )
{
  var link   = menu.options[menu.selectedIndex];
  var url    = link.value;
  var target      = link.target;
  if (link.popup == "true")
  {
    openPopup(url, link.popupwidth, link.popupheight, target);
  }
  else if (isValidUrl(url))
  {
    if (url.indexOf("javascript:") != -1)
    {
      eval(url.substr(url.indexOf(":")+1));
    } else if (target && target != "")
    {
      if (target == "_top")
        window.top.location.href = url;
```

```
      else if (target.substr(0,1) != "_")
        window.parent.frames[target].location.href = url;
      else window.location.href = url;
    }
    else
    {
      window.location.href = url;
    }
  }
  menu.selectedIndex = 0;
}
</script>
```

Describing how this JavaScript functions is beyond the scope of the book. However, you can see near the bottom that the code moves the browser to the link specified in the **<option>** tag. The following line of code performs this function.

```
window.location.href = url;
```

The **window.location.href** property allows JavaScript to move the browser to a new page. This is often the line of code that a bot programmer will be interested in. Recipe 9.1 shows how to parse the JavaScript and access all pages in this article.

Working with JavaScript Includes

Not all JavaScript is necessarily located on the page that is making use of it. JavaScript includes allowing an HTML form to import JavaScript from an external file. This allows commonly used JavaScript code to be placed into files that can easily be included across many HTML documents.

To see an example of JavaScript includes examine the following URL:

http://www.httprecipes.com/1/9/includes.php

You can see this page in Figure 9.2.

Figure 9.2: JavaScript Includes

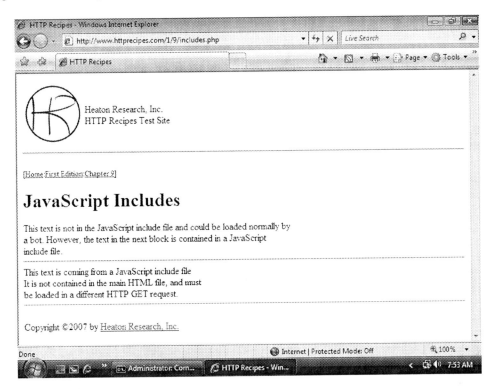

If you examine the HTML at the above URL, you will notice that not all of the text is on that page. If you look at Figure 9.2, you will notice the text "This text is coming from a JavaScript include file". However, if you examine the HTML from the above URL you will not see this text. You can see the HTML from the page here:

```
<!DOCTYPE HTML PUBLIC "-//W3C//DTD HTML 4.01 Transitional//EN">

<HTML>
<HEAD>
    <TITLE>HTTP Recipes</TITLE>
    <meta http-equiv="Content-Type" content="text/html;
charset=UTF-8">
    <meta http-equiv="Cache-Control" content="no-cache">
</HEAD>

<BODY>

<table border="0"><tr><td>
<a href="http://www.httprecipes.com/">
<img src="/images/logo.gif" alt="Heaton Research Logo" bor-
der="0"></a>
```

```
</td><td valign="top">Heaton Research, Inc.<br>
HTTP Recipes Test Site
</td></tr>
</table>
<hr><p><small>[<a href="/">Home</a>:<a href="/1/">
First Edition</a>:<a href="/1/9/">Chaper 9</a>]</small></p>

<h1>JavaScript Includes</h1>
This text is not in the JavaScript include file and could be load-
ed normally by<br>

a bot.  However, the text in the next block is contained in a
JavaScript<br>
include file.<br>
<hr>
<script type="text/javascript" src="include.js"></script>
<hr>
<p>Copyright 2006 by <a href="http://www.heatonresearch.com/
">Heaton Research, Inc.</a></p>
</BODY>
</HTML>
```

The JavaScript include statement includes another file, named **include.js**. You can see this include statement here:

```
<script type="text/javascript" src="include.js"></script>
```

This will cause the file **include.js** to be included as part of the HTML file. However, the **include.js** file is assumed to be JavaScript, so no **<script>** tags are necessary inside **include.js**. The file **include.js** is shown here.

```
document.write('This text is coming from a JavaScript include
file<br>');
document.write('It is not contained in the main HTML file, and
must<br>');
document.write('be loaded in a different HTTP GET request.<br>');
```

The web browser, as a separate request, loads the **include.js** file. It is a regular web document, which could be found at the following address:

http://www.httprecipes.com/1/9/include.js

To process JavaScript includes with a bot you must examine what they contain and how you will obtain what you need from them. Like the other JavaScript techniques, it is a matter of providing the correct HTTP requests to the server and processing the responses. Recipe 9.2 shows how to process this URL.

Working with JavaScript Forms

One of the most common uses for JavaScript is to validate forms. JavaScript allows you to conduct basic validation checks on data before that data is sent to the web server. The following URL has an example of a JavaScript enabled form.

`http://www.httprecipes.com/1/9/form.php`

This form can be seen in Figure 9.3.

Figure 9.3: A JavaScript Enabled Form

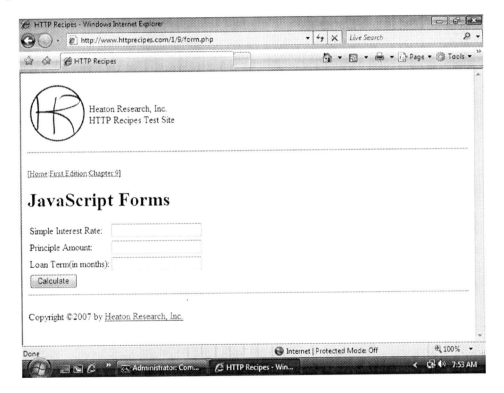

This form allows the user to enter information about a loan. Once the user clicks the "Calculate" button, a loan amortization schedule will be calculated. You can see this amortization schedule in Figure 9.4.

Figure 9.4: Amortization Data

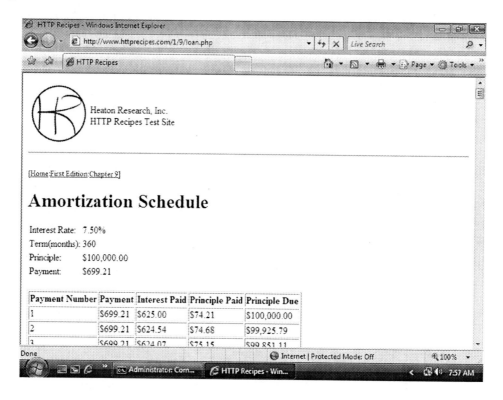

To see how this form is implemented we will examine its HTML. You can see the form **<input>** tag form the "Calculate" button here:

```
<input type="button" name="action" value="Calculate" onclick="form
Validate(this.form);">
```

As you can see from the above code, the "calculate" button calls the **formValidate** function when it is clicked. The **formValidate** function is shown here.

```
<script type="text/javascript">
<!--
function formValidate(form){

if( form.interest.value.length==0 )
      alert("You must enter an interest rate.");
else if( form.principle.value.length==0 )
      alert("You must enter a principle.");
else if( form.term.value.length==0 )
      alert("You must enter a term.");
else
      form.submit();
```

```
}
//-->
</script>
```

This is a very simple form checker. This form checker validates to ensure that the user has entered a value for each of the three fields. If all fields have been entered, the form is submitted.

Processing JavaScript forms is usually fairly easy for a bot. A JavaScript validation form often works just like a regular form. Your bot can usually ignore the validations and just post the form like a normal form would be posted. Recipe 9.3 shows how to write a bot for this page.

Working with AJAX

AJAX is a relatively new technique used by many web sites. It uses JavaScript and XML to exchange data with the web server. AJAX stands for "Asynchronous JavaScript and XML". This allows the web site to interact with a user without moving to a new page. Many AJAX web sites more closely resemble traditional GUI applications than web sites.

AJAX is heavily dependent on JavaScript. Special considerations must be made for web sites that make use of AJAX. Chapter 10 will show you how to create bots for AJAX sites.

Other JavaScript Techniques

This chapter discusses some of the most common JavaScript techniques. However, this is only the beginning. Web sites use JavaScript in many different ways. JavaScript sites are much more complex for bots than non-JavaScript sites. There is no one single method to create a bot for all JavaScript sites.

Creating bots for JavaScript sites means that you, the bot programmer, must understand how these JavaScript sites work and generate the correct HTTP requests and process the responses. It is important to remember that generating the correct HTTP requests is really all there is to creating a bot.

After all, the web server is not aware of JavaScript. JavaScript simply helps the browser to generate HTTP requests. Your bot can generate these same requests, if you understand how the site is using JavaScript. There are many good books and online tutorials for learning JavaScript.

Interpreting JavaScript

It is possible to interpret and execute JavaScript in C#. This can be done by using JavaScript DotNet. This is a complex topic that is beyond the scope of this book. However, we will explain enough to get you started.

To use JavaScript DotNet you should use the JScript.NET Expression Evaluator. First, you should create a JScript.NET "package" that includes a publicly-callable method that calls the JScript.NET **eval** function:

```
package JScript
{
  class Eval
  {
    public function DoEval(expr : String) : String
    {
      return eval(expr);
    }
  }
}
```

Then add a reference to the package's assembly to your C# application. Finally, use the above class to evaluate JScript.NET expressions:

```
JScript.Eval E = new JScript.Eval();

String Expression = ExpressionTextBox.Text;

try
{
  ResultTextBox.Text = E.DoEval(Expression);
}
catch(Microsoft.JScript.JScriptException jse)
{
// Handle exceptions.
}
```

This technique will work for simple JavaScript expressions.

Recipes

This chapter includes three recipes. These recipes demonstrate how to construct bots that navigate and extract data from JavaScript enabled web pages. Specifically, you will see how to process these JavaScript techniques:

- Automatic Choice Lists
- JavaScript Includes
- JavaScript Forms

These recipes will show you how a bot can be adapted to several very common JavaScript techniques. The first recipe demonstrates automatic choice lists.

Recipe #9.1: Automatic Choice Lists

Automatic choice lists are a common use for JavaScript. They are usually used as a navigational aid. You are allowed to select an option from a choice list. Once you select an item from the choice list, you will be taken immediately to the web page that corresponds to the option you chose.

This recipe will show how to extract data from a site that makes use of automatic choice lists. This site presents a multi-page article that allows you to select which page to view using an automatic choice list. This recipe will extract data from the following URL:

http://www.httprecipes.com/1/9/article.php

This recipe is shown in Listing 9.1.

Listing 9.1: Automatic Choice Lists (DownloadAtricle.cs)

```
using System;
using System.Collections.Generic;
using System.Text;
using System.Net;
using System.IO;
using HeatonResearch.Spider.HTML;


namespace Recipe9_1
{
    class DownloadArticle
    {
        /// <summary>
        /// This method downloads the specified URL into a C#
        /// String. This is a very simple method, that you can
        /// reused anytime you need to quickly grab all data from
        /// a specific URL.
        /// </summary>
        /// <param name="url">The URL to download.</param>
        /// <returns>The contents of the URL that was
        /// downloaded.</returns>
        public String DownloadPage(Uri url)
        {
            WebRequest http = HttpWebRequest.Create(url);
            HttpWebResponse response =
                (HttpWebResponse)http.GetResponse();
            StreamReader stream = new StreamReader(
        response.GetResponseStream(), System.Text.Encoding.ASCII);

            String result = stream.ReadToEnd();
```

```
        response.Close();
        stream.Close();
        return result;
}

/// <summary>
/// This method is very useful for grabbing
/// information from a
/// HTML page.  It extracts text from between two
/// tokens, the tokens need not be case sensitive.
/// </summary>
/// <param name="str">The string to extract from.</param>
/// <param name="token1">The text, or tag, that comes
/// before the desired text</param>
/// <param name="token2">The text, or tag, that comes
/// after the desired text</param>
/// <param name="count">Which occurrence of token1 to
/// use, 1 for the first</param>
/// <returns></returns>
public String ExtractNoCase(String str,
  String token1, String token2,
    int count)
{
    int location1, location2;

    // convert everything to lower case
    String searchStr = str.ToLower();
    token1 = token1.ToLower();
    token2 = token2.ToLower();

    // now search
    location1 = location2 = 0;
    do
    {
        location1 = searchStr.IndexOf(token1,
                location1 + 1);

        if (location1 == -1)
            return null;

        count--;
    } while (count > 0);

    // return the result from the original string that
    // has mixed case
```

```
    location1 += token1.Length;
    location2 = str.IndexOf(token2, location1 + 1);
    if (location2 == -1)
        return null;

    return str.Substring(location1, location2 -
        location1);
}


/// <summary>
/// This method is called to download article text
/// from each article page.
/// </summary>
/// <param name="url">The URL to download from.</param>
/// <returns>The article text from the specified page.
/// </returns>
private String DownloadArticlePage(Uri url)
{
    const String token = "<center>";
    String contents = DownloadPage(url);
    String result = ExtractNoCase(contents, token,
        token, 0);
    return token + result;
}


/// <summary>
/// This method looks for each of the <option> tags
/// that contain
/// a link to each of the pages.  For each page found the
/// DownloadArticlePage method is called.
/// </summary>
public void Process()
{
    Uri url = new Uri(
        "http://www.httprecipes.com/1/9/article.php");
    WebRequest http = HttpWebRequest.Create(url);
    http.Timeout = 30000;
    WebResponse response = http.GetResponse();
    Stream stream = response.GetResponseStream();
    ParseHTML parse = new ParseHTML(stream);

    int ch;
    while ((ch = parse.Read()) != -1)
    {
        if (ch == 0)
        {
```

```
                    HTMLTag tag = parse.Tag;
                    if (String.Compare(tag.Name, "option", true)
                        == 0)
                    {
                        String str = tag["value"];
                        Uri u = new Uri(url, str);
                        Console.WriteLine(DownloadArticlePage(u));
                    }
                }
            }
        }


        static void Main(string[] args)
        {
            DownloadArticle parse = new DownloadArticle();
            parse.Process();
        }
    }
}
```

This recipe is structured around two functions. The first function, named **Process**, reads the automatic choice list and extracts URLs from it. These URLs will be the URLs of all of the pages in the article. Next the **Process** method calls the **DownloadArticlePage** method for each URL extracted.

The next two sections will describe these two functions. First, we will examine the **Process** function.

Reading the Choice List

The **Process** function reads the **<option>** tags that will be passed to the Java-Script. This provides a complete list of where all seven pages are stored. You can see the option tags that we will be parsing here:

```
<option SELECTED VALUE="/1/9/article.php?id=1">
Page 1 - Introduction</option>
<option  VALUE="/1/9/article.php?id=2">
Page 2 - Using the BinaryFile Class</option>
<option  VALUE="/1/9/article.php?id=3">
Page 3 - String Datatypes</option>
<option  VALUE="/1/9/article.php?id=4">
Page 4 - Numeric Datatypes</option>
<option  VALUE="/1/9/article.php?id=5">
Page 5 - Alignment</option>
<option  VALUE="/1/9/article.php?id=6">
Page 6 - Reading a GIF Header</option>
```

```
<option  VALUE="/1/9/article.php?id=7">
Page 7 - Summary</option>
```

The **VALUE** attribute of each of the above option tags defines the URL we will access to find that page.

This function begins by opening the URL that contains the first page.

```
Uri url = new Uri("http://www.httprecipes.com/1/9/article.php");
WebRequest http = HttpWebRequest.Create(url);
http.Timeout = 30000;

WebResponse response = http.GetResponse();
Stream stream = response.GetResponseStream();
```

We will use a **ParseHTML** object to parse the HTML. The **ParseHTML** class was discussed in Chapter 6.

```
ParseHTML parse = new ParseHTML(stream);

int ch;
while ((ch = parse.Read()) != -1)
{
```

As the data is read from the HTML page, each tag is processed. If the tag found is an **<option>** tag, then we will look for a page's URL.

```
  if (ch == 0)
if (ch == 0)
{
  HTMLTag tag = parse.Tag;
  if (String.Compare(tag.Name, "option", true) == 0)
  {
```

If an **<option>** tag is found, construct a URL object for it and call the **DownloadArticlePage** function.

```
    String str = tag["value"];
    Uri u = new Uri(url, str);

    Console.WriteLine(DownloadArticlePage(u));
    }
  }
}
```

The **DownloadArticlePage** function returns a string for every page downloaded. This string is displayed.

Reading Each Article Page

Reading the data from each of the article pages is fairly straightforward. First, let's examine the HTML page containing each page of the article. You can see this HTML here:

```
<center>
<h1>Programming Binary Files in Java</h1>
<h3>Introduction</h3></center>
<p><p>Java contains an extensive array of classes for file access.
A series of readers, writers and filters make up

... article continues here ...

</p>
<center><select onchange="menuLink(this)">
```

To extract the article text, we must find the HTML tags that completely enclose the article. The article begins with a **<center>** tag. The article also ends with a **<center>** tag (not a **</center>** tag). This is because the ending **<center>** tag is actually used to center the automatic choice list; and the automatic choice list occurs at the end of the article text.

If you are extracting data from other web sites, you must find the bounding tags for that article. It may even be a series of tags, for example **</p></center>** could be the ending tag for a page. It depends on the data you are reading.

To do this, the **ExtractNoCase** function is used.

```
const String token = "<center>";
String contents = DownloadPage(url);
String result = ExtractNoCase(contents, token, token, 0);
return token + result;
```

Once the page has been read, the article text is returned.

Recipe #9.2: JavaScript Includes

JavaScript includes are another common use of JavaScript. They allow an HTML document to include JavaScript from another HTML document. This recipe will demonstrate how to read an HTML document that includes JavaScript includes. This recipe outputs a "compound document" that will replace the JavaScript include statements with the text contained in the included JavaScript documents.

This recipe will read the HTML text located at the following URL:

http://www.httprecipes.com/1/9/includes.php

This recipe is shown in Listing 9.2.

Listing 9.2: JavaScript Includes (Includes.cs)

```csharp
using System;
using System.Collections.Generic;
using System.Text;
using System.Net;
using System.IO;
using HeatonResearch.Spider.HTML;


namespace Recipe9_2
{
    class Includes
    {
        /// <summary>
        /// This method downloads the specified URL into a C#
        /// String. This is a very simple method, that you can
        /// reused anytime you need to quickly grab all data from
        /// a specific URL.
        /// </summary>
        /// <param name="url">The URL to download.</param>
        /// <returns>The contents of the URL that was
        /// downloaded.</returns>
        public String DownloadPage(Uri url)
        {
            WebRequest http = HttpWebRequest.Create(url);
            HttpWebResponse response =
                    (HttpWebResponse)http.GetResponse();
            StreamReader stream = new StreamReader(
                    response.GetResponseStream(),
                    System.Text.Encoding.ASCII);

            String result = stream.ReadToEnd();

            response.Close();
            stream.Close();
            return result;
        }

        /// <summary>
        /// This method is very useful for grabbing
        /// information from a HTML page.  It extracts text
        /// from between two tokens, the tokens need not be
        /// case sensitive.
        /// </summary>
        /// <param name="str">The string to extract from.</param>
```

```csharp
/// <param name="token1">The text, or tag, that comes
/// before the desired text</param>
/// <param name="token2">The text, or tag, that
/// comes after the desired text</param>
/// <param name="count">Which occurrence of token1
/// to use, 1 for the first</param>
/// <returns></returns>
public String ExtractNoCase(String str,
    String token1, String token2,
    int count)
{
    int location1, location2;

    // convert everything to lower case
    String searchStr = str.ToLower();
    token1 = token1.ToLower();
    token2 = token2.ToLower();

    // now search
    location1 = location2 = 0;
    do
    {
        location1 = searchStr.IndexOf(token1,
            location1 + 1);

        if (location1 == -1)
            return null;

        count--;
    } while (count > 0);

    // return the result from the original string
    // that has mixed case
    location1 += token1.Length;
    location2 = str.IndexOf(token2, location1 + 1);
    if (location2 == -1)
        return null;

    return str.Substring(location1, location2 -
        location1);
}



/// <summary>
/// Called to download the text from a page.  If any
```

```
/// JavaScript
/// include is found, the text from that page is read too.
/// </summary>
public void Process()
{
    Uri url = new Uri(
    "http://www.httprecipes.com/1/9/includes.php");
    WebRequest http = HttpWebRequest.Create(url);
    http.Timeout = 30000;
    WebResponse response = http.GetResponse();
    Stream stream = response.GetResponseStream();
    ParseHTML parse = new ParseHTML(stream);
    StringBuilder buffer = new StringBuilder();

    int ch;
    while ((ch = parse.Read()) != -1)
    {
        if (ch == 0)
        {
            HTMLTag tag = parse.Tag;
            if (String.Compare(tag.Name, "script", true)
                == 0 && tag["src"] != null)
            {
                String src = tag["src"];
                Uri u = new Uri(url, src);
                String include = DownloadPage(u);
                buffer.Append("<script>");
                buffer.Append(include);
                buffer.Append("</script>");
            }
            else
            {
                buffer.Append(tag.ToString());
            }
        }
        else
        {
            buffer.Append((char)ch);
        }
    }

    Console.WriteLine(buffer.ToString());
}

static void Main(string[] args)
{
```

```
                    Includes parse = new Includes();
                    parse.Process();
                }
            }
        }
```

The recipe begins by opening a connection to the URL it will download from.

```
Uri url = new Uri("http://www.httprecipes.com/1/9/includes.php");
WebRequest http = HttpWebRequest.Create(url);
http.Timeout = 30000;
WebResponse response = http.GetResponse();
Stream stream = response.GetResponseStream();
```

A **ParseHTML** object will be used to parse the HTML. The **ParseHTML** class was discussed in Chapter 6.

```
ParseHTML parse = new ParseHTML(stream);
StringBuilder buffer = new StringBuilder();
```

As the data is read from the HTML page, each tag is processed. If the tag found is a **<script>** tag, then we will look to see if it is a JavaScript include. Additionally, a **StringBuilder** is setup to hold the compound document.

```
int ch;
while ((ch = parse.Read()) != -1)
{
  if (ch == 0)
  {
```

If this tag is a **<script>** tag, and it has a **src** attribute, the tag will be processed as a JavaScript include.

```
    HTMLTag tag = parse.Tag;
    if (String.Compare(tag.Name, "script", true) == 0 &&
tag["src"] != null)
    {
```

The included page is loaded and appended to the main document. Included JavaScript pages do not have beginning **<script>** and ending **</script>** tags of their own, so these tags are added.

```
      String src = tag["src"];
      Uri u = new Uri(url, src);
      String include = DownloadPage(u);
      buffer.Append("<script>");
      buffer.Append(include);
      buffer.Append("</script>");
    }
    else
```

```
  {
```
If this is a regular HTML tag, append it to the **StringBuilder**.

```
    buffer.Append(tag.ToString());
  }
}
```
If this is a regular HTML text character, append it to the **StringBuilder**.

```
  else
  {
    buffer.Append((char)ch);
  }
}
```

```
Console.WriteLine(buffer.ToString());
```
Finally, once the entire document has been read, it is displayed.

Recipe #9.3: JavaScript Forms

Another very common use for JavaScript is to validate forms. Usually these forms can be treated as normal forms. However, sometimes these forms will make use of an **<input   type="button">** tag to submit, rather than the usual **<input type="submit">**. If an **<input>** tag makes use of the **button** type, rather than **submit**, JavaScript must be used to submit the form. This recipe shows how to process such a form. You can see the form that this recipe will process at the following URL:

http://www.httprecipes.com/1/9/form.php

This recipe is shown in Listing 9.3:

Listing 9.3: JavaScript Forms (JavaScriptForms.cs)

```
using System;
using System.Collections.Generic;
using System.Text;
using System.Net;
using System.IO;
using HeatonResearch.Spider.HTML;

namespace Recipe9_3
{
    class JavaScriptForms
    {
        /// <summary>
        /// Advance to the specified HTML tag.
```

```csharp
        /// </summary>
        /// <param name="parse">The HTML parse object to use.
        /// </param>
        /// <param name="tag">The HTML tag.</param>
        /// <param name="count">How many tags like this to find.
        /// </param>
        /// <returns>True if found, false otherwise.</returns>
        private bool Advance(ParseHTML parse, String tag,
            int count)
        {
            int ch;
            while ((ch = parse.Read()) != -1)
            {
                if (ch == 0)
                {
                    if (String.Compare(parse.Tag.Name, tag, true)
                        == 0)
                    {
                        count--;
                        if (count <= 0)
                            return true;
                    }
                }
            }
            return false;
        }


        /// <summary>
        /// This method is called once for each table row
        /// located, it
        /// contains a list of all columns in that row.
        /// The method provided
        /// simply prints the columns to the console.
        /// </summary>
        /// <param name="list">Columns that were found on
        /// this row.</param>
        private void ProcessTableRow(List<String> list)
        {
            StringBuilder result = new StringBuilder();
            foreach (String item in list)
            {
                if (result.Length > 0)
                    result.Append(",");
                result.Append('\"');
                result.Append(item);
```

```
        result.Append('\"');

    }
    Console.WriteLine(result.ToString());
}

/// <summary>
/// This method will download an amortization table
/// for the specified parameters.
/// </summary>
/// <param name="interest">The interest rate for
/// the loan.</param>
/// <param name="term">The term(in months) of the
/// loan.</param>
/// <param name="principle">The principle amount of
/// the loan.</param>
public void process(double interest, int term,
    int principle)
{
    Uri url = new Uri(
        "http://www.httprecipes.com/1/9/loan.php");
    WebRequest http = HttpWebRequest.Create(url);
    http.Timeout = 30000;
    http.ContentType =
        "application/x-www-form-urlencoded";
    http.Method = "POST";
    Stream ostream = http.GetRequestStream();

    FormUtility form = new FormUtility(ostream, null);
    form.Add("interest", "" + interest);
    form.Add("term", "" + term);
    form.Add("principle", "" + principle);
    form.Complete();
    ostream.Close();
    WebResponse response = http.GetResponse();

    Stream istream = response.GetResponseStream();
    ParseHTML parse = new ParseHTML(istream);
    StringBuilder buffer = new StringBuilder();
    List<String> list = new List<String>();
    bool capture = false;

    Advance(parse, "table", 3);

    int ch;
    while ((ch = parse.Read()) != -1)
```

```
                        {
                           if (ch == 0)
                           {
                              HTMLTag tag = parse.Tag;
                              if (String.Compare(tag.Name, "tr", true) == 0)
                              {
                                 list.Clear();
                                 capture = false;
                                 buffer.Length = 0;
                              }
                              else if (String.Compare(tag.Name, "/tr", true)
                                   == 0)
                              {
                                 if (list.Count > 0)
                                 {
                                    ProcessTableRow(list);
                                    list.Clear();
                                 }
                              }
                              else if (String.Compare(tag.Name, "td", true)
                                   == 0)
                              {
                                 if (buffer.Length > 0)
                                    list.Add(buffer.ToString());
                                 buffer.Length = 0;
                                 capture = true;
                              }
                              else if (String.Compare(tag.Name, "/td", true)
                                    == 0)
                              {
                                 list.Add(buffer.ToString());
                                 buffer.Length = 0;
                                 capture = false;
                              }
                              else if (String.Compare(tag.Name, "/table",
                                   true) == 0)
                              {
                                 break;
                              }
                           }
                           else
                           {
                              if (capture)
                                 buffer.Append((char)ch);
                           }
                        }
```

```
        }


        static void Main(string[] args)
        {
            JavaScriptForms parse = new JavaScriptForms();
            parse.process(7.5, 12, 10000);
        }
    }
}
```

This recipe submits data to a JavaScript enabled form. This form collects information about a loan and displays the loan's amortization table. Figure 9.4, from earlier in this chapter, shows the amortization schedule.

To produce an amortization schedule, the user must enter the principal loan amount, the interest rate and the term. These values will all be transmitted to the form, by the bot, and the resulting amortization table will be parsed.

This recipe begins by opening a connection to the **loan.php** page. This is the page that the form will **POST** to.

```
Uri url = new Uri("http://www.httprecipes.com/1/9/loan.php");
WebRequest http = HttpWebRequest.Create(url);
http.Timeout = 30000;
http.ContentType = "application/x-www-form-urlencoded";
http.Method = "POST";
```

First, a **FormUtility** object is built to construct our response to the form. Chapter 7 explains how to use the **FormUtility** class.

```
Stream ostream = http.GetRequestStream();

FormUtility form = new FormUtility(ostream, null);
```

The three form variables of interest, term and principal are added to the form.

```
form.Add("interest", "" + interest);
form.Add("term", "" + term);
form.Add("principle", "" + principle);
form.Complete();
ostream.Close();
```

The form is now posted. We will parse the results that were returned.

```
WebResponse response = http.GetResponse();

Stream istream = response.GetResponseStream();
ParseHTML parse = new ParseHTML(istream);
```

```
StringBuilder buffer = new StringBuilder();
List<String> list = new List<String>();
bool capture = false;
```

The data we are looking for is in the third table. We begin parsing the HTML, looking for the tags comprising the table that holds the amortization schedule. The data contained here is in a table. Table parsing was covered in more detail in Chapter 6.

```
Advance(parse, "table", 3);
```

```
int ch;
while ((ch = parse.Read()) != -1)
{
  if (ch == 0)
  {
```

If the tag is an opening table row, **\<tr>** tag, we clear the list to begin capturing a table row.

```
    HTMLTag tag = parse.Tag;
    if (String.Compare(tag.Name, "tr", true) == 0)
    {
      list.Clear();
      capture = false;
      buffer.Length = 0;
```

If the tag is an ending table row, **\</tr>** tag, we can display the row we just extracted. This display is handled by the **ProcessTableRow** method.

```
    }
    else if (String.Compare(tag.Name, "/tr", true) == 0)
    {
      if (list.Count > 0)
      {
        ProcessTableRow(list);
        list.Clear();
      }
    }
```

If the tag is an opening table column, **\<td>** tag, begin capturing the data contained in that column.

```
    else if (String.Compare(tag.Name, "td", true) == 0)
    {
      if (buffer.Length > 0)
        list.Add(buffer.ToString());
      buffer.Length = 0;
      capture = true;
    }
```

If the tag is an ending table column, **</td>** tag, we have captured one complete column. Add that column to the row's list and stop capturing text.

```
else if (String.Compare(tag.Name, "/td", true) == 0)
{
  list.Add(buffer.ToString());
  buffer.Length = 0;
  capture = false;
}
```

Finally, if we reach an ending **</table>** tag, we have finished.

```
else if (String.Compare(tag.Name, "/table", true) == 0)
{
  break;
}
}
```

When characters are encountered, we should append them to the **buffer**, if we are capturing.

```
else
{
  if (capture)
    buffer.Append((char)ch);
}
```

Once the loop ends, the entire amortization table will be parsed.

Summary

This chapter explained how to handle JavaScript enabled web sites when writing a bot. The web server does not handle JavaScript; it is a web browser only technology. As a result your bot does not need to be directly concerned with JavaScript. Rather, as a bot programmer, you must understand the JavaScript code and ensure that your bot sends the same HTTP requests that a browser running the JavaScript would.

There are several common JavaScript techniques. One of the most common is using JavaScript to validate data entered into a form. JavaScript is also often used to provide automatic choice lists, as well as JavaScript includes. This chapter showed recipes demonstrating how to manage each of these situations.

Additionally, you can include a JavaScript interpreter in your programs. The JavaScript DotNet language allows you to execute some JavaScript within your program. A bot program rarely needs this functionality.

The next chapter will examine one of the most popular ways to use JavaScript. AJAX is a technology combining JavaScript and asynchronous HTTP messages to provide very rich interactive experiences for the user. AJAX processing requires special considerations.

CHAPTER 10: WORKING WITH AJAX SITES

- Understanding AJAX
- Understanding the Components of AJAX
- Parsing XML
- Generating XML

AJAX is a web development technology that has become very popular. AJAX web sites look much more like traditional GUI applications than regular web sites. When you access a regular web site you move from one web page to another, as you use the web site. AJAX applications usually use a single page, and update only what needs to be updated.

In an attempt to respond quicker to the user and behave more like traditional applications, AJAX web applications attempt to limit the movement from one web page to another. Your browser's URL line stays the same, and only the part of the page that actually changed is updated. There are many commercial websites that make use of AJAX, such as:

- Google
- Digg
- Yahoo Mail
- Writely

There are still HTTP requests and responses being transmitted between the web browser and web server. However, the HTTP responses do not move the user to a new page. Rather JavaScript interprets these HTTP responses on the web browser. This allows much more real-time interaction with the user.

AJAX is an acronym for Asynchronous JavaScript and XML. AJAX employs a number of existing web technologies. Because AJAX is based on existing web technologies AJAX works on nearly every web browser. Table 10.1 summarizes the technologies used by AJAX.

Table 10.1: AJAX Components

Technology	AJAX Use
HTML/XHTML and CSS	CSS allows AJAX applications to format their display. By using CSS the HTML documents can be kept relatively simple, which makes it easier for them to be modified by the DOM.
DOM	The Document Object Model allows JavaScript to modify the data displayed on the web browser. The DOM also allows JavaScript to parse XML.
XMLHttpRequest object	The XMLHttpRequest object allows you to exchange data asynchronously with the web server through HTTP requests and responses. Some AJAX applications use an embedded <iframe> to accomplish this as well.
XML	XML, or some other textual format, is the format usually used for AJAX applications to communicate with the web server.

It may be easier to create a bot for an AJAX web site than for a regular web site. AJAX web sites tend to be designed so that their JavaScript can request information from the server in short simple XML packets. This can be ideal for a bot and requires an understanding what format these small requests will be in.

Understanding AJAX

To understand this format you must understand how AJAX works. There are entire books dedicated to AJAX. This chapter will present a brief introduction to AJAX.

Other than understanding how AJAX works, you may simply to use a network analyzer. If you use a network analyzer you can watch the web browser communicate to the web server. This enables you to see the AJAX requests and responses. From this information you could then build a bot to send these same requests. Using a network analyzer to analyze AJAX will be discussed later in this chapter.

In the next few sections this chapter will present a brief overview of how AJAX works.

Using HTML/XHTML and CSS

AJAX web sites use the Document Object Model (DOM) to modify their HTML programmatically. Rather than calling on the web server to completely redraw the entire HTML page, AJAX applications request data from the server and then modify the page the user is already looking at. This means it is best to keep the HTML as simple as possible. Cascading Style Sheets (CSS) is a great way to do this.

Consider if you wanted to use traditional HTML to display the message "This is a note" in a red font and bold type. The following HTML would have to be used:

```
<font color="red"><p><b>This is a note</b></p></font>
```

Here there is quite a bit of "overhead" HTML that has nothing to do with the text being displayed. For each place that you want to use this style of text you need to include the additional "overhead" HTML that specifies the formatting properties for the text.

With CSS, you can define styles. Styles are either included in a separate style file, or defined between a beginning **<style>** and an ending **</style>** tag. Using CSS to format the text above, simply include the following style:

```
.note {
    color: red;
    font-weight: bold;
}
```

Now, anytime you want to apply this style simply use a class attribute, such as:

```
<p class="note">This is a note</p>
```

This is very advantageous for bots. The above HTML example is far easier to parse than the preceding traditional HTML example.

XHTML is often used in place of HTML in AJAX applications. XHTML looks almost identical to HTML. The main difference is that XHTML must follow XML formatting rules. For instance, the following example is fine under HTML, but is unacceptable in XHTML:

```
Line 1<br>
Line 2<br>
<ul>
   <li>Option 1
   <li>Option 2
   <li>Option 3
</ul>
```

There are several missing end tags. The above document, re-created as XHTML looks like this:

```
Line 1<br/>
Line 2<br/>
<ul>
   <li>Option 1</li>
   <li>Option 2</li>
   <li>Option 3</li>
</ul>
```

The advantage is that this method makes it much easier for a parser, such as the DOM, to understand the document.

Understanding Document Object Model

The Document Object Model (DOM) is a series of JavaScript objects that allows a Java-Script application to access and modify both XML and HTML information. There are two primary functions that most AJAX web sites use the DOM for. They are summarized here:

- Parsing XML received from the web server
- Allowing dynamic changes to web page displayed on the browser

When the web server sends an HTML document to the web browser, the web browser now has a copy of the document, separate from the web server. This separate copy, which the web browser stores in memory, is the copy of the web page the user is looking at. Using the DOM, it is possible for a JavaScript program to make changes to the copy of the web page that the user is viewing. This allows the browser to update only parts of the document, and does not change the document on the web server.

This is how AJAX gets by with not having to update the entire page. AJAX applications use the DOM to update parts of the page in response to packets sent to the AJAX application from the web server.

It is very easy to view a web page as it is seen from the DOM. The FireFox web browser includes a function, under the "Tools" menu, called "DOM Inspector. For example, consider the web page stored at the following URL:

`http://www.httprecipes.com/1/10/example1.html`

This page stores a simple table and some text. You can see this web page in Figure 10.1.

Figure 10.1: A Simple HTML Page

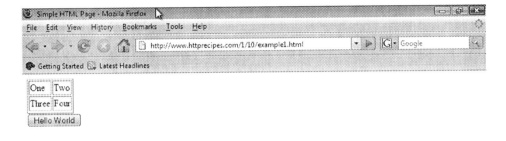

The FireFox web browser includes a special tool named "DOM Inspector" that allows you to see your document as the DOM sees it. The DOM inspector can be found under the tools menu in Firefox. Some versions of FireFox require you to do a "custom" install and choose "developer tools" to access the "DOM Inspector". Selecting the "DOM Inspector" shows you how this page is viewed by the DOM. Figure 10.2 shows what this page looks like in the "DOM Inspector".

Figure 10.2: A Simple Page in the DOM Inspector

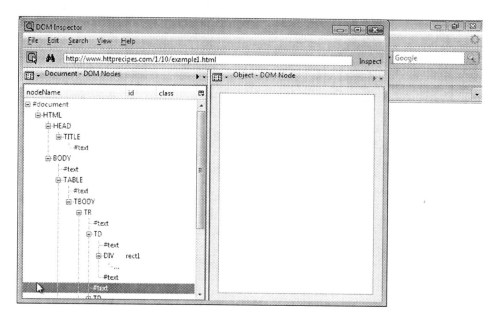

The DOM provides a programmatic way to access the contents of the web site. For example, the following JavaScript code will change the text "One", from Figure 10.1 to "Hello World".

```
document.getElementById('rect1').innerHTML='Hello World';
```

As you can see from the above code, the value of the **<div>** tag, named **rect1** can be changed as needed. Here it is being changed to the words "Hello World".

This is the heart of AJAX programming. You modify the page currently being displayed. This limits the number of times the web browser has to go back to the web server for a complete page.

Communicating using the XMLHttpRequest Object

The **XMLHttpRequest** object allows JavaScript to communicate directly with the web server. This communication occurs through the HTTP protocol. However, the data exchanged with the **XMLHttpRequest** objects goes to the JavaScript program and does not redisplay the entire page. The AJAX browser application can then interpret the HTTP response as needed and update itself using the DOM.

Despite the fact that the **XMLHttpRequest** object has the XML acronym as part of its name, it does not require that you use XML. You can use the **XMLHttpRequest** object to exchange text information just as well as XML. However, if you are using XML, the **XMLHttpRequest** object will conveniently package the incoming XML with the DOM.

The **XMLHttpRequest** object is not the only method that can be used to exchange information with the web server. Another common technique is to use an **<iframe>**. The **<iframe>** tag allows you to embed one web page inside another.

The **<iframe>** tag has a URL that defines what HTML is to be displayed. This URL property can be modified with JavaScript. If the URL is modified, the **<iframe>** will load the data contained at the new URL. Some sites hide the **<iframe>** and change its URL to the page they would like to retrieve a message from. The browser then fills the **<iframe>** element with the data received from the URL. The JavaScript can now harvest the data. Because the **<iframe>** element is hidden, the user will not see any of this.

Interpreting XML

XML is an ideal protocol to exchange information between the web server and the AJAX program running on the web browser. Because the DOM can easily parse XML, JavaScript is very well equipped to handle XML messages.

To see what XML messages might be sent, consider an AJAX web application that maintains an employee database. This type of AJAX application may need to implement an employee search. Consider an employee search function where the user enters the first and last name of an employee and the system attempts to locate that employee's record.

For such a system, the AJAX application running on the web browser could construct and send the following XML message:

```
<request type="employeeSearch">
  <searchFor>
    <first>John</first>
    <last>Smith</last>
  </searchFor>
</request>
```

When the server sends back the requested employee, it will be as an XML message. The following message could be returned:

```
<response type="employeeSearch">
  <employee>
    <first>John</first>
    <last>John</last>
    <phone>636-555-1212</phone>
    <address>102 Main Street</address>
    <city>St. Louis</city>
```

```
      <state>MO</state>
      <zip>63017</zip>
   </employee>
</response>
```

The AJAX web browser application will take the above XML information and use the DOM to parse it. The data extracted from the message will be displayed on the current web page using the DOM.

It is not necessary to use XML with an AJAX application. Some AJAX applications will transmit HTML or raw text messages. XML is particularly convenient because JavaScript can use the DOM to parse it.

What AJAX Means to Bots

Supporting AJAX from a bot is similar to supporting JavaScript from a bot. As with JavaScript, the user's web browsing experience is simply a series of HTTP requests. The web server is not aware that AJAX is being used. The web server simply accepts HTTP requests and issues HTTP responses. How these responses are interpreted is up to the web browser.

To create a bot that supports an AJAX site you must provide the same HTTP requests as the AJAX web application would. The bot then examines the responses and extracts the needed information from these responses.

There are two ways to do this. If you know JavaScript and how to use AJAX you can examine the target AJAX site and learn to construct the same requests as the AJAX application. An easier approach is to use a network analyzer to examine the AJAX web site as you use it. The network analyzer can show you the format of the HTTP requests and responses. This approach also means you do not need an in-depth knowledge of AJAX.

Recipes

The first recipe for this chapter will show how to use a network analyzer to construct the bot. This chapter will demonstrate two different recipes:

- Extract data from a non-XML based AJAX site
- Extract data from a XML based AJAX site

We will begin with a non-XML based AJAX site.

Recipe #10.1: A non-XML Based AJAX Site

Some AJAX sites do not use XML to transfer messages between the web browser and web server. One common format is HTML. It is often very convenient for an AJAX application to transmit new HTML that must be displayed to part of the web browser. To see an example of this visit the following URL:

http://www.httprecipes.com/1/10/ajaxnonxml.php

This page contains two AJAX features. First, as you type the name of a US state a drop list is shown to help you narrow in on what state you would like to view. You can see this in Figure 10.3.

Figure 10.3: An AJAX Drop-List

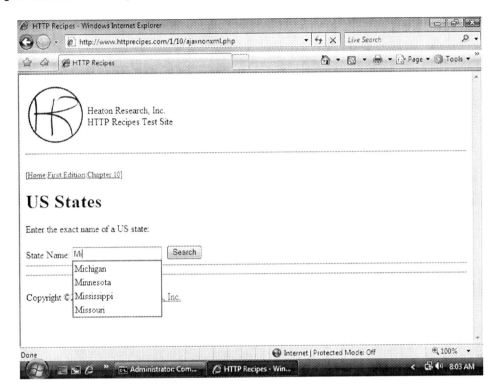

Once you select a state and click the "Search" button you will see the second AJAX feature of this web site. Information about the state you choose is displayed. However, only the information about the state you choose was transmitted to the web server. You will notice that you are still at the same URL. You can see a state displayed here in Figure 10.4.

Figure 10.4: Viewing Missouri

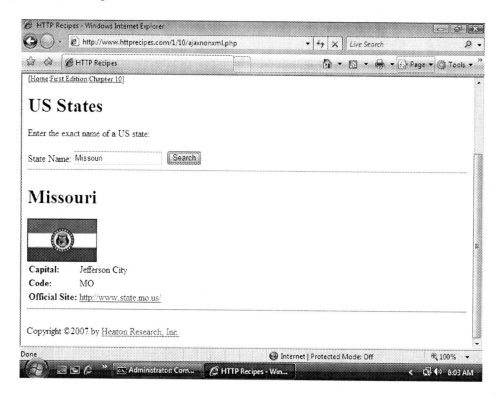

In the next section we will analyze the traffic that supports these AJAX requests.

Analyzing the HTTP Traffic

To display this drop list, as well as information about the selected state, HTML is downloaded from the web server as needed. To observe this, use the WireShark network analyzer. This was covered in Chapter 2. You can see WireShark following the AJAX traffic in Figure 10.5.

Figure 10.5: WireShark Examining AJAX

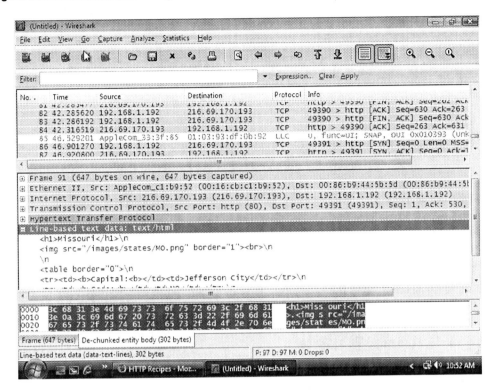

Only the very top request, in Figure 10.5, is used to display a complete HTTP page. All of the other requests occur as a result of typing in a state's name, and displaying the drop-down.

As you type part of the state's name the web browser requests a list of states that match what you have requested so far. This data is obtained from the following URL:

`http://www.httprecipes.com/1/10/states.php`

As the state name is typed, the JavaScript on the page sends requests to the above URL to obtain a list of states that match what has been typed so far. For example, if the user had typed "Mi", the following message would be returned.

```
<ul>
<li>Michigan
<li>Minnesota
<li>Mississippi
<li>Missouri
</ul>
```

This list will be displayed in the drop down list.

Once you actually select a state, the following request is sent.

http://www.httprecipes.com/1/10/statehtml.php?state=MO

The above URL requests state information for Missouri, which has the postal code of "MO". The following HTML would be returned.

```
<h1>Missouri</h1>
<img src="/images/states/MO.png" border="1"><br>

<table border="0">
<tr><td><b>Capital:<b></td><td>Jefferson City</td></tr>
<tr><td><b>Code:<b></td><td>MO</td></tr>
<tr><td><b>Official Site:<b></td><td><a href="http://www.state.
mo.us/">http://www.state.mo.us/</a></td></tr>
</table>
```

This is not a complete page of HTML. The complete page will be displayed just below the search box.

Writing a Bot for the non-XML AJAX Site

We will now construct a bot that can download the state information. When you want to write a bot for an AJAX site, your job is to send the same requests as the web browser would. The bot being created sends the same request as the web server did when the state information was requested. You can see this recipe in Listing 10.1.

Listing 10.1: Non-XML AJAX Bot (AjaxNonXML.cs)

```csharp
using System;
using System.Collections.Generic;
using System.Text;
using System.Net;
using System.IO;


namespace Recipe10_1
{
    class AjaxNonXML
    {
        /// <summary>
        /// This method downloads the specified URL into a C#
        /// String. This is a very simple method, that you can
        /// reused anytime you need to quickly grab all data from
        /// a specific URL.
```

```csharp
/// </summary>
/// <param name="url">The URL to download.</param>
/// <returns>The contents of the URL that was
/// downloaded.</returns>
public String DownloadPage(Uri url)
{
    WebRequest http = HttpWebRequest.Create(url);
    HttpWebResponse response =
            (HttpWebResponse)http.GetResponse();
    StreamReader stream = new
            StreamReader(response.GetResponseStream(),
            System.Text.Encoding.ASCII);

    String result = stream.ReadToEnd();

    response.Close();
    stream.Close();
    return result;
}


/// <summary>
/// This method is very useful for grabbing
/// information from a
/// HTML page.  It extracts text from between two tokens,
/// the tokens need not be case sensitive.
/// </summary>
/// <param name="str">The string to extract from.</param>
/// <param name="token1">The text, or tag, that comes
/// before the desired text</param>
/// <param name="token2">The text, or tag, that comes
/// after the desired text</param>
/// <param name="count">Which occurrence of token1 to
/// use, 1 for the first</param>
/// <returns></returns>
public String ExtractNoCase(String str,
    String token1, String token2, int count)
{
    int location1, location2;

    // convert everything to lower case
    String searchStr = str.ToLower();
    token1 = token1.ToLower();
    token2 = token2.ToLower();

    // now search
    location1 = location2 = 0;
```

```csharp
        do
        {
            location1 = searchStr.IndexOf(token1, location1
                + 1);

            if (location1 == -1)
                return null;

            count--;
        } while (count > 0);

        // return the result from the original string
        // that has mixed case
        location1 += token1.Length;
        location2 = str.IndexOf(token2, location1 + 1);
        if (location2 == -1)
            return null;

        return str.Substring(location1, location2 -
            location1);
    }


    /// <summary>
    /// This method will download data from the
    /// specified state.
    /// This data will come in as a partial HTML document,
    /// the necessary data will be extracted from there.
    /// </summary>
    /// <param name="state">The state you want to
    /// download (i.e. Missouri)</param>
    public void Process(String state)
    {
        Uri url = new Uri(
"http://www.httprecipes.com/1/10/statehtml.php?state=" + state);
        String buffer = DownloadPage(url);
        String name = this.ExtractNoCase(buffer, "<h1>",
            "</h1>", 0);
        String capital = this.ExtractNoCase(buffer,
            "Capital:<b></td><td>", "</td>", 0);
        String code = this.ExtractNoCase(buffer,
            "Code:<b></td><td>", "</td>", 0);
        String site = this.ExtractNoCase(buffer,
    "Official Site:<b></td><td><a href=\"", "\"", 0);

        Console.WriteLine("State name:" + name);
        Console.WriteLine("State capital:" + capital);
```

```
            Console.WriteLine("Code:" + code);
            Console.WriteLine("Site:" + site);
        }


        static void Main(string[] args)
        {
            if (args.Length != 1)
            {
                Console.WriteLine(
                    "Usage: Recipe10_1 [state, i.e. Missouri]");
            }
            else
            {
                AjaxNonXML d = new AjaxNonXML();
                d.Process(args[0]);
            }
        }
    }
}
```

Most of the work for this recipe is done inside the **Process** method. The **Process** method begins by downloading the contents of the URL.

```
Uri url = new Uri("http://www.httprecipes.com/1/10/statehtml.
php?state=" + state);
String buffer = DownloadPage(url);
```

Next the state name, capital, code and site are all extracted from the HTML downloaded.

```
String name = this.ExtractNoCase(buffer, "<h1>", "</h1>", 0);
String capital = this.ExtractNoCase(buffer, "Capital:<b></
td><td>", "</td>", 0);
String code = this.ExtractNoCase(buffer, "Code:<b></td><td>", "</
td>", 0);
String site = this.ExtractNoCase(buffer, "Official Site:<b></
td><td><a href=\"", "\"", 0);
```

Once the data has been extracted it is displayed.

```
Console.WriteLine("State name:" + name);
Console.WriteLine("State capital:" + capital);
Console.WriteLine("Code:" + code);
Console.WriteLine("Site:" + site);
```

This recipe can be adapted to web sites that transfer HTML data with AJAX.

Recipe #10.2: A XML Based AJAX Site

Many AJAX sites use XML to transfer messages between the web browser and web server. This recipe demonstrates how to write a bot for an AJAX web site that uses XML. To see a web site that makes use of AJAX XML communication examine the following URL:

`http://www.httprecipes.com/1/10/ajaxxml.php`

This page allows you to search for a list of states. For example, if you enter the string "Miss" you will see the states "Mississippi" and "Missouri". You can see this in Figure 10.6.

Figure 10.6: Searching for States

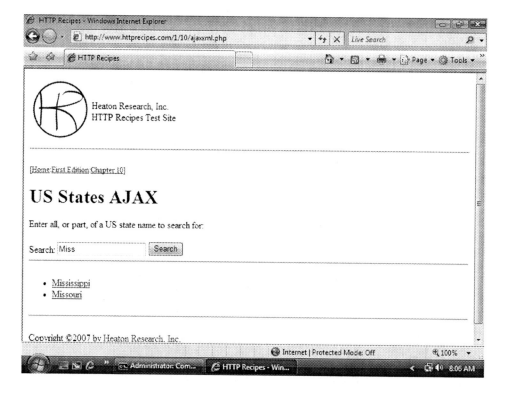

You can open any of the states returned for more information. Clicking on Missouri will produce Figure 10.7.

Figure 10.7: Displaying a State

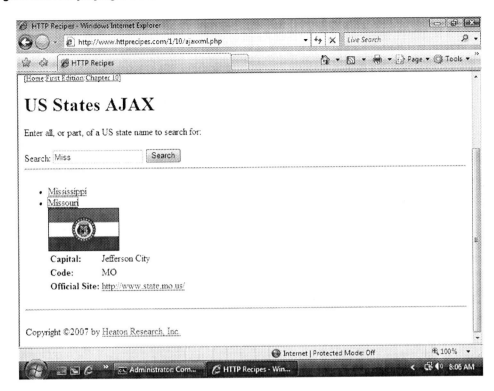

You can click on as many states as are returned from the search. The HTML will be built dynamically to add the additional information for the states.

We will now examine the XML messages that the web browser exchanges with the web server to preset this information.

XML AJAX Messages

Two different XML request/response pairs are sent. The first request/response pair performs the search. If you enter the string "Miss" and select search, the following XML message will be sent to the web server:

```
<request type="search">
  <search>Miss</search>
</request>
```

There is no specified XML format for AJAX websites. You will have to analyze the messages sent by an AJAX site to see what their structure is. This can be done with a tool such as WireShark. WireShark was covered in Chapter 2.

When the above search request is sent to the web server, it makes the following response:

```
<result>
  <state>
    <code>MS</code>
    <name>Mississippi</name>
  </state>
  <state>
    <code>MO</code>
    <name>Missouri</name>
  </state>
</result>
```

Once you have decided on a state that you would like displayed and click on it, the following request will be sent.

```
<request type="state">
  <code>MO</code>
</request>
```

This requests information about the state of Missouri. The web server will respond as follows:

```
<result>
  <state id="25">
    <code>MO</code>
    <name>Missouri</name>
    <capital>Jefferson City</capital>
    <url>http://www.state.mo.us/</url>
  </state>
</result>
```

The above response is used by the JavaScript to display information about Missouri.

Writing a Bot for the XML AJAX Site

We will now create a bot that can download and process the XML data from the AJAX web site. This recipe is shown in Listing 10.2.

Listing 10.2: XML AJAX Bot (AjaxXML.cs)

```
using System;
using System.Collections.Generic;
using System.Text;
using System.Net;
using System.IO;
using System.Xml;

namespace Recipe10_2
```

```
{

    class AjaxXML
    {
        /// <summary>
        /// Obtains a XML node.  Specify a name such as
        /// "state.name"
        /// to nest several layers of nodes.
        /// </summary>
        /// <param name="e">The parent node.</param>
        /// <param name="name">The child node to search for.
        /// Specify levels with .'s.</param>
        /// <returns>Returns the node found.</returns>
        private XmlNode GetXMLNode(XmlNode e, String name)
        {
            char[] split = { '.' };
            String[] tok = name.Split(split);
            XmlNode node = e;
            foreach (String currentName in tok)
            {
                XmlNodeList list = node.ChildNodes;
                int len = list.Count;
                for (int i = 0; i < len; i++)
                {
                    XmlNode n = list[i];
                    if (n.Name.Equals(currentName))
                    {
                        node = n;
                        break;
                    }
                }
            }
            return node;
        }


        /// <summary>
        /// Obtain the specified XML attribute from the
        /// specified node.
        /// </summary>
        /// <param name="e">The XML node to obtain an
        /// attribute from.</param>
        /// <param name="name">The name of the attribute.</param>
        /// <returns>Returns the value of the attribute.</returns>
        private String GetXMLAttribute(XmlNode e, String name)
        {
```

```
        XmlNamedNodeMap map = e.Attributes;
        XmlNode attr = map.GetNamedItem(name);
        return attr.Value;
    }


    /// <summary>
    /// Download the information for the specified
    /// state.  This bot uses
    /// a AJAX web site to obtain the XML message.
    /// </summary>
    /// <param name="state">The state code to look
    /// for(i.e. MO).</param>
    public void Process(String state)
    {
        Uri url = new Uri(
        "http://www.httprecipes.com/1/10/request.php");

        WebRequest http = HttpWebRequest.Create(url);
        http.Timeout = 30000;
        http.Method = "POST";

        String request = "<request type=\"state\"><code>"
                + state + "</code></request>";

        http.Timeout = 30000;
        http.ContentType =
                "application/x-www-form-urlencoded";

        http.Method = "POST";
        Stream ostream = http.GetRequestStream();

        System.Text.ASCIIEncoding enc =
                new System.Text.ASCIIEncoding();
        byte[] b = enc.GetBytes(request);
        ostream.Write(b, 0, b.Length);
        ostream.Close();
        WebResponse response = http.GetResponse();
        Stream istream = response.GetResponseStream();

        XmlDocument d = new XmlDocument();
        d.Load(istream);

        XmlElement e = d.DocumentElement;
        XmlNode stateNode = GetXMLNode(e, "state");
        String id = GetXMLAttribute(stateNode, "id");
        Console.WriteLine("State Name:" + GetXMLNode(e,
```

```
              "state.name").InnerText);
      Console.WriteLine("Code:" + GetXMLNode(e,
          "state.code").InnerText);
      Console.WriteLine("Capital:" + GetXMLNode(e,
      "state.capital").InnerText);
      Console.WriteLine("URL:" +
          GetXMLNode(e, "state.url").InnerText);
      Console.WriteLine("ID:" + id);
    }

    static void Main(string[] args)
    {
        if (args.Length != 1)
        {
            Console.WriteLine(
              "Usage: Recipe10_2 [state code, i.e. MO]");
        }
        else
        {
            AjaxXML d = new AjaxXML();
            d.Process(args[0]);
        }
    }
  }
}
```

The **Process** method is called to download a state's information. The Process method is passed a variable, named state that contains the code for the state that is to be downloaded.

The process method begins by constructing a URL that the XML request will be posted to.

```
Uri url = new Uri("http://www.httprecipes.com/1/10/request.php");

WebRequest http = HttpWebRequest.Create(url);
http.Timeout = 30000;
http.Method = "POST";
```

Next the XML request is constructed.

```
String request = "<request type=\"state\"><code>" + state +
      "</code></request>";
```

A connection is opened, and the request is posted to the web server.

```
System.Text.ASCIIEncoding enc = new System.Text.ASCIIEncoding();
byte[] b = enc.GetBytes(request);
ostream.Write(b, 0, b.Length);
```

```
ostream.Close();
WebResponse response = http.GetResponse();
Stream istream = response.GetResponseStream();
```

The response will be in XML format, as discussed earlier. C# contains many classes to support the parsing of XML. To do this we must first create an **XmlDocument**. Once an **XmlDocument** is constructed, we can pass it the **Stream** from the HTTP connection. The XML from the **Stream** will be parsed and loaded into an **XmlDocument** object. The Document implements the Document Object Model (DOM) for C#. As already discussed, the DOM allows C# to parse XML and HTML.

```
XmlDocument d = new XmlDocument();
d.Load(istream);
```

The root element is obtained form the DOM.

```
XmlElement e = d.DocumentElement;
```

The **GetXMLNode** function is called to obtain the state node from the XML. The implementation of the **GetXMLNode** function will be explained later in this chapter. The **GetXMLAttribute** function is also called to read the **id** attribute from the **state** node.

```
XmlNode stateNode = GetXMLNode(e, "state");
String id = GetXMLAttribute(stateNode, "id");
```

Each of the attributes is read from the state node.

```
Console.WriteLine("State Name:" +
GetXMLNode(e, "state.name").InnerText);
Console.WriteLine("Code:" +
GetXMLNode(e, "state.code").InnerText);
Console.WriteLine("Capital:" +
GetXMLNode(e, "state.capital").InnerText);
Console.WriteLine("URL:" + GetXMLNode(e, "state.url").InnerText);
Console.WriteLine("ID:" + id);
```

We made use of **GetXMLNode** and **GetXMLAttribute**. These are not built in C# functions. These functions were created to make working with the DOM easier. They will be discussed in the next two sections.

Implementing getXMLNode

The **GetXMLNode** function is a simple function that allows you to quickly take apart XML and get to the data you need. To understand how it works consider the following XML:

```
<firstLevel>
  <secondLevel>
    <thirdLevel>
```

```
    </thirdLevel>
  </secondLevel>
</firstLevel>
```

If you wanted to access the **<thirdLevel>** node, using only the DOM, you would have to iterate through each level.

Using the **GetXMLNode** function makes this much easier.   To return the **<thirdLevel>** node, use the following code:

```
XmlNode node = GetXMLNode(e, documentRoot,"firstLevel.secondLevel.
thirdLevel");
```

The **GetXMLNode** method is fairly short. It begins by splitting the name by periods(.). For example, the name "firstLevel.secondLevel.thirdLevel" would be broken in to three names.

```
char[] split = { '.' };
String[] tok = name.Split(split);
XmlNode node = e;
foreach (String currentName in tok)
{
```

As each component of the name is parsed, we attempt to find it at the current level.

```
  XmlNodeList list = node.ChildNodes;
  int len = list.Count;
  for (int i = 0; i < len; i++)
  {
```

Once the current name segment is found, we move it to the **node** variable and **break** out of the search loop. The function will now return if there are no more search elements, or continue searching if there are.

```
    XmlNode n = list[i];
    if (n.Name.Equals(currentName))
    {
      node = n;
      break;
    }
  }
}
```

Finally the node that was found is returned.

```
return node;
```

Once you have read a node you will either want to get its content text, or obtain an attribute from that node. To access the content text, use the **InnerText** property of the node, as follows:

```
Console.WriteLine("Value is: " + node.InnerText );
```

Obtaining an attribute from a node is discussed in the next section.

Implementing getXMLAttribute

Some XML tags have attributes. The **GetXMLAttribute** method can be called to quickly retrieve the attribute from a XML tag. Consider the following XML tag:

```
<state id="25">
```

This XML tag has one property named **id** with a value of **25**. To access this value the **GetXMLAttribute** function is used. This function begins by obtaining a map of all attributes. Calling **GetNamedItem** looks up the attribute; the node value is then returned.

```
XmlNamedNodeMap map = e.Attributes;
XmlNode attr = map.GetNamedItem(name);
return attr.Value;
```

This obtains the attribute value.

Summary

This chapter explained how to create bots that access those sites which use AJAX. AJAX stands for Asynchronous JavaScript with XML. AJAX web sites usually use HTML/XML, CSS and the **XMLHttpRequestObject**. However, some of these components can be exchanged for other components. For example, some web sites use **<iframe>** tags instead of the **XMLHttpRequestObject**. Additionally, not all AJAX websites use XML.

This chapter presented two recipes showing how to communicate with the different types of AJAX web sites. You were shown how to process data from an AJAX web site that exchanges information using XML. You were also shown how to access data from an AJAX web site that did not use XML.

The biggest challenge in creating a bot for an AJAX web site is identifying the communication protocol between the web server and the web browser. You must understand what HTTP requests and responses are flowing between the web server and the web browser. This allows your bot to send the same requests and process the same responses as a web browser would. The challenges are similar to working with JavaScript, as was covered in the last chapter; this is because AJAX sites are just an advanced application of JavaScript.

Some web sites are designed to allow you to transfer XML requests with them. Such services are called web services. Exchanging XML with a web service is very similar to communicating with an AJAX web site. Building bots to work with web services will be explained in the next chapter.

Chapter 11: Handling Web Services

- Understanding Web Services
- Notable Public Web Services
- Using the Google Search API
- Creating Hybrid Bots

A bot is a program that accesses HTML and AJAX web sites designed for human visitors. Often this is complex for the bot because the HTML is formatted for a human to read. This is not the case with a web service. A web service is a web site that was designed, from the start, to be accessed by other computers.

Web Services are an important aspect of HTTP programming. Web Services communicate using HTTP. The data exchanged between a Web Service server and client is usually in XML form. This makes it very easy for a C# program to interpret.

A program that accesses a web service is not typically called a bot. However, some bots make use of Web Services to help them find other HTML sites to process. Such a bot is called a hybrid bot. Hybrid bots will be discussed later in this chapter. This chapter will also present one recipe that implements a hybrid bot.

Notable Public Web Services

Many different companies offer web services. Many major web sites offer some sort of web service. If the web site you wish to work with offers a web service, this is the preferred means of communicating with that site. Table 11.1 lists some of the most commonly used Web Services.

Table 11.1: Large Websites Offering Web Services

Web Site	Web Services Offered
Alexa	Alexa web services allow access to their web site directory and web site thumbnails.
Amazon	Amazon allows access to their product database through their web services. This allows web sites to create a complete Amazon based online store, complete with a shopping cart.
Blogger	Blogger web services allow blog entries to be posted.

Digg	Digg web services allow you to digg a web link, as well as other access to the Digg API.
EBay	EBay web services allow you to place and modify auction listings.
Flickr	Flickr web services allow access to their image database.
Google	Google web services allow access to their search database, and other services.
MSN	MSN web services allow access to their search database.
Paypal	Paypal web services allow you to process payments.
United States Postal Service	The USPS web services allow you to calculate shipping rates.
Yahoo	Yahoo web services allow access to their search database.

For more information on any of these web services you should consult their web site. Most web sites that make web services available have documentation explaining how to implement their service using C#.

Using the Google API

Google offers a wide variety of web services. One of the most useful to bot programmers is the Google Search API. Information about the Google Search API can be found at the following address:

`http://www.google.com/apis/index.html`

The Google Search API allows access to Google search information. You can perform any of the following using the Google search API.

- Spell check
- Search for a term
- View Google's cache for a site
- Find sites that link to a URL
- Plus more

In the next two sections you will be shown how to make use of the Google Search API. First you will have to register with Google. Secondly, you will have to create a reference to Google's search API in your C# project.

Registering for the Google API

When you request information from the Google API you must send a key along with your request. This key allows Google to track where requests are coming from. Before you can use the Google Search API you must register to obtain one of these keys. Once you register with Google your key will be mailed to you.

The Google key is just a long stream of seemingly random characters. For example, the Google key might look something like:

```
jWKfuw78WHdiwe8dfHs
```

This is not an actual Google key, and as a result would not work properly with the Google Search API. To use any of the Google examples in this chapter, you will have to obtain a Google API key of your own.

Once you have obtained a Google key, you can make use of the Google SOAP web services. You will learn to access SOAP web services later in this chapter.

Hybrid Bots

A hybrid bot makes use of both web services and conventional HTML based web access. The Google web services API is very useful for creating hybrid bots. The Google search API allows you to quickly locate pages for your bot to visit.

Consider if you wanted to create a bot that downloaded information about "George Washington". It would take a very long time to construct a bot that would visit every site on the web looking for information about "George Washington".

Thanks to the Google search API you do not need to construct such a bot. You can submit a search request to the Google API, and you will be given a list of all web pages that contain the name "George Washington". Your bot can then access these sites using the methods previously discussed in this book. Recipe 11.3 demonstrates a hybrid bot.

Understanding SOAP

When you make use of the Google API, your computer is sending requests to Google and receiving responses. You might be wondering what format the requests and responses take. Most web services use the HTTP protocol to send and receive Simple Object Access Protocol (SOAP) formatted requests and responses.

SOAP is a standard format for representing these requests and responses. SOAP is XML based and can be processed using the Document Object Model (DOM) or any of a large number of framework libraries designed to make it easy to access SOAP. Later in this chapter you will be shown how to use .NET to access SOAP services. For now we will examine SOAP directly, and see what messages are sent and received by it.

You can see a simple SOAP server at the following URL:

http://www.httprecipes.com/1/11/

This SOAP server translates English to "Pig Latin". Pig Latin is a simple language game based on English. English can be quickly translated to Pig Latin by following a set of rules. For more information on Pig Latin visit the following URL:

http://en.wikipedia.org/wiki/Pig latin

It is not necessary to understand Pig Latin for this example. It is simply used to create a simple web service.

Using WSDL Information

Most web services use a single HTTP page that describes the types of requests that a SOAP server can handle. This page is in a special XML format called Web Service Definition Language (WSDL). The Pig Latin web server supports such a page. To see the WSDL from the Pig Latin SOAP server visit the following URL:

http://www.httprecipes.com/1/11/soap/?wsdl

You can see the output from the above URL in Listing 11.1:

Listing 11.1: Pig Latin Server's WSDL

```
<?xml version="1.0" encoding="ISO-8859-1"?>
<definitions
  xmlns:SOAP-ENV="http://schemas.xmlsoap.org/soap/envelope/"
  xmlns:xsd="http://www.w3.org/2001/XMLSchema"
  xmlns:xsi="http://www.w3.org/2001/XMLSchema-instance"
  xmlns:SOAP-ENC="http://schemas.xmlsoap.org/soap/encoding/"
  xmlns:tns="http://www.httprecipes.com/1/11/soap/"
  xmlns:soap="http://schemas.xmlsoap.org/wsdl/soap/"
  xmlns:wsdl="http://schemas.xmlsoap.org/wsdl/"
  xmlns="http://schemas.xmlsoap.org/wsdl/"
  targetNamespace="http://www.httprecipes.com/1/11/soap/">

  <types>
    <xsd:schema
targetNamespace="http://www.httprecipes.com/1/11/soap/">
      <xsd:import
namespace="http://schemas.xmlsoap.org/soap/encoding/" />
      <xsd:import namespace="http://schemas.xmlsoap.org/wsdl/" />
    </xsd:schema>
  </types>
```

```
<message name="translateRequest">
  <part name="inputString" type="xsd:string" />
</message>
<message name="translateResponse">
  <part name="return" type="xsd:string" />
</message>

<portType name="PigLatinTranslatorPortType">
  <operation name="translate">
    <input message="tns:translateRequest"/>
    <output message="tns:translateResponse"/>
  </operation>
</portType>

<binding name="PigLatinTranslatorBinding"
  type="tns:PigLatinTranslatorPortType">
  <soap:binding style="rpc"
    transport="http://schemas.xmlsoap.org/soap/http"/>
    <operation name="translate">
    <soap:operation
      soapAction=
"http://www.httprecipes.com/1/11/soap/index.php/translate"
      style="rpc"/>
      <input>
        <soap:body use="encoded"
namespace="http://www.httprecipes.com/1/11/soap/"
    encodingStyle="http://schemas.xmlsoap.org/soap/encoding/"/>
      </input>
      <output>
        <soap:body use="encoded"
namespace="http://www.httprecipes.com/1/11/soap/"
encodingStyle="http://schemas.xmlsoap.org/soap/encoding/"/>
      </output>
    </operation>
  </binding>
  <service name="PigLatinTranslator">
    <port name="PigLatinTranslatorPort"
binding="tns:PigLatinTranslatorBinding">
      <soap:address
location="http://www.httprecipes.com/1/11/soap/index.php"/>
    </port>
  </service>
</definitions>
```

It is not important to understand the exact format of WSDL unless you are going to implement a SOAP framework. Later in this chapter you will see how to use the .NET framework to generate C# class files from the above WSDL.

In the next two sections you will see how to use the Pig Latin server to translate "Hello World" into Pig Latin. You will be shown both the request and response for this operation. Finally, you will be shown how to use .NET to generate C# classes that perform all of these operations for you.

SOAP Requests

SOAP requests and responses work in a similar way to C# method calls. For the Pig Latin server, think of it as calling a very simple function, such as:

```
public String translate(String str);
```

The **translate** function accepts a string, which is the text to be translated, then returns a translated string. To do this, an XML request is built, according to the SOAP specification that contains the name of the function to call, as well as the text to translate. Listing 11.2 shows how you would call the translate function with the text "Hello World".

Listing 11.2: Pig Latin SOAP Request

```
<?xml version="1.0" encoding="UTF-8" standalone="no"?>
<SOAP-ENV:Envelope
  xmlns:SOAP-ENV="http://schemas.xmlsoap.org/soap/envelope/"
  xmlns:xsd="http://www.w3.org/2001/XMLSchema"
  xmlns:xsi="http://www.w3.org/2001/XMLSchema-instance"
  xmlns:tns="http://www.httprecipes.com/1/11/soap/"
  xmlns:soap="http://schemas.xmlsoap.org/wsdl/soap/"
  xmlns:wsdl="http://schemas.xmlsoap.org/wsdl/"
  xmlns:SOAP-ENC="http://schemas.xmlsoap.org/soap/encoding/">
  <SOAP-ENV:Body>
    <mns:translate
    xmlns:mns="http://www.httprecipes.com/1/11/soap/"
    SOAP-ENV:encodingStyle="http://schemas.xmlsoap.org/soap/encod-
ing/">
      <inputString xsi:type="xsd:string">Hello World</inputString>
    </mns:translate>
  </SOAP-ENV:Body>
</SOAP-ENV:Envelope>
```

There is considerable overhead XML that tells the SOAP server what kind of request this is, however, you can still see the function name (translate) and the text passed to the function (Hello World).

SOAP Responses

Once the SOAP server receives the request, the text is translated and returned. The text is returned as a SOAP formatted response. The response is seen in Listing 11.3.

Listing 11.3: Pig Latin Server's SOAP Response

```
<?xml version="1.0" encoding="ISO-8859-1"?>
<SOAP-ENV:Envelope
  SOAP-ENV:encodingStyle="http://schemas.xmlsoap.org/soap/encod-
ing/"
  xmlns:SOAP-ENV="http://schemas.xmlsoap.org/soap/envelope/"
  xmlns:xsd="http://www.w3.org/2001/XMLSchema"
  xmlns:xsi="http://www.w3.org/2001/XMLSchema-instance"
  xmlns:SOAP-ENC="http://schemas.xmlsoap.org/soap/encoding/">
  <SOAP-ENV:Body>
    <ns1:translateResponse xmlns:ns1="http://www.httprecipes.
com/1/11/soap/">
      <return xsi:type="xsd:string">ellohay orldway</return>
  </ns1:translateResponse></SOAP-ENV:Body>
</SOAP-ENV:Envelope>
```

As you can see, the translated text is returned.

C# makes it very easy to use web services. By using C# references you can register web services and have them appear as classes inside your project. The next section shows how to do this.

Using Web Services in C#

C# references allow you to access other external objects in your projects. These references allow you to access objects in programs and dynamic link libraries (DLLs). You can also create a web reference to access objects provided by a web service. Figure 11.1 shows a simple C# project. Notice the "References" folder.

Figure 11.1: Simple Project

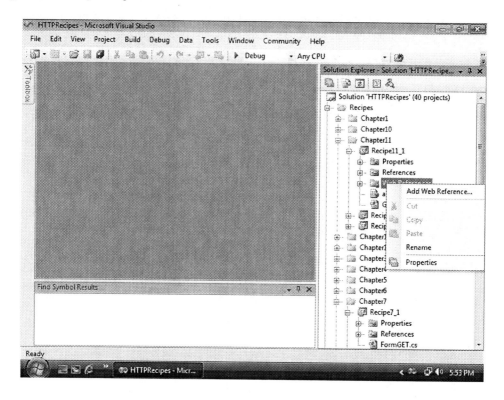

To add a reference right-click the "References" folder; this will give you the following two options:

- Add Reference
- Add Web Reference

Select the "Add Web Reference" option. This will reveal Figure 11.2.

Figure 11.2: Adding a Web Reference

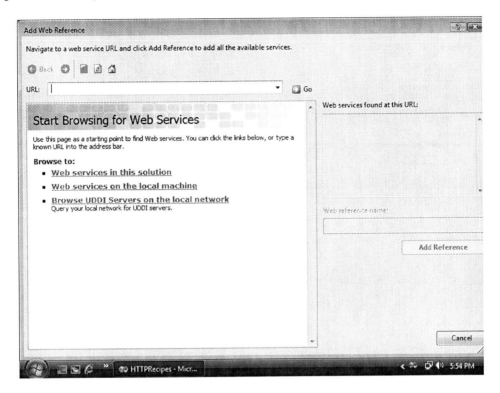

To add a web service, you must provide the URL of the web service's WSDL. To add the Google Search, use the following URL:

```
http://api.google.com/GoogleSearch.wsdl
```

Once you enter the URL, you will be shown the Google Search Service as seen in Figure 11.3.

Figure 11.3: The Google Search Service

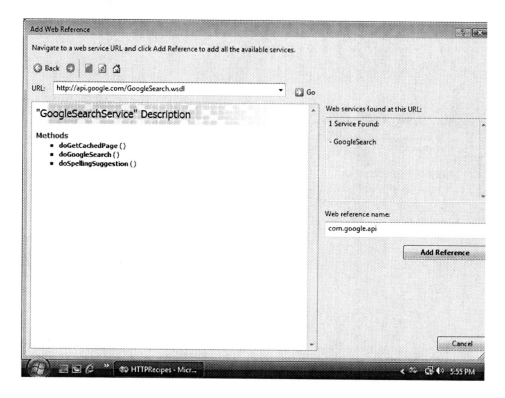

Click the "Add Reference" and the Google Search will be added as a web reference. You will now be able to see the Google Search API listed under the "Web References", as seen in Figure 11.4.

Figure 11.4: The Google Search Service Added

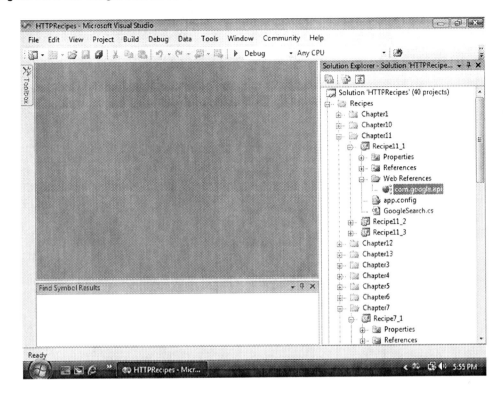

You can now access the Google Search API by adding the following **using** statement:

```
using com.google.api
```

These instructions are not unique to the Google API. Any web service that you would like to access will follow similar steps.

Recipes

This chapter includes three recipes. These recipes demonstrate how to construct bots that work with web services or a combination of web services and regular HTTP programming. Specifically, you will see how to perform the following techniques:

- Using the Google Search API
- Using a Simple Web Service
- Hybrid Bots

These recipes will show you how a bot can be adapted to several very common web service techniques. The first recipe demonstrates the Google SOAP Search API.

Recipe #11.1: Scanning for Links

One of the key components to how high a search engine will place a particular site is how many other sites are linking to that site. Because of this it can be very beneficial to scan what sites are linking to a particular site.

This recipe will display all inbound links to a particular site, based on the Google Search API. This recipe also displays how many links each of those sites has as well. Consider 11.5.

Figure 11.5: Links Between Sites

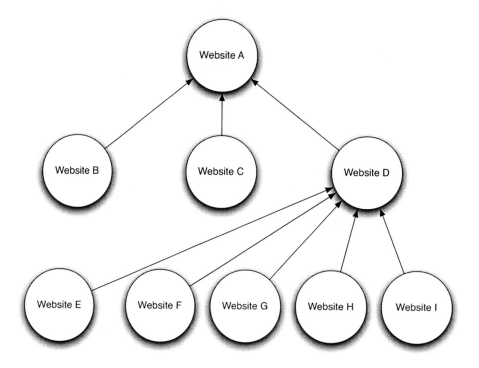

Our website is site A. You can see that we have three inbound links, from sites B, C and D. Site B and C have no links of their own, so they are not highly valued by a search engine. Site D, on the other hand, has five links of its own. As a result, site D is far more valuable as a link to Site A than Site B and Site C.

That is why this recipe shows how many links each inbound link has. The inbound links with the higher number, and therefore more links, are more valuable.

A very useful technique is to run this recipe for a competitor's web site. You will quickly see which links are most valuable to your competitor. You can then investigate getting links from those sites to your site as well.

Listing 11.4 shows this recipe.

Listing 11.4: Scanning for Links (GoogleSearch.cs)

```csharp
using System;
using System.Collections.Generic;
using System.Text;
using Recipe11_1.com.google.api;

namespace Recipe11_1
{
    class GoogleSearch
    {
        /// <summary>
        /// The key that Google provides anyone who uses
        /// their API.
        /// </summary>
        static String key;

        /// <summary>
        /// The search object to use.
        /// </summary>
        static GoogleSearchService search;

        /// <summary>
        /// Perform a Google search and return the results.
        /// Only return 100 results.
        /// </summary>
        /// <param name="query">What to search for.</param>
        /// <returns>The URL's that google returned
        /// for the search.</returns>
        public static List<ResultElement> GetResults(String query)
        {
            List<ResultElement> result =
                new List<ResultElement>();
            int resultCount = 0;
            int top = 0;

            do
            {
                GoogleSearchResult r = search.doGoogleSearch(key,
                    query, top, 10, false, "", false, "",
                  "latin1", "latin1");
```

```csharp
            resultCount = r.resultElements.GetLength(0);

            if (r != null)
            {
                foreach (ResultElement element
                    in r.resultElements)
                {
                    result.Add(element);
                }
            }
            top = top + 10;
            Console.WriteLine("Searching Google: " + top);
        } while ((resultCount >= 10) && (top < 100));

        return result;
    }

    /// <summary>
    /// For the given URL check how many links the URL has.
    /// </summary>
    /// <param name="url">The URL to check.</param>
    /// <returns>The number of links that URL has.</returns>
    public static int getLinkCount(String url)
    {
        int result = 0;

        String query = "link:" + url;
        GoogleSearchResult r = search.doGoogleSearch(key,
            query, 0, 10, false, "", false, "",
                "latin1", "latin1");

        result = r.estimatedTotalResultsCount;
        return result;
    }


    static void Main(string[] args)
    {
        if (args.Length < 2)
        {
            Console.WriteLine(
                "Recipe11_1 [Google Key] [Site to Scan]");
        }
        else
        {
            key = args[0];
```

```
        search = new GoogleSearchService();

        List<ResultElement> c = GetResults("\"" + args[1]
            + "\"");

        foreach (ResultElement element in c)
        {
            StringBuilder str = new StringBuilder();
            str.Append(getLinkCount(element.URL));
            str.Append(":");
            str.Append(element.title);
            str.Append("(");
            str.Append(element.URL);
            str.Append(")");
            Console.WriteLine(str.ToString());
        }
      }
    }
  }
}
```

This recipe should be run with two parameters. The first parameter is the "your Google key", which was obtained from Google. The second parameter is the URL of the site you wish to scan. For example, to scan the HTTP Recipes site, use the following command:

```
Recipe11_1 [Google Key] [URL to Scan]
```

The main method begins by obtaining the key and passing it onto the **GoogleSearch** object.

```
key = args[0];
search = new GoogleSearchService();
```

Next, the URL to be scanned is passed to the **GetResults** function. This function will be discussed in the next section.

```
List<ResultElement> c = GetResults("\"" + args[1]
+ "\"");
```

The **GetResults** function returns a **Collection** of **ResultElement** objects. These objects are displayed.

```
foreach (ResultElement element in c)
{
```

Each element is displayed. For each element the **GetLinkCount** function is called to display the number of links found.

```
    StringBuilder str = new StringBuilder();
    str.Append(getLinkCount(element.URL));
```

```
   str.Append(":");
   str.Append(element.title);
   str.Append(" (");
   str.Append(element.URL);
   str.Append(")");
   Console.WriteLine(str.ToString());
}
```

Each of the elements will be displayed.

Searching Google

In the last section we saw that the **GetResults** function returns a list of pages from the Google search engine. In this section we will see how the **GetResults** functions. It begins by creating a collection of **ResultElement** objects.

```
List<ResultElement> result = new List<ResultElement>();
int resultCount = 0;
int top = 0;
```

Next, the **GetResults** function begins a loop and obtains the search results. Google returns the search results ten items at a time. The search is performed.

```
do
{
  GoogleSearchResult r = search.doGoogleSearch(key,
    query, top, 10, false, "", false, "", "latin1", "latin1");
  resultCount = r.resultElements.GetLength(0);
```

For each search, a **GoogleSearchResult** object is returned. This object is accessed to obtain the **ResultElement** objects, which contain the actual URLs found by the Google search.

```
  if (r != null)
  {
```

Look through and obtain all of the **ResultElement** objects.

```
    top = top + 10;
    Console.WriteLine("Searching Google: " + top);
  } while ((resultCount >= 10) && (top < 100));
```

If fewer than ten items were returned in the search, we have reached the end of the search. When the **GetResults** function completes, we will have a list of all pages that contain a reference to the target web site.

Getting a Link Count

It is also very easy to get a link count from Google. Simply search on the target URL, with the prefix "link:", as seen here:

```
int result = 0;

String query = "link:" + url;
GoogleSearchResult r = search.doGoogleSearch(key,
  query, 0, 10, false, "", false, "", "latin1", "latin1");
```

Next, the search is performed.

```
result = r.estimatedTotalResultsCount;
return result;
```

Now, rather than looping through all the results, as was done in the last section, we simply access the **getEstimatedTotalResultsCount** property to see how many links were found. The number of results found is returned.

Recipe #11.2: Using .NET to Access a SOAP Server

In the previous recipe we accessed the Google Search API. The C# web references can be used to access any web service. The HTTP Recipes site provides a simple web service that will translate any string into Pig Latin. This recipe demonstrates how to access this very simple web service. You can see this recipe in Listing 11.5.

Listing 11.5: Using .NET to Access a SOAP Server (PigLatinTranslate.cs)

```
using System;
using System.Collections.Generic;
using System.Text;


namespace Recipe11_2
{
    class PigLatinTranslate
    {
        static void Main(string[] args)
        {
            Recipe11_2.com.httprecipes.www.PigLatinTranslator
translator
                =
      new Recipe11_2.com.httprecipes.www.PigLatinTranslator();
            Console.WriteLine( translator.translate(
                "Hello World!") );
        }
    }
}
```

The WSDL URL for this web service can be found at the following address:

```
http://www.httprecipes.com/1/11/soap/
```

Once a reference is created for the above WSDL URL it is very easy to use the Pig Latin translator. First a new object is created.

```
Recipe11_2.com.httprecipes.www.PigLatinTranslator translator
                 = new Recipe11_2.com.httprecipes.www.PigLatinT-
ranslator();
```

Next, the translate function is called just like any regular C# object.

```
Console.WriteLine( translator.translate("Hello World!") );
```

The above code will translate "Hello World" into Pig Latin.

Recipe #11.3: A Google Hybrid Bot

It is also possible to create a hybrid bot. A hybrid bot uses both traditional HTML parsing, as discussed in the preceding chapters, as well as web services. The Google Search API is a great choice for hybrid bots. You can use the Google Search API to locate web pages that match your criteria, and then use a traditional HTML bot to scan these sites for what you are looking for.

This recipe will create a bot that will scan sites that contain information about a famous person who you choose. The bot will attempt to obtain the person's birth year. The bot works by calling on Google to find web sites that contain the person's name. The bot then scans the HTML of each of these pages looking for the person's birth year.

This recipe is shown in Listing 11.6.

Listing 11.6: A Google Hybrid Bot (WhenBorn.cs)

```
using System;
using System.Collections.Generic;
using System.Text;
using System.IO;
using System.Net;
using System.Globalization;
using Recipe11_3.com.google.api;

using HeatonResearch.Spider.HTML;

namespace Recipe11_3
{
    class WhenBorn
    {
        /// <summary>
        /// The key that Google provides anyone who uses
        /// their API.
        /// </summary>
```

```
static String key;

/// <summary>
/// The search object to use.
/// </summary>
static GoogleSearchService search;

/// <summary>
/// This map stores a mapping between a year, and how
/// many times that year
/// has come up as a potential birth year.
/// </summary>
private Dictionary<int, int> results =
    new Dictionary<int, int>();


/// <summary>
/// Perform a Google search and return the results.
/// Only return 100 results.
/// </summary>
/// <param name="query">What to search for.</param>
/// <returns>The URL's that google returned
/// for the search.</returns>
public static List<ResultElement> GetResults(String query)
{
    List<ResultElement> result =
          new List<ResultElement>();
    int resultCount = 0;
    int top = 0;

    do
    {
        GoogleSearchResult r = search.doGoogleSearch(
          key, query, top, 10, false, "", false, "",
          "latin1", "latin1");
        resultCount = r.resultElements.GetLength(0);

        if (r != null)
        {
            foreach (ResultElement element
                in r.resultElements)
            {
                result.Add(element);
            }
        }
        top = top + 10;
```

```csharp
            Console.WriteLine("Searching Google: " + top);
        } while ((resultCount >= 10) && (top < 100));

        return result;
    }

    /// <summary>
    /// Examine a sentence and see if it contains
    /// the word born and a number.
    /// </summary>
    /// <param name="sentence">The sentence to search.</param>
    /// <returns>The number that was found.</returns>
    private int ExtractBirth(String sentence)
    {
        bool foundBorn = false;
        Int32 result = -1;
        char[] sep = { ' ' };
        String[] tok = sentence.Split(sep);
        foreach (String word in tok)
        {

            if (String.Compare(word, "born", true) == 0)
                foundBorn = true;
            else
            {
                Int32 temp;
                int.TryParse(word, NumberStyles.Integer,
                    null, out temp);
                if (temp != 0)
                    result = temp;
            }
        }


        if (!foundBorn)
            result = -1;

        return result;
    }


    /// <summary>
    /// Increase the count for the specified year.
    /// </summary>
    /// <param name="year">The year.</param>
    private void IncreaseYear(int year)
```

```
{
    int count;
    if (!results.ContainsKey(year))
    {
        count = 0;
        results.Add(year, count);
    }
    else
        results[year]++;


}



/// <summary>
/// Check the specified URL for a birth year.  This
/// will occur if one sentence is found that has the
/// word born, and a numeric value less than 3000.
/// </summary>
/// <param name="url">The URL to check.</param>
public void CheckURL(Uri url)
{
    int ch;
    StringBuilder sentence = new StringBuilder();

    try
    {
        WebRequest http = HttpWebRequest.Create(url);
        HttpWebResponse response =
          (HttpWebResponse)http.GetResponse();
        Stream istream = response.GetResponseStream();
        ParseHTML html = new ParseHTML(istream);
        do
        {
            ch = html.Read();
            if ((ch != -1) && (ch != 0))
            {
                if (ch == '.')
                {
                    String str = sentence.ToString();
                    int year = ExtractBirth(str);
                    if ((year > 1) && (year < 3000))
                    {
                        Console.WriteLine(
                            "URL supports year: " + year);
                        IncreaseYear(year);
                    }
```

```
                                sentence.Length = 0;
                        }
                        else
                            sentence.Append((char)ch);
                    }
                } while (ch != -1);

            }
            catch (WebException)
            {
            }
            catch (IOException)
            {
            }
        }

        /// <summary>
        /// Get birth year that occurred the largest
        /// number of times.
        /// </summary>
        /// <returns>The birth year that occurred the largest
        /// number of times.</returns>
        public int GetResult()
        {
            int result = -1;
            int maxCount = 0;

            foreach (int year in results.Keys)
            {
                int count = results[year];
                if (count > maxCount)
                {
                    result = year;
                    maxCount = count;
                }
            }

            return result;
        }

        /// <summary>
        /// This method is called to determine the birth
        /// year for a person.  It obtains 100 web pages that
        /// Google returns for that person.  Each of these pages
        /// is then searched for the birth year of that person.
        /// Which ever year is selected the largest number of
```

```csharp
/// times is selected as the birth year.
/// </summary>
/// <param name="name">The name of the person you are
/// seeing the birth year for.</param>
public void Process(String name)
{
    search = new GoogleSearchService();

    Console.WriteLine(
        "Getting search results form Google.");
    List<ResultElement> c = GetResults(name);
    int i = 0;

    Console.WriteLine("Scanning URL's from Google.");
    foreach (ResultElement element in c)
    {
        try
        {
            i++;
            Uri u = new Uri(element.URL);
            Console.WriteLine(
            "Scanning URL: " + i + "/" + c.Count + ":" + u);
            CheckURL(u);
        }
        catch (IOException)
        {

        }
    }

    int resultYear = GetResult();
    if (resultYear == -1)
    {
        Console.WriteLine(
        "Could not determine when " + name + " was born.");
    }
    else
    {
        Console.WriteLine(name +
            " was born in " + resultYear);
    }
}


static void Main(string[] args)
```

```
        {
            if (args.Length < 2)
            {
                Console.WriteLine(
                    "Recipe13_3 [Google Key] [Site to Scan]");
            }
            else
            {
                key = args[0];
                WhenBorn when = new WhenBorn();
                when.Process(args[1]);
            }
        }
    }
}
```

This program completes three phases to obtain the information needed. First, the famous person is presented to Google, to get a list of web sites that contain this person's name. Secondly, each of the search results is scanned for a birth year. These birth years are accumulated in a list. Finally, the program determines which birth year was the most prevalent. This birth year is then assumed to be the birth year of the famous person.

This recipe begins by submitting the name of the famous person to Google. The results are read by calling the **GetResults** function.

```
search = new GoogleSearchService();

Console.WriteLine("Getting search results form Google.");
List<ResultElement> c = GetResults(name);
int i = 0;
```

Next, each of the URLs returned from Google are checked. A try/catch block is used inside the loop to catch errors. This is because some of the URLs returned from Google may no longer be valid. This is not really an issue to the program, such URLs are simply skipped. The loop simply continues to the next iteration.

Each URL that is found is passed to the **CheckURL** method. This method will be covered in a later section.

```
Console.WriteLine("Scanning URL's from Google.");
foreach (ResultElement element in c)
{
  try
  {
    i++;
    Uri u = new Uri(element.URL);
    Console.WriteLine("Scanning URL: " + i + "/" + c.Count + ":" +
u);
```

```
      CheckURL(u);
  }
  catch (IOException)
  {
  }
}
```

Once all of the URLs have been processed, the **GetResult** function is called to deter-mine which birth year is the famous person's actual birth year.

```
int resultYear = GetResult();
if (resultYear == -1)
{
  Console.WriteLine("Could not determine when " + name +
          " was born.");
}
else
{
  Console.WriteLine(name + " was born in " + resultYear);
}
```

The program may not be able to determine the person's birth year. If this is the case, the user is informed.

Searching Google

The first step is to submit the search to Google and get the results back.

```
List<ResultElement> result = new List<ResultElement>();
int resultCount = 0;
int top = 0;
```

The search is submitted.

```
GoogleSearchResult r = search.doGoogleSearch(key,
  query, top, 10, false, "", false, "", "latin1", "latin1");
  resultCount = r.resultElements.GetLength(0);
```

If search results were found, add them to the list and continue. Google returns **ResultElement** objects for each URL found.

```
if (r != null)
{
  foreach (ResultElement element in r.resultElements)
  {
    result.Add(element);
  }
}

top = top + 10;
```

```
Console.WriteLine("Searching Google: " + top);
```

Only look at up to 100 pages.

```
} while ((resultCount >= 10) && (top < 100));
```

```
return result;
```

Finally, the complete list is returned.

Checking a Search Result

Each URL located by Google must be processed. These URLs will be downloaded and parsed into sentences. If a sentence contains both the word "born" and a number that looks like a year then that number is assumed to be a birth year. Numbers between 1 and 3000 are considered as possible years.

The **CheckURL** method begins by creating a **StringBuilder** that will hold each sentence as it is parsed.

```
int ch;
StringBuilder sentence = new StringBuilder();
```

A connection is opened to the URL and a **ParseHTML** object is constructed to parse the HTML found at this site. We are not really interested in the HTML. The main purpose of the parser is to strip the HTML tags away from the text. We are only interested in the text. The **ParseHTML** class was explained in Chapter 6.

```
WebRequest http = HttpWebRequest.Create(url);
HttpWebResponse response = (HttpWebResponse)http.GetResponse();
Stream istream = response.GetResponseStream();
ParseHTML html = new ParseHTML(istream);
```

Next we loop across all of the characters in the HTML file. A value of zero is returned if an HTML tag is encountered. Any HTML tags are ignored.

```
do
{
  ch = html.Read();
  if ((ch != -1) && (ch != 0))
  {
    if (ch == '.')
    {
```

Once we have accumulated a complete sentence, which ends in a period, we check the sentence for the birth year. This is not the most accurate way to break up sentences, but it works well enough for this recipe. If a few sentences run on, or are cut short, it does not significantly affect the final output of the program. This program is attempting to find many birth years and then uses a form of "majority rules" to find the correct one. If a few are lost in the noise, it does not affect the outcome.

If a valid birth year is found, it is recorded and the program continues.

```
String str = sentence.ToString();
int year = ExtractBirth(str);
if ((year > 1) && (year < 3000))
{
  Console.WriteLine("URL supports year: " + year);
  IncreaseYear(year);
}
sentence.Length = 0;
}
else
  sentence.Append((char)ch);
}
} while (ch != -1);
```

This process is continued until the end of the HTML document is reached.

Extracting a Birth Year

Each "sentence" that is found must be scanned for a birth year. To do this, the sentence is broken up into "words", which are defined as groups of characters separated by spaces.

```
bool foundBorn = false;
Int32 result = -1;
char[] sep = { ' ' };
String[] tok = sentence.Split(sep);
foreach (String word in tok)
{
```

First, each word must be checked to see if it is a number. If it is a number, that number is recorded and the program sentence parsing continues. If more than one number is found in a sentence, only the last number is used.

```
if (String.Compare(word, "born", true) == 0)
  foundBorn = true;
else
{
  Int32 temp;
  int.TryParse(word, NumberStyles.Integer, null, out temp);
  if (temp != 0)
    result = temp;
}
```

If the word "born" is found, a boolean variable is set to record that it was found.

```
if (!foundBorn)
  result = -1;
```

```
return result;
```

If a number and the word "born" were both found, the number is returned. We have found a potential birth year. If only one, or neither is found, return a negative one.

Finding the Correct Birth Year

Once the program finishes scanning the URLs identified with a famous person, we are left with a list of potential birth years. The program also tracks how many times each of those potential birth years were located. The **GetResult** function is now called to determine which year had the largest number of "votes".

The function begins by creating two variables. The **result** variable holds the year with the largest count. The second variable, named **maxCount**, holds the number of votes held by the current value of the **result** variable.

```
int result = -1;
int maxCount = 0;
```

Next, a **Set** is created that contains each birth year. Each birth year is checked and at the end, the birth year with the largest count is held in the **result** variable.

```
foreach (int year in results.Keys)
{
  int count = results[year];
  if (count > maxCount)
  {
    result = year;
    maxCount = count;
  }
}
```

```
return result;
```

If no birth years were found, then the result variable stays at negative one. This will indicate to the calling method that no birth year was found.

Summary

HTML was designed primarily for humans to access web sites. If a web site is designed for computers to access, usually XML and web services are used. This chapter showed how to access a variety of web services.

Many web services use Simple Object Access Protocol (SOAP). SOAP is an XML based protocol that specifies how a web service server and client should communicate. Most SOAP web services include a Web Service Definition Language (WSDL) file that provides information to the program on how to access the web service.

The Google Search API is a very commonly used web service. It is based on SOAP, however, Google provides a set of classes you can download and use. The Google Search API allows you to easily construct and submit search requests to the Google search engine.

You can also construct Hybrid bots. A hybrid bot uses both web services and traditional HTML parsing. The Google search API is commonly used to construct hybrid bots. You can submit a search term to Google, then use a traditional HTML bot to scan all of the results returned from Google.

Three recipes were presented in this chapter. The first showed how to use the Google Search API to display information regarding all of the sites linking to a particular site. The second recipe showed how to use the .NET framework to use a web service. The third recipe showed how to create a hybrid bot that used both the Google Search API, as well as a traditional HTML bot.

The next chapter will discuss Real-time Site Syndication (RSS). RSS is an XML format that allows you to keep up with new content on web sites.

Chapter 12: Working with RSS Feeds

- Understanding RSS
- Differences Between RSS 1.0 and RSS 2.0
- Parsing RSS
- Find the RSS Link Tag

RSS feeds are a means by which web sites can communicate links to their newest content. Users interested in particular web sites can instruct their browsers and other software, to follow the RSS feeds from a particular web site. When new content is posted to the feed, the user will be informed about it.

RSS is communicated using the HTTP protocol. The "file format" used for RSS is XML based. Because of these two features, it is easy to add RSS support to a bot. RSS data can be valuable to bots that monitor web sites. In this chapter you will be shown how to access RSS with C#.

RSS is an acronym. It has several meanings, which are spelt out here:

- Really Simple Syndication (RSS 2.0)
- Rich Site Summary (RSS 0.91, RSS 1.0)
- RDF Site Summary (RSS 0.9 and 1.0)

For the end user, all versions of RSS operate similarly. In the next section we will see how users typically use RSS.

Using RSS with a Web Browser

Most modern web browsers include support for RSS. An RSS feed is usually implemented as a sort of dynamic bookmark in most web browsers. Internet Explorer alerts you to the presence of RSS with a simple icon. If you access the following URL, you will see a RSS icon in Internet Explorer.

```
http://www.httprecipes.com/
```

Figure 12.1 shows this icon.

Figure 12.1: A RSS Enabled Site

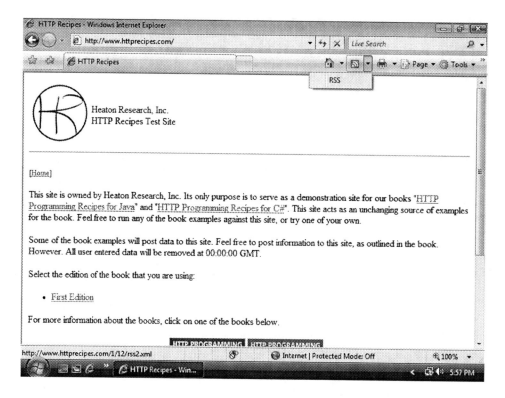

Can you see the RSS icon in Figure 12.1? It looks like several small waves on an orange background. It is found to the far right of the tab bar area.

Clicking this icon will allow you to add the RSS Feed to your browser. Now, whenever you click on the RSS feed icon for that site, you will be shown the new RSS items. Figure 12.2 shows a user access the HTTP Recipes RSS feed.

Figure 12.2: The HTTP Recipes Feed

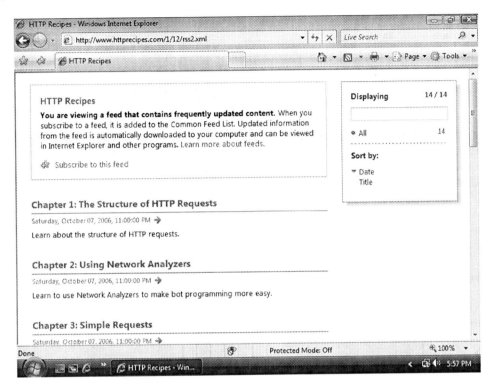

This allows the user to easily keep up with new pages posted to a web site of interest.

RSS Format

RSS follows a specific format. This book will cover the two most common RSS formats:

- RSS 1.0
- RSS 2.0

The next two sections will cover RSS 1.0 and RSS 2.0. A sample will be shown for each format. This sample will contain the same data, so you can easily see the differences between the two formats.

Understanding RSS 1.0

RSS 1.0 allows a web site to publish a list of links to that site's newest content. An RSS 1.0 feed is always accessed directly from a URL. To see a sample RSS 1.0 feed from the HTTP recipes site, access the following URL.

```
http://www.httprecipes.com/1/12/rss1.xml
```

The contents of this URL are shown in Listing 12.1.

Listing 12.1: A RSS 1.0 File

```xml
<?xml version="1.0"?>

<rdf:RDF
 xmlns:rdf="http://www.w3.org/1999/02/22-rdf-syntax-ns#"
 xmlns="http://purl.org/rss/1.0/">

 <channel rdf:about="http://www.httprecipes.com/1/12/rss1.xml">
   <title>HTTP Recipes</title>
   <link>http://www.httprecipes.com/</link>
   <description>
     A collection of HTTP programming recipes.
   </description>

 </channel>

 <item rdf:about="http://www.httprecipes.com/1/1/">
   <title>Chapter 1: The Structure of HTTP Requests</title>
   <link>http://www.httprecipes.com/1/1/</link>
   <description>
    Learn about the structure of HTTP requests.
   </description>
 </item>

 <item rdf:about="http://www.httprecipes.com/1/2/">
   <title>Chapter 2: Using Network Analyzers</title>
   <link>http://www.httprecipes.com/1/2/</link>
   <description>
    Learn to use Network Analyzers to make bot programming
    more easy.
   </description>
 </item>
 <item rdf:about="http://www.httprecipes.com/1/3/">

   <title>Chapter 3: Simple Requests</title>
   <link>http://www.httprecipes.com/1/3/</link>
   <description>
    Learn to construct simple HTTP requests in Java.
   </description>
 </item>


... Chapters 4-13 continue here ...
```

```
<item rdf:about="http://www.httprecipes.com/1/14/">
  <title>Chapter 14: Well Behaved Spiders and Bots</title>
  <link>http://www.httprecipes.com/1/14/</link>
  <description>
   Learn create bots that are well behaved.
  </description>

</item>

</rdf:RDF>
```

The file begins with some header information about the feed. The **<title>** tag specifies the title of the RSS feed. The **<link>** tag specifies the location of the site producing the RSS feed. The **<description>** tag gives a description of the feed.

There are also several **<item>** tags. These are the individual items, or articles, about which the feed provides information. Inside the **<item>** tag you will find several other tags defining this item. The **<title>** tag gives the name of this item. The **<link>** tag gives a link to this item, which is a URL. The **<description>** tag provides a description of this item.

Understanding RSS 2.0

RSS 2.0, like RSS 1.0, allows a web site to publish a list of links to that site's newest content. Like RSS 1.0, a RSS 2.0 feed is always accessed directly from a URL. To see a sample RSS 2.0 feed from the HTTP recipes site, access the following URL.

http://www.httprecipes.com/1/12/rss2.xml

The contents of this URL are shown in Listing 12.2.

Listing 12.2: A RSS 2.0 File

```
<?xml version="1.0"?>
<rss version="2.0">
  <channel>
    <title>HTTP Recipes</title>
    <link>http://www.httprecipes.com/</link>
    <description>A collection of HTTP programming recipes.
</description>
    <language>en-us</language>
    <pubDate>Sun, 8 Oct 2006 04:00:00 GMT</pubDate>

    <docs>http://blogs.law.harvard.edu/tech/rss</docs>

    <item>
```

```
        <title>Chapter 1: The Structure of HTTP Requests</title>
        <pubDate>Sun, 8 Oct 2006 04:00:00 GMT</pubDate>
        <link>http://www.httprecipes.com/1/1/</link>
        <description>

        Learn about the structure of HTTP requests.
        </description>
    </item>
    <item>
        <title>Chapter 2: Using Network Analyzers</title>
        <pubDate>Sun, 8 Oct 2006 04:00:00 GMT</pubDate>
        <link>http://www.httprecipes.com/1/2/</link>
        <description>

        Learn to use Network Analyzers to make bot programming
        more easy.
        </description>
    </item>
    <item>
        <title>Chapter 3: Simple Requests</title>
        <pubDate>Sun, 8 Oct 2006 04:00:00 GMT</pubDate>
        <link>http://www.httprecipes.com/1/3/</link>
        <description>

        Learn to construct simple HTTP requests in Java.
        </description>
    </item>


... Chapters 4-13 continue here ...


    <item>
        <title>Chapter 14: Well Behaved Spiders and Bots</title>
        <pubDate>Sun, 8 Oct 2006 04:00:00 GMT</pubDate>
        <link>http://www.httprecipes.com/1/14/</link>
        <description>

        Learn create bots that are well behaved.
        </description>
    </item>

  </channel>
</rss>
```

The main difference between the RSS 2.0 and RSS 1.0 formats that we will need to understand is the placement of the **<item>** elements. RSS 2.0 places the **<item>** elements inside the **<channel>** element. RSS 1.0 places the **<item>** elements at the same level as the **<channel>** element.

Additionally, RSS 1.0 **<item>** elements do not contain a **<pubDate>** element. However, RSS 2.0 includes a **<pubDate>** element. The **<pubDate>** element contains the date that the article or channel was last updated. RSS stores dates in the following format:

```
Sun, 8 Oct 2006 04:00:00 GMT
```

To work with RSS in C#, this date will need to be converted to a C# **Date** object.

Parsing RSS Files

In this section we will develop a package of classes that can parse RSS data. This package will be used by the RSS recipes presented in this chapter. There will be only two classes in this relatively simple package. These classes are:

- RSS
- RSSItem

The **RSS** class is the main entry point for this package. Using the RSS class you will be able to parse RSS data. The **RSSItem** class holds data about individual RSS items, or articles, found when parsing the RSS feed. In the next two sections we will examine each of these classes.

This RSS parser is designed to work with either RSS 1.0 or RSS 2.0 feeds. The program automatically adapts to each type of feed.

The RSS Class

The **RSS** class is the main class of the RSS parsing package. The RSS class is the class that you will instruct to parse **RSS**. Additionally, the **RSS** class is the class that you will use to navigate the RSS data that was retrieved. The **RSS** class is shown in Listing 12.3.

Listing 12.3: The RSS Class (RSS.cs)

```csharp
using System;
using System.Collections.Generic;
using System.Text;
using System.Xml;
using System.Net;
using System.IO;

namespace HeatonResearch.Spider.RSS
{
    /// <summary>
```

```csharp
/// RSS: This is the class that actually parses the
/// RSS and builds a collection of RSSItems.  To make use
/// of this class call the load method with a URL that
/// points to RSS.
/// </summary>
public class RSS
{
    /// <summary>
    /// All of the attributes for this RSS document.
    /// </summary>
    public Dictionary<String, String> Attributes
    {
        get
        {
            return attributes;
        }
    }

    /// <summary>
    /// All RSS items, or stories, found.
    /// </summary>
    public List<RSSItem> Items
    {
        get
        {
            return items;
        }
    }

    /// <summary>
    /// All of the attributes for this RSS document.
    /// </summary>
    private Dictionary<String, String> attributes =
      new Dictionary<String, String>();

    /// <summary>
    /// All RSS items, or stories, found.
    /// </summary>
    private List<RSSItem> items = new List<RSSItem>();

    /// <summary>
    /// Simple utility function that converts a RSS
    /// formatted date
    /// into a C# date.
    /// </summary>
    /// <param name="datestr">A date</param>
```

```
/// <returns>A C# DateTime object.</returns>
public static DateTime ParseDate(String datestr)
{
    DateTime date = DateTime.Parse(datestr);
    return date;
}


/// <summary>
/// Load the specified RSS item, or story.
/// </summary>
/// <param name="item">A XML node that contains a
/// RSS item.</param>
private void LoadItem(XmlNode item)
{
    RSSItem rssItem = new RSSItem();
    rssItem.Load(item);
    items.Add(rssItem);
}


/// <summary>
/// Load the channle node.
/// </summary>
/// <param name="channel">A node that contains a
/// channel.</param>
private void LoadChannel(XmlNode channel)
{

    foreach (XmlNode node in channel.ChildNodes)
    {
        String nodename = node.Name;
        if (String.Compare(nodename, "item", true) == 0)
        {
            LoadItem(node);
        }
        else
        {
            attributes.Remove(nodename);
            attributes.Add(nodename, channel.InnerText);
        }
    }
}


/// <summary>
/// Load all RSS data from the specified URL.
/// </summary>
/// <param name="url">URL that contains XML data.</param>
```

```csharp
public void Load(Uri url)
{
    WebRequest http = HttpWebRequest.Create(url);
    HttpWebResponse response =
            (HttpWebResponse)http.GetResponse();
    Stream istream = response.GetResponseStream();

    XmlDocument d = new XmlDocument();
    d.Load(istream);

    foreach (XmlNode node in d.DocumentElement.ChildNodes)
    {

        String nodename = node.Name;

        // RSS 2.0
        if (String.Compare(nodename, "channel", true)
                == 0)
        {
            LoadChannel(node);
        }
        // RSS 1.0
        else if (String.Compare(nodename, "item", true)
                == 0)
        {
            LoadItem(node);
        }
    }

}

/// <summary>
/// Convert the object to a String.
/// </summary>
/// <returns>The object as a String.</returns>
public override String ToString()
{
    StringBuilder str = new StringBuilder();

    foreach (String item in attributes.Keys)
    {
        str.Append(item);
        str.Append('=');
        str.Append(attributes[item]);
        str.Append('\n');
    }
```

```
        str.Append("Items:\n");
        foreach (RSSItem item in items)
        {
            str.Append(item.ToString());
            str.Append('\n');
        }
        return str.ToString();
    }
  }
}
```

It is very easy to use the **RSS** class. Simply call the **Load** method, and pass a **Uri** that contains RSS data. Once you have loaded the RSS data, you can use the **Attributes** property of the RSS class to access any attributes of the **<channel>** element. Additionally, you can use the **Items** property to access any **RSSItems** that were parsed.

This chapter includes two recipes that demonstrate exactly how to use the **RSS** class to parse RSS data. In the following sections you will see how the RSS parsing class was constructed.

Loading the RSS File

Calling the **Load** method of the **RSS** class will load RSS data at the specified URL. The first thing that the **Load** method does is to open a connection and obtain a **Stream** to the URL that contains the RSS data.

```
WebRequest http = HttpWebRequest.Create(url);
HttpWebResponse response = (HttpWebResponse)http.GetResponse();
Stream istream = response.GetResponseStream();
```

Next the DOM is setup to parse the XML data from the **Stream**.

```
XmlDocument d = new XmlDocument();
d.Load(istream);
```

We will iterate over all of the top-level document elements of the RSS data.

```
foreach (XmlNode node in d.DocumentElement.ChildNodes)
{
  String nodename = node.Name;
```

Once we find the **<channel>** element, the **LoadChannel** method is called to load the channel data.

```
  // RSS 2.0
  if (String.Compare(nodename, "channel", true) == 0)
  {
    LoadChannel(node);
  }
```

If this is an RSS 1.0 feed, there will be **<item>** elements at the top level. If any item tags are encountered, then we call **LoadItem** to process them.

```
// RSS 1.0
else if (String.Compare(nodename, "item", true) == 0)
{
  LoadItem(node);
}
}
```

This process continues until all top level elements have been processed.

Loading the Channel

The **LoadChannel** method is called to load a **<channel>** element. This method begins by looping across all of the child elements of the **<channel>** element.

```
foreach (XmlNode node in channel.ChildNodes)
{
```

Once a child node is located we examine the name of that node.

```
String nodename = node.Name;
```

If this is an **<item>** element, then we call **LoadItem** to load that item.

```
if (String.Compare(nodename, "item", true) == 0)
{
  LoadItem(node);
}
```

Otherwise, we add the item to the **attributes** collection.

```
else
{
  attributes.Remove(nodename);
  attributes.Add(nodename, channel.InnerText);
}
```

The **attributes** collection stores all of the attributes that were loaded with the **<channel>** element.

The RSSItem Class

The **RSSItem** class is the class that holds individual RSS items, or articles. The **RSSItem** class holds all of the attributes that were parsed from each of the **<item>** elements in the RSS feed. The **RSSItem** class is shown in Listing 12.4.

Listing 12.4: The RSSItem Class (RSSItem.cs)

```csharp
using System;
using System.Collections.Generic;
using System.Text;
using System.Xml;

namespace HeatonResearch.Spider.RSS
{
    /// <summary>
    /// RSSItem: This is the class that holds individual RSS
    /// RSS items, or stories, for the RSS class.
    /// </summary>
    public class RSSItem
    {
        /// <summary>
        /// The title of this item.
        /// </summary>
        public String Title
        {
            get
            {
                return title;
            }
            set
            {
                title = value;
            }
        }

        /// <summary>
        /// The hyperlink to this item.
        /// </summary>
        public String Link
        {
            get
            {
                return link;
            }
            set
            {
                link = value;
            }
        }
```

```csharp
/// <summary>
/// The description of this item.
/// </summary>
public String Description
{
    get
    {
        return description;
    }
    set
    {
        description = value;
    }
}

/// <summary>
/// The date this item was published.
/// </summary>
public DateTime Date
{
    get
    {
        return date;
    }
    set
    {
        date = value;
    }
}

/// <summary>
/// The title of this item.
/// </summary>
private String title;

/// <summary>
/// The hyperlink to this item.
/// </summary>
private String link;

/// <summary>
/// The description of this item.
/// </summary>
private String description;
```

```
/// <summary>
/// The date this item was published.
/// </summary>
private DateTime date;


/// <summary>
/// Load an item from the specified node.
/// </summary>
/// <param name="node">The Node to load the item
/// from.</param>
public void Load(XmlNode node)
{

    foreach(XmlNode n in node.ChildNodes )
    {
        String name = n.Name;

        if (String.Compare(name, "title", true) == 0)
            title = n.InnerText;
        else if (String.Compare(name, "link", true) == 0)
            link = n.InnerText;
        else if (String.Compare(name, "description", true)
           == 0)
            description = n.InnerText;
        else if (String.Compare(name, "pubDate", true)
          == 0)
        {
            String str = n.InnerText;
            if (str != null)
                date = RSS.ParseDate(str);
        }

    }
}


/// <summary>
/// Convert the object to a String.
/// </summary>
/// <returns>The object as a String.</returns>
public override String ToString()
{
    StringBuilder builder = new StringBuilder();
    builder.Append('[');
    builder.Append("title=\"");
```

```
            builder.Append(title);
            builder.Append("\",link=\"");
            builder.Append(link);
            builder.Append("\",date=\"");
            builder.Append(date);
            builder.Append("\"]");
            return builder.ToString();
        }
    }
}
```

The **RSSItem** class holds all of the attributes that are parsed from individual **<item>** elements. These attributes, which can be accessed using getters, are:

- title
- description
- link
- date

The **RSSItem** class includes a method, named **Load**, which loads the item from an **<item>** element. This method begins by looping through all of the child elements of the **<item>** element.

```
foreach(XmlNode n in node.ChildNodes )
{
  String name = n.Name;
```

Each of the elements are checked to see if it is a **<title>**, **<description>**, **<link>** or **<date>** element. If the element is one of these, then the value of that element is copied into the correct property.

```
if (String.Compare(name, "title", true) == 0)
  title = n.InnerText;
else if (String.Compare(name, "link", true) == 0)
  link = n.InnerText;
else if (String.Compare(name, "description", true) == 0)
  description = n.InnerText;
else if (String.Compare(name, "pubDate", true) == 0)
{
```

If the element is a date, the date is parsed.

```
  String str = n.InnerText;
  if (str != null)
    date = RSS.ParseDate(str);
}
```

This continues until all child elements of the **<item>** element have been processed.

Recipes

This chapter includes two recipes. These recipes demonstrate how to parse RSS feeds. In particular, you will learn how to perform the following techniques:

- Parse a RSS Feed
- Find a RSS Feed from a Link Tag

These recipes will show you how a bot can be adapted to work with RSS feeds. The first recipe demonstrates how to display an RSS feed.

Recipe #12.1: Display an RSS Feed

This recipe demonstrates how to open an RSS feed and parse it. This recipe works with either a RSS 1.0 or RSS 2.0 feed. It relies on the RSS parser, which was constructed earlier in this chapter. This recipe is shown in Listing 12.5.

Listing 12.5: Display an RSS Feed (LoadRSS.cs)

```
using System;
using System.Collections.Generic;
using System.Text;
using HeatonResearch.Spider.RSS;

namespace Recipe12_1
{
    class LoadRSS
    {
        /// <summary>
        /// Display an RSS feed.
        /// </summary>
        /// <param name="url">The URL of the RSS feed.</param>
        public void Process(Uri url)
        {
            RSS rss = new RSS();
            rss.Load(url);
            Console.WriteLine(rss.ToString());
        }

        static void Main(string[] args)
        {
            Uri url;

            if (args.Length != 0)
                url = new Uri(args[0]);
            else
                url = new Uri(
            "http://www.httprecipes.com/1/12/rss1.xml");
```

```
                    LoadRSS load = new LoadRSS();
                    load.Process(url);
                }
            }
        }
```

This recipe is very simple. It begins by creating a new **RSS** object. The **RSS** class was constructed earlier in this chapter.

```
RSS rss = new RSS();
```

Next the **load** method is called to load a RSS feed.

```
rss.Load(url);
```

Finally, the RSS feed is displayed by calling the RSS object's **ToString** function.

```
Console.WriteLine(rss.ToString());
```

If you wanted to access the RSS items directly, you can easily use the **Items** property to obtain a list of **RSSItem** objects.

Recipe #12.2: Find an RSS Feed

Many web sites contain a special **<link>** tag that shows you where the RSS feed for that site resides. By parsing for this **<link>** tag you can easily obtain the RSS feed for a web site. The HTTP Recipes site contains such a tag. If you examine the source, at the following URL, you will see this tag.

http://www.httprecipes.com/

The above URL contains the following **<link>** tag.

```
<link rel="alternate"
type="application/rss+xml"
href="http://www.httprecipes.com/1/12/rss2.xml">
```

The **href** attribute of this tag tells us that we can find the RSS feed for the HTTP Recipes site at the following URL.

http://www.httprecipes.com/1/12/rss2.xml

This recipe explains how to access the HTTP Recipes site, find the **<link>** tag for the RSS Feed, and then download the RSS feed. This recipe is shown in Listing 12.6.

Listing 12.6: Find an RSS Feed (FindRSS.cs)

```
using System;
using System.Collections.Generic;
```

```
using System.Text;
using System.IO;
using System.Net;
using HeatonResearch.Spider.RSS;
using HeatonResearch.Spider.HTML;


namespace Recipe12_2
{
    class FindRSS
    {

        /// <summary>
        /// Display an RSS feed.
        /// </summary>
        /// <param name="url">The URL of the RSS feed.</param>
        public void ProcessRSS(Uri url)
        {
            RSS rss = new RSS();
            rss.Load(url);
            Console.WriteLine(rss.ToString());
        }

        /// <summary>
        /// This method looks for a link tag at the
        /// specified URL.  If a link
        /// tag is found that specifies an RSS feed, then
        /// that feed is displayed.
        /// </summary>
        /// <param name="url">The URL of the web site.</param>
        public void Process(Uri url)
        {
            String href = null;
            WebRequest http = HttpWebRequest.Create(url);
            http.Timeout = 30000;
            WebResponse response = http.GetResponse();
            Stream stream = response.GetResponseStream();
            ParseHTML parse = new ParseHTML(stream);

            int ch;
            do
            {
                ch = parse.Read();
                if (ch == 0)
                {
                    HTMLTag tag = parse.Tag;
                    if (String.Compare(tag.Name, "link", true)
```

```
                              == 0)
                    {
                        String type = tag["type"];
                        if (type != null && type.IndexOf("rss")
                              != -1)
                        {
                            href = tag["href"];
                        }
                    }
                }
            } while (ch != -1);

            if (href == null)
            {
                Console.WriteLine("No RSS link found.");
            }
            else
                ProcessRSS(new Uri(href));
        }

        static void Main(string[] args)
        {

            Uri url;

            if (args.Length != 0)
                url = new Uri(args[0]);
            else
                url = new Uri("http://www.httprecipes.com/");

            FindRSS load = new FindRSS();
            load.Process(url);
        }
    }
}
```

This recipe begins by opening a connection to the web site that we will scan for a URL. A **ParseHTML** object is setup to parse the HTML. The **ParseHTML** class was discussed in Chapter 6.

```
String href = null;
WebRequest http = HttpWebRequest.Create(url);
http.Timeout = 30000;
WebResponse response = http.GetResponse();
Stream stream = response.GetResponseStream();
ParseHTML parse = new ParseHTML(stream);
```

```
int ch;
```

The program will look through all of the tags in the document, ignoring the text between HTML tags. Because this program is only looking for a **<link>** tag, the actual text does not matter.

```
do
{
  ch = parse.Read();
  if (ch == 0)
  {
    HTMLTag tag = parse.Tag;
```

Once a **<link>** tag is found, check to see if its **type** attribute specifies RSS. If this is the type tag, then we store the **<link>** tag's **href** attribute into a variable also named **href**.

```
if (String.Compare(tag.Name, "link", true) == 0)
{
  String type = tag["type"];
  if (type != null && type.IndexOf("rss") != -1)
  {
    href = tag["href"];
  }
}
```

This process continues until the end of the HTML document is reached.

```
} while (ch != -1);
```

If no RSS tag was found, then we inform the user.

```
if (href == null)
{
  Console.WriteLine("No RSS link found.");
}
else
  ProcessRSS(new Uri(href));
```

Once the link has been found, call the **ProcessRSS** method to display the RSS feed. The **ProcessRSS** method works the same as the process method from Recipe 12.1.

Summary

This chapter showed how to create C# applications that can work with RSS. RSS is a very simple way of keeping up with new content on web sites. Using RSS your bot can quickly query a web site and discover which new documents are available.

There are two major versions of RSS. RSS 1.0 and RSS 2.0. Though these formats are similar, there are some important differences. This chapter showed how to construct an RSS parser class that is capable of parsing either type of RSS feed.

RSS feeds return a list of new articles on the web site, as well as hyperlinks to the original article. Because of this, bots can easily use RSS to get a listing of URLs on a web site containing new content. Some web sites also include a `<link>` tag that specifies the location of the site's RSS feed. By looking for this tag your bot can automatically locate the RSS feed for most web sites.

This chapter included two recipes. The first recipe simply displays the contents of a RSS feed from a web site. The second recipe scans a web site, looking for a RSS `<link>` tag. Once the site's RSS feed is located, it is displayed.

The next chapter will show how to construct a spider. A spider is a program that crawls a web site. Spiders can be used to download the contents of web site, or scan a site for specific information.

CHAPTER 13: USING A SPIDER

- Understanding when to Use a Spider
- Introducing the Heaton Research Spider
- Using Thread Pools
- Using Memory to Track URLs
- Using SQL to Track URLs
- Spidering Many Web Sites

A spider is a special type of bot designed to crawl the World Wide Web, just like a biological spider crawls its web. While bots are usually designed to work with one specific site, spiders are usually designed to work with a vast number of web sites.

A spider always starts on a single page. This page is scanned for links. Any links to other pages, are stored in a list. The spider will then visit the next URL on the list and scan for links again. This process continues endlessly as the spider finds new pages.

Usually some restriction is placed on the spider to limit what pages it will visit. If no restrictions were placed on the spider, it would theoretically visit every single page on the Internet.

Most of the recipes in this book have been fairly self-contained, usually requiring only a class or two to function. This presents the reader with an efficient solution and a minimum of overhead. This strategy does not work so well with a spider. To create an effective spider there are many considerations, including:

- Thread pooling and synchronization
- Storing a very large URL list
- HTML parsing
- Working with a SQL database
- Reporting results

These considerations do not lend themselves to a concise example. This book will show you how to use the "Heaton Research Spider". The Heaton Research Spider is an ever-evolving open source spider produced by the publisher of this book. The Heaton Research Spider is also available in C#, as well as Java. The Heaton Research Spider can be obtained from the following URL:

```
http://www.heatonresearch.com/spider/
```

This book uses v1.0 of the Heaton Research Spider. New releases will likely be available after the publication of this book. Version 1.0 of the spider is included with the companion download of this book. Adapting to later versions of the spider should be relatively easy as backwards compatibility is a very important design consideration for the spider.

The Heaton Research Spider is not an immense project. The spider seeks to be as capable as possible, without including in a great deal of overhead. In addition to proving four recipes that use the spider, this chapter will also take you through every aspect of the spider's construction. The next section will show you how to use the spider.

Using the Heaton Research Spider

In this section you will learn to use the Heaton Research Spider. The Heaton Research Spider can be configured to perform a wide variety of tasks. There are three primary steps to using the Heaton Research Spider:

- Configure the spider
- Provide a class for the spider to report its findings to
- Start the spider

In the following sections you will learn to use the Heaton Research Spider.

Configuring the Spider

You will now be shown how to configure the Heaton Research Spider. The Heaton Research Spider is easy to configure. There are two ways to do this:

- Configuring Programmatically
- Configuring with a File

Each of these methods will be discussed in the next two sections.

Configuring the Spider Directly

To configure the Heaton Research Spider, use the **SpiderOptions** class. The **SpiderOptions** class contains several properties, implemented as public members. We chose to use public members to allow the class to be quickly loaded from a file using C# reflection. These properties are shown in Table 13.1.

Table 13.1: Spider Configuration Options

Configuration Option	Purpose
Timeout	How long to wait for a connection/read (in milliseconds).
MaxDepth	How deep to search for links (1 for homepage only, -1 infinite depth).
UserAgent	What user agent to report, blank to report the C# user agent.
DbConnectionString	The OLEDB connection string of a database to use (only needed if using a SQL workload).
WorkloadManager	The full class name of a workload manager to use.
Startup	What to do on startup. Specify "clear" to clear the workload or "resume" to resume processing.
Filter	The full class path of a filter class. More than one filter can be specified.

The **Timeout** value allows you to define the amount of time, in milliseconds that you will wait for a page to load.

The **UserAgent** property allows you to specify the User-Agent header that the spider will report when accessing web sites. It is usually a good idea to create a specific user agent for your spider so that it can be identified. If you set this value to **null**, then the default C# user agent will be used.

The **DbURL** and **DbClass** properties allow you to define an ADO database. For more information on what to set these values to, refer to the section "Configuring a SQL Workload", later in this chapter.

The **WorkloadManager** property allows you to specify what sort of a workload manager should handle the URL list. To specify an in-memory workload manager, use the following option:

```
HeatonResearch.Spider.Workload.Memory.MemoryWorkloadManager
```

To specify a SQL based workload manager, use the following option:

```
HeatonResearch.Spider.Workload.SQL.SQLWorkloadManager
```

If you are going to use a SQL workload manager, you must also specify **DbURL** and **DbClass**. Additionally, you must create a database that has the required tables. This is covered in the later section "Configuring a SQL Workload". There are no options that need to be specified for a memory workload.

A memory workload is much more simple to setup than an SQL workload. However, a memory workload can only hold so many URLs. The memory workload manager is only capable of spidering a single host. If you would like to spider multiple hosts or very large hosts, use an SQL workload manager.

There are two values you can specify for the **Startup** property. First, if you specify the value of **clear**, the entire workload will be erased, and the spider will start over. Secondly, if you specify the value of **resume**, the spider will resume where it left off from the last run.

The **Filter** property allows you to specify one or more filters to use. You should always make sure you use at least the **RobotsFilter**. This filter ensures that your bot complies with the "Bot Exclusion Standard". The Bot Exclusion Standard will be covered in Chapter 14.

The following code shows how you might initialize a **SpiderOptions** object.

```
SpiderOptions options = new SpiderOptions();

options.Timeout = 60000;
options.MaxDepth = -1;
options.UserAgent = null;
options.DbConnectionString = "Provider=Microsoft.Jet.
OLEDB.4.0;Data Source=c:\spider.mdb"
options.WorkloadManager = "HeatonResearch.Spider.Workload.SQL.SQL-
WorkloadManager";
options.Startup = "clear";
options.Filter.Add("HeatonResearch.Spider.Filter.RobotsFilter");
```

You can also configure the spider using a configuration file. This is discussed in the next section.

Configuring with a Configuration File

It is often more convenient to use a configuration file than directly setting the values of the **SpiderOptions**. To use a configuration file, create a text file that contains a single line for each configuration option. Each configuration option is a name-value pair. A colon separates the name and value (:). The name corresponds to the property names in the **SpiderOptions** class. See Table 13.1 for a complete list of configuration options.

A sample configuration file is shown in Listing 13.1.

Listing 13.1: A Configuration file for the Spider (spider.conf)

```
timeout:     60000
maxDepth:    -1
userAgent:
```

```
dbConnectionString: Provider=Microsoft.Jet.OLEDB.4.0;Data
Source=c:\spider.mdb
workloadManager:HeatonResearch.Spider.Workload.SQL.
SQLWorkloadManager
```

```
startup:      clear
filter:                 HeatonResearch.Spider.Filter.RobotsFilter
```

Once the configuration file is setup, it is relatively easy to tell the spider to make use of it. Simply call the load method on the **SpiderOptions** object. The following demonstrates this:

```
SimpleReport report = new SimpleReport();
SpiderOptions options = new SpiderOptions();
options.Load("c:\\spider.conf");
Spider spider = new Spider(options,report);
```

Once the **SpiderOptions** object has been loaded, it is passed to the spider's constructor. You will notice that a report variable is passed to the spider. The spider uses this object to report its findings. It will be discussed later in this chapter.

Setting up the Database

If you are going to use the **SQLWorkloadManager**, you will have to prepare a database for use with the workload manager. The **SQLWorkloadManager** requires that two tables be present in the database. They are:

- spider_host
- spider_workload

There can be tables other than these two, the spider will simply ignore them.

The **spider_host** table keeps a list of hosts that the spider has encountered. The fields contained in the **spider_host** table are summarized in Table 13.2.

Table 13.2: The spider_host Table

Field Name	SQL Type	Purpose
host_id	int(10)	The primary key for the table.
host	varchar(255)	The host name (i.e. www.httprecipes.com).
status	varchar(1)	The status of the host.
urls_done	int(11)	The number of URLs successfully processed for this host.
urls_error	int(11)	The number of URLs that resulted in an error, for this host.

The **spider_workload** table contains a complete list of every URL that the spider has encountered. The fields contained in the **spider_workload** table are summarized in Table 13.3.

Table 13.3: the spider_workload Table

Field Name	SQL Type	Purpose
workload_id	int(10)	The primary key for this table.
host	int(10)	The host id this URL corresponds to.
url	varchar(2083)	The URL used for this workload element.
status	varchar(1)	This status of this workload element.
depth	int(10)	The depth of this URL.
url_hash	int(11)	A hash code that allows the URL to be looked up quickly.
source_id	int(11)	The ID of the URL where this URL was found.

Both of the tables can be created using data definition language (DDL) scripts. The DDL script for Microsoft Access is shown in Listing 13.2.

Listing 13.2: Example CREATE TABLE DDL for Microsoft Access

```
CREATE TABLE [spider_host] (
  [host_id] counter  NOT NULL,
  [host] varchar(255) NOT NULL,
  [status] varchar(1) NOT NULL,
  [urls_done] int NOT NULL,
  [urls_error] int NOT NULL,
  PRIMARY KEY  ([host_id]),
  CONSTRAINT `host` UNIQUE  (`host`)
);

CREATE TABLE [spider_workload] (
  [workload_id] counter NOT NULL,
  [host] integer  NOT NULL,
  [url] varchar(255) NOT NULL,
  [status] varchar(1) NOT NULL,
  [depth] integer NOT NULL,
  [url_hash] integer NOT NULL,
  [source_id] integer NOT NULL,
  PRIMARY KEY  ([workload_id])
);

create index idx_status on spider_workload (status);
```

```
create index idx_url_hash on spider_workload (url_hash);
```

There is a status field contained in both tables. The status field contains a single character that specifies the status of either the host or workload entry. These status codes are summarized in Table 13.4.

Table 13.4: Spider Statuses

Status Code	Purpose
D	Processed successfully.
E	Error while processing.
P	Currently processing.
W	Waiting to be processed.

For more information on setting up your database, including examples for databases other than Microsoft Access, refer to Appendix D.

How the Spider Reports its Findings

The spider uses the **SpiderReportable** interface to report its findings. For each spider you create, you should create your own class that implements the **SpiderReportable** interface. The **SpiderReportable** interface is shown in Listing 13.3.

Listing 13.3: The SpiderReportable Interface (SpiderReportable.cs)

```csharp
using System;
using System.Collections.Generic;
using System.Text;
using System.IO;

namespace HeatonResearch.Spider
{
    /// <summary>
    /// The SpiderReportable interface defines how the spider
    /// reports its findings to an outside class.
    /// </summary>
    public interface SpiderReportable
    {
        /// <summary>
        /// This function is called when the spider is ready to
        /// process a new host.
        /// </summary>
        /// <param name="host">The new host that is about
```

```
/// to be processed.</param>
/// <returns>True if this host should be processed,
/// false otherwise.</returns>
bool BeginHost(String host);

/// <summary>
/// Called when the spider is starting up. This method
/// provides the SpiderReportable class with the spider
/// object.
/// </summary>
/// <param name="spider">The spider that will be
/// working with this object.</param>
void Init(Spider spider);

/// <summary>
/// Called when the spider encounters a URL.
/// </summary>
/// <param name="url">The URL that the spider found.
/// </param>
/// <param name="source">The page that the URL was found
/// on.</param>
/// <param name="type">The type of link this URL is.
/// </param>
/// <returns>True if the spider should scan for links
/// on this page.</returns>
bool SpiderFoundURL(Uri url, Uri source,
    Spider.URLType type);

/// <summary>
/// Called when the spider is about to process a NON-HTML
/// URL.
/// </summary>
/// <param name="url">The URL that the spider found.
/// </param>
/// <param name="stream">An InputStream to read the
/// page contents from.</param>
void SpiderProcessURL(Uri url, Stream stream);

/// <summary>
/// Called when the spider is ready to process an HTML
/// URL.
/// </summary>
/// <param name="url">The URL that the spider is
/// about to process.</param>
/// <param name="parse">An object that will allow
/// you you to parse the
```

```
/// HTML on this page.</param>
void SpiderProcessURL(Uri url, SpiderParseHTML parse);

/// <summary>
/// Called when the spider tries to process a URL
/// but gets an error.
/// </summary>
/// <param name="url">The URL that generated an
/// error.</param>
void SpiderURLError(Uri url);
    }
}
```

Any class that implements this interface must provide implementations for each of the methods and functions contained in the above listing. These methods and function are summarized in Table 13.5.

Table 13.5: Functions and Methods of the SpiderReportable Interface

Name	Purpose
BeginHost	Called when the spider begins processing a new host.
Init	Called to setup the object.. The object is provided with a reference to the spider at this point.
SpiderFoundURL	Called when the spider finds a URL. Return true if links from this URL should be processed.
SpiderProcessURL (HTML)	Called when the spider encounters an HTML page, a SpiderHTMLParse object is provided to parse the HTML.
SpiderProcesURL (binary)	Called to download a binary page, such as an image, an InputStream is provided to download the page.
SpiderURLError	Called when a URL results in an error while loading.

By providing a class that implements the **SpiderReportable** interface, you are able to process all of the data the spider finds. This is how you really define what sort of a spider you are creating. The recipes section of this chapter will demonstrate several **SpiderReportable** implementations.

Starting the Spider

Now that you have seen now to configure and setup the spider you are ready to see how to actually start the spider. The spider can be started with the following lines of code:

```
Uri base = new Uri("http://www.httprecipes.com/");
SimpleReport report = new SimpleReport();
SpiderOptions options = new SpiderOptions();
options.Load("spider.conf");
Spider spider = new Spider(options,report);
spider.AddURL(base, null, 1);
spider.Process();
Console.WriteLine(spider.Status);
```

First a variable named **base** is created that contains the **base** URL the spider will begin with. Next a **SimpleReport** object is created named **report**. The **SimpleReport** class implements a spider **ReportableInterface**, and is provided by the Heaton Research Spider. However, the **SimpleReport** does nothing more than allow the spider to continue crawling, no data is processed. It is suitable only for testing the spider.

Next a **SpiderOptions** object, named **options** is created. The **options** object loads configuration data from a file named **spider.conf**. Now that we have both a configuration and report object, we can create a Spider object named **spider**.

Finally, the base URL is added to the spider object, and the **Process** method is called. The **Process** method will not return until the spider is finished. If you wish to cancel the spider processing early, you should call the **Cancel** method on the **spider** object.

Of course you could also directly create the **SpiderOptions** object, as discussed earlier in the chapter. To set options directly, remove the call to the **Load** method and set each of the properties of the **options** object directly.

Recipes

This chapter includes four recipes. These recipes demonstrate how to construct spiders that check links, download sites and attempt to access a large number of sites. Additionally, a recipe is provided that tracks the progress of a spider. Specifically, you will learn how to:

- Find all of the broken links on a site
- Download the contents of a site
- Access a large number of sites on the Internet
- Track the progress of a spider

These recipes will show you how a bot can be adapted to several very common spider techniques. The first recipe demonstrates how to find bad links.

Recipe #13.1: Broken Links

A broken link is a link on a web site that leads to a non-existent page or image. Broken links make a web site look unprofessional. Spiders are particularly adept at finding broken links on a web site. This recipe shows how to create a spider that will scan a web site for broken links.

To run this spider, pass the URL of the website you wish to check as the first argument. For example, to spider the HTTP Recipes site, use the following command:

```
Recipe13_1 http://www.httprecipes.com
```

This recipe is made up of two classes. The first, named **CheckLinks**, configures the spider and then begins processing. The next class, named **LinkReport** receives information from the spider and compiles a list of bad links. We will examine each of these classes, starting with **CheckLinks**.

Creating the Broken Links Spider

The **CheckLinks** class contains the **main** method for the recipe. Listing 13.4 shows the **CheckLinks** class.

Listing 13.4: Find Broken Links (CheckLinks.cs)

```csharp
using System;
using System.Collections.Generic;
using System.Text;
using HeatonResearch.Spider;
using HeatonResearch.Spider.Workload.Memory;


namespace Recipe13_1
{
    class CheckLinks
    {
        /// <summary>
        /// This method is called by main to check a link. After
        /// spidering through the site, the final list of
        /// bad links is displayed.
        /// </summary>
        /// <param name="url">The URL to check for bad
        /// links.</param>
        public void check(Uri url)
        {
            SpiderOptions options = new SpiderOptions();
            options.WorkloadManager =
                    typeof(MemoryWorkloadManager).FullName;
            LinkReport report = new LinkReport();
            Spider spider = new Spider(options, report);
```

```
        spider.AddURL(url, null, 1);

        spider.Process();
        Console.WriteLine(spider.Status);

        if (report.Bad.Count > 0)
        {
            Console.WriteLine("Bad Links Found:");
            foreach (String str in report.Bad)
            {
                Console.WriteLine(str);
            }
        }
        else
        {
            Console.WriteLine("No bad links were found.");
        }

    }


    static void Main(string[] args)
    {

        if (args.Length != 1)
        {
            Console.WriteLine(
              "Usage: Recipe13_1 [website to check]");
        }
        else
        {
            CheckLinks links = new CheckLinks();
            links.check(new Uri(args[0]));
        }

    }
}
}
```

All of the work performed by this recipe is accomplished inside the **CheckLink** method. This method begins by creating a **SpiderOptions** object named **options**. A **MemoryWorkloadManager** is then specified. A **MemoryWorkloadManager** will work with relatively large sites, however, if you are going to check an extremely large site, you may want to use a **SQLWorkloadManager**.

```
SpiderOptions options = new SpiderOptions();
```

```
options.WorkloadManager = typeof(MemoryWorkloadManager).FullName;
```

Next a **LinkReport** object is created. The **LinkReport** class will be discussed in the next section. The spider is then created and which URL to check is added to the spider's workload.

```
LinkReport report = new LinkReport();
Spider spider = new Spider(options, report);
spider.AddURL(url, null, 1);
```

Calling the **Process** method starts the spider. Once the spider is completed, its status is displayed.

```
spider.Process();
Console.WriteLine(spider.Status);
```

If bad links are found, they are displayed in a list.

```
if (report.Bad.Count > 0)
{
  Console.WriteLine("Bad Links Found:");
  foreach (String str in report.Bad)
  {
    Console.WriteLine(str);
  }
}
```

Finally, if no bad links are found, the user is informed.

```
else
{
  Console.WriteLine("No bad links were found.");
}
```

The **LinkReport** class processes all of the bad links. The **LinkReport** class will be described in the next section.

Receiving Data for the Broken Links Spider

The Heaton Research Spider requires that any spider include a class that implements the **SpiderReportable** interface. This object manages the spider and receives all information found by the spider. The broken links spider uses the **LinkReport** class to implement the **SpiderReportable** interface.

Listing 13.5 shows the **LinkReport** class.

Listing 13.5: Report Broken Links (LinkReport.cs)

```
using System;
using System.Collections.Generic;
using System.Text;
```

```csharp
using System.IO;
using HeatonResearch.Spider;
using HeatonResearch.Spider.Workload;
using HeatonResearch.Spider.Logging;

namespace Recipe13_1
{
    class LinkReport : SpiderReportable
    {
        /// <summary>
        /// The host we are working with.
        /// </summary>
        private String baseHost;

        /// <summary>
        /// The Spider object that this object reports to.
        /// </summary>
        private Spider spider;

        /// <summary>
        /// The bad URL's.
        /// </summary>
        private List<String> bad = new List<String>();

        /// <summary>
        /// This function is called when the spider is ready to
        /// process a new host. This function simply stores the
        /// value of the current host.
        /// </summary>
        /// <param name="host"></param>
        /// <returns></returns>
        public bool BeginHost(String host)
        {
            if (this.baseHost == null)
            {
                this.baseHost = host;
                return true;
            }
            else
            {
                return false;
            }
        }

        /// <summary>
        /// The bad link's found.
```

```
/// </summary>
public List<String> Bad
{
    get
    {
        return this.bad;
    }
    set
    {
        bad = value;
    }
}


/// <summary>
/// Called when the spider is starting up. This method
/// provides the SpiderReportable class with the spider
/// object.
/// </summary>
/// <param name="spider">The spider that will be working
/// with this object.</param>
public void Init(Spider spider)
{
    this.spider = spider;
}


/// <summary>
/// Called when the spider finds a URL.
/// </summary>
/// <param name="url">The URL that was found.</param>
/// <param name="source">Where the URL was found.</param>
/// <param name="type">What sort of tag produced
/// this URL.</param>
/// <returns>True if this URL should be spidered</returns>
public bool SpiderFoundURL(Uri url, Uri source,
    Spider.URLType type)
{
    if ((this.baseHost != null) &&
(String.Compare(this.baseHost, url.Host, true) != 0))
    {
        return false;
    }

    return true;
}
```

```csharp
/// <summary>
/// Not used by the link checker.
/// </summary>
/// <param name="url">Not used.</param>
/// <param name="stream">Not used.</param>
public void SpiderProcessURL(Uri url, Stream stream)
{
}

/// <summary>
/// Called when the spider is ready to process an HTML
/// URL.
/// </summary>
/// <param name="url">The URL that the spider is
/// about to process.</param>
/// <param name="parse">An object that will allow you
/// you to parse the HTML on this page.</param>
public void SpiderProcessURL(Uri url,
    SpiderParseHTML parse)
{
    try
    {
        parse.ReadAll();
    }
    catch (IOException)
    {
        spider.Logging.Log(Logger.Level.INFO,
            "Error reading page:" + url.ToString());
    }
}

/// <summary>
/// Called when the spider tries to process a URL but gets
/// an error.
/// </summary>
/// <param name="url">The URL that generated an
/// error.</param>
public void SpiderURLError(Uri url)
{
    Uri source;
    try
    {
        source = this.spider.Workload.GetSource(url);
        StringBuilder str = new StringBuilder();
        str.Append("Bad URL:");
        str.Append(url.ToString());
```

```
              str.Append(" found at ");
              str.Append(source.ToString());
              this.bad.Add(str.ToString());
          }
          catch (WorkloadException e)
          {
              Console.WriteLine(e.StackTrace);
          }
      }
   }
}
```

The **ReportLinks** class implements all of the functions and methods defined by the **SpiderReportable** interface. To review what these methods and functions are for refer to Table 13.1.

The **FoundURL** function is called each time a new URL is found. Because this spider only checks a single web server, the **FoundURL** method ensures that all new URLs are on the same server.

```
if ((this.baseHost != null) && (String.Compare(this.baseHost, url.
Host, true) != 0))
{
  return false;
}

return true;
```

If the new URLs host varies from the starting host, returning **false** ignores the new URL. The above lines of code can be reused in any spider that is to operate only on a single host.

The **ProcessURL** method, which usually downloads a URL, is fairly simple. Because we are only checking links, we do not need to actually download the page. This can be done by calling the **ReadAll** method of the **ParseHTML** object.

```
try
{
  parse.ReadAll();
}
catch (IOException)
{
  spider.Logging.Log(Logger.Level.INFO, "Error reading page:" +
url.ToString());
}
```

We do not need to record the **IOException** that was caught. This is most likely a timeout on the web server and not a missing page. Timeouts are caused by a variety of purposes, such as an overloaded web server. Missing pages throw an exception when they are first opened, not during the transfer of information. Because a timeout is only a temporary server issue, we do not record that page as a bad link.

The Heaton Research Spider calls the **SpiderURLError** method whenever a bad URL is found. This URL is displayed, along with the page it was found on, and added to the **bad** list.

```
Uri source;
try
{
  source = this.spider.Workload.GetSource(url);
  StringBuilder str = new StringBuilder();
  str.Append("Bad URL:");
  str.Append(url.ToString());
  str.Append(" found at ");
  str.Append(source.ToString());
  this.bad.Add(str.ToString());
}
catch (WorkloadException e)
{
  Console.WriteLine(e.StackTrace);
}
```

These bad URLs are accumulated in the **LinkReport** class until the spider is finished. Then the bad URL list is displayed.

Recipe #13.2: Downloading HTML and Images

Another common use for spiders is to create an offline copy of a web site. This recipe will show how to do this. To start this spider you must provide three arguments. The first argument is the name of the spider configuration file. Through the spider configuration file you can specify whether to use an SQL or a memory based workload manager. Listing 13.1 shows an example of a spider configuration file. Next, the local directory to download the site to must be specified. Finally, the starting URL must be specified.

The following shows how you might start the spider.

```
Recipe13_2 c:\spider.conf c:\temp http://www.jeffheaton.com/
```

Now that you have seen how to use the download spider, we will see how it was constructed.

Creating the Download Spider

The **DownloadSite** class contains the main method for the recipe. Listing 13.6 shows the **DownloadSite** class.

Listing 13.6: Download a Site (DownloadSite.cs)

```
using System;
using System.Collections.Generic;
using System.Text;
using HeatonResearch.Spider;

namespace Recipe13_2
{
    class DownloadSite
    {
        /// <summary>
        /// Download an entire site.
        /// </summary>
        /// <param name="config">The spider configuration file
        /// to use.</param>
        /// <param name="baseURL">The URL to start from.></param>
        /// <param name="local">The local path to save
        /// files to.</param>
        public void Download(String config, Uri baseURL,
            String local)
        {
            SpiderReport report = new SpiderReport(local);
            SpiderOptions options = new SpiderOptions();
            options.Load(config);
            Spider spider = new Spider(options, report);
            spider.Logging.Console = true;
            spider.Logging.Filename = "c:\\spider.log";
            spider.Logging.Clear();

            spider.AddURL(baseURL, null, 1);
            spider.Process();
            Console.WriteLine(spider.Status);
        }


        static void Main(string[] args)
        {
            if (args.Length < 3)
            {
                Console.WriteLine(
                "Usage: Recipe13_2 [Path to spider.conf] " +
```

```
                              "[Path to download to] [URL to download]");
                }
                else
                {
                    try
                    {
                        DownloadSite download = new DownloadSite();
                        download.Download(args[0],
                        new Uri(args[2]), args[1]);
                    }
                    catch (Exception e)
                    {
                        Console.WriteLine(e.StackTrace);

                    }


                }

            }
        }
}
```

The majority of the work done by this recipe is performed inside the **download** method. The download method is very similar to Recipe 13.1, except that the configuration is read from a file. This recipe begins by creating a **SpiderReport** object, named **report**, and a **SpiderOptions** object, named **options**. The configuration is then loaded from a file.

```
SpiderReport report = new SpiderReport(local);
SpiderOptions options = new SpiderOptions();
options.Load(config);
```

Next the spider is constructed and the starting URL added.

```
Spider spider = new Spider(options, report);
spider.AddURL(base, null, 1);
```

Once the spider has been created, it can be started by calling the **process** method. Once the spider has finished, its status is displayed.

```
spider.Process();
Console.WriteLine(spider.Status);
```

The actual downloading is performed by the **SpiderReport** class, which is discussed in the next section.

Receiving Data for the Download Spider

Just like the last recipe, you must have a class that implements the **SpiderReportable** interface. This object manages the spider and receives all information found by the spider. The site download spider uses the **SpiderReport** class to implement the **SpiderReportable** interface.

Listing 13.7 shows the **SpiderReport** class.

Listing 13.7: Report Download Information (SpiderReport.cs)

```
using System;
using System.Collections.Generic;
using System.Text;
using System.IO;
using System.Net;
using HeatonResearch.Spider;
using HeatonResearch.Spider.HTML;


namespace Recipe13_2
{
    class SpiderReport : SpiderReportable
    {
        /// <summary>
        /// The base host. Only URL's from this host will be
        /// downloaded.
        /// </summary>
        private String baseHost;

        /// <summary>
        /// The local path to save downloaded files to.
        /// </summary>
        private String path;

        /// <summary>
        /// Construct a SpiderReport object.
        /// </summary>
        /// <param name="path">The local file path to store
        /// the files to.</param>
        public SpiderReport(String path)
        {
            this.path = path;
        }

        /// <summary>
        /// This function is called when the spider is ready to
        /// process a new host. This function simply stores the
```

```csharp
/// value of the current host.
/// </summary>
/// <param name="host">The new host that is about
/// to be processed.</param>
/// <returns>True if this host should be processed,
/// false otherwise.</returns>
public bool BeginHost(String host)
{
    if (this.baseHost == null)
    {
        this.baseHost = host;
        return true;
    }
    else
    {
        return false;
    }
}


/// <summary>
/// Not used.
/// </summary>
/// <param name="spider">Not used.</param>
public void Init(Spider spider)
{
}


/// <summary>
/// Called when the spider encounters a URL. If the URL is
/// on the same host as the base host, then the function
/// will return true, indicating that the URL is to be
/// processed.
/// </summary>
/// <param name="url">The URL that the spider
/// found.</param>
/// <param name="source">The page that the URL was
/// found on.</param>
/// <param name="type">The URL type.</param>
/// <returns>True if the spider should scan for
/// links on this page.</returns>
public bool SpiderFoundURL(Uri url, Uri source,
    Spider.URLType type)
{

    if ((this.baseHost != null) &&
    (string.Compare(this.baseHost, url.Host, true) != 0))
```

```
    {
        return false;
    }

    return true;
}


/// <summary>
/// Called when the spider is about to process a NON-HTML
/// URL.
/// </summary>
/// <param name="url">The URL that the spider
/// found.</param>
/// <param name="stream">An InputStream to read the
/// page contents from.</param>
public void SpiderProcessURL(Uri url, Stream stream)
{
    byte[] buffer = new byte[1024];

    int length;
    String filename = URLUtility.convertFilename(
            this.path, url, true);

    Stream os = new FileStream(filename, FileMode.Create);
    do
    {
        length = stream.Read(buffer, 0, buffer.Length);
        if (length >0)
        {
            os.Write(buffer, 0, length);
        }
    } while (length >0 );
    os.Close();
}


/// <summary>
/// Called when the spider is ready to process an HTML
/// URL. Download the contents of the URL to a local file.
/// </summary>
/// <param name="url">The URL that the spider is about
/// to process.</param>
/// <param name="parse">An object that will allow you
/// you to parse the HTML on this page.</param>
public void SpiderProcessURL(Uri url,
        SpiderParseHTML parse)
{
```

```
        String filename = URLUtility.convertFilename(
                this.path, url, true);

        Stream os = new FileStream(filename, FileMode.Create);
        parse.Stream.OutputStream = os;
        parse.ReadAll();
        os.Close();

    }

    /// <summary>
    /// Not used.
    /// </summary>
    /// <param name="url">Not used.</param>
    public void SpiderURLError(Uri url)
    {

    }
  }
}
```

Quite a bit of the **SpiderReportable** implementation of Recipe 13.2 is similar to Recipe 13.1. However, the main difference is that Recipe 13.2 will download what it finds. This downloading is implemented in the **spiderProcessURL** methods. The first **SpiderProcessURL** method is designed to take an **InputStream**.

```
public void SpiderProcessURL(Uri url, Stream stream)
```

This method is called to download images and other binary objects. Anything that is not HTML is downloaded by this method. HTML is handled differently because HTML contains links to other pages. This method begins by creating a buffer to read the binary data with.

```
byte[] buffer = new byte[1024];
int length;
```

Next, a filename is created. The filename uses the **ConvertFilename** function to convert the URL into a file that can be saved to the local computer. The **ConvertFilename** function also creates the directory structure to hold the specified file.

```
String filename = URLUtility.ConvertFilename(this.path, url,
true);
```

Next the data is read in. It is read using the buffer created earlier.

```
Stream os = new FileStream(filename, FileMode.Create);
do
{
  length = stream.Read(buffer, 0, buffer.Length);
  if (length >0)
  {
```

```
    os.Write(buffer, 0, length);
  }
} while (length >0 );
```

Once the data has been read, the output stream can be closed.

```
os.Close();
```

This recipe also has to handle HTML data. If a URL has HTML data, the second form of the **SpiderProcessURL** method is used.

```
public void SpiderProcessURL(Uri url, SpiderParseHTML parse)
```

First a filename is generated, just as was done for a binary URL. A **Stream** is opened to write the file to.

```
String filename = URLUtility.convertFilename(this.path, url,
true);
Stream os = new FileStream(filename, FileMode.Create);
```

The **Stream** is then attached to the **ParseHTML** object so that any data ready from the HTML stream is also written to the **OutputStream**. This saves the HTML file to the local computer.

```
parse.Stream.OutputStream = os;
```

Finally, **ReadAll** is called to read the entire HTML file. The HTML file will be written to the attached output **Stream** as it is parsed.

```
parse.ReadAll();
os.Close();
```

The output **Stream** can now be closed, because the file has been written.

Recipe #13.3: Spider the World

Perhaps the most well known of all spiders are the search engine spiders. These are the spiders used by sites such as Google to add new sites to their search engines. Such spiders are not designed to stay on a specific site. In this recipe I will show you how to create a spider that will not restrict itself to one site, rather this spider will keep following links endlessly. It is very unlikely that this spider would ever finish, since it would have to visit nearly every public URL on the Internet to do so.

To start this spider you must provide three arguments. The first argument is the name of a spider configuration file. Using the spider configuration file, you can specify whether to use an SQL or a memory based workload manager. Listing 13.1 shows an example spider configuration file. Next, a local directory to download the site to must be specified. Finally, the starting URL must be specified.

The following shows how you might start the spider.

```
Recipe13_3 c:\spider.conf c:\temp http://www.jeffheaton.com/
```

This spider is designed to access a large number of sites. You should use the **SQLWorkloadManager** class with this spider. Because the **MemoryWorkloadManager** is only designed to work with one single host, it would not be compatible with this spider.

Now that you have seen how to use the world spider we will see how it was constructed.

Creating the World Spider

The **WorldSpider** class contains the main method for the recipe. Listing 13.8 shows the **WorldSpider** class.

Listing 13.8: Download the World (WorldSpider.cs)

```csharp
using System;
using System.Collections.Generic;
using System.Text;
using HeatonResearch.Spider;


namespace Recipe13_3
{
    class WorldSpider
    {
        /// <summary>
        /// Download an entire site.
        /// </summary>
        /// <param name="config">
        /// The spider configuration file to use.</param>
        /// <param name="baseHost">The URL to start from.</param>
        /// <param name="local">The local path to save files to.
        /// </param>
        public void Download(String config, Uri baseHost,
            String local)
        {
            WorldSpiderReport report =
                new WorldSpiderReport(local);
            SpiderOptions options = new SpiderOptions();
            options.Load(config);
            Spider spider = new Spider(options, report);
            spider.AddURL(baseHost, null, 1);
            spider.Process();
            Console.WriteLine(spider.Status);
        }
```

```
    static void Main(string[] args)
    {
        if (args.Length < 3)
        {
            Console.WriteLine(
              "Usage: Recipe13_3 [Path to spider.conf] " +
              "[Path to download to] [URL to download]");
        }
        else
        {
            WorldSpider download = new WorldSpider();
            download.Download(args[0],
                    new Uri(args[2]), args[1]);
        }
    }

}
}
```

The **download** method for the world spider is essentially the same as Recipe 13.2. The difference is in the **WorldSpiderReport** class, which manages the spider.

Receiving Data for the World Spider

Just like the last two recipes, you must have a class that implements the **SpiderReportable** interface. This object manages the spider and receives all information found by the spider. The site world spider uses the **WorldSpiderReport** class to implement the **SpiderReportable** interface.

Listing 13.9 shows the **SpiderReport** class.

Listing 13.9: Report for World Spider (WorldSpiderReport.cs)

```
using System;
using System.Collections.Generic;
using System.Text;
using System.IO;
using HeatonResearch.Spider;
using HeatonResearch.Spider.HTML;


namespace Recipe13_3
{
    class WorldSpiderReport : SpiderReportable
    {
        /// <summary>
        /// The base host. Only URL's from this host will be
        /// downloaded.
```

```csharp
/// </summary>
private String baseHost;

/// <summary>
/// The local path to save downloaded files to.
/// </summary>
private String path;

/// <summary>
/// Construct a SpiderReport object.
/// </summary>
/// <param name="path">The local file path to
/// store the files to.</param>
public WorldSpiderReport(String path)
{
    this.path = path;
}

/// <summary>
/// This function is called when the spider is ready to
/// process a new host. This function simply stores the
/// value of the current host.
/// </summary>
/// <param name="host">The new host that is about
/// to be processed.</param>
/// <returns>True if this host should be processed,
/// false otherwise.</returns>
public bool BeginHost(String host)
{
    if (this.baseHost == null)
    {
        this.baseHost = host;
        return true;
    }
    else
    {
        return false;
    }
}

/// <summary>
/// Not used.
/// </summary>
/// <param name="spider">Not used.</param>
public void Init(Spider spider)
{
```

```
}

/// <summary>
/// Called when the spider encounters a URL. This function
/// will always return true. Because this spider will
/// theoretically visit every URL on the Internet, all
/// URL's will be processed.
/// </summary>
/// <param name="url">The URL that the spider found.
/// </param>
/// <param name="source">The page that the URL was
/// found on.</param>
/// <param name="type">The type of link this URL
/// is.</param>
/// <returns>True if the spider should scan for
/// links on this page.</returns>
public bool SpiderFoundURL(Uri url, Uri source,
    Spider.URLType type)
{
    return true;
}


/// <summary>
/// Called when the spider is about to process a NON-HTML
/// URL.
/// </summary>
/// <param name="url">The URL that the spider
/// found.</param>
/// <param name="stream">An InputStream to read the
/// page contents from.</param>
public void SpiderProcessURL(Uri url, Stream stream)
{
    byte[] buffer = new byte[1024];

    int length;
    String filename = URLUtility.convertFilename(
            this.path, url, true);

    Stream os = new FileStream(filename, FileMode.Create);
    do
    {
        length = stream.Read(buffer, 0, buffer.Length);
        if (length > 0)
        {
            os.Write(buffer, 0, length);
        }
```

```
            } while (length > 0);
            os.Close();
        }

        /// <summary>
        /// Called when the spider is ready to process an HTML
        /// URL. Download the contents of the URL to a local file.
        /// </summary>
        /// <param name="url">The URL that the spider is
        /// about to process.</param>
        /// <param name="parse">An object that will allow you to
        /// parse the HTML on this page.</param>
        public void SpiderProcessURL(Uri url,
            SpiderParseHTML parse)
        {
            String filename = URLUtility.convertFilename(
                this.path, url, true);
            Stream os = new FileStream(filename, FileMode.Create);
            parse.Stream.OutputStream = os;
            parse.ReadAll();
            os.Close();
        }

        /// <summary>
        /// Not used.
        /// </summary>
        /// <param name="url">Not used.</param>
        public void SpiderURLError(Uri url)
        {
        }
    }
}
```

The primary difference with the world spider is the way that it handles new URLs when **SpiderFoundURL** is called. Unlike the previous spiders, no checks are made to determine if the URL is on the same host. Any URL is a candidate to be visited.

```
public bool SpiderFoundURL(Uri url, Uri source,
            Spider.URLType type)
{
    return true;
}
```

As you can see, the **SpiderFoundURL** simply returns true.

This spider shows how you would setup a spider that would access a large number of web sites. Of course this spider is only the beginning of a search engine. But it demonstrates how you would configure the Heaton Research Spider to access a large amount of sites.

Recipe #13.4: Display Spider Statistics

Because the **SQLWorkloadManager** class stores the workload in a database, it is possible for other programs to monitor the progress of the spider. This recipe shows you how to create a simple program that monitors the progress of the database of a Heaton Research spider.

This recipe makes use of a Heaton Research Spider configuration file, just like previous recipes. To start this recipe, specify the name of the configuration file as the first argument. The following shows how you might start the spider.

```
Recipe13_4 c:\spider.conf
```

Figure 13.1 shows this program monitoring a spider's progress.

Figure 13.1: Monitoring a Spider

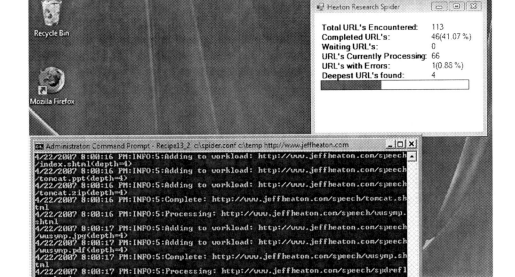

The spider monitor is shown in Listing 13.10.

Listing 13.10: Display Spider Statistics (SpiderStats.cs)

```csharp
using System;
using System.Collections.Generic;
using System.Windows.Forms;
using HeatonResearch.Spider;
using System.Data.OleDb;

namespace Recipe13_4
{
    static class SpiderStats
    {
        /// <summary>
        /// The main entry point for the application.
        /// </summary>
        [STAThread]
        static void Main(String[] args)
        {
            Application.EnableVisualStyles();
            Application.SetCompatibleTextRenderingDefault(false);

            MainForm form = new MainForm();
            if (args.Length < 1)
            {
                MessageBox.Show("Please pass a path to a spider
configuration file as an argument to this program (i.e. Recipe13_4
c:\\spider.conf).", "Heaton Research Spider");
                return;
            }

            SpiderOptions options = new SpiderOptions();
            options.Load(args[0]);
            form.Options = options;

            Application.Run(form);
        }
    }
}
```

This program begins by creating its window and then creating a timer. The timer allows the application to update the statistics on a regular basis. The timer is contained in the **timer_Tick** method. The **timer_Tick** method begins by opening a connection to the database and obtaining a Graphics object.

```csharp
Graphics g = this.CreateGraphics();
```

The database connection is established by calling the **Open** method, which will be covered in the next section. If the **Graphics** object, named **g**, was obtained successfully, the **GetStats** method is called to obtain the current statistics from the database. Next, the **DisplayStats** method is called to display the current statistics.

```
if (this.connection == null)
{
  Open();
}

if (g != null)
{
  GetStats();
  DisplayStats(g);
}

g.Dispose();
```

This process will continue as long as the program is allowed to run.

Opening a Database Connection

Before any SQL commands can be issued to obtain stats, a connection must be opened to the database. This is done by the **Open** method. The **Open** method will also create several **DbCommand** that will execute the two SQL statements that this program uses to obtain its statistics. The **Open** method begins by using the information from a **SpiderOptions** object to establish a connection. The **SpiderOptions** object was loaded from a spider configuration file, as discussed in previous recipes in this chapter.

```
connection = new OleDbConnection(this.options.DbConnectionString);
connection.Open();
```

Next, two prepared statements are created for the two SQL statements that this program uses to obtain statistics.

```
stmtStatus = this.connection.CreateCommand();
stmtStatus.CommandText = MainForm.sqlStatus;
stmtStatus.Prepare();

stmtDepth = this.connection.CreateCommand();
stmtDepth.CommandText = MainForm.sqlDepth;
stmtDepth.Prepare();
```

Finally, catch statements are used to trap any of the errors that can occur while establishing a **database** connection.

```
catch (Exception e)
{
```

```
    errorMessage = e.Message;
}
```

If any error does occur, a stack trace is printed and the method ends.

Obtaining the Statistics

Now that the database connection has been opened, the statistics can be obtained. Calling the **GetStats** method does this. The **GetStats** method begins by clearing out all of the totals and executing the **stmtStatus** query. This query obtains a count for each of the status types in the **spider_workload** table.

```
this.waiting = this.processing = this.error = this.done = 0;
DbDataReader rs = this.stmtStatus.ExecuteReader();
```

Next, the results will be examined. The SQL was constructed so that each of the status types will be returned in a separate row, along with a count. As we loop over everything that was returned, we examine the **status** of each row and assign it to the correct total variable.

```
while (rs.NextResult())
{
  String status = rs.GetString(1);
  int count = rs.GetInt32(2);
  if (String.Compare(status, "W", true) == 0)
  {
    this.waiting = count;
  }
  else if (String.Compare(status, "P", true) == 0)
  {
    this.processing = count;
  }
  else if (String.Compare(status, "E", true) == 0)
  {
    this.error = count;
  }
  else if (String.Compare(status, "D", true) == 0)
  {
    this.done = count;
  }
}
rs.Close();
```

Once this is complete, we can close the result set.

Next, we execute the **stmtDepth** query. This simple SQL query obtains the maximum depth recorded in the **spider_workload** table.

```
this.depth = 0;
```

```
rs = this.stmtDepth.ExecuteReader();
if (rs.NextResult())
{
  this.depth = rs.GetInt32(1);
}
rs.Close();
```

Once the depth has been obtained, the result set can be closed.

```
catch (Exception e)
{
  errorMessage = e.Message;
}
```

If any errors occur, a stack trace is displayed.

Displaying the Statistics

Now that we have obtained the statistics from the database, we can display the xxx. First, a string is created for each of the statistics that will be displayed.

```
const String stat1 = "Total URL\'s Encountered:";
const String stat2 = "Completed URL\'s:";
const String stat3 = "Waiting URL\'s:";
const String stat4 = "URL\'s Currently Processing:";
const String stat5 = "URL\'s with Errors:";
const String stat6 = "Deepest URL\'s found:";
```

Next, two **Font** objects are created to display the text. A bold font is used to display the headings, and a regular font is used to display the text values. Drawing a white rectangle clears the display area.

```
Font drawFont = new Font(FontFamily.GenericSansSerif, 10.0F, Font-
Style.Regular);
Font boldFont = new Font(FontFamily.GenericSansSerif, 10.0F, Font-
Style.Bold);

int y = boldFont.Height;
```

If an error message has been set, do not display the stats. If this is the case, the error message will be displayed.

```
if (errorMessage == null)
{
```

If a percent done can be calculated, calculate it. Otherwise, put a zero into percent done.

```
if ((this.waiting + this.processing + this.done) == 0)
{
```

```
      this.donePercent = 0;
}
else
{
   this.donePercent = (double)this.done / (double)(this.waiting +
this.processing + this.done);
}
```

If a percent error can be calculated, calculate it. Otherwise, put a zero into percent error.

```
if (total == 0)
{
   this.errorPercent = 0;
}
else
{
   this.errorPercent = (double)this.error / (double)total;
}
```

Display the total URLs found and move the **y** variable down by the correct amount.

```
g.DrawString(stat1, boldFont, Brushes.Black, new PointF(10, y));
g.DrawString("" + total, drawFont, Brushes.Black, new PointF(200,
y));
y += boldFont.Height;
```

Display the total URLs done and the percent done. Move the **y** variable down by the correct amount.

```
g.DrawString(stat2, boldFont, Brushes.Black, new PointF(10, y));
g.DrawString(this.done.ToString("G") + "("
+ this.donePercent.ToString("P") + ")", drawFont, Brushes.Black,
new PointF(200, y));
y += boldFont.Height;
```

Display the total URLs waiting to be processed and move the **y** variable down by the correct amount.

```
g.DrawString(stat3, boldFont, Brushes.Black, new PointF(10, y));
g.DrawString(this.waiting.ToString("G"), drawFont, Brushes.Black,
new PointF(200, y));
y += boldFont.Height;
```

Display the total URLs currently being processed and move the **y** variable down by the correct amount.

```
g.DrawString(stat4, boldFont, Brushes.Black, new PointF(10, y));
g.DrawString(this.processing.ToString("G"), drawFont, Brushes.
Black, new PointF(200, y));
```

```
y += boldFont.Height;
```

Display the total URLs that resulted in an error, and the error percent. Move the **y** variable down by the correct amount.

```
g.DrawString(stat5, boldFont, Brushes.Black, new PointF(10, y));
g.DrawString(this.error.ToString("G") + "("
+ this.errorPercent.ToString("P") + ")", drawFont, Brushes.Black,
new PointF(200, y));
y += boldFont.Height;
```

Display the deepest URL processed and move the **y** variable down by the correct amount.

```
g.DrawString(stat6, boldFont, Brushes.Black, new PointF(10, y));
g.DrawString(this.depth.ToString("G"), drawFont, Brushes.Black,
new PointF(200, y));
y += boldFont.Height;
```

Finally, display a progress bar indicating how close we are to completion.

```
DisplayProgressBar(g, y);
```

Of course, the progress bar is a very rough approximation. The spider does not know ahead of time how many URLs it will find. So the percent done is simply the ratio of the number of URLs processed against the total number of URLs found.

Displaying the Progress Bar

The progress bar is a simple green rectangle drawn to show a percent done. The percent done was calculated in the previous section. First the total width is calculated.

```
int width = this.Width;
int progressWidth = width - 20;
```

Next, a green bar that is a percent of the total width is drawn. This bar is drawn with a white background.

```
g.FillRectangle(Brushes.White, new Rectangle(10, y, progressWidth,
16));
g.FillRectangle(Brushes.Green, new Rectangle(10, y,
(int)(progressWidth * this.donePercent), 16));
```

Finally, a black border is drawn around the total width of the progress bar. This allows the user to see a white region that represents how much longer it will take to process.

```
g.DrawRectangle(Pens.Black, new Rectangle(10, y, progressWidth,
16));
```

The bar will be updated until it reaches 100%.

Summary

A spider is a special kind of bot. A spider scans HTML pages and looks for more pages to visit. Theoretically, a spider would continue finding URLs forever, or until it had visited every URL on the internet. However, there are two factors that prevent a spider from doing this. First, a spider is often given a maximum depth to visit. If a page is deeper, relative to the home page, than the maximum depth, the spider will not visit it. Secondly, spiders are often instructed to stay within a specified set of hosts. This set is often just one host.

This chapter explained how to use the Heaton Research Spider. The Heaton Research Spider is an open source Java and C# spider available free from Heaton Research, Inc. To use the Heaton Research Spider, you must create two objects.

A **SpiderOptions** object must be created to provide the spider with some basic configuration options. The **SpiderOptions** properties can either be set directly, or loaded from a file.

A **WorkloadManager** is required. For simple spiders you may choose to use the **MemoryWorkloadManager**. This will store all URLs in the computer's memory. For larger spiders, use the **SQLWorkloadManager**. The **SQLWorkloadManager** stores the URL workload on a SQL database.

This chapter provided four recipes. The first recipe showed how to use a spider to check for bad links on a web site. The second recipe showed how to use a spider to download a site. The third recipe showed how to create a spider that accesses a large number of URLs and does not restrict itself to a single host. The fourth recipe showed how to display the statistics from the database, as a spider executes.

Now that you know how to use the Heaton Research Spider, the next chapter will take you through the internals of how the Heaton Research Spider works. If you are content with only using the Heaton Research Spider and do not yet wish to learn the internals of how to build a spider, you may skip safely to Chapter 15 and learn how to create well behaved bots. Otherwise, we will continue to Chapter 14 and learn the internals of the Heaton Research Spider.

CHAPTER 14: INSIDE THE HEATON RESEARCH SPIDER

- The Spider Class
- How Workloads are Managed
- Reading Configuration files
- Thread Pools
- The Memory-Based Workload Manager
- Spider HTML Parsing
- Spider Streams

Chapter 13 taught you to use the Heaton Research Spider. The Heaton Research Spider is an advanced and very extensible spider that can be applied to both small and large spider tasks. Chapter 13 only showed you how to use the Heaton Research Spider. This chapter will show you how the Heaton Research Spider is constructed. Because the Heaton Research Spider is open source, you are free to make your own modifications.

The Heaton Research Spider is an ongoing open source project. Because of this, there may have been enhancements made to the spider after the publication of this book. You can always check the Heaton Research Spider's home page for the latest updates. The latest version of the Heaton Research Spider can always be found at the following URL:

`http://www.heatonresearch.com/spider/`

If you are content using the Heaton Research Spider, and are not currently interested in how it works internally, you can safely skip to Chapter 15. However, you may still wish to visit the above URL to obtain the latest version. Additionally, there is a forum at the above URL where you can discuss using and modifying the Heaton Research Spider.

The Heaton Research Spider is made up of several different classes. These classes are summarized in Table 14.1.

Table 14.1: The Heaton Research Spider Classes

Class	Purpose
MemoryWorkloadManager	Manage the set of URLs the spider knows about using the computer's memory.
OracleHolder	Holds the SQL statements used by the OracleWorkload-Manager.
OracleWorkloadManager	Manage the set of URLs the spider knows about using an Oracle Database.
RepeatableStatement	Holds an SQL statement that can be repeated. SQL statements are repeated if the connection is broken.
RobotsFilter	Filter URLs using the bot exclusion file (robots.txt).
SimpleReport	A very simple SpiderReportable implementation. This class does nothing with the data reported by the spider.
Spider	The main class for the spider. You will command the spider through this class.
SpiderException	Thrown when the spider encounters an error it cannot handle.
SpiderFilter	An interface that defines how to create filters for the spider. Filters allow specific URLs to be excluded.
SpiderFormatter	A JDK logging formatter to display the spider's log output in a simple way.
SpiderInputStream	A special InputStream that also writes everything it reads to an OutputStream. This class allows the spider to both save HTML and parse it, at the same time.
SpiderOptions	Holds configuration items for the spider. Also loads configuration from a file.
SpiderParseHTML	A special version of the HTML parser for the spider. This version records any links found, as the user program parses the HTML.
SpiderReportable	An interface that defines a class to which the spider can report its findings.
SQLHolder	All of the SQL statements used by the spider are contained here.
SQLWorkloadManager	Manage the set of URLs the spider knows about using an SQL database.

Status	The status of a URL, held in the SQL workload manager.
URLStatus	The status of a URL, held in the memory workload manager.
WorkloadException	Thrown when the workload manager encounters a problem.
WorkloadManager	An interface that defines the spider's workload manager. Workload managers hold all of the URLs that the spider has encountered.

We will review all but the simplest classes shown in Table 14.1. We will begin with the Spider class.

The Spider Class

As you will recall from Chapter 14, one of the most important classes in the Heaton Research Spider is the **Spider** class. In this section we will examine the spider class. The Spider class is shown in Listing 14.1.

Listing 14.1: The Spider Class (Spider.cs)

```
using System;
using System.Collections.Generic;
using System.Threading;
using System.Reflection;
using System.Text;
using System.Net;
using System.IO;
using HeatonResearch.Spider.Workload;
using HeatonResearch.Spider.Filter;
using HeatonResearch.Spider.Logging;

namespace HeatonResearch.Spider
{
    /// <summary>
    /// Spider: This is the main class that implements the Heaton
    /// Research Spider.
    /// </summary>
    public class Spider
    {
        /// <summary>
        /// The workload manager for the spider.
        /// </summary>
        public WorkloadManager Workload
        {
            get
```

```csharp
        {
            return workloadManager;
        }
    }

    /// <summary>
    /// A list of URL filters to use.
    /// </summary>
    public List<SpiderFilter> Filters
    {
        get
        {
            return filters;
        }
    }

    /// <summary>
    /// The SpiderReportable object for the spider.
    /// The spider
    /// will report all information to this class.
    /// </summary>
    public SpiderReportable Report
    {
        get
        {
            return report;
        }
    }

    /// <summary>
    /// Used to log spider events.  Using this object
    /// you can configure how the spider logs information.
    /// </summary>
    public Logger Logging
    {
        get
        {
            return logging;
        }
    }

    /// <summary>
    /// The configuration options for the spider.
    /// </summary>
    public SpiderOptions Options
    {
```

```
    get
    {
        return options;
    }
}

/// <summary>
/// The object that the spider reports its findings to.
/// </summary>
private SpiderReportable report;

/**
 * A flag that indicates if this process should be
 * canceled.
 */
private bool cancel = false;

/// <summary>
/// The workload manager, the spider can use any of
/// several different workload managers. The workload
/// manager tracks all URL's found.
/// </summary>
private WorkloadManager workloadManager;

/// <summary>
/// The options for the spider.
/// </summary>
private SpiderOptions options;

/// <summary>
/// Filters used to block specific URL's.
/// </summary>
private List<SpiderFilter> filters =
    new List<SpiderFilter>();

/// <summary>
/// The time that the spider began.
/// </summary>
private DateTime startTime;

/// <summary>
/// The time that the spider ended.
/// </summary>
private DateTime stopTime;

/// <summary>
```

```csharp
        /// The logger.
        /// </summary>
        private Logger logging = new Logger();

        /// <summary>
        /// The types of link that can be encountered.
        /// </summary>
        public enum URLType
        {
            /// <summary>
            /// Hyperlinks from the &lt;A&gt; tag.
            /// </summary>
            HYPERLINK,
            /// <summary>
            /// Images from the &lt;IMG&gt; tag.
            /// </summary>
            IMAGE,
            /// <summary>
            /// External scripts from the &lt;SCRIPT&gt; tag.
            /// </summary>
            SCRIPT,
            /// <summary>
            /// External styles from the &lt;STYLE&gt; tag.
            /// </summary>
            STYLE
        }

        /// <summary>
        /// Construct a spider object. The options parameter
        /// specifies the options for this spider. The report
        /// parameter specifies the class that the spider is to
        /// report progress to.
        /// </summary>
        /// <param name="options">The configuration options
        /// for this spider.</param>
        /// <param name="report">A SpiderReportable class to
        /// report progress to</param>
        public Spider(SpiderOptions options,
            SpiderReportable report)
        {
            this.options = options;
            this.report = report;

            this.workloadManager = (WorkloadManager)
            Assembly.GetExecutingAssembly().CreateInstance(
            this.options.WorkloadManager);
```

```
    this.workloadManager.Init(this);
    report.Init(this);

    // add filters
    if (options.Filter != null)
    {
        foreach (String name in options.Filter)
        {
            SpiderFilter filter = (SpiderFilter)
Assembly.GetExecutingAssembly().CreateInstance(name);
            if (filter == null)
                throw new SpiderException(
                "Invalid filter specified: " + name);
            this.filters.Add(filter);
        }
    }

    // perform startup
    if (String.Compare(options.Startup,
        SpiderOptions.STARTUP_RESUME) == 0)
    {
        this.workloadManager.Resume();
    }
    else
    {
        this.workloadManager.Clear();
    }
}


/// <summary>
/// Add a URL for processing. Accepts a SpiderURL.
/// </summary>
/// <param name="url">The URL to add.</param>
/// <param name="source">Where this URL was found.</param>
/// <param name="depth">The depth of this URL.</param>
public void AddURL(Uri url, Uri source, int depth)
{
    // Check the depth.
    if ((this.options.MaxDepth != -1) &&
        (depth > this.options.MaxDepth))
    {
        return;
    }

    // Check to see if it does not pass any of the fil-
```

ters.

```csharp
            foreach (SpiderFilter filter in this.filters)
            {
                if (filter.IsExcluded(url))
                {
                    return;
                }
            }

            // Add the item.
            if (this.workloadManager.Add(url, source, depth))
            {
                StringBuilder str = new StringBuilder();
                str.Append("Adding to workload: ");
                str.Append(url);
                str.Append(" (depth=");
                str.Append(depth);
                str.Append(")");
                logging.Log(Logger.Level.INFO, str.ToString());
            }
        }

        /// <summary>
        /// This will halt the spider.
        /// </summary>
        public void Cancel()
        {
            this.cancel = true;
        }

        /// <summary>
        /// Generate basic status information about the spider.
        /// </summary>
        public String Status
        {
            get
            {
                StringBuilder result = new StringBuilder();
                TimeSpan duration = stopTime - startTime;
                result.Append("Start time:");
                result.Append(this.startTime.ToString());
                result.Append('\n');
                result.Append("Stop time:");
                result.Append(this.stopTime.ToString());
                result.Append('\n');
                result.Append("Minutes Elapsed:");
```

```
        result.Append(duration);
        result.Append('\n');

        return result.ToString();
    }
}

/// <summary>
/// Called to start the spider.
/// </summary>
public void Process()
{
    this.cancel = false;
    this.startTime = DateTime.Now;

    // Process all hosts/
    do
    {
        ProcessHost();
    } while (this.workloadManager.NextHost() != null);

    this.stopTime = DateTime.Now;
}

/// <summary>
/// Process one individual host.
/// </summary>
private void ProcessHost()
{
    Uri url = null;

    String host = this.workloadManager.GetCurrentHost();

    // First, notify the manager.
    if (!this.report.BeginHost(host))
    {
        return;
    }

    // Second, notify any filters of a new host/
    foreach (SpiderFilter filter in this.filters)
    {
        try
        {
            filter.NewHost(host, this.options.UserAgent);
        }
```

```
            catch (IOException e)
            {
                logging.Log(Logger.Level.INFO,
            "Error while reading robots.txt file:"
                    + e.Message);
            }
        }

        // Now process this host.
        do
        {
            url = this.workloadManager.GetWork();
            if (url != null)
            {

                WaitCallback w =
                    new WaitCallback(SpiderWorkerProc);
                ThreadPool.QueueUserWorkItem(w, url);
            }
            else
            {
                this.workloadManager.WaitForWork(60);
            }
        } while (!this.cancel &&
            !workloadManager.WorkloadEmpty());
    }



    /// <summary>
    /// This method is called by the thread pool to
    /// process one single URL.
    /// </summary>
    /// <param name="stateInfo">Not used.</param>
    private void SpiderWorkerProc(Object stateInfo)
    {
        Stream istream = null;
        WebRequest http;
        HttpWebResponse response;
        Uri url = null;
        try
        {
            url = (Uri)stateInfo;
            logging.Log(Logger.Level.INFO,
              "Processing: " + url);
            // Get the URL's contents.
```

```
    http = HttpWebRequest.Create(url);
    http.Timeout = this.options.Timeout;
    if (this.options.UserAgent != null)
    {
        http.Headers["User-Agent"] =
            this.options.UserAgent;
    }
    response = (HttpWebResponse)http.GetResponse();


    // Read the URL.
    istream = response.GetResponseStream();

    // Parse the URL.
    if (String.Compare(response.ContentType,
      "text/html") == 0)
    {
        SpiderParseHTML parse =
            new SpiderParseHTML(response.ResponseUri,
            new SpiderInputStream(istream, null),
             this);
        this.report.SpiderProcessURL(url, parse);
    }
    else
    {
        this.report.SpiderProcessURL(url, istream);
    }

}
catch (IOException e)
{
    logging.Log(Logger.Level.INFO,
      "I/O error on URL:" + url);
    try
    {
        this.workloadManager.MarkError(url);
    }
    catch (WorkloadException)
    {
        logging.Log(Logger.Level.ERROR,
            "Error marking workload(1).", e);
    }
    this.report.SpiderURLError(url);
    return;
}
catch (WebException e)
```

```
{
    logging.Log(Logger.Level.INFO,
      "Web error on URL:" + url);
    try
    {
        this.workloadManager.MarkError(url);
    }
    catch (WorkloadException)
    {
        logging.Log(Logger.Level.ERROR,
            "Error marking workload(2).", e);
    }
    this.report.SpiderURLError(url);
    return;
}
catch (Exception e)
{
    try
    {
        this.workloadManager.MarkError(url);
    }
    catch (WorkloadException)
    {
        logging.Log(Logger.Level.ERROR,
            "Error marking workload(3).", e);
    }

    logging.Log(Logger.Level.ERROR,
      "Caught exception at URL:" + url.ToString(), e);
    this.report.SpiderURLError(url);
    return;
}
finally
{
    if (istream != null)
    {

        istream.Close();

    }
}

try
{
    // Mark URL as complete.
    this.workloadManager.MarkProcessed(url);
```

```
        logging.Log(Logger.Level.INFO,
                "Complete: " + url);
        if (!url.Equals(response.ResponseUri))
        {
            // save the URL(for redirect's)
            this.workloadManager.Add(
                response.ResponseUri, url,
                this.workloadManager.GetDepth(
                response.ResponseUri));
            this.workloadManager.MarkProcessed(
                response.ResponseUri);
        }
    }
    catch (WorkloadException e)
    {
        logging.Log(Logger.Level.ERROR,
                "Error marking workload(3).", e);
    }

    }
  }
}
```

As you can see from the above listing, the spider uses a number of instance variables. The spider uses these to track its current state, as well as to remember configuration information. These instance variables are summarized in Table 14.2.

Table 14.2: Instance Variables for the Spider Class

Instance Variable	Purpose
cancel	A flag that indicates if this process should be canceled.
filters	Filters used to block specific URLs.
logger	The object to which the spider reports its findings.
options	The configuration options for the spider.
startTime	The time that the spider began.
stopTime	The time that the spider finished.
workloadManager	The workload manager. The spider can use any of several different workload managers. The workload manager tracks all URLs found.

There are also a number of methods and functions that perform important tasks for the **Spider** class. These will be discussed in the next few sections.

The Spider Constructor

The **Spider** class's constructor begins by saving the **SpiderOptions** and **WorkloadManager** that were passed as parameters. This will allow the spider to refer to these important objects later.

```
this.options = options;
this.report = report;
```

Next, a workload manager is instantiated from the class name provided in the **SpiderOptions** class. The **Init** method is also called on the workload manager.

```
this.workloadManager = (WorkloadManager)Assembly.GetExecutingAs-
sembly().CreateInstance(this.options.WorkloadManager);

this.workloadManager.Init(this);
report.Init(this);
```

Next, the thread pool is setup. This uses the JDK 1.5 **ThreadPoolExecutor** to implement the spider's thread pool. The thread pool is started with the options specified in the **SpiderOptions** object.

If any filters were specified, they are loaded at this point.

```
// add filters
if (options.Filter != null)
{
  foreach (String name in options.Filter)
  {
    SpiderFilter filter = (SpiderFilter)Assembly.GetExecutingAs-
sembly().CreateInstance(name);
    if (filter == null)
      throw new SpiderException("Invalid filter specified: "
            + name);
    this.filters.Add(filter);
  }
}
```

Finally, we are ready to perform the startup operation that was specified in the **SpiderOptions** configuration. If the user requests **STARUP_RESUME,** the workload manager is instructed to setup to resume from the last spider run. Otherwise, the workload will be cleared.

```
// perform startup
if (String.Compare(options.Startup,
      SpiderOptions.STARTUP_RESUME) == 0)
{
  this.workloadManager.Resume();
}
```

```
else
{
  this.workloadManager.Clear();
}
```

After the constructor completes, the spider is ready to run. The Heaton Research Spider is designed so that you should create a new Spider object for each spider run.

Adding a URL

When you first create a Spider object, you are to add one or more URLs to begin processing. If you do not add a URL, the spider will have no work. These URLs are added through the spider's **AddURL** method. Additionally, when the spider finds other URLs the spider itself uses its own **AddURL** method to add URLs. This is helpful because the spiders **AddURL** method performs some checks to make sure the URL should be added to the workload.

First, the spider checks to see if the URL being added is beyond the specified maximum depth.

```
// Check the depth.
if ((this.options.MaxDepth != -1) && (depth > this.options.Max-
Depth))
{
  return;
}
```

Next, the spider makes sure that any filters have not excluded the URL.

```
// Check to see if it does not pass any of the filters.
foreach (SpiderFilter filter in this.filters)
{
  if (filter.IsExcluded(url))
  {
    return;
  }
}
```

Finally, the URL is passed onto the workload manager. If the workload manager returns **true**, the URL was added. The workload manager does some additional filtering on URLs. Specifically, if the workload manager determines that the URL has already been found, then the URL is not reprocessed.

```
// Add the item.
if (this.workloadManager.Add(url, source, depth))
{
  StringBuilder str = new StringBuilder();
  str.Append("Adding to workload: ");
  str.Append(url);
  str.Append(" (depth=");
```

```
str.Append(depth);
str.Append(")");
logging.Log(Logger.Level.INFO, str.ToString());
}
```

Finally, if the URL was added, it is then logged.

Processing All Hosts

When the **Process** method is called, the spider begins working. The **Process** method will not return until the spider has no more work to do. The process method begins by clearing the **cancel** flag and recording the starting time for the spider.

```
this.cancel = false;
this.startTime = DateTime.Now;
```

Next, the spider begins looping until there are no more hosts to process. If at least one URL has been added, there will be at least one host to process. You should always add at least one URL to the spider, otherwise it has no work to do.

```
// Process all hosts/
do
{
  ProcessHost();
} while (this.workloadManager.NextHost() != null);
```

Finally, the spider shuts down the thread pool, and records the stopping time.

```
this.stopTime = DateTime.Now;
```

At this point the spider is complete, and the **Process** method returns.

Processing One Host

The **ProcessHost** method is called for each host the spider needs to process. This method will begin processing URLs on the workload that corresponds to the current host. The **ProcessHost** method is called in a loop, by the **Process** method, until all hosts have been processed.

The **ProcessHost** method begins by obtaining the current host.

```
Uri url = null;

String host = this.workloadManager.GetCurrentHost();
```

Next, spider manager is notified that a new host is beginning.

```
// First, notify the manager.
if (!this.report.BeginHost(host))
{
```

```
    return;
}
```

Next, any filters are notified that we are moving to a new host.

```
// Second, notify any filters of a new host/
foreach (SpiderFilter filter in this.filters)
{
  try
  {
    filter.NewHost(host, this.options.UserAgent);
  }
  catch (IOException e)
  {
    logging.Log(Logger.Level.INFO, "Error while reading robots.txt
file:"
    + e.Message);
  }
}
```

Now that everything has been notified, we can begin processing the host. To do this we attempt to obtain a URL from the workload manager. If no URL was available, we wait for up to 60 seconds and try the process again.

```
// Now process this host.
do
{
  url = this.workloadManager.GetWork();
  if (url != null)
  {

    WaitCallback w = new WaitCallback(SpiderWorkerProc);
    ThreadPool.QueueUserWorkItem(w, url);
  }
  else
  {
    this.workloadManager.WaitForWork(60);
  }
} while (!this.cancel && !workloadManager.WorkloadEmpty());
```

This process continues until there is no work left for the current host.

Other Important Classes in the Heaton Research Spider

When you use the Heaton Research Spider, you will deal primarily with the Spider class. However, there are other important classes in the Heaton Research Spider that you will also use. In particular, the Heaton Research Spider supports several interfaces and is also capable of throwing several exceptions.

Spider Interfaces

There are two interfaces that the Heaton Research Spider uses. These interfaces allow you to define how the spider acts. These interfaces will be discussed in this section.

The first interface is the **SpiderReportable** interface. To use the Heaton Research Spider, you must provide a class that implements the **SpiderReportable** interface. This class is responsible for processing the data that the spider finds.

The second interface is the **WorkloadManager** interface. The **WorkloadManager** class allows the spider to use more than one different type of workload manager. There are two workload managers provided with the spider. The **SQLWorkloadManager** stores URLs in a SQL database. The **MemoryWorkloadManager** stores URLs in memory.

Spider Exceptions

There are two exceptions that can be thrown by the spider. These exceptions must be caught when you are working with the spider. Which exception you must catch is determined by what operation you are performing with the spider.

The first exception is the **SpiderException**. The **Spider** class throws the **SpiderException** when a severe error occurs. This must be a real error that prevents the spider from continuing. Errors that are internal to individual web pages are not thrown as spider errors.

The second exception is the **WorkloadException**. The **WorkloadException** is thrown when there is an error with the workload. That can be a SQL exception, or other communication error when dealing with an SQL based workload manager. Usually classes external to the spider are not exposed to the **WorkloadException**. Rather, these classes will throw the **WorkloadException** as a **SpiderException**.

Configuring the Spider

The **SpiderOptions** class is used to configure the spider. This class can accept configuration directly from other C# classes. Modifying the public properties on the **SpiderOptions** object does this. The **SpiderOptions** class can also load configuration options from a file. Listing 14.2 shows the **SpiderOptions** class.

Listing 14.2: Configuring the Spider (SpiderOptions.cs)

```
using System;
using System.Collections.Generic;
using System.Text;
using System.IO;
using System.Reflection;
```

```
namespace HeatonResearch.Spider
{
    /// <summary>
    /// SpiderOptions: This class contains options for the
    /// spider's execution.
    /// </summary>
    public class SpiderOptions
    {
        /// <summary>
        /// Specifies that when the spider starts up it
        /// should clear the workload.
        /// </summary>
        public const String STARTUP_CLEAR = "CLEAR";

        /// <summary>
        /// Specifies that the spider should resume processing
        /// its workload.
        /// </summary>
        public const String STARTUP_RESUME = "RESUME";

        /// <summary>
        /// How many milliseconds to wait when downloading pages.
        /// </summary>
        public int Timeout
        {
            get
            {
                return timeout;
            }
            set
            {
                timeout = value;
            }
        }

        /// <summary>
        /// The maximum depth to search pages. -1 specifies
        /// no maximum depth.
        /// </summary>
        public int MaxDepth
        {
            get
            {
                return maxDepth;
            }
```

```
        set
        {
            maxDepth = value;
        }
    }

    /// <summary>
    /// What user agent should be reported to the web site.
    ///  This allows the web site to determine what browser
    /// is being used.
    /// </summary>
    public String UserAgent
    {
        get
        {
            return userAgent;
        }
        set
        {
            userAgent = value;
        }
    }


    /// <summary>
    /// The connection string for databases. Used to hold
    /// the workload.
    /// </summary>
    public String DbConnectionString
    {
        get
        {
            return dbConnectionString;
        }
        set
        {
            dbConnectionString = value;
        }
    }


    /// <summary>
    /// What class to use as a workload manager.
    /// </summary>
    public String WorkloadManager
    {
```

```csharp
    get
    {
        return workloadManager;
    }
    set
    {
        workloadManager = value;
    }
}


/// <summary>
/// How to startup the spider, either clear or resume.
/// </summary>
public String Startup
{
    get
    {
        return startup;
    }
    set
    {
        startup = value;
    }
}

/// <summary>
///  Specifies a class to be used a filter.
/// </summary>
public List<String> Filter
{
    get
    {
        return filter;
    }
}


private int timeout = 60000;
private int maxDepth = -1;
private String userAgent = null;
private String dbConnectionString;
private String workloadManager;
private String startup = STARTUP_CLEAR;
private List<String> filter = new List<String>();
```

```csharp
/// <summary>
/// Load the spider settings from a configuration file.
/// </summary>
/// <param name="inputFile">The name of the
/// configuration file.</param>
public void Load(String inputFile)
{
    StreamReader r = File.OpenText(inputFile);

    String line;
    while ((line = r.ReadLine()) != null)
    {
            ParseLine(line);

    }
    r.Close();
}


/// <summary>
/// The line of text read from the configuration file.
/// </summary>
/// <param name="line">The line of text read from the
/// configuration file.</param>
private void ParseLine(String line)
{
    String name, value;
    int i = line.IndexOf(':');
    if (i == -1)
    {
        return;
    }
    name = line.Substring(0, i).Trim();
    value = line.Substring(i + 1).Trim();

    if (value.Trim().Length == 0)
    {
        value = null;
    }


    Type myType = typeof(SpiderOptions);
    FieldInfo field = myType.GetField(name,
        BindingFlags.NonPublic | BindingFlags.Instance);
    if (field == null)
```

```
      {
          throw new SpiderException(
            "Unknown configuration file element: "
            + name + " .");
      }
      else if (field.FieldType.Equals(typeof(String)))
      {
          field.SetValue(this, value);
      }
      else if (field.FieldType.Equals(typeof(List<String>)))
      {
          List<String> list =
            (List<String>)field.GetValue(this);
          list.Add(value);
      }
      else
      {
          int x = int.Parse(value);
          field.SetValue(this, x);
      }
    }


  }
}
```

The **Load** and **LoadLine** methods of the **SpiderOptions** class are used to load data from a spider configuration file. The **Load** method works by reading a simple configuration file that consists of named value pairs. For each name found in the file, the **LoadLine** method uses C# reflection to determine how to set the variable in a **SpiderOptions** object. This allows us to quickly add new variables by adding them to the **SpiderOptions** object. No additional parsing code is needed for any new property.

Reading a Configuration File

The **Load** method reads the spider configuration file. For each line encountered by the load method, the **LoadLine** method is called. The **Load** method begins by opening the file and creating a **BufferedReader**. The **BufferedReader** will allow us to read the file on a line-by-line basis.

```
StreamReader r = File.OpenText(inputFile);
```

Next, a single line is read from the file, if the line is null, then the program is done reading the file.

```
String line;
while ((line = r.ReadLine()) != null)
{
```

```
    ParseLine(line);
}
```

The line that was read is passed on to the **ParseLine** method. Finally, the file is closed.

```
r.Close();
```

The real work of loading the configuration file is done by the **LoadLine** method, which is discussed in the next section.

Reading a Line from the Configuration File

The **LoadLine** method begins by checking for a colon (:) character. This character separates a name from a value. If no colon is found, then the line is invalid, so it is ignored.

```
String name, value;
int i = line.IndexOf(':');
if (i == -1)
{
   return;
}

name = line.Substring(0, i).Trim();
value = line.Substring(i + 1).Trim();

name = line.substring(0, i).trim();
value = line.substring(i + 1).trim();
```

If the value has no length, then it is assumed to be **null**.

```
if (value.Trim().Length == 0)
{
   value = null;
}
```

Next, reflection is used to look up the **name** variable. The names in the configuration file must match the names of the properties in the **SpiderOptions** class. If the variable cannot be found, an error will be thrown, which is caught by the **Load** method.

```
Type myType = typeof(SpiderOptions);
FieldInfo field = myType.GetField(name,
   BindingFlags.NonPublic | BindingFlags.Instance);
```

If the variable is of type **String**, then we simply set the variable to the **value** variable that was parsed earlier.

```
if (field.FieldType.Equals(typeof(String)))
{
   field.SetValue(this, value);
```

```
}
```

If the variable is a **List**, then the value variable is simply added to the **List**.

```
else if (field.FieldType.Equals(typeof(List<String>)))
{
  List<String> list = (List<String>)field.GetValue(this);
  list.Add(value);
}
```

Finally, if the variable is numeric, then the **value** variable is parsed as an integer.

```
else
{
  int x = int.Parse(value);
  field.SetValue(this, x);
}
```

This process is repeated for each line read in the configuration file.

Understanding the Thread Pool

The spider uses a thread pool to perform its tasks. A thread pool programming pattern creates N number of threads to perform tasks. These tasks are organized in a queue. This queue then feeds a workload to the number of threads. As soon as a thread completes its task, it will request the next task from the queue until all tasks have been completed. At this point, the thread can then terminate or sleep until new tasks are available. The number of threads is tuned to increase overall performance.

Thread pools address two different problems. First, they usually provide improved performance when executing large numbers of asynchronous tasks. This is due to a reduced overhead of recreating threads. Secondly, a thread pool provides a means of managing the resources, including threads, consumed when executing a collection of tasks.

C# includes support for thread pools. This is done through the use of the **ThreadPool** class. The **ThreadPool** class is static. As a result, you do not create instances of the **ThreadPool** class; rather you make use of the static methods provided by the **ThreadPool** class.

To use the thread pool, submit tasks to run. These tasks are delegates that point to a worked method. As new tasks are submitted to the thread pool, they are moved to the queue, until the thread pool has time to execute them.

The thread pool is particularly valuable to a spider. Even on a single processor computer, using a thread pool considerably improves the performance of the spider. This is because a spider spends a good deal of time waiting. When a spider submits a request to a web sever, the spider immediately begins waiting for the response. It is much better to be waiting on several web pages than just one.

Constructing the SpiderWorkerProc Method

To use a C# thread pool you must add delegates. These delegates point to a method that will perform the work being performed by the thread pool. The Heaton Research Spider uses the **SpiderWorkerProc** method of the **Spider** class for this purpose.

As the thread pool processes, the **SpiderWorkerProc** method begins by logging the URL it is currently processing. Then a connection is opened to that URL.

```
Stream istream = null;
WebRequest http;
HttpWebResponse response;
Uri url = null;
try
{
  url = (Uri)stateInfo;
  logging.Log(Logger.Level.INFO, "Processing: " + url);
  // Get the URL's contents.
  http = HttpWebRequest.Create(url);
```

Next the timeout value is set. The same timeout value is used both for connection and read timeouts.

```
  http.Timeout = this.options.Timeout;
```

If a **User-Agent** was specified, then the user agent is set.

```
if (this.options.UserAgent != null)
{
  http.Headers["User-Agent"] = this.options.UserAgent;
}
```

The spider is now ready to read the contents of the URL. First, the spider checks to see if the data from the URL is of the MIME type **text/html**. If this is a **text/html** document, a new **SpiderParseHTML** object is created and the **SpiderProcessURL** method is called for the **SpiderReportable** object.

The **SpiderParseHTML** works exactly the same as a **PasrseHTML** class, except that it allows the spider to gather links as the **SpiderProcessURL** method parses the HTML. This allows the spider link gathering to remain transparent to the class using the spider.

```
response = (HttpWebResponse)http.GetResponse();


// Read the URL.
istream = response.GetResponseStream();

// Parse the URL.
```

```
if (String.Compare(response.ContentType, "text/html") == 0)
{
  SpiderParseHTML parse = new SpiderParseHTML(
     response.ResponseUri,
     new SpiderInputStream(istream, null), this);
  this.report.SpiderProcessURL(url, parse);
}
else
{
  this.report.SpiderProcessURL(url, istream);
}
```

If an I/O exception occurs while reading the page, the exception is logged.

```
logging.Log(Logger.Level.INFO, "I/O error on URL:" + url);
try
{
```

In addition to logging the exception, the page is also marked as "error" in the workload manager.

```
  this.workloadManager.MarkError(url);
}
catch (WorkloadException)
{
  logging.Log(Logger.Level.ERROR,
    "Error marking workload(1).", e);
}

this.report.SpiderURLError(url);
return;
```

The spider also traps the catch-all **Exception**. This prevents errors that occur in the **SpiderReportable** class from causing the spider to crash. If an exception occurs, it is logged, and the spider continues.

```
catch (Exception e)
{
  try
  {
    this.workloadManager.MarkError(url);
  }
  catch (WorkloadException)
  {
    logging.Log(Logger.Level.ERROR,
      "Error marking workload(3).", e);
  }

  logging.Log(Logger.Level.ERROR, "Caught exception at URL:"
```

```
      + url.ToString(), e);
   this.report.SpiderURLError(url);
   return;
}
```

A finally block ensures that the **InputStream** is closed.

```
finally
{
  if (istream != null)
  {
    istream.Close();
  }
}
```

If no exceptions have occurred to this point, the URL can be marked as processed in the workload Manager.

```
try
{
  // Mark URL as complete.
  this.workloadManager.MarkProcessed(url);
  logging.Log(Logger.Level.INFO, "Complete: " + url);
  if (!url.Equals(response.ResponseUri))
  {
```

Sometimes the spider will request one URL and get another. This is the case with an HTTP redirect. One requested URL could redirect the browser to another. If this happens, we need to mark the redirected URL 'processed' as well. The following lines of code do this.

```
  // Save the URL(for redirect's).
  this.workloadManager.Add(response.ResponseUri, url,
    this.workloadManager.GetDepth(response.ResponseUri));
  this.workloadManager.MarkProcessed(response.ResponseUri);
}
```

If any errors occur marking the workload, they are logged.

```
catch (WorkloadException e)
{
  logging.Log(Logger.Level.ERROR, "Error marking workload(3).",
      e);
}
```

The thread pool will continue processing until the spider has no more work to do.

Spider HTML Parsing

The Heaton Research Spider provides a **SpiderHTMLParse** object to the **piderProcessURL** method of a **SpiderReportable** object. This object allows the HTML found by the spider to be parsed. However, it also allows the spider to extract links from the HTML. The **SpiderHTMLParse** class is shown in Listing 14.3.

Listing 14.3: HTML Parsing (SpiderParseHTML.cs)

```
using System;
using System.Collections.Generic;
using System.Text;
using System.IO;
using HeatonResearch.Spider.HTML;
using HeatonResearch.Spider.Workload;
using HeatonResearch.Spider.Logging;


namespace HeatonResearch.Spider
{
    /// <summary>
    /// SpiderParseHTML: This class layers on top of the
    /// ParseHTML class and allows the spider to extract what
    /// link information it needs. A SpiderParseHTML class can be
    /// used just like the ParseHTML class, with the spider
    /// gaining its information in the background.
    /// </summary>
    public class SpiderParseHTML : ParseHTML
    {
        /// <summary>
        /// The stream that the parser is reading from.
        /// </summary>
        public SpiderInputStream Stream
        {
            get
            {
                return stream;
            }
        }


        /// <summary>
        /// The Spider that this page is being parsed for.
        /// </summary>
        private Spider spider;

        /// <summary>
        /// The URL that is being parsed.
```

```csharp
    /// </summary>
    private Uri baseURL;

    /// <summary>
    /// The depth of the page being parsed.
    /// </summary>
    private int depth;

    /// <summary>
    /// The InputStream that is being parsed.
    /// </summary>
    private SpiderInputStream stream;

    /// <summary>
    /// Construct a SpiderParseHTML object. This object allows
    /// you to parse HTML, while the spider collects link
    /// information in the background.
    /// </summary>
    /// <param name="baseURL">The URL that is being parsed,
    /// this is used for relative links.</param>
    /// <param name="istream">The InputStream being
    /// parsed.</param>
    /// <param name="spider">The Spider that is
    /// parsing.</param>
    public SpiderParseHTML(Uri baseURL,
            SpiderInputStream istream, Spider spider)
        : base(istream)
    {
        this.stream = istream;
        this.spider = spider;
        this.baseURL = baseURL;
        this.depth = spider.Workload.GetDepth(baseURL);
    }

    /// <summary>
    /// Read a single character. This function will
    /// process any tags that the spider needs for
    /// navigation, then pass the character on to the
    /// caller. This allows the spider to transparently
    /// gather its links.
    /// </summary>
    /// <returns></returns>
    public override int Read()
    {
        int result = base.Read();
        if (result == 0)
```

```
    {
        HTMLTag tag = Tag;

        if (String.Compare(tag.Name, "a", true) == 0)
        {
            String href = tag["href"];
            HandleA(href);
        }
        else if (String.Compare(tag.Name, "img", true)
                == 0)
        {
            String src = tag["src"];
            AddURL(src, Spider.URLType.IMAGE);
        }
        else if (String.Compare(tag.Name, "style", true)
                == 0)
        {
            String src = tag["src"];
            AddURL(src, Spider.URLType.STYLE);
        }
        else if (String.Compare(tag.Name, "link", true)
                == 0)
        {
            String href = tag["href"];
            AddURL(href, Spider.URLType.SCRIPT);
        }
        else if (String.Compare(tag.Name, "base", true)
                == 0)
        {
            String href = tag["href"];
            this.baseURL = new Uri(this.baseURL, href);
        }

    }
    return result;
}

/// <summary>
/// Read all characters on the page. This will discard
/// these characters, but allow the spider to examine the
/// tags and find links.
/// </summary>
public void ReadAll()
{
    while (Read() != -1)
    {
```

```
        }
    }

/// <summary>
/// Used internally, to add a URL to the spider's
/// workload.
/// </summary>
/// <param name="u">The URL to add.</param>
/// <param name="type">What type of link this is.</param>
private void AddURL(String u, Spider.URLType type)
{
    if (u == null)
    {
        return;
    }

    try
    {
        Uri url = URLUtility.constructURL(this.baseURL,
          u, true);
        url = this.spider.Workload.ConvertURL(
          url.ToString());

        if ((String.Compare(url.Scheme, "http", true)
          == 0)
            || (String.Compare(url.Scheme, "https",
                true) == 0))
        {
            if (this.spider.Report.SpiderFoundURL(
                url, this.baseURL, type))
            {
                try
                {
                    this.spider.AddURL(url,
                      this.baseURL, this.depth + 1);
                }
                catch (WorkloadException e)
                {
                    throw new IOException(e.Message);
                }
            }
        }
    }

    catch (UriFormatException)
    {
```

```
            spider.Logging.Log(Logger.Level.INFO,
              "Malformed URL found:" + u);
        }
        catch (WorkloadException)
        {
            spider.Logging.Log(Logger.Level.INFO,
              "Invalid URL found:" + u);
        }
    }


    /// <summary>
    /// This method is called when an anchor(A) tag is found.
    /// </summary>
    /// <param name="href">The link found.</param>
    private void HandleA(String href)
    {

        String cmp = null;
        if (href != null)
        {
            href = href.Trim();
            cmp = href.ToLower();
        }


        if ((cmp != null) &&
            !URLUtility.containsInvalidURLCharacters(href))
        {
            if (!cmp.StartsWith("javascript:")
                && !cmp.StartsWith("rstp:")
                && !cmp.StartsWith("rtsp:")
                && !cmp.StartsWith("news:")
                && !cmp.StartsWith("irc:")
                && !cmp.StartsWith("mailto:"))
            {
                AddURL(href, Spider.URLType.HYPERLINK);
            }
        }
    }
  }
}
```

Several methods and functions make up the **SpiderParseHTML** class. These will be discussed in the next sections.

Constructing a SpiderParseHTML Object

The constructor for the **SpiderParseHTML** class is relatively simple. It accepts several parameters and uses them to initialize the object. As you can see from the following lines of code, each of the instance variables is initialized in the constructor.

```
this.stream = istream;
this.spider = spider;
this.baseURL = baseURL;
this.depth = spider.Workload.GetDepth(baseURL);
```

Once the instance variables are initialized, the **SpiderParseHTML** object is ready for use.

Reading Data from a SpiderParseHTML Object

The **Read** function is called to read individual characters as the HTML is parsed. This works the same as a regular **ParseHTML** object. The **ParseHTML** class was covered in Chapter 5. The **Read** function begins by calling the parent's read function.

```
int result = base.Read();
if (result == 0)
{
```

If the **Read** function returns zero then a tag was found. The tag is checked to see if it is of any of the tag types that contain a link.

```
HTMLTag tag = Tag;

if (String.Compare(tag.Name, "a", true) == 0)
{
  String href = tag["href"];
  HandleA(href);
}
else if (String.Compare(tag.Name, "img", true) == 0)
  {
    String src = tag["src"];
    AddURL(src, Spider.URLType.IMAGE);
  }
  else if (String.Compare(tag.Name, "style", true) == 0)
  {
    String src = tag["src"];
    AddURL(src, Spider.URLType.STYLE);
  }
  else if (String.Compare(tag.Name, "link", true) == 0)
  {
    String href = tag["href"];
    AddURL(href, Spider.URLType.SCRIPT);
  }
```

```
    else if (String.Compare(tag.Name, "base", true) == 0)
    {
      String href = tag["href"];
      this.baseURL = new Uri(this.baseURL, href);
    }
}
return result;
```

For most tag types the **AddURL** method will be called. However, the anchor tag is handled differently with a call to the **HandleA** method.

Adding a URL to the SpiderParseHTML

The **AddURL** method, of the **SpiderParseHTML** class, is called to add a URL. It begins by rejecting any **null** URLs.

```
if (u == null)
{
  return;
}
```

First the URL is converted to fully qualified form. If the **href** of "images/me.gif" were found on the page, the fully qualified URL would be `http://www.httprecipes.com/1/images/me.gif`.

```
try
{
  Uri url = URLUtility.constructURL(this.baseURL, u, true);
  url = this.spider.Workload.ConvertURL(url.ToString());
```

Next the protocol is checked. If the URL's protocol is anything other than **http** or **https**, the URL is ignored.

```
if ((String.Compare(url.Scheme, "http", true) == 0)
    || (String.Compare(url.Scheme, "https", true) == 0))
{
```

The **SpiderFoundURL** function is called to determine if the URL should be added. If the URL should be added, the spider's **AddURL** method is called.

```
if (this.spider.Report.SpiderFoundURL(url, this.baseURL, type))
{
    try
    {
      this.spider.AddURL(url, this.baseURL, this.depth + 1);
    }
    catch (WorkloadException e)
    {
      throw new IOException(e.Message);
    }
}
```

```
    }
}
```

Some URLs require additional processing. The anchor tag is discussed in the next section.

Adding an Anchor URL

Anchor tags sometimes have a prefix such as "javascript:". These are not valid URLs so they cannot be parsed through the **Uri** class. The **HandleA** method takes care of these prefixes. The **HandleA** method begins by trimming the **href** value.

```
if (href != null)
{
  href = href.Trim();
  cmp = href.ToLower();
}
```

If the URL has any of the following well-known prefixes then it will be ignored. Otherwise the URL will be added to the spider's workload.

```
if ((cmp != null) &&
    !URLUtility.containsInvalidURLCharacters(href))
{
  if (!cmp.StartsWith("javascript:")
     && !cmp.StartsWith("rstp:")
     && !cmp.StartsWith("rtsp:")
     && !cmp.StartsWith("news:")
     && !cmp.StartsWith("irc:")
     && !cmp.StartsWith("mailto:"))
  {
    AddURL(href, Spider.URLType.HYPERLINK);
  }
}
```

This allows non-standard URLs to be ignored without throwing a **FormatException**.

Spider Input Stream

The spider also includes a **Stream** derived class named **SpiderInputStream**. This stream works just like a regular **Stream**, except that it holds a **Stream**. This **Stream** is sent a copy of everything read by the **SpiderInputStream**. This allows the raw HTML to be written out to a file as it is parsed. The **SpiderInputStream** is shown in Listing 14.4.

Listing 14.4: Spider Input Stream (SpiderInputStream.cs)

```
using System;
```

```csharp
using System.Collections.Generic;
using System.Text;
using System.IO;

namespace HeatonResearch.Spider
{
    /// <summary>
    /// SpiderInputStream: This class is used by the spider to
    /// both parse and save an InputStream.
    /// </summary>
    public class SpiderInputStream:Stream
    {
        /// <summary>
        /// Reports that this Stream can read.
        /// </summary>
        public override bool CanRead
        {
            get { return true; }
        }

        /// <summary>
        /// Reports that this Stream can not seek.
        /// </summary>
        public override bool CanSeek
        {
            get { return false; }
        }

        /// <summary>
        /// Reports that this Stream can not write.
        /// </summary>
        public override bool CanWrite
        {
            get { return false; }
        }

        /// <summary>
        /// Flush the underlying output stream.
        /// </summary>
        public override void Flush()
        {
            ostream.Flush();
        }

        /// <summary>
        /// Getting the length is not supported.  This will
```

```csharp
/// throw an exception.
/// </summary>
public override long Length
{
    get { throw new Exception(
    "The method or operation is not implemented."); }
}

/// <summary>
/// Getting or setting the position is not supported, this
/// will throw an exception.
/// </summary>
public override long Position
{
    get
    {
        throw new Exception(
          "The method or operation is not implemented.");
    }
    set
    {
        throw new Exception(
          "The method or operation is not implemented.");
    }
}

/// <summary>
/// The OutputStream that this class will send all
/// output to.
///</summary>
public Stream OutputStream
{
    get { return ostream; }
    set { this.ostream = value; }
}

/// <summary>
/// The input stream to read from.
/// </summary>
private Stream istream;


/// <summary>
/// The output stream to write to.
/// </summary>
private Stream ostream;
```

```csharp
/// <summary>
/// Construct a SpiderInputStream object.
/// </summary>
/// <param name="istream">The input stream.</param>
/// <param name="ostream">The output stream.</param>
public SpiderInputStream(Stream istream, Stream ostream)
{
    this.istream = istream;
    this.ostream = ostream;
}


/// <summary>
/// Read bytes from the underlying input stream and also
/// write them to the output stream.
/// </summary>
/// <param name="buffer">The buffer to read into.</param>
/// <param name="offset">The offset into the buffer to
/// begin reading at.</param>
/// <param name="count">The maximum number of bytes
/// to read.</param>
/// <returns></returns>
public override int Read(byte[] buffer, int offset,
    int count)
{
    int result = istream.Read(buffer, offset, count);
    if (ostream != null)
    {
        ostream.Write(buffer, offset, count);
    }
    return result;
}


/// <summary>
/// This operation is not supported, and will throw an
/// exception.
/// </summary>
/// <param name="offset">The offset.</param>
/// <param name="origin">The origin.</param>
/// <returns>How many bytes were read.</returns>
public override long Seek(long offset, SeekOrigin origin)
{
    throw new Exception(
        "The method or operation is not implemented.");
}
```

```
/// <summary>
/// This operation is not supported, and will throw an
/// exception.
/// </summary>
/// <param name="value">The length</param>
public override void SetLength(long value)
{
    throw new Exception(
        "The method or operation is not implemented.");
}

/// <summary>
/// This operation is not supported, and will throw an
/// exception.
/// </summary>
/// <param name="buffer">The buffer to write.</param>
/// <param name="offset">The offset.</param>
/// <param name="count">The count.</param>
public override void Write(byte[] buffer,
        int offset, int count)
{
    throw new Exception(
        "The method or operation is not implemented.");
}
    }
}
```

The **read** function performs the work done by this class. The **read** function reads from the parent class and writes that value to the **Stream**. Then the value is returned to the calling method or function.

Workload Management

A workload manager is a class that manages the list of URLs for the spider. The workload manager tracks which URLs the spider has yet to visit, as well as which URLs resulted in an error.

As URLs are found by the spider, they are added to the workload. Initially, they are in a waiting state. However, as the URL is processed by the spider it will enter other states as well. Table 14.3 lists the states that a URL will go through as it is processed.

Table 14.3: URL States

State	Purpose
ERROR	The URL has resulted in an error. The URL will not enter a new state after this one.
PROCESSED	The URL was processed successfully. The URL will not enter a new state after this one.
WAITING	The URL is waiting to be processed. The URL will enter the WORKING state once the spider is ready to process it.
WORKING	The spider is currently processing the URL. If processing the URL is successful, the URL will enter the PROCESSED state after this state. If processing the URL results in an error, the URL will enter the ERROR state after this state.

Figure 14.1 summarizes these states as a state diagram.

Figure 14.1: URL State Diagram

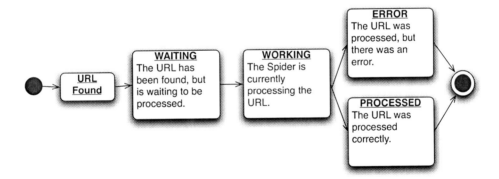

Any class that is to serve as a workload manager must implement the **WorkloadManager** interface. This interface defines the methods and functions necessary to track a list of URLs for the spider. The workload management class is shown in Listing 14.5.

Listing 14.5: Workload Management (WorkloadManager.cs)

```
using System;
using System.Collections.Generic;
using System.Text;
```

```csharp
namespace HeatonResearch.Spider.Workload
{
    /// <summary>
    /// WorkloadManager: This interface defines a workload
    /// manager. A workload manager handles the lists of URLs
    /// that have been processed, resulted in an error, and
    /// are waiting to be processed.
    /// </summary>
    public interface WorkloadManager
    {
        /// <summary>
        /// Add the specified URL to the workload.
        /// </summary>
        /// <param name="url">The URL to be added.</param>
        /// <param name="source">The page that contains
        /// this URL.</param>
        /// <param name="depth">The depth of this URL.</param>
        /// <returns>True if the URL was added, false
        /// otherwise.</returns>
        bool Add(Uri url, Uri source, int depth);

        /// <summary>
        /// Clear the workload.
        /// </summary>
        void Clear();

        /// <summary>
        /// Determine if the workload contains the specified URL.
        /// </summary>
        /// <param name="url">The URL to check.</param>
        /// <returns>True if the URL is contained in the
        /// workload.</returns>
        bool Contains(Uri url);

        /// <summary>
        /// Convert the specified String to a URL. If the
        /// string is too long or has other issues, throw a
        /// WorkloadException.
        /// </summary>
        /// <param name="url">A String to convert into
        /// a URL.</param>
        /// <returns>The URL.</returns>
        Uri ConvertURL(String url);

        /// <summary>
        /// Get the current host.
```

```
/// </summary>
/// <returns>The current host.</returns>
String GetCurrentHost();

/// <summary>
/// Get the depth of the specified URL.
/// </summary>
/// <param name="url">The URL to get the depth of.</param>
/// <returns>The depth of the specified URL.</returns>
int GetDepth(Uri url);

/// <summary>
/// Get the source page that contains the specified URL.
/// </summary>
/// <param name="url">The URL to seek the source
/// for.</param>
/// <returns>The source of the specified URL</returns>
Uri GetSource(Uri url);

/// <summary>
/// Get a new URL to work on. Wait if there are no
/// URL's currently available. Return null if done with
/// the current host. The URL being returned will be
/// marked as in progress.
/// </summary>
/// <returns>The next URL to work on.</returns>
Uri GetWork();

/// <summary>
/// Setup this workload manager for the specified spider.
/// </summary>
/// <param name="spider">The spider using this
/// workload manager.</param>
void Init(Spider spider);

/// <summary>
/// Mark the specified URL as error.
/// </summary>
/// <param name="url">The URL that had an error.</param>
void MarkError(Uri url);

/// <summary>
/// Mark the specified URL as successfully processed.
/// </summary>
/// <param name="url">The URL to mark as
/// processed.</param>
```

```
void MarkProcessed(Uri url);

/// <summary>
/// Move on to process the next host. This should only
/// be called after getWork returns null.
/// </summary>
/// <returns>The name of the next host.</returns>
String NextHost();

/// <summary>
/// Setup the workload so that it can be resumed
/// from where the last spider left the workload.
/// </summary>
void Resume();

/// <summary>
/// If there is currently no work available, then wait
/// until a new URL has been added to the workload.
/// </summary>
/// <param name="time">The amount of time to wait.</param>
void WaitForWork(int time);

/// <summary>
/// Return true if there are no more workload units.
/// </summary>
/// <returns></returns>
bool WorkloadEmpty();


    }
}
```

As you can see from the above listing there are quite a few required functions and methods that a class must implement to serve as a workload manager. These methods and functions are summarized in Table 14.4.

Table 14.4: Methods and Functions in the WorkloadManager Interface

Method or Function	Purpose
add	Add the specified URL to the workload. Return true if the URL was added, false otherwise.
clear	Clear the workload.
contains	Returns true if the workload contains the specified URL.
convertURL	Convert the specified String to a URL. If the string is too long or has other issues, throw a WorkloadException. Returns the URL with any necessary conversion.
getCurrentHost	Returns the current host.
getDepth	Returns the depth for the specified URL.
getSource	Returns the source for the specified URL.
getWork	Returns the next URL that needs to be processed. Also mark this URL as currently being processed.
init	Setup the workload manager.
markError	Mark the specified URL as having an error.
markProcessed	Mark the specified URL as successfully processed.
nextHost	Return the next host to be processed.
resume	Called to setup the workload to resume from a previous attempt.
waitForWork	If there is currently no work available, then wait until a new URL has been added to the workload.
workloadEmpty	Return true if the workload is empty.

By defining a workload management interface, the Heaton Research Spider can be programmed to use a variety of workload managers. Currently there are only two workload managers defined for the Heaton Research Spider. These workload managers are:

- Memory Workload Management
- SQL Workload Management

This chapter will explain the **MemoryWorkloadManager**. The following chapter will explain the **SQLWorkloadManager**.

Memory Workload Management

The most basic workload management type provided by the spider is the memory-based workload. The memory-based workload is contained in the class **MemoryWorkloadManager**. This class stores the complete list of URLs in memory.

The advantage of the **MemoryWorkloadManager** is that it is very easy to setup. Just create a new instance of the **MemoryWorkloadManager** and your spider is ready to go. Because everything is stored in memory, there is no database or file system set up.

The main disadvantage of a **MemoryWorkloadManager** is that it is unable to hold a large number of URLs. Because of this, the **MemoryWorkloadManager** is limited to processing URLs from only a single host. If you would like to process URLs from many different web hosts you will need to use the **SQLWorkloadManager**.

SQL Workload Management

The **SQLWorkloadManager** uses an SQL database to hold the list of URLs. This allows the **SQLWorkloadManager** to process a much larger amount of data than the **MemoryWorkloadManager**. Additionally, the **SQLWorkloadManager** can process multiple hosts.

The main disadvantage of the **SQLWorkloadManager** is that it is complex to setup. You must create a database, with the correct table structure. You must make sure that the spider has the correct login information and drivers for the database. None of this is terribly difficult; however it is more complex than the simple **MemoryWorkloadManager**.

Other Workload Managers

Some databases require specialized workload managers. One such example is Oracle. A specialized workload manager is provided for Oracle named **OracleWorkloadManager**. Oracle requires slightly different forms of a few of the SQL statements used by the workload manager. As a result, it is necessary to create a special workload manager for Oracle. The **OracleWorkloadManager** class is very short. It simply derives from **WorkloadManagement** and replaces a few of the SQL statements.

Currently, the **OracleWorkloadManager**, the **MemoryWorkloadManager** and the **SQLWorkloadManager** are the only supported workload managers. Others may be supported in the future. One example would be a **FileSystemWorkloadManager**. This workload manager uses a directory on the file system to store the URL list. This has a similar capacity to the **SQLWorkloadManager**, but would not require a relational database.

Implementing a Memory Based WorkloadManager

You will now see how the **MemoryWorkloadManager** class is implemented. The memory workload manager stores the list of URLs in several memory-based objects. The **MemoryWorkloadManager** is shown in Listing 14.6.

Listing 14.6: Memory Workload Manager (MemoryWorkloadManager.cs)

```csharp
using System;
using System.Collections.Generic;
using System.Text;
using System.Threading;

namespace HeatonResearch.Spider.Workload.Memory
{
    /// <summary>
    /// MemoryWorkloadManager: This class implements a workload
    /// manager that stores the list of URL's in memory. This
    /// workload manager only supports spidering against a single
    /// host.
    /// </summary>
    public class MemoryWorkloadManager : WorkloadManager
    {
        /// <summary>
        /// The current workload, a map between URL and URLStatus
        /// objects.
        /// </summary>
        private Dictionary<Uri, URLStatus> workload =
            new Dictionary<Uri, URLStatus>();

        /// <summary>
        /// The list of those items, which already in the
        /// workload, that are waiting for processing.
        /// </summary>
        private Queue<Uri> waiting = new Queue<Uri>();

        /// <summary>
        /// How many URL's are currently being processed.
        /// </summary>
        private int workingCount = 0;

        /// <summary>
        /// Because the MemoryWorkloadManager only supports a
        /// single host, the currentHost is set to the host of the
        /// first URL added.
        /// </summary>
        private String currentHost;

        /// <summary>
        /// Allows other threads to wait for the status of the
```

```csharp
/// workload to change.
/// </summary>
private AutoResetEvent workloadEvent =
    new AutoResetEvent(true);

/// <summary>
/// Add the specified URL to the workload.
/// </summary>
/// <param name="url">The URL to be added.</param>
/// <param name="source">The page that contains
/// this URL.</param>
/// <param name="depth">The depth of this URL.</param>
/// <returns>True if the URL was added, false
/// otherwise.</returns>
public bool Add(Uri url, Uri source, int depth)
{
    if (!Contains(url))
    {
        this.waiting.Enqueue(url);
        SetStatus(url, source,
          URLStatus.Status.WAITING, depth);
        if (this.currentHost == null)
        {
            this.currentHost = url.Host.ToLower();
        }
        this.workloadEvent.Set();
        return true;
    }
    return false;

}

/// <summary>
/// Clear the workload.
/// </summary>
public void Clear()
{
    this.workload.Clear();
    this.waiting.Clear();
    this.workingCount = 0;
    this.workloadEvent.Set();
}

/// <summary>
/// Determine if the workload contains the specified URL.
/// </summary>
```

```
/// <param name="url">The URL to check.</param>
/// <returns>Returns true if the specified URL is
/// contained in the workload</returns>
public bool Contains(Uri url)
{
    return (this.workload.ContainsKey(url));
}


/// <summary>
/// Convert the specified String to a URL. If the
/// string is too long or has other issues, throw a
/// WorkloadException.
/// </summary>
/// <param name="url">A String to convert into
/// a URL.</param>
/// <returns>The URL converted.</returns>
public Uri ConvertURL(String url)
{
    try
    {
        return new Uri(url);
    }
    catch (UriFormatException e)
    {
        throw new WorkloadException(e);
    }
}



/// <summary>
/// Get the current host.
/// </summary>
/// <returns>The current host.</returns>
public String GetCurrentHost()
{
    return this.currentHost;
}


/// <summary>
/// Get the depth of the specified URL.
/// </summary>
/// <param name="url">The URL to get the depth of.</param>
/// <returns>The depth of the specified URL.</returns>
public int GetDepth(Uri url)
{
```

```
        URLStatus s = this.workload[url];
        if (s != null)
        {
            return s.Depth;
        }
        else
        {
            return 1;
        }
    }

    /// <summary>
    /// Get the source page that contains the specified URL.
    /// </summary>
    /// <param name="url">The URL to seek the source
    /// for.</param>
    /// <returns>The source of the specified URL.</returns>
    public Uri GetSource(Uri url)
    {
        URLStatus s = this.workload[url];
        if (s == null)
        {
            return null;
        }
        else
        {
            return s.Source;
        }
    }

    /// <summary>
    /// Get a new URL to work on. Wait if there are no URL's
    /// currently available. Return null if done with the
    /// current host. The URL being returned will be marked as
    /// in progress.
    /// </summary>
    /// <returns>The next URL to work on.</returns>
    public Uri GetWork()
    {
        Uri url = null;

        if (this.waiting.Count > 0)
        {
            url = this.waiting.Dequeue();
            SetStatus(url, null,
              URLStatus.Status.WORKING, -1);
```

```
                this.workingCount++;
        }
        return url;
}


/// <summary>
/// Setup this workload manager for the specified spider.
/// This method is not used by the MemoryWorkloadManager.
/// </summary>
/// <param name="spider">The spider using this
/// workload manager.</param>
public void Init(Spider spider)
{
}


/// <summary>
/// Mark the specified URL as error.
/// </summary>
/// <param name="url">The URL that had an error.</param>
public void MarkError(Uri url)
{
        this.workingCount--;
        SetStatus(url, null, URLStatus.Status.ERROR, -1);

}


/// <summary>
/// Mark the specified URL as successfully processed.
/// </summary>
/// <param name="url">The URL to mark as
/// processed.</param>
public void MarkProcessed(Uri url)
{
        this.workingCount--;
        SetStatus(url, null, URLStatus.Status.PROCESSED, -1);
}

/// <summary>
/// Move on to process the next host. This should only be
/// called after getWork returns null. Because the
/// MemoryWorkloadManager is single host only, this
/// function simply returns null.
/// </summary>
```

```csharp
/// <returns>The name of the next host.</returns>
public String NextHost()
{
    return null;
}


/// <summary>
/// Setup the workload so that it can be
/// resumed from where
/// the last spider left the workload.
/// </summary>
public void Resume()
{
    throw (new WorkloadException(
      "Memory based workload managers can not resume."));
}


/// <summary>
/// If there is currently no work available, then wait
/// until a new URL has been added to the workload.
/// </summary>
/// <param name="time">The amount of time to wait.</param>
public void WaitForWork(int time)
{
    DateTime start = DateTime.Now;
    while (!WorkloadEmpty() && this.workingCount > 0)
    {
        if (!workloadEvent.WaitOne(1000, false))
        {
            TimeSpan span = DateTime.Now - start;
            if (span.TotalSeconds > time)
                return;
        }

    }
}

/// <summary>
/// Return true if there are no more workload units.
/// </summary>
/// <returns>Returns true if there are no more
/// workload units.</returns>
public bool WorkloadEmpty()
{
```

```
    try
    {
        Monitor.Enter(this);

        if (this.waiting.Count != 0)
        {
            return false;
        }

        if (this.workingCount < 1)
            return true;
        else
            return false;
    }
    finally
    {
        Monitor.Exit(this);
    }
}

/// <summary>
/// Set the source, status and depth for the
/// specified URL.
/// </summary>
/// <param name="url">The URL to set.</param>
/// <param name="source">The source of this URL.</param>
/// <param name="status"> The status of this URL.</param>
/// <param name="depth">The depth of this URL.</param>
private void SetStatus(Uri url, Uri source,
    URLStatus.Status status, int depth)
{
    URLStatus s;
    if (!this.workload.ContainsKey(url))
    {
        s = new URLStatus();
        this.workload.Add(url, s);
    }
    else
        s = this.workload[url];

    s.CurrentStatus = status;

    if (source != null)
    {
        s.Source = source;
    }
```

```
        if (depth != -1)
        {
            s.Depth = depth;
        }

        workloadEvent.Set();
    }
  }
}
```

There are several instance variables used by the **MemoryWorkloadManager**. These instance variables are summarized in Table 14.5.

Table 14.5: Instance Variables of the MemoryWorkloadManager

Property	Purpose
workload	The current workload, a map between URL and URLStatus objects.
waiting	The list of those items, already in the workload, waiting for processing.
workingCount	The number of URLs being processed.
currentHost	Because the MemoryWorkloadManager only supports a single host, the currentHost is set to the host of the first URL added.

The **MemoryWorkloadManager** class must implement all of the methods and functions in the **WorkloadManager** interface. These functions and methods will be covered in the next few sections.

Adding URLs to the Workload

The **AddURL** method, of the **MemoryWorkloadManager**, is called to add a URL to the workload. First, the workload is checked to see if the URL is already part of the workload. If the URL has not previously been added to the workload, then it is processed.

```
if (!Contains(url))
{
```

The URL is added to the waiting list, and the URL's status is set to waiting. Additionally, the depth is recorded.

```
    this.waiting.Enqueue(url);
    SetStatus(url, source, URLStatus.Status.WAITING, depth);
```

If the **currentHost** variable has not been set, set it to the host of the URL being added. The **MemoryWorkloadManager** can only process one host. If you would like to process more than one host, use the **SQLWorkloadManager**.

```
    this.waiting.Enqueue(url);
    SetStatus(url, source, URLStatus.Status.WAITING, depth);
    if (this.currentHost == null)
    {
      this.currentHost = url.Host.ToLower();
    }
    this.workloadEvent.Set();
    return true;
}
return false;
```

If the URL was not added to the workload then return **false**, otherwise return **true**.

Clearing the Workload

Clearing the workload is easy. The **workload** and **waiting** variables are cleared and the **workingCount** is set to zero.

```
this.workload.Clear();
this.waiting.Clear();
this.workingCount = 0;
this.workloadEvent.Set();
```

The **resume** method is not implemented because the memory workload will not save its data between runs of the program. There will be nothing to resume.

Getting the Depth of a URL

An important aspect of the workload management is to track the depth of each URL encountered. The depth of the URL was stored when the URL was added to the workload. To determine the URL of a workload, the **URLStatus** is read from the map.

```
URLStatus s = this.workload[url];
if (s != null)
{
  return s.Depth;
}
else
{
  return 1;
}
```

The depth of the specified URL is returned.

Getting the Source of a URL

Along with the depth of a URL, the source of a URL is also tracked. The source of a URL is the page on which the URL was found. Finding the source of a URL is very similar to finding the depth of a URL. It is read from the **URLStatus** entry in the map.

```
URLStatus s = this.workload[url];
if (s == null)
{
  return null;
}
else
{
  return s.Source;
}
```

If a URL status is not found for the specified URL, then **null** is returned.

Getting Work

The **GetWork** method is used by the spider to receive individual URLs for the **SpiderWorkerProc** to work on. The **GetWork** method begins by polling the **waiting** queue. The program will wait up to five seconds for something to be placed in the queue.

```
Uri url = null;

if (this.waiting.Count > 0)
{
  url = this.waiting.Dequeue();
  SetStatus(url, null, URLStatus.Status.WORKING, -1);
```

Once a URL is located, the URLs status is set to **WORKING** and the **workingCount** is increased.

```
  this.workingCount++;
}
            return url;
```

Return any URL that was found.

Marking a URL as Error

If an error occurs while processing a URL, that URL is marked as **ERROR**. The **workingCount** is decreased. If this value falls below zero, this is an error. The URL is removed from the waiting queue.

```
this.workingCount--;
SetStatus(url, null, URLStatus.Status.ERROR, -1);
```

Finally, the URLs status is set to **ERROR**.

Marking a URL as Processed

If a URL has been successfully processed, that URL is marked as **PROCESSED**. The **workingCount** is decreased. If this value falls below zero, this is an error. The URL is removed from the waiting queue.

```
this.workingCount--;
SetStatus(url, null, URLStatus.Status.PROCESSED, -1);
```

Finally, the URLs status is set to **PROCESSED**.

Setting a URL Status

Both the **MarkProcessed** and **MarkError** methods rely on the **SetStatus** method to set the status for a URL. The **SetStatus** accepts a URL, a **status**, a page **source** and a page **depth**. Setting the **status** and **depth** is optional. If you do not wish to affect the **source,** pass **null** for source. If you do not wish to affect **depth**, then pass negative one for **depth**.

The **SetStatus** method begins by attempting to access the **URLStatus** object in the map for the specified URL. If no status object is found, then one is created.

```
URLStatus s;
if (!this.workload.ContainsKey(url))
{
  s = new URLStatus();
  this.workload.Add(url, s);
}
else
  s = this.workload[url];

s.CurrentStatus = status;
```

If a value was specified for **source**, set the source for the **URLStatus** object.

```
if (source != null)
{
  s.Source = source;
}
```

If a value was specified for **depth**, then set the source for the **URLStatus** object.

```
if (depth != -1)
{
  s.Depth = depth;
}
```

```
workloadEvent.Set();
```

The workload manager uses this method internally any time the status should be set.

Summary

In Chapter 13 you learned how to use the Heaton Research Spider. In this chapter you saw how the Heaton Research Spider was constructed. This chapter is intended for those who want to see the inner workings of the Heaton Research Spider, rather than simply using it.

The spider uses thread pools to work more efficiently. In addition to allowing the spider to execute more effectively on multi processor systems, the thread pool allows even a single processor system to execute more efficiently. This is because the spider spends a great deal of time waiting. A thread pool allows the spider to be waiting on a large number of URLs.

The spider also uses workload managers. Any workload manager used by the spider must implement the **WorkloadManager** interface. The workload managers manage the URL list. There are two workload managers provided with the Heaton Research Spider. The **MemoryWorkloadManager** class stores the workload in memory. The **SQLWorkloadManager** class stores the workload in an SQL database.

This chapter introduced the internals of the Heaton Research Spider. You also saw how the **MemoryWorkloadManager** was constructed. In the next chapter you will learn how the **SQLWorkloadManager** class was constructed and how the Heaton Research Spider interacts with a SQL based workload manager.

CHAPTER 15: USING A SQL WORKLOAD

- Dealing with Broken Connections
- Using DbCommands
- Creating Hash Codes for URLs
- Working with Multiple Hosts

The Heaton Research Spider includes a SQL based workload manager. The SQL workload manager allows the Heaton Research Spider to store its lists of URLs to an ADO SQL data source. This allows the spider to manage a very large set of URLs. This chapter will discuss the internals of implementing the **SQLWorkloadManager** class.

If you are only interested in using the **SQLWorkloadManager**, refer to Chapter 13. Chapter 13 contains a complete description of how to use the Heaton Research Spider. Chapter 14 explains how the Heaton Research Spider was constructed. This chapter focuses exclusively on how the **SQLWorkloadManager** class was constructed.

There are three different classes making up the SQL workload manager. All three of these classes are in the following package:

HeatonResearch.Spider.Workload.SQL

The classes contained in the above package are listed here:

- RepeatableStatement
- SQLWorkloadManager
- Status

The **RepeatableStatement** holds an SQL statement that can be repeated, if the connection to the database is broken. The **SQLWorkloadManager** is the main class for the SQL workload manager. The **Status** class is used to hold the status of each URL in the workload. The **Status** class is just a simple data holder. The **RepeatableStatement** and **SQLWorkloadManager** classes will be discussed in the next sections.

Repeatable Statements

C# provides a class, named **DbCommand** that allows you to compile SQL into objects that can be quickly executed. Because the SQL workload manager only executes a little over a dozen unique SQL statements, it makes sense to package each of these SQL statements as a **DbCommand**. This will allow the SQL statements to be executed more quickly. However, it is very important that no two threads use the same **DbCommand**. Because of this, it is necessary to create a class that will keep the **DbCommand** objects from different threads apart.

Additionally, we need to build in the ability to repeat an SQL statement. The spider is designed to potentially run for days or weeks when using an SQL workload. The connection to the database could be broken in that time period. We need a way to continue re-executing an SQL statement if it fails. To accomplish both of these design goals, the **RepeatableStatement** class was developed.

Before I show you how the **RepeatableStatement** class was constructed we will briefly examine how it is used. The following code uses a **RepeatableStatement** to execute a simple SQL query.

```
String sql = "SELECT * from table_name where name = ?";

statement.Parameters.Clear();
DbParameter dbParam = statement.CreateParameter();
dbParam.Value = "Fred";
statement.Parameters.Add(dbParam);
DbDataReader reader = statement.ExecuteReader();
Results results = new Results(this, statement, reader);
```

You will notice that the SQL contains a question mark (?). This is a parameter. The parameters you pass on the **ExecuteNonQuery** or **ExecuteReader** function calls will be substituted for the question mark. In the above example, the value of "Fred" is passed in for the question mark.

The **RepeatableStatement** class is shown in Listing 15.1.

Listing 15.1: Repeatable Statements (RepeatableStatement.cs)

```
using System;
using System.Collections.Generic;
using System.Text;
using System.Data.Common;
using System.Data;
using System.Threading;

using HeatonResearch.Spider.Logging;
```

```csharp
namespace HeatonResearch.Spider.Workload.SQL
{
    /// <summary>
    /// RepeatableStatement: Holds a SQL command that can
    /// be repeated if the SQL connection fails.
    /// </summary>
    class RepeatableStatement
    {
        /// <summary>
        /// The results of a query.
        /// </summary>
        public class Results
        {
            /// <summary>
            /// The DataReader associated with these results.
            /// </summary>
            public DbDataReader DataReader
            {
                get
                {
                    return resultSet;
                }
            }

            /// <summary>
            /// The PreparedStatement that generated these
            /// results.
            /// </summary>
            private DbCommand statement;

            /// <summary>
            /// The ResultSet that was generated.
            /// </summary>
            private DbDataReader resultSet;

            /// <summary>
            /// The RepeatableStatement object that this
            /// belongs to.
            /// </summary>
            private RepeatableStatement parent;

            /// <summary>
            /// Construct a Results object.
            /// </summary>
            /// <param name="parent">The parent object, the
```

```csharp
        /// RepeatableStatement.</param>
        /// <param name="statement">The PreparedStatement
        /// for these results.</param>
        /// <param name="resultSet">The ResultSet.</param>
        public Results(RepeatableStatement parent,
              DbCommand statement, DbDataReader resultSet)
        {
            this.statement = statement;
            this.resultSet = resultSet;
            this.parent = parent;
        }

        /// <summary>
        /// Close the ResultSet.
        /// </summary>
        public void Close()
        {
            this.resultSet.Close();
            parent.ReleaseStatement(this.statement);
        }

    }


    /// <summary>
    /// The SQLWorkloadManager that created this object.
    /// </summary>
    private SQLWorkloadManager manager;


    /// <summary>
    /// The SQL for this statement.
    /// </summary>
    private String sql;


    /// <summary>
    /// The PreparedStatements that are assigned to
    /// each thread.
    /// </summary>
    private List<DbCommand> statementCache =
        new List<DbCommand>();


    /// <summary>
    /// Construct a repeatable statement based on the
```

```
/// specified SQL.
/// </summary>
/// <param name="sql">The SQL to base this statement on.
/// </param>
public RepeatableStatement(String sql)
{
    this.sql = sql;
}


/// <summary>
/// Close the statement.
/// </summary>
public void Close()
{
    try
    {
        Monitor.Enter(this);


        foreach (DbCommand statement in
          this.statementCache)
        {

            statement.Dispose();

        }
    }
    finally
    {
        Monitor.Exit(this);
    }
}


/// <summary>
/// Create the statement, so that it is ready to assign
/// PreparedStatements.
/// </summary>
/// <param name="manager">The manager that created
/// this statement.</param>
public void Create(SQLWorkloadManager manager)
{
    Close();
    this.manager = manager;
}
```

```csharp
/// <summary>
/// Execute SQL that does not return a result set. If an
/// error occurs, the statement will be retried until
/// it is successful. This handles broken connections.
/// </summary>
/// <param name="parameters">The parameters for
/// this SQL.</param>
public void Execute(params Object[] parameters)
{
    DbCommand statement = null;

    try
    {
        statement = ObtainStatement();

        for (; ; )
        {
            try
            {
                statement.Parameters.Clear();
                foreach (Object parameter in parameters)
                {
                    DbParameter dbParam =
                      statement.CreateParameter();

                    if (parameter == null)
                    {
                        dbParam.Value = DBNull.Value;
                    }
                    else
                    {
                        dbParam.Value = parameter;
                    }
                    statement.Parameters.Add(dbParam);
                }

                statement.ExecuteNonQuery();
                return;
            }
            catch (Exception e)
            {
                this.manager.Spider.Logging.Log(
                    Logger.Level.ERROR,
                "SQL Exception", e);
```

```
                    this.manager.TryOpen();
            }
        }
    }
    catch (Exception e)
    {
        throw (new WorkloadException(e));
    }
    finally
    {
        if (statement != null)
        {
            ReleaseStatement(statement);
        }
    }
}


/// <summary>
/// Execute an SQL query that returns a result set. If an
/// error occurs, the statement will be retried until
/// it is successful. This handles broken connections.
/// </summary>
/// <param name="parameters">The parameters for
/// this SQL.</param>
/// <returns>The results of the query.</returns>
public Results ExecuteQuery(params Object[] parameters)
{
    DbCommand statement = null;
    try
    {
        statement = ObtainStatement();

        for (; ; )
        {
            try
            {
                statement.Parameters.Clear();
                foreach (Object parameter in parameters)
                {
                    DbParameter dbParam =
                        statement.CreateParameter();

                    if (parameter == null)
                    {
```

```
                                    dbParam.Value = DBNull.Value;
                                }
                                else
                                {
                                    dbParam.Value = parameter;
                                }
                                statement.Parameters.Add(dbParam);
                            }

                            DbDataReader reader =
                                    statement.ExecuteReader();
                            Results results =
                                new Results(this, statement, reader);
                            return results;
                        }
                        catch (Exception e)
                        {
                            this.manager.Spider.Logging.Log(
                                Logger.Level.ERROR,
                                "SQL Exception", e);

                            this.manager.TryOpen();
                        }
                    }
                }
                catch (Exception e)
                {
                    throw (new WorkloadException(e));
                }

            }

        /// <summary>
        /// Obtain a statement. Each thread should use their own
        /// statement, and then call the releaseStatement method
        /// when they are done.
        /// </summary>
        /// <returns>A PreparedStatement object.</returns>
        private DbCommand ObtainStatement()
        {
            DbCommand result = null;

            try
            {
                Monitor.Enter(this);
                if (this.statementCache.Count == 0)
```

```
        {
    result = this.manager.Connection.CreateCommand();
        result.CommandText = this.sql;
        result.Prepare();
    }
    else
    {
        result = this.statementCache[0];
        this.statementCache.Remove(result);
        result.Parameters.Clear();
    }

}
finally
{
    Monitor.Exit(this);
}

return result;
}

/// <summary>
/// This method releases statements after the thread is
/// done with them. These statements are not closed, but
/// rather cached until another thread has need of them.
/// </summary>
/// <param name="stmt">The statement that is to be
/// released.</param>
private void ReleaseStatement(DbCommand stmt)
{
    try
    {
        Monitor.Enter(this);
        if( !this.statementCache.Contains(stmt))
            this.statementCache.Add(stmt);
    }
    finally
    {
        Monitor.Exit(this);
    }
}
}
}
```

As you can see from the above listing, the **RepeatableStatement** class defines several instance variables. These instance variables are defined in Table 15.1.

Table 15.1: Instance Variables of the RepeatableStatement Class

Instance Variable	Purpose
manager	The SQLWorkloadManager that created this object. This is used to reopen the database connection, when needed.
sql	The SQL for this statement. This is used to recreate the DbCommand when needed.
statementCache	The DbCommands that are assigned to each thread.

There are also several methods and functions that make up the `RepeatableStatement` class. These methods and functions will be discussed in the next few sections.

Executing SQL Commands

The `ExecuteNonQuery` method is used to execute SQL commands that do not return a `DbDataReader`. The `ExecuteNonQuery` method makes use of the variable argument count feature of JDK 1.5. This allows a number of parameters to be included with the SQL command. Parameters were discussed earlier in this chapter.

```
public void Execute(params Object[] parameters)
{
  DbCommand statement = null;
```

Next a statement is obtained by calling the `ObtainStatement` function. The `ObtainStatement` function will be covered later in this chapter.

```
try
{
  statement = ObtainStatement();
```

Now we enter a loop to execute the statement. This loop will execute until the statement executes successfully.

```
for (; ; )
{
  try
  {
```

The arguments are copied to the statement.

```
    statement.Parameters.Clear();
    foreach (Object parameter in parameters)
    {
      DbParameter dbParam = statement.CreateParameter();

      if (parameter == null)
```

```
    {
      dbParam.Value = DBNull.Value;
    }
    else
    {
      dbParam.Value = parameter;
    }

    statement.Parameters.Add(dbParam);
  }

  for (int i = 0; i < parameters.length; i++) {
    if (parameters[i] == null) {
  statement.setNull(i, Types.INTEGER);
    } else {
      statement.setObject(i + 1, parameters[i]);
    }
  }
}
```

The current time is taken before and after the SQL is executed. Adding a statement to log this time can be helpful when tuning the SQL statements and queries.

```
statement.ExecuteNonQuery();
return;
```

If an **Exception** is thrown while trying to execute the SQL statement, the connection is reopened and the SQL is tried again.

```
catch (Exception e)
{
  throw (new WorkloadException(e));
}
finally
{
  if (statement != null)
  {
    ReleaseStatement(statement);
  }
}
```

Once the SQL statement has been executed, the statement can be released.

The **ExecuteQuery** function works almost identically to the execute method. The only difference is that the **ExecuteQuery** function returns a **DbDataReader**.

Obtaining a DbCommand

Other than allowing statements to be repeated, the other major function provided by the **RepeatableStatement** class is the ability to allocate **DbCommand** objects to threads. Two threads cannot use the same **DbCommand** object at the same time. To keep threads from using the same **DbCommand** object, the **ObtainStatement** and **ReleaseStatement** functions are used.

The first thing that the **ObtainStatement** function does is to check to see if it can acquire a lock from the **Monitor**. The monitor enforces a critical section. A critical section is a section of code that only one thread may execute at a time. This ensures that no two threads obtain a **DbCommand** at exactly the same time. This prevents two threads from calling **ObtainStatement** at exactly the same time.

```
DbCommand result = null;

try
{
  Monitor.Enter(this);
```

If there are no extra statements already in the cache, create a new **DbCommand**.

```
  if (this.statementCache.Count == 0)
  {
    result = this.manager.Connection.CreateCommand();
    result.CommandText = this.sql;
    result.Prepare();
  }
```

If there is an extra **DbCommand** in the cache, return that **DbCommand** and remove it from the cache.

```
  else
  {
    result = this.statementCache[0];
    this.statementCache.Remove(result);
    result.Parameters.Clear();
  }
```

Once we are done, we can release the **Montitor**. The monitor is released in a **finally** block so that we can be sure that it is actually released, even if an error occurs.

```
  finally
  {
    Monitor.Exit(this);
  }

  return result;
```

Once you are done with the **DbCommand** that we obtained, call **ReleaseStatement** to return it to the cache.

Releasing a DbCommand

When a **DbCommand** is released, with a call to **ReleaseStatment**, the **DbCommand** is not actually released. Rather, it is simply returned to the **DbCommand** cache. This saves the program the overhead of allocating and releasing large numbers of **DbCommand** objects.

The **ReleaseStatement** method first obtains a lock from the **Monitor**. This is the same method as was used by the **ObtainStatement** function. This ensures that no two threads are accessing the **DbCommand** cache at the same time.

```
try
{
  Monitor.Enter(this);
  if( !this.statementCache.Contains(stmt))
    this.statementCache.Add(stmt);
}
```

The **DbCommand** is also added to the cache.

Finally, the **Monitor** is released.

```
finally
{
  Monitor.Exit(this);
}
```

Once the **ReleaseStatement** method is complete, the **DbCommand** is back on the cache awaiting the next thread that needs it.

Implementing a SQL Based Workload Manager

The SQL based workload manager is implemented in the **SQLWorkloadManager** class. In this section I will show you some of the internals of how this class works. This class makes extensive use of SQL. Teaching SQL is beyond the scope of this book. Many of the methods and functions of the **SQLWorkloadManager** are simply wrappers for SQL statements. All of the SQL statements used by the spider are relatively simple, if you know SQL. This section will focus on explaining how the class works and not what the actual SQL does.

The SQL queries used by this class should work with nearly any SQL database, once you get the database setup. For more information about how to setup the database for your particular database see Appendix D. The **SQLWorkloadManager** class is shown in Listing 15.2.

Listing 15.2: SQL Workload Management (SQLWorkloadManager.cs)

```csharp
using System;
using System.Collections.Generic;
using System.Text;
using System.Threading;
using System.Data.Common;
using System.Data;
using System.Reflection;
using HeatonResearch.Spider.Logging;
using System.Data.OleDb;

namespace HeatonResearch.Spider.Workload.SQL
{
    /// <summary>
    /// SQLWorkloadManager: This workload manager stores the URL
    /// lists in an SQL database. This workload manager uses two
    /// tables, which can be created as follows:
    /// <pre>
    /// CREATE TABLE 'spider_host' (
    /// 'host_id' int(10) unsigned NOT NULL auto_increment,
    /// 'host' varchar(255) NOT NULL default '',
    /// 'status' varchar(1) NOT NULL default '',
    /// 'urls_done' int(11) NOT NULL,
    /// 'urls_error' int(11) NOT NULL,
    /// PRIMARY KEY  ('host_id')
    /// )
    ///
    /// CREATE TABLE 'spider_workload' (
    /// 'workload_id' int(10) unsigned NOT NULL auto_increment,
    /// 'host' int(10) unsigned NOT NULL,
    /// 'url' varchar(2083) NOT NULL default '',
    /// 'status' varchar(1) NOT NULL default '',
    /// 'depth' int(10) unsigned NOT NULL,
    /// 'url_hash' int(11) NOT NULL,
    /// 'source_id' int(11) NOT NULL,
    /// PRIMARY KEY  ('workload_id'),
    /// KEY 'status' ('status'),
    /// KEY 'url_hash' ('url_hash'),
    /// KEY 'host' ('host')
    /// )</pre>
    /// </summary>
    public class SQLWorkloadManager : WorkloadManager
    {
        /// <summary>
        /// The database connection being used.
        /// </summary>
```

```csharp
public DbConnection Connection
{
    get
    {
        return connection;
    }
}

/// <summary>
/// The spider being used.
/// </summary>
public Spider Spider
{
    get
    {
        return spider;
    }
}


private SQLHolder holder = new SQLHolder();
private RepeatableStatement stmtClear;
private RepeatableStatement stmtClear2;
private RepeatableStatement stmtAdd;
private RepeatableStatement stmtAdd2;
private RepeatableStatement stmtGetWork;
private RepeatableStatement stmtGetWork2;
private RepeatableStatement stmtWorkloadEmpty;
private RepeatableStatement stmtSetWorkloadStatus;
private RepeatableStatement stmtSetWorkloadStatus2;
private RepeatableStatement stmtGetDepth;
private RepeatableStatement stmtGetSource;
private RepeatableStatement stmtResume;
private RepeatableStatement stmtResume2;
private RepeatableStatement stmtGetWorkloadID;
private RepeatableStatement stmtGetHostID;
private RepeatableStatement stmtGetNextHost;
private RepeatableStatement stmtSetHostStatus;
private RepeatableStatement stmtGetHost;

/// <summary>
/// The connection string for the connection.
/// </summary>
private String connectionString;

/// <summary>
```

```csharp
/// Only one thread at a time is allowed to add to the
/// workload.
/// </summary>
private Semaphore addLock;

/// <summary>
/// Is there any work?
/// </summary>
private AutoResetEvent workLatch;

/// <summary>
/// The maximum size a Uri can be.
/// </summary>
private int maxURLSize;

/// <summary>
/// The maximum size that a host can be.
/// </summary>
private int maxHostSize;

/// <summary>
/// All of the RepeatableStatement objects.
/// </summary>
private List<RepeatableStatement> statements =
    new List<RepeatableStatement>();

/// <summary>
/// Used to obtain the next URL.
/// </summary>
private RepeatableStatement.Results workResultSet = null;

/// <summary>
/// Used to obtain the next host.
/// </summary>
private RepeatableStatement.Results hostResultSet = null;

/// <summary>
/// A connection to a OLEDB database.
/// </summary>
private DbConnection connection;

/// <summary>
/// The current host.
/// </summary>
private String currentHost;
```

```
/// <summary>
/// The ID of the current host.
/// </summary>
private int currentHostID = -1;

/// <summary>
/// The spider that this object is being used with.
/// </summary>
private Spider spider;


/// <summary>
/// Add the specified Uri to the workload.
/// </summary>
/// <param name="url">The URL to be added.</param>
/// <param name="source">The page that contains
/// this URL.</param>
/// <param name="depth">The depth of this URL.</param>
/// <returns>True if the URL was added, false
/// otherwise.</returns>
public virtual bool Add(Uri url, Uri source, int depth)
{
    bool result = false;
    try
    {
        this.addLock.WaitOne();
        if (!Contains(url))
        {
            String strURL = Truncate(url.ToString(),
                this.maxURLSize);
            String strHost = Truncate(url.Host,
                this.maxHostSize).ToLower();
            result = true;

            // get the host
            int hostID = GetHostID(url, false);

            if (hostID == -1)
            {
                this.stmtAdd2.Execute(strHost,
                Status.STATUS_WAITING, 0, 0);
                hostID = GetHostID(url, true);
            }

            // need to set the current host for the
            // first time?
```

```csharp
                if (this.currentHostID == -1)
                {
                    this.currentHostID = hostID;
                    this.currentHost = strHost;
                    this.stmtSetHostStatus.Execute(
        Status.STATUS_PROCESSING, this.currentHostID);
                }

                // now add workload element
                if (source != null)
                {
                    int sourceID = GetWorkloadID(source,
                         true);
                    this.stmtAdd.Execute(hostID, strURL,
                        Status.STATUS_WAITING, depth,
                        ComputeHash(url), sourceID);
                }
                else
                {
                    this.stmtAdd.Execute(hostID, strURL,
                        Status.STATUS_WAITING, depth,
                        ComputeHash(url), 0);
                }

                this.workLatch.Set();
            }

        }
        catch (Exception e)
        {
            throw (new WorkloadException(e));
        }
        finally
        {
            this.addLock.Release();
        }
        return result;
    }

    /// <summary>
    /// Clear the workload.
    /// </summary>
    public virtual void Clear()
    {
        this.stmtClear.Execute();
        this.stmtClear2.Execute();
```

```
    }

    /// <summary>
    /// Close the workload.
    /// </summary>
    public void Close()
    {
        if (this.workResultSet != null)
        {
            try
            {
                this.workResultSet.Close();
            }
            catch (Exception)
            {
                spider.Logging.Log(Logger.Level.ERROR,
"Error trying to close workload result set, ignoring...");
            }
            this.workResultSet = null;
        }

        foreach (RepeatableStatement
            statement in this.statements)
        {
            statement.Close();
        }

        if (this.connection != null)
        {
            this.connection.Close();
        }
    }

    /// <summary>
    /// Determine if the workload contains the specified URL.
    /// </summary>
    /// <param name="url">The Uri to search the w
    /// orkload for.</param>
    /// <returns>True if the workload contains the
    /// specified URL.</returns>
    public virtual bool Contains(Uri url)
    {
        try
        {
            return (GetWorkloadID(url, false) != -1);
        }
```

```
        catch (Exception e)
        {
            throw (new WorkloadException(e));
        }
    }

    /// <summary>
    /// Convert the specified String to a URL. If the
    /// string is too long or has other issues, throw a
    /// WorkloadException.
    /// </summary>
    /// <param name="url">A String to convert into a URL.
    /// </param>
    /// <returns>The URL.</returns>
    public virtual Uri ConvertURL(String url)
    {
        Uri result = null;

        url = url.Trim();
        if (url.Length > this.maxURLSize)
        {
            throw new WorkloadException(
                "Uri size is too big, must be under "
                  + this.maxURLSize + " bytes.");
        }

        try
        {
            result = new Uri(url);
        }
        catch (UriFormatException e)
        {
            throw new WorkloadException(e);
        }
        return result;
    }

    /// <summary>
    /// Get the current host.
    /// </summary>
    /// <returns>The current host.</returns>
    public virtual String GetCurrentHost()
    {
        return this.currentHost;
    }
```

```csharp
/// <summary>
/// Get the depth of the specified URL.
/// </summary>
/// <param name="url">The URL to get the depth of.</param>
/// <returns>The depth of the specified URL.</returns>
public virtual int GetDepth(Uri url)
{
    RepeatableStatement.Results rs = null;
    try
    {
        rs = this.stmtGetDepth.ExecuteQuery(
          ComputeHash(url));
        while (rs.DataReader.Read())
        {
            String u = (String)rs.DataReader[0];
            if (u.Equals(url.ToString()))
            {
                return (int)rs.DataReader[1];
            }
        }
        return 1;
    }
    catch (Exception e)
    {
        throw (new WorkloadException(e));
    }
    finally
    {
        if (rs != null)
        {
            rs.Close();
        }
    }
}

/// <summary>
/// Get the source page that contains the specified URL.
/// </summary>
/// <param name="url">The Uri to seek the source for.
/// </param>
/// <returns>The source of the specified URL.</returns>
public virtual Uri GetSource(Uri url)
{
    RepeatableStatement.Results rs = null;
    try
    {
```

```
        rs = this.stmtGetSource.ExecuteQuery(
          ComputeHash(url));
        while (rs.DataReader.Read())
        {
            String u = (String)rs.DataReader[0];
            if (u.Equals(url.ToString()))
            {
                return (new Uri((String)
                      rs.DataReader[0]));
            }
        }
        return null;
    }
    catch (UriFormatException e)
    {
        throw (new WorkloadException(e));
    }
    catch (Exception e)
    {
        throw (new WorkloadException(e));
    }
    finally
    {
        if (rs != null)
        {
            rs.Close();
        }
    }
}

/// <summary>
/// Get a new Uri to work on. Wait if there are no URL's
/// currently available. Return null if done with the
/// current host. The Uri being returned will be marked as
/// in progress.
/// </summary>
/// <returns>The next URL to work on.</returns>
public virtual Uri GetWork()
{
    Uri url = null;
    do
    {
        url = GetWorkInternal();
        if (url == null)
        {
            if (WorkloadEmpty())
```

```
                    {
                        break;
                    }

                }
            } while (url == null);

            return url;
        }

        /// <summary>
        /// Setup this workload manager for the specified spider.
        /// </summary>
        /// <param name="spider">
            The spider using this workload manager.</param>
        public virtual void Init(Spider spider)
        {
            this.spider = spider;
            this.addLock = new Semaphore(1, 1);
            this.workLatch = new AutoResetEvent(false);

            this.connectionString =
                    spider.Options.DbConnectionString;

            this.statements.Add(this.stmtClear =
new RepeatableStatement(this.holder.getSQLClear()));
            this.statements.Add(this.stmtClear2 =
new RepeatableStatement(this.holder.getSQLClear2()));
            this.statements.Add(this.stmtAdd =
new RepeatableStatement(this.holder.getSQLAdd()));
            this.statements.Add(this.stmtAdd2 =
new RepeatableStatement(this.holder.getSQLAdd2()));
            this.statements.Add(this.stmtGetWork =
new RepeatableStatement(this.holder.getSQLGetWork()));
            this.statements.Add(this.stmtGetWork2 =
new RepeatableStatement(this.holder.getSQLGetWork2()));
            this.statements
                .Add(this.stmtWorkloadEmpty =
new RepeatableStatement(this.holder.getSQLWorkloadEmpty()));
            this.statements.Add(this.stmtSetWorkloadStatus =
new RepeatableStatement(
                this.holder.getSQLSetWorkloadStatus()));
            this.statements.Add(this.stmtSetWorkloadStatus2 =
new RepeatableStatement(
                this.holder.getSQLSetWorkloadStatus2()));
            this.statements.Add(this.stmtGetDepth =
```

```
new RepeatableStatement(this.holder.getSQLGetDepth()));
        this.statements.Add(this.stmtGetSource =
new RepeatableStatement(this.holder.getSQLGetSource()));
        this.statements.Add(this.stmtResume =
new RepeatableStatement(this.holder.getSQLResume()));
        this.statements.Add(this.stmtResume2 =
new RepeatableStatement(this.holder.getSQLResume2()));
        this.statements
            .Add(this.stmtGetWorkloadID =
new RepeatableStatement(this.holder.getSQLGetWorkloadID()));
        this.statements.Add(this.stmtGetHostID =
new RepeatableStatement(this.holder.getSQLGetHostID()));
        this.statements.Add(this.stmtGetNextHost =
new RepeatableStatement(this.holder.getSQLGetNextHost()));
        this.statements
            .Add(this.stmtSetHostStatus =
new RepeatableStatement(this.holder.getSQLSetHostStatus()));
        this.statements.Add(this.stmtGetHost =
new RepeatableStatement(this.holder.getSQLGetHost()));

            try
            {
                Open();

                this.maxURLSize = GetColumnSize(
                  "spider_workload", "url");
                this.maxHostSize = GetColumnSize(
                  "spider_host", "host");
            }
            catch (Exception e)
            {
                throw (new WorkloadException(e));
            }
        }

        /// <summary>
        /// Mark the specified Uri as error.
        /// </summary>
        /// <param name="url">The URL that had an error.</param>
        public virtual void MarkError(Uri url)
        {
            try
            {
                SetStatus(url, Status.STATUS_ERROR);
                this.workLatch.Set();
            }
```

```
    catch (Exception e)
    {
        throw (new WorkloadException(e));
    }
}


/// <summary>
/// Mark the specified Uri as successfully processed.
/// </summary>
/// <param name="url">The Uri to mark as
/// processed.</param>
public virtual void MarkProcessed(Uri url)
{
    try
    {
        SetStatus(url, Status.STATUS_DONE);
        this.workLatch.Set();
    }
    catch (Exception e)
    {
        throw (new WorkloadException(e));
    }
}


/// <summary>
/// Move on to process the next host. This should only be
/// called after getWork returns null.
/// </summary>
/// <returns>The name of the next host.</returns>
public virtual String NextHost()
{
    if (this.currentHostID == -1)
    {
        throw new WorkloadException(
    "Attempting to obtain host before adding first URL.");
    }
    else
    {
        MarkHostProcessed(this.currentHost);
    }

    try
    {
        bool requery = false;

        if (this.hostResultSet == null)
```

```csharp
        {
            requery = true;
        }
        else
        {
            if (!this.hostResultSet.DataReader.Read())
            {
                requery = true;
            }
        }

        if (requery)
        {
            if (this.hostResultSet != null)
            {
                this.hostResultSet.Close();
            }

            this.hostResultSet =
this.stmtGetNextHost.ExecuteQuery(Status.STATUS_WAITING);

            if (!this.hostResultSet.DataReader.Read())
            {
                return null;
            }
        }

        this.currentHostID = (int)
                this.hostResultSet.DataReader[0];
        this.currentHost = (String)
                this.hostResultSet.DataReader[1];
        this.stmtSetHostStatus.Execute(
          Status.STATUS_PROCESSING, this.currentHostID);
        spider.Logging.Log(Logger.Level.INFO,
          "Moving to new host: " + this.currentHost);
        return this.currentHost;

    }
    catch (Exception e)
    {
        throw (new WorkloadException(e));
    }

}

/// <summary>
```

```
/// Setup the workload so that it can be resumed
/// from where the last spider left the workload.
/// </summary>
public virtual void Resume()
{
    RepeatableStatement.Results rs = null;

    try
    {
        rs = this.stmtResume.ExecuteQuery();

        if (!rs.DataReader.Read())
        {
            throw (new WorkloadException(
  "Can't resume, unable to determine current host."));
        }

        this.currentHostID = (int)rs.DataReader[0];
        this.currentHost = (String)GetHost(
                this.currentHostID);
    }
    catch (Exception e)
    {
        throw (new WorkloadException(e));
    }
    finally
    {
        if (rs != null)
        {
            rs.Close();
        }
    }

    this.stmtResume2.Execute();


}

/// <summary>
/// If there is currently no work available, then wait
/// until a new Uri has been added to the workload.
/// </summary>
/// <param name="time">The amount of time to wait.</param>
public virtual void WaitForWork(int time)
{

    this.workLatch.WaitOne();
```

```csharp
}

/// <summary>
/// Return true if there are no more workload units.
/// </summary>
/// <returns>Returns true if there are no more workload
/// units.</returns>
public virtual bool WorkloadEmpty()
{
    RepeatableStatement.Results rs = null;

    try
    {
        rs = this.stmtWorkloadEmpty.ExecuteQuery(
          this.currentHostID);
        if (!rs.DataReader.Read())
        {
            return true;
        }
        return ((int)rs.DataReader[0] < 1);
    }
    catch (Exception e)
    {
        throw (new WorkloadException(e));
    }
    finally
    {
        if (rs != null)
        {
            rs.Close();
        }
    }
}

/// <summary>
/// Compute a hash for a URL.
/// </summary>
/// <param name="url">The Uri to compute the hash
/// for.</param>
/// <returns>The hash code.</returns>
protected virtual int ComputeHash(Uri url)
{
    String str = url.ToString().Trim();
```

```
        int result = str.GetHashCode();
        result = (result % 0xffff);
        return result;
    }


    /// <summary>
    /// Return the size of the specified column.
    /// </summary>
    /// <param name="table">The table that contains the
    /// column.</param>
    /// <param name="column">The column to get the size
    /// for.</param>
    /// <returns>The size of the column.</returns>
    public virtual int GetColumnSize(String table,
        String column)
    {
        try
        {
            DataTable datatable = connection.
GetSchema("Columns");
// Unfortunatly the hard coded string values below are not really
// standardized, even amoung Microsoft products.  If you find that
// this method is always returning -1 for the column length, try
// the following lines of code, they will dump all information
// from the schema to the console.  Then you can find out what
// your database/driver uses for column_length.
//foreach (DataRow row in datatable1.Rows)
//{
//    foreach (DataColumn col in datatable.Columns)
//    {
//        Console.WriteLine(col.ToString() + " = " +
// row[col].ToString());
//    }
//}

            foreach (System.Data.DataRow row in
              datatable.Rows)
            {

                if (String.Compare(
    row["COLUMN_NAME"].ToString(), column, true) == 0)
                {
                    return int.Parse(
    row["CHARACTER_MAXIMUM_LENGTH"].ToString());
                }
            }
```

```csharp
        }
        catch (Exception)
        {
            // Like was stated above, different databases
            // seem to name things
            // differently.  If an error occurs, then just
            // report that we can't
            // get the length, by falling through to the -1.
        }

        return 1;
    }

    /// <summary>
    /// Get the host name associated with the specified
    /// host id.
    /// </summary>
    /// <param name="hostID">The host id to look up.</param>
    /// <returns>The name of the host.</returns>
    protected virtual String GetHost(int hostID)
    {
        RepeatableStatement.Results rs = null;

        try
        {
            rs = this.stmtGetHost.ExecuteQuery(hostID);
            if (!rs.DataReader.Read())
            {
                throw new WorkloadException(
                    "Can't find previously created host.");
            }
            return (String)rs.DataReader[0];
        }
        catch (Exception e)
        {
            throw new WorkloadException(e);
        }
        finally
        {
            if (rs != null)
            {
                rs.Close();
            }
        }
```

```
}

/// <summary>
/// Get the id for the specified host name.
/// </summary>
/// <param name="host">The host to lookup.</param>
/// <param name="require">Should an exception be thrown
/// if the host is not located.</param>
/// <returns>The id of the specified host name.</returns>
protected virtual int GetHostID(String host, bool require)
{
    RepeatableStatement.Results rs = null;

    // is this the current host?
    if (this.currentHostID != -1)
    {
        if (String.Compare(this.currentHost, host,
          true) == 0)
        {
            return this.currentHostID;
        }
    }

    // use the database to find it
    try
    {
        rs = this.stmtGetHostID.ExecuteQuery(host);

        if (rs.DataReader.Read())
        {
            return (int)rs.DataReader[0];
        }

    }
    finally
    {
        if (rs != null)
        {
            rs.Close();
        }
    }

    if (require)
    {
        StringBuilder str = new StringBuilder();
        str.Append(
```

```
            "Failed to find previously visited Host,");
        str.Append("Host=\"");
        str.Append(host);
        str.Append("\".");
        throw (new WorkloadException(str.ToString()));
    }
    else
    {
        return -1;
    }
}

/// <summary>
/// Get the ID for the given host. The host name is
/// extracted from the specified URL.
/// </summary>
/// <param name="url">The Uri that specifies the host
/// name to lookup.</param>
/// <param name="require">Should an exception be thrown
/// if the host is not located.</param>
/// <returns></returns>
protected virtual int GetHostID(Uri url, bool require)
{
    String host = url.Host.ToLower();
    return GetHostID(host, require);
}

/// <summary>
/// Called internally to get a work unit. This function
/// does not wait for work, rather it simply returns null.
/// </summary>
/// <returns>The next Uri to process.</returns>
protected virtual Uri GetWorkInternal()
{
    if (this.currentHostID == -1)
    {
        throw new WorkloadException(
    "Attempting to obtain work before adding first URL.");
    }

    try
    {
        bool requery = false;

        if (this.workResultSet == null)
        {
```

```
            requery = true;
        }
        else
        {
            if (!this.workResultSet.DataReader.Read())
            {
                requery = true;
            }
        }

        if (requery)
        {
            if (this.workResultSet != null)
            {
                this.workResultSet.Close();
            }

            this.workResultSet =
this.stmtGetWork.ExecuteQuery(Status.STATUS_WAITING,
                this.currentHostID);

            if (!this.workResultSet.DataReader.Read())
            {
                return null;
            }
        }

        int id = (int)this.workResultSet.DataReader[0];
        String url =
            (String)this.workResultSet.DataReader[1];

        this.stmtGetWork2.Execute(
            Status.STATUS_PROCESSING, id);
        return new Uri(url);
    }
    catch (UriFormatException e)
    {
        throw (new WorkloadException(e));
    }
    catch (Exception e)
    {
        throw (new WorkloadException(e));
    }
}
```

```csharp
/// <summary>
/// Get the workload ID, given a URL.
/// </summary>
/// <param name="url"> The URL to look up.</param>
/// <param name="require">Should an exception be thrown
/// if the workload
/// is not located.</param>
/// <returns>The ID of the workload.</returns>
protected virtual int GetWorkloadID(Uri url, bool require)
{
    int hash = 0;
    RepeatableStatement.Results rs = null;
    try
    {
        hash = ComputeHash(url);
        rs = this.stmtGetWorkloadID.ExecuteQuery(hash);
        while (rs.DataReader.Read())
        {
            if (rs.DataReader[1].Equals(url.ToString()))
            {
                return (int)rs.DataReader[0];
            }
        }
    }
    finally
    {
        if (rs != null)
        {
            rs.Close();
        }
    }

    if (require)
    {
        StringBuilder str = new StringBuilder();
        str.Append(
"Failed to find previously visited URL, hash=\"");
        str.Append(hash);
        str.Append("\", URL=\"");
        str.Append(url.ToString());
        str.Append("\".");
        throw (new WorkloadException(str.ToString()));
    }
    else
    {
        return -1;
```

```
    }
}

/// <summary>
/// Mark the specified host as processed.
/// </summary>
/// <param name="host">The host to mark.</param>
protected virtual void MarkHostProcessed(String host)
{
    try
    {
        int hostID = this.GetHostID(host, true);
        this.stmtSetHostStatus.Execute(
            Status.STATUS_DONE, hostID);
    }
    catch (Exception e)
    {
        throw new WorkloadException(e);
    }
}


/// <summary>
/// Open a database connection.
/// </summary>
protected virtual void Open()
{
    connection = new OleDbConnection(
            this.spider.Options.DbConnectionString);
    connection.Open();

    foreach (RepeatableStatement statement
            in this.statements)
    {
        statement.Create(this);
    }
}

/// <summary>
/// Set the status for the specified URL.
/// </summary>
/// <param name="url">The Uri to set the status for.
/// </param>
/// <param name="status">What to set the
/// status to.</param>
protected virtual void SetStatus(Uri url, String status)
```

```
{
    int id = GetWorkloadID(url, true);
    this.stmtSetWorkloadStatus.Execute("" + status, id);
    if (String.Compare(status,
            Status.STATUS_ERROR, true) == 0)
    {
        this.stmtSetWorkloadStatus2.Execute(0, 1,
                url.Host.ToLower());
    }
    else if (String.Compare(status, Status.STATUS_DONE,
            true) == 0)
    {
        this.stmtSetWorkloadStatus2.Execute(1, 0,
                url.Host.ToLower());
    }

}

/// <summary>
/// Truncate a string to the specified length.
/// </summary>
/// <param name="str">The string to truncate.</param>
/// <param name="length">The length to truncate the
/// string to.</param>
/// <returns>The truncated string.</returns>
protected virtual String Truncate(String str, int length)
{
    if (str.Length < length)
    {
        return str;
    }
    else
    {
        return str.Substring(0, length);
    }
}

/// <summary>
/// Try to open the database connection.
/// </summary>
public virtual void TryOpen()
{
    Exception ex = null;

    this.spider.Logging.Log(Logger.Level.ERROR,
    "Lost connection to database, trying to reconnect.");
```

```
for (int i = 1; i < 120; i++)
{
    try
    {
        Close();
    }
    catch (Exception e1)
    {
        this.spider.Logging.Log(Logger.Level.ERROR,
"Failed while trying to close lost connection, ignoring...", e1);
    }

    ex = null;

    try
    {
        this.spider.Logging.Log(Logger.Level.ERROR,
      "Attempting database reconnect");
        Open();
        this.spider.Logging.Log(Logger.Level.ERROR,
      "Database connection reestablished");
        break;
    }
    catch (Exception e)
    {
        ex = e;
        this.spider.Logging.Log(Logger.Level.ERROR,
            "Reconnect failed", ex);
    }

    if (ex != null)
    {

        this.spider.Logging.Log(Logger.Level.ERROR,
            "Reconnect attempt " + i
          + " failed.  Waiting to try again.");
        Thread.Sleep(30000);

    }
}

if (ex != null)
{
    throw (new WorkloadException(ex));
}
```

```
        }

        /// <summary>
        /// Create the correct type of SQLHolder to go
        /// along with this workload manager.
        /// </summary>
        /// <returns>A SQLHolder.</returns>
        public virtual SQLHolder CreateSQLHolder()
        {
            return new SQLHolder();
        }
    }
}
```

As you can see from the above listing, the **SQLWorkloadManager** class defines several instance variables. These instance variables are defined in Table 15.2.

Table 15.2: Instance Variables of the RepeatableStatement Class

Instance Variable	Purpose
connection	A connection to a ADO database connection.
currentHost	The current host.
currentHostID	The ID of the current host.
driver	The driver for the ADO connection.
hostResultSet	Used to obtain the next host.
maxHostSize	The maximum size that a host can be. Determined from the column size of the HOST field of the SPIDER_HOST table.
maxURLSize	The maximum size a URL can be. Determined from the column size of the URL field of SPIDER_WORKLOAD table.
statements	All of the DbCommand objects.
url	The URL for the ADO connection.

There are also several methods and functions that make up the **RepeatableStatement** class. These methods and functions will be discussed in the following sections.

Generating Hash Codes

URLs can become quite long. Sometimes they will exceed 2,000 characters. In reality, very few URLs will ever reach this length. However, since they can, they must be supported. This is why the **URL** field of the **SPIDER_WORKLOAD** table is 2,083, which is the maximum URL size supported by many web browsers.

This large field size presents a problem. The spider will often need to lookup and see if a URL has already been processed. The long URL length makes this field very difficult to index in a database. To get around this issue, we create a hash of the URL and store this into a field named **URL_HASH**. Using the hash we can quickly narrow the search down to just a few rows. Additionally, because the hash is a number, it can very efficiently be indexed.

You may be wondering what a hash is. A hash is a very common computer programming technique where you convert a String, or other object type, to a number. C# includes support for hash all the way down to the **Object** level. The **Object** class contains a method called **hashCode**. The **GetHashCode** function returns a hash for any C# object.

A hash code is not a unique identifier. Hash codes are never guaranteed to be unique. Though they are not unique, they allow us to break large sets of data down into small manageable sets that can be accessed very quickly.

To compute a hash for a URL, the **SQLWorkloadManager** class uses the **ComputeHash** method. The **ComputeHash** function relies heavily on C#s built in **GetHashCode** function. The **ComputeHash** method begins by converting the URL to a **String** and trimming it.

```
String str = url.ToString().Trim();
```

Next the **GetHashCode** function is called to generate a hash code for the trimmed URL.

```
int result = str.GetHashCode();
result = (result % 0xffff);
return result;
```

The hash code is trimmed to 16-bits in length. This allows the hash code to be stored as a regular integer column type.

Workload Synchronization

The SQL workload manager must synchronize access to the workload. There are two synchronization objects used by the **SQLWorkloadManager**. The first, named **addLock**, is defined as:

```
private Semaphore addLock;
```

The **addLock** semaphore is used to ensure that no two threads add to the workload at exactly the same time. This prevents the workload from getting two or more of the same URLs added. A semaphore is a synchronization object that allows a specified number of threads to simultaneously access a resource. The **addLock** resource was created to allow only one thread to access it at a time. A semaphore that allows only one thread to access at a time is sometimes called a mutex.

The second synchronization object used by the **SQLWorkloadManager**, named **workLatch**, is defined as:

```
private AutoResetEvent workLatch;
```

The **workLatch** synchronization object allows threads to wait until a workload becomes available. A latch allows several threads to wait for an event to occur. When the event occurs, the latch allows the resource to be accessed.

Multiple Hosts

The ability to spider multiple hosts is one of the main reasons to use the SQL workload manager. First, let me define what I mean by multiple hosts. Consider the following two URLs. These URLs are on the same host:

```
http://www.httprecipes.com/index.php
```

```
http://www.httprecipes.com/1/index.php
```

The above URLs both specify different internet resources; however, they are both on the same host. They both are on the host **www.httprecipes.com**.

The following two URLs are on different hosts:

```
http://www.httprecipes.com/index.php
```

```
http://www.heatonresearch.com/index.php
```

Even though both of these URLs access the file **index.php**, they are both on different hosts. The first URL is on the **www.httprecipes.com** host, and the second is on the **www.heatonresearch.com** host.

If any part of the host is different, the two hosts are considered to be different. For example **www1.heatonresearch.com** and **www2.heatonresearch.com** are two different hosts.

To support multiple hosts, the SQL workload manager uses the **SPIDER_HOST** table. The **SPIDER_HOST** table keeps a list of all of the hosts that a spider has encountered.

The Heaton Research Spider only processes one host at a time. Once all the URLs from one host have been processed, then the Heaton Research Spider moves on to the next host. Future versions of the Heaton Research Spider may add an option to mix hosts, but for now, it is one host at a time. Processing one host at a time makes it easier to work with **robots.txt** files, which are used by site owners to restrict portions of their site to spiders. You will learn more about **robots.txt** files in Chapter 16.

The workload manager uses two variables to work with multiple hosts. The **currentHost** variable tracks the String value of the current host. The **currentHostID** variable tracks the table ID of the current host.

Determining Column Sizes

The SQL workload manager scans **String** columns to determine their size. This allows URL and host names that are too long to be discarded. It is suggested that you always use a column size of 2,083 for URLs and a column size of 255 for host names. However, these are only suggestions. You can set the size of these fields to any length, and the spider will adapt.

The **GetColumnSize** function can be used to determine the column's size. The **GetColumnSize** function begins by calling the ADO **GetSchema** function. This function will return a **DataTable** that contains information about the specified table.

```
String[] restriction = { null, null, table, null };
DataTable dt = connection.GetSchema("Columns", restriction);
```

Next, the **GetColumnSize** function loops through the results and finds the specified column.

```
foreach (System.Data.DataRow row in datatable.Rows)
{
  if (String.Compare(row["COLUMN_NAME"].ToString(), column, true)
== 0)
  {
    return
      int.Parse(row["CHARACTER_MAXIMUM_LENGTH"].ToString());
  }
}
```

If the specified column is not found, or an exception thrown, negative one is returned.

Summary

The **SQLWorkloadManager** allows the Heaton Research Spider to process large workloads. To use the **SQLWorkloadManager**, you require a database with the **SPIDER_WORKLOAD** and **SPIDER_HOST** tables.

The **SQLWorkloadManager** will automatically reestablish an ADO connection if an error occurs. Using the **RepeatableStatement** class supports this. The **RepeatableStatement** class encapsulates a **DbCommand**. However, unlike a **DbCommand**, the **RepeatableStatement** class will automatically reestablish broken connections.

Not all web sites welcome spiders and bots. You should never create a spider or bot that accesses a site in such a way that damages the site. You should always respect the wishes of the web site owner. Creating well behaved bots is discussed in the next chapter.

CHAPTER 16: WELL BEHAVED BOTS

- Understanding the Ethical Use of Bots
- Understanding CAPTCHAs
- Using User-Agent Filtering
- Working with the Bot Exclusion Standard
- Implementing a robots.txt Filter

Not all sites are welcoming, or even indifferent to bots. Some sites actively take steps to curtail bot usage. These web sites often have good reason. Unethical bots can be a real nuisance to a web master. Some of the common problems:

- Posting advertising to BLOG comments
- Posting advertising to forums
- Registering fake users in forums
- Creating large number of web postings
- Spamming the referrer logs of web sites
- Harvesting email addresses from web sites

You should never create a bot that performs any of these actions. It simply bogs down the Internet with useless information and annoys people using the Internet for legitimate purposes.

Most web sites do not object to bots that simply scan for information. However, there are exceptions to this as well. Unsolicited email, or SPAM, is becoming illegal in many parts of the world. Harvesting email addresses using a spider is not something you should do. Further, it is not something this book will teach you to do. However, just gathering information from sites is generally acceptable, so long as you intend to use the information for a legal purpose.

Where you really have to be careful is when your bot posts information to a site. Posting information to web sites is where bots and web masters most often clash. It really just comes down to common sense. You could create a bot that posts a link to your site on 100s of forums. But do the forum owners really want their systems clogged with a ton of useless information?

Not every bot programmer uses bots ethically. Because of this, web sites are forced to curtail bot usage. This chapter will cover some of the ways that web sites do this. The purpose of this chapter is not to teach you to circumvent any of these mechanisms. Rather, this chapter makes you aware of them so your bots always act in a well-behaved manor. The most common methods used to curtail bot usage are:

- CAPTCHAs
- Bot Exclusion File
- User-Agent Filtering

This chapter will explore each of these methods.

Using a CAPTCHA

One of the most common methods used to thwart bot access is the CAPTCHA. You have likely seen CAPTCHAs on popular web sites. A CAPTCHA displays an image of distorted text and asks the user to enter the characters displayed. Figure 16.1 shows four CAPTCHAs from popular web sites.

Figure 16.1: Four CAPTCHAs

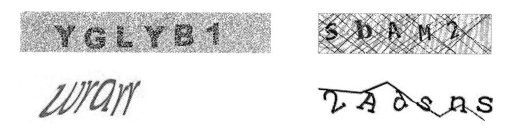

CAPTCHA is an acronym for "Completely Automated Public Turing Test to Tell Computers and Humans Apart". The term CAPTCHA is trademarked by Carnegie Mellon University. Luis von Ahn, Manuel Blum, Nicholas J. Hopper of Carnegie Mellon University and John Langford of IBM coined the term in 2000. Most CAPTCHAs require that the user type the letters of a distorted image, sometimes with the addition of an obscured sequence of letters or digits that appears on the screen.

Origin of CAPTCHAs

The first discussion of automated tests, which distinguish humans from computers for the purpose of controlling access to web services, appeared in a 1996 manuscript of Moni Naor from the Weizmann Institute of Science. Primitive CAPTCHAs seem to have been later developed in 1997 at AltaVista by Andrei Broder and his colleagues to prevent bots from adding URLs to their search engine. The team sought to make their CAPTCHA resistant to Optical Character Recognition (OCR) attack. The team looked at the manual to their Brother scanner, which included recommendations for improving OCR results.

These recommendations included similar typefaces and plain backgrounds. The team created puzzles by attempting to simulate what the manual claimed would cause bad OCR. In 2000, von Ahn and Blum developed and publicized the notion of a CAPTCHA, which included any program that can distinguish humans from computers. They invented multiple examples of CAPTCHAs, including the first CAPTCHAs to be widely used (at Yahoo!).

Accessibility Concerns

CAPTCHAs are usually based on reading text. This can present a problem for blind or visually impaired users who would like to access the protected resource. However, CAPT-CHAs do not necessarily have to be visual. Any hard artificial intelligence problem, such as speech recognition, could be used as the basis of a CAPTCHA. Some implementations of CAPTCHAs permit visually impaired users to opt for an audio CAPTCHA.

Because CAPTCHAs are designed to be unreadable by machines, common assistive technology tools such as screen readers, cannot interpret them. Since sites may use CAPTCHAs as part of the initial registration process, or even every login, this challenge can completely block access. In certain jurisdictions, site owners could become the target of litigation if they are using CAPTCHAs that discriminate against certain people with disabilities. For example, a CAPTCHA may make a site incompatible with Section 508 in the United States.

Circumvention of CAPTCHAs

There are a number of means that unethical bot writers use to defeat CAPTCHAs. This chapter will not demonstrate how to circumvent a CAPTCHA. If a web master has taken the time to insert a CAPTCHA, they surely do not want bots to access their site. I will discuss some of the methods used to circumvent a CAPTCHA so you are aware of both sides of this "battle". Some of the more common means to circumvent CAPTCHAs are:

- Optical Character Recognition (OCR)
- Cheap or unwitting human labor
- Insecure implementation

Optical Character Recognition is a computer process that converts images to ASCII text. This is often used for FAX documents. Using OCR you can capture the text image of the FAX and import it into a word processor for editing. OCR technology can also be used to circumvent a CAPTCHA. However, most modern CAPTCHAs take steps to make it very difficult for traditional OCR technology to read them.

CAPTCHAs are designed to make sure that a human is using the system. The obvious circumvention is to have a human identify hundreds of CAPTCHAs an hour in a highly automated fashion. Low-wage human workers could perform this task.

Some poorly designed CAPTCHA protection systems can be bypassed without using OCR simply by re-using the session ID of a known CAPTCHA image. Sometimes, if part of the software generating the CAPTCHA is client-side, the non-image-text can easily be lifted from the HTML page. As web sites become more sophisticated to bot spamming, client side CAPTCHAs are becoming increasingly rare.

Overall, CAPTCHAs are an effective defense against bots. Using a CAPTCHA on a site will require the spammer, or other malicious bot programmer, to go to great lengths to access the site.

User Agent Filtering

Some web server software allows you to exclude certain clients based on their **User-Agent**. If you are using the Apache web server, this is configured using the **.htaccess** file. For example, to exclude the **User-Agent**'s of **BadBot** and **AnotherBadBot**, use the following **.htaccess** file:

```
RewriteEngine On
RewriteCond %{HTTP_USER_AGENT} ^BadBot [OR]
RewriteCond %{HTTP_USER_AGENT} ^AnotherBadBot
```

If either of these bots tries to access a URL on the sever, they will receive the following error:

```
403 Access Denied
```

Simply changing the **User-agent** name of your bot can circumvent this. Of course, this is an unethical thing to do!

Using agent filtering is generally very effective against commercial spiders that do not allow their **User-agent** to be changed.

Robots Exclusion Standard

The robots exclusion standard, or **robots.txt** protocol, allows a web site to specify what portions of that site can be accessed by bots. The information specifying the parts that should not be accessed is specified in a file called **robots.txt** in the top-level directory of the website.

The **robots.txt** protocol was created by consensus in June 1994 by members of the robots mailing list (**robots-request@nexor.co.uk**). There is no official standards body or RFC for this protocol.

The robots.txt file is simply placed at the root level of a domain. It can be viewed by a web browser. For example to see the **robots.txt** file for Wikipedia, visit the following URL:

```
http://en.wikipedia.org/wiki/Robots.txt
```

The Wikipedia **robots.txt** file is fairly long. The format itself is actually quite simple. The following section will describe it.

Because the **robots.txt** file is publicly accessible, it is not an effective way to hide "private" parts of your web site. Any user with a browser can quickly examine your **robots.txt** file. To make a part of your web site truly secure you must use more advanced methods than **robots.txt**. It is generally best to list a private section in **robots.txt** and additionally, assign a password to this part of your web site.

Understanding the robots.txt Format

The two lines that you will most often see in a **robots.txt** file are **User-agent:** and **Disallow:**. The **Disallow** prefixed lines specify what URLs should not be accessed. The **User-agent** prefixed lines tell you which program the **Disallow** lines refer to.

As discussed in Chapter 13, you should create a **User-agent** name to identify your spider. This will allow a site to exclude your spider, if they so desire. By default, the Heaton Research Spider uses C#'s own **User-agent** string. Because many programs use this **User-agent** you should chose another. If a site were to exclude the C# **User-agent**, your spider would be excluded as well.

You may also see **User-agent** prefixed lines that specify a user agent of "*". This means all bots. Any instructions following a **User-agent** of "*" should be observed by all bots, including yours.

The **robots.txt Disallow** patterns are matched by simple substring comparisons, so care should be taken to make sure that patterns matching directories have the final '/' character appended, otherwise all files with names starting with that substring will match, rather than just those in the directory intended.

This following **robots.txt** file allows all robots to visit all files because the wildcard "*" specifies all robots:

```
User-agent: *
Disallow:
```

The following **robots.txt** is the opposite of the preceding one as it blocks all bot access:

```
User-agent: *
Disallow: /
```

To block four directories on your site, use the following **robots.txt** file.

```
User-agent: *
Disallow: /cgi-bin/
Disallow: /images/
Disallow: /tmp/
Disallow: /private/
```

If you would like to exclude a specific bot, named **BadBot**, from your **/private/** directory, use the following **robots.txt** file.

```
User-agent: BadBot
Disallow: /private/
```

The pound "#" character can be used to insert comments, such as:

```
# This is a comment
User-agent: * # match all bots
Disallow: / # keep them out
```

The wildcard character can only be used with the **User-Agent** directive. The following line would be invalid:

```
Disallow: *
```

Rather, to disallow everything, simply disallow your document root, as follows:

```
Disallow: /
```

In the next section we will see how to use a filter with the Heaton Research Spider to follow the **robots.txt** files posted on sites.

Using Filters with the Heaton Research Spider

The Heaton Research Spider allows you to provide one or more filter classes. These filter classes instruct the spider to skip certain URLs. You can specify a filter class as part of the spider configuration file. The spider comes with one built-in filter, named **RobotsFilter**. This filter scans a **robots.txt** file and instructs the spider to skip URLs that were marked as Disallowed in the robots.txt file.

Listing 16.1 shows a spider configuration file that specifies the **RobotsFilter**.

Listing 16.1: Spider Configuration (Spider.conf)

```
timeout:          60000
maxDepth:         -1
userAgent:
corePoolSize:     100
maximumPoolSize:100
keepAliveTime:    60
dbURL:  Driver={Microsoft Access Driver (*.mdb)};DBQ=c:\spider.
mdb;DriverID=22;READONLY=false}
dbClass:          System.Data.Odbc
workloadManager:HeatonResearch.Spider.Workload.SQL.SQLWorkloadMa-
nager
startup:          clear
filter:                 HeatonResearch.Spider.Filter.RobotsFilter
```

As you can see from the above listing, the **filter** line specifies the filter. If you would like to use more than one filter, simply specify more than one **filter** line.

You should always make use of the **RobotsFilter**. If a web master specifies to skip parts of their site, or the entire site, through the **robots.txt** file, you should honor this request. Including the **RobotsFilter** honors this file automatically.

The Filter Interface

To create a filter class for the Heaton Research spider, that class must implement the **SpiderFilter** interface. This interface defines the two necessary functions that must be implemented to create a filter.

The **SpiderFilter** interface is shown in Listing 16.2.

Listing 16.2: The SpiderFilter Interface (SpiderFilter.cs)

```
using System;
using System.Collections.Generic;
using System.Text;
using System.Net;
```

```
namespace HeatonResearch.Spider.Filter
{
    /// <summary>
    /// SpiderFilter: Filters will cause the spider to skip
    /// URL's.
    /// </summary>
    public interface SpiderFilter
    {
        /// <summary>
        /// Check to see if the specified URL is to be excluded.
        /// </summary>
        /// <param name="url">The URL to be checked.</param>
        /// <returns>Returns true if the URL should be
        /// excluded.</returns>
        bool IsExcluded(Uri url);

        /// <summary>
        /// Called when a new host is to be processed.
        /// SpiderFilter classes can not be shared among hosts.
        /// </summary>
        /// <param name="host">The new host.</param>
        /// <param name="userAgent">The user agent being used
        /// by the spider. Leave
        /// null for default.</param>
        void NewHost(String host, String userAgent);
    }
}
```

The first required function is named **IsExcluded**. The **IsExcluded** function will be called for each URL that the spider finds, for the current host. If the URL is to be excluded, then a value of **true** will be returned.

The second required method is named **NewHost**. The **NewHost** method is called whenever the spider is processing a new host. As you will recall from Chapter 14, the spider processes one host at a time. As a result, **NewHost** will be called when a new host is being processed. It will also be called when the first host is being processed. After **NewHost** is called, **IsExcluded** will be called for each URL found at that host. Hosts will not be overlapped, once **NewHost** is called, you will not receive URLs from the previous host.

Implementing a robots.txt Filter

The **RobotsFilter** class, provided by the Heaton Research Spider, implements the **SpiderFilter** interface. This section will show the **RobotsFilter** filter was implemented. The **RobotsFilter** class is shown in Listing 16.3.

Listing 16.3: A robots.txt Filter (RobotsFilter.cs)

```csharp
using System;
using System.Collections.Generic;
using System.Text;
using System.Net;
using System.IO;

namespace HeatonResearch.Spider.Filter
{
    /// <summary>
    /// This filter causes the spider so skip URL's from a
    /// robots.txt file.
    /// </summary>
    class RobotsFilter : SpiderFilter
    {
        /// <summary>
        /// Returns a list of URL's to be excluded.
        /// </summary>
        public List<String> Exclude
        {
            get
            {
                return exclude;
            }
        }

        /// <summary>
        /// The full URL of the robots.txt file.
        /// </summary>
        public Uri RobotURL
        {
            get
            {
                return robotURL;
            }
        }

        /// <summary>
        /// The full URL of the robots.txt file.
        /// </summary>
        private Uri robotURL;

        /// <summary>
        /// A list of full URL's to exclude.
        /// </summary>
        private List<String> exclude = new List<String>();
```

```csharp
/// <summary>
/// Is the parser active? It can become inactive when
/// parsing sections of the file for other user agents.
/// </summary>
private bool active;

/// <summary>
/// The user agent string we are to use. null for default.
/// </summary>
private String userAgent;


/// <summary>
/// Check to see if the specified URL is to be excluded.
/// </summary>
/// <param name="url">The URL to be checked.</param>
/// <returns>Returns true if the URL should be
/// excluded.</returns>
public bool IsExcluded(Uri url)
{
    foreach (String str in this.exclude)
    {
        if (url.PathAndQuery.StartsWith(str))
        {
            return true;
        }
    }
    return false;
}


/// <summary>
/// Called when a new host is to be processed.
/// SpiderFilter
/// classes can not be shared among hosts.
/// </summary>
/// <param name="host">The new host.</param>
/// <param name="userAgent">The user agent being used
/// by the spider. Leave null for default.</param>
public void NewHost(String host, String userAgent)
{
    try
    {
        String str;
        this.active = false;
        this.userAgent = userAgent;
```

```
        StringBuilder robotStr = new StringBuilder();
        robotStr.Append("http://");
        robotStr.Append(host);
        robotStr.Append("/robots.txt");
        this.robotURL = new Uri(robotStr.ToString());

        WebRequest http = HttpWebRequest.Create(
          this.robotURL);

        if (userAgent != null)
        {
            http.Headers.Set("User-Agent", userAgent);
        }

        HttpWebResponse response =
          (HttpWebResponse)http.GetResponse();
        StreamReader reader = new StreamReader(
response.GetResponseStream(), System.Text.Encoding.ASCII);

        exclude.Clear();

        try
        {
            while ((str = reader.ReadLine()) != null)
            {

                LoadLine(str);
            }
        }
        finally
        {
            reader.Close();
        }
    }
    catch (Exception)
    {
        // Site does not have a robots.txt file
        // this is common.
    }
}

/// <summary>
/// Add the specified string to the exclude list.
/// </summary>
/// <param name="str">This string to add.  This is
```

```csharp
/// the path part of a URL.</param>
private void Add(String str)
{
    if (!this.exclude.Contains(str))
    {
        this.exclude.Add(str);
    }
}

/// <summary>
/// Called internally to process each line of the
/// robots.txt file.
/// </summary>
/// <param name="str">The line that was read in.</param>
private void LoadLine(String str)
{
    str = str.Trim();
    int i = str.IndexOf(':');

    if ((str.Length == 0) || (str[0] == '#') || (i == -1))
    {
        return;
    }

    String command = str.Substring(0, i);
    String rest = str.Substring(i + 1).Trim();
    if (String.Compare(command, "User-agent", true) == 0)
    {
        this.active = false;
        if (rest.Equals("*"))
        {
            this.active = true;
        }
        else
        {
            if ((this.userAgent != null) &&
          String.Compare(rest, this.userAgent, true) == 0)
            {
                this.active = true;
            }
        }
    }
    if (this.active)
    {
        if (String.Compare(command, "disallow", true) ==
0)
```

```
        {
            if (rest.Trim().Length > 0)
            {
                Uri url = new Uri(this.robotURL, rest);
                Add(url.PathAndQuery);
            }
        }
      }
    }
  }
}
```

The **RobotsFilter** class defines four instance variables, which are listed here:

- robotURL
- exclude
- active
- userAgent

The **robotURL** variable holds the URL to the **robots.txt** file that was most recently received. Each time the **NewHost** method is called, a new **robotURL** variable is constructed by concatenating the string "robots.txt" to the host name.

The **Exclude** variable contains a list of the URLs to be excluded. This list is built each time a new host is encountered. The **Exclude** list must be cleared for each new host.

The **active** variable tracks whether the loading process is actively tracking Disallow lines. The loader becomes active when a **User-agent** line matches the user agent string being used by the spider.

The **userAgent** variable holds the user agent string that the spider is using. This variable is passed into the **newHost** method.

There are also several methods and functions that make up the **RobotsFilter**. These will be discussed in the next sections.

Processing a New Host

When a new host is about to be processed, the spider calls the **NewHost** method of any filters that are in use. When the **NewHost** method is called for the **RobotsFilter** class, the host is scanned for a **robots.txt** file. If one is found it is processed.

The first action that the **NewHost** method performs is to declare a **String**, which will be used to hold lines read from the **robots.txt** file, and to set the **active** variable to **false**.

```
String str;
```

```
this.active = false;
this.userAgent = userAgent;
```

Next, a connection is opened to the **robots.txt** file. The **robots.txt** file is always located at the root of the host.

```
StringBuilder robotStr = new StringBuilder();
robotStr.Append("http://");
robotStr.Append(host);
robotStr.Append("/robots.txt");
this.robotURL = new Uri(robotStr.ToString());

WebRequest http = HttpWebRequest.Create(this.robotURL);
```

If a user agent was specified, using the **userAgent** variable, then the user agent is set for the connection. If the **userAgent** variable is **null**, then the default C# user agent will be used.

```
if (userAgent != null)
{
  http.Headers.Set("User-Agent", userAgent);
}
```

Next a **StreamReader** is setup to read the **robots.txt** file on a line-by-line basis.

```
HttpWebResponse response = (HttpWebResponse)http.GetResponse();
          StreamReader reader = new StreamReader(response.GetRe-
sponseStream(), System.Text.Encoding.ASCII);
```

We are now about to begin parsing the file, so it is important to clear any previous list of excluded URLs.

```
Exclude.Clear();
```

A **while** loop is used to read each line from the **robots.txt** file. Each line read is passed onto the **LoadLine** method. The **LoadLine** method actually interprets the command given for each line of the **robots.txt** file.

```
try
{
  while ((str = reader.ReadLine()) != null)
  {
    LoadLine(str);
  }
}
```

Once complete, the streams are closed. The **Close** commands are placed inside a **finally** block to ensure that they are executed, even if an exception is thrown while reading from the **robots.txt** file.

```
finally
{
  reader.Close();
}
```

Each line read by the **NewHost** method is passed onto the **LoadLine** method. This method will be discussed in the next section.

Loading a Line from the robots.txt File

The **LoadLine** method interprets each of the lines contained in the robots.txt file. The **LoadLine** method begins by trimming the line passed in and searching for the first occurrence of a colon (:). As you will recall from earlier in the chapter, lines in the robots.txt file consist of a command and value separated by a colon.

```
str = str.Trim();
int i = str.IndexOf(':');
```

If the colon is not found, the line starts with a pound sign (#), or the line is empty, then the method returns. As you will recall from earlier in the chapter, a pound sign signifies a comment line.

```
if ((str.Length == 0) || (str[0] == '#') || (i == -1))
{
  return;
}
```

Next, the line is parsed into a command, and another variable named rest. The rest variable contains whatever text occurred to the right of the colon.

```
String command = str.Substring(0, i);
String rest = str.Substring(i + 1).Trim();
```

First we check to see if this is a **User-agent** command.

```
if (String.Compare(command, "User-agent", true) == 0)
{
  this.active = false;
}
```

If an asterisk (*) is specified as the user agent, the program becomes "active" immediately, since this applies to all bots. Being "active" implies that the program will begin tracking **Disallow** commands.

```
  if (rest.Equals("*"))
  {
    this.active = true;
  }
```

If an asterisk was not specified, the user agent command must match the user agent for the spider. If they do match, the program begins actively checking for **Disallow** commands.

```
else
{
  if ((this.userAgent != null) && String.Compare(rest, this.
userAgent, true) == 0)
  {
    this.active = true;
  }
}
```

If we are currently active, then we need to check for additional commands.

```
if (this.active)
{
```

Next, check to see if this is a **Disallow** command. If it is a **Disallow** command, then we create a new URL from the information provided.

```
  if (String.Compare(command, "disallow", true) == 0)
  {
    if (rest.Trim().Length > 0)
    {
      Uri url = new Uri(this.robotURL, rest);
      Add(url.PathAndQuery);
    }
  }
}
```

At this point the line is now parsed, and we are ready for the next line.

Determining if a URL is to be Excluded

To determine if a URL should be excluded, the **IsExcluded** function is called. If the URL should be excluded, this method will return a value of **false**. This method begins by looping through all URLs in the **exclude** list. If the specified URL matches one, a value of **true** is returned.

```
foreach (String str in this.exclude)
{
  if (url.PathAndQuery.StartsWith(str))
  {
    return true;
  }
}
```

Return a value of **false** if the URL was not found.

```
return false;
```

The spider, prior to adding any URL to the workload, will call this method.

Summary

Not all sites welcome bots. This is particularly true of bots that post information to web sites. You should never create a bot that accesses web sites unethically. If a web site does not wish to be accessed with a bot, you should respect that site's wishes. Web sites use a number of means to prevent bots from accessing their site.

CAPTCHAs are a very common method for preventing bot access. CAPTCHA is an acronym for "Completely Automated Public Turing Test to Tell Computers and Humans Apart". A CAPTCHA displays an image and makes the user enter the text in the image. Because a bot cannot easily read the image, the bot is unable to continue.

User agent filtering is another common method for denying access to bots. Most web servers allow the web master to enter a list of user agents, which identify bots that they wish to block. If any bot that is on the blocked list attempts to access the site, they will receive an HTTP error.

The Bot Exclusion Standard is another method that is commonly used to restrict bots. Web site owners can place a file, named `robots.txt`, in the root of their web server. The bots will access this file for information about what parts of the web site to stay away from.

You now know how to create a variety of bots that can access web sites in many different ways. This chapter ends the book by showing you how to use bots ethically. How you use bots is ultimately up to you. It is our hope that you use bots to make the Internet a better place for all!

Remember, with great power, comes great responsibility.

– Uncle Ben, Spider Man 2002

APPENDIX A: DOWNLOADING EXAMPLES

This book contains many source code examples. You do not need to retype any of these examples; they all can be downloaded from the Internet.

Simply go to the site:

```
http://www.heatonresearch.com/download/
```

This site will give you more information on how to download the example programs.

APPENDIX B: SETTING UP EXAMPLES

- From a Command Prompt
- From Visual Studio
- Compiling without Visual Studio

The examples in this book require the .Net Framework 2.0, as included with Visual Studio 2005. These examples will not compile with versions of Visual Studio prior to 2005. It is likely that these examples will work just fine with later releases of Visual Studio 2005.

All of the examples were tested with Windows XP, Windows Vista and Windows 2000. The examples should work just fine on any computer system that is capable of running Visual Studio 2005.

Some of the examples make use of a database. A sample Microsoft Access MDB database is provided. You are not required to have a copy of Microsoft Access to use this MDB file. The examples will work just fine without Microsoft Access installed. Appendix D shows how to use the examples with several popular databases.

When you download the examples, as covered in Appendix A, you will be given a file named `CSharpHTTPRecipes.zip`. This file's contents are shown in Figure B.1.

Figure B.1: The Examples Archive

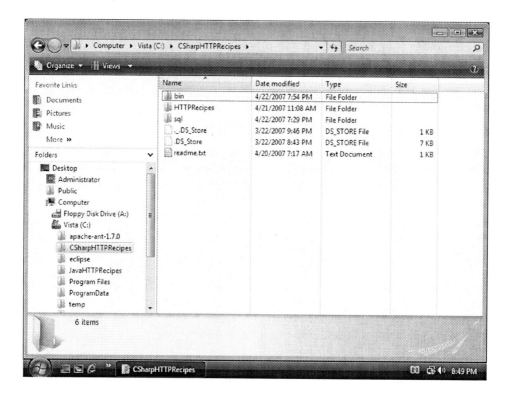

The examples can be ran by several methods. The examples can be ran from a command prompt. The examples can also be ran from an IDE, usually Visual Studio 2005. The next section will cover running the examples from a command prompt.

Running from a Command Prompt

As you saw from Figure B.1 there is a **bin** directory included with the example download. This **bin** directory contains compiled **EXE** files for all of the recipes in this book. To run a example from a command prompt, first open a command prompt. Next move to the bin directory of the HTTP recipes download. If you installed the examples to c:\ the following command would move you to the correct directory.

```
C:
cd \CSharpHTTPRecipes\bin
```

Once you are in the correct directory you can run any of the recipes by simply typing the name of the recipes. For example, to run Recipe 3.3 execute the following command.

```
Recipe3_3
```

Once you run Recipe 3.3 you will see Figure B.2.

Figure B.2: Running an Example from the Command Prompt

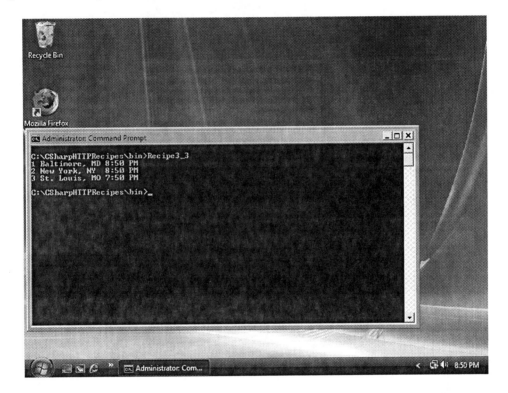

Of course some of the recipes will require command line arguments. If the recipe requires command line arguments, they should entered after the command. Perhaps the easiest way to run the examples is from Visual Studio. This is covered in the next section.

Running from Visual Studio

To run the examples from Visual Studio launch Visual Studio and open the file `HTTPRecipes.sln`. This file is located in the `HTTPRecipes` directory of the download. Figure B.3 shows this file opened in Visual Studio.

Figure B.3: The Recipes in Visual Studio

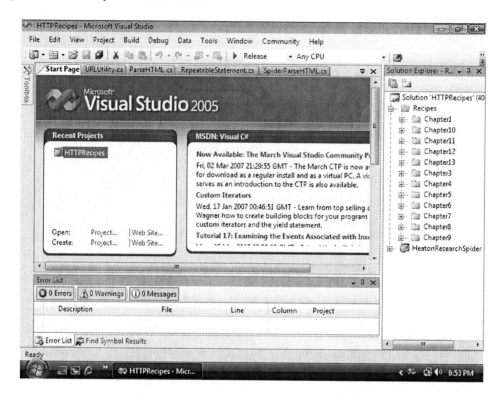

You can now run and debug the recipes just like you would any Visual Studio project. Of course some off the recipes will require command line arguments. These can be specified under the project properties.

Compiling without Visual Studio

There are ways beyond visual Studio 2005 to compile and run the examples in this book. One project is called Mono. Mono is an open source implementation of .NET. As of the writing of this book Mono does not fully support .NET 2.0. Many of the examples require .NET 2.0. Because of this Mono is not currently an option for this book. If later releases of Mono support .NET 2.0, the examples may work.

Of course no IDE is required to execute the examples from the command prompt. Visual Studio is only needed when you would like to compile the examples.

Another possibility is to use a free third party IDE. Once such IDE is SharpDevelop. SharpDevelop can be downloaded from the following URL:

```
http://www.icsharpcode.net/OpenSource/SD/
```

APPENDIX C: USEFUL CLASSES, METHODS AND FUNCTIONS

The recipes in this book present many useful classes, methods and functions. This appendix summarizes them. This appendix also presents a list of all of the book's recipes.

Reusable Functions and Methods

The following functions and methods were used as parts of recipes. These functions and methods would be useful in other classes and programs. Table C.1 summarizes them.

Table C.1: Reusable Functions and Methods

Method/Function	Introduced in Recipe	Purpose
DownloadPage	Recipe 3.1	Download a URL into a string.
Extract	Recipe 3.2	Extract a string from a page bounded by two substrings.
SaveBinaryPage	Recipe 3.4	Save a downloaded page as binary.
DownloadText	Recipe 3.5	Download a page as text.
ExtractNoCase	Recipe 4.2	Extract a string from a page bounded by two case-insensitive substrings.
DownloadText	Recipe 4.3	Download a text page and covert line endings to match the Operating System.
DownloadBinary	Recipe 4.3	Download a binary page.
Advance	Recipe 6.1	Advance the HTML parser to a specified tag.
GetXMLNode	Recipe 10.2	Extract an XML node.
GetXMLAttribute	Recipe 10.2	Extract an XML attribute.

Reusable Classes

Some examples in this book were large enough for their own class or package. Table C.2 summarizes them.

Table C.2: Reusable Classes

Package/Class	Purpose
HeatonResearch.Spider.HTML.FormUtility	Form handling utilities.
HeatonResearch.Spider.HTML.ParseHTML	An HTML parser.
HeatonResearch.Spider.HTML.URLUtility	Many useful URL utilities.
HeatonResearch.Spider.RSS.RSS	Parse RSS feeds.
HeatonResearch.Spider.Spider	The Heaton Research Spider.

These classes are all contained in the reusable DLL named **HeatonResearchSpider.dll**. These classes are part of the open source Heaton Research Spider project.

All Recipes

The following is a listing of all of the recipes in this book.

- Recipe #1.1: A Simple Web Server
- Recipe #1.2: File Based Web Server
- Recipe #2.1: Examining Cookies
- Recipe #2.2: Examining Forms
- Recipe #3.1: Downloading the Contents of a Web Page
- Recipe #3.2: Extract Simple Information from a Web Page
- Recipe #3.3: Parsing Dates and Times
- Recipe #3.4: Downloading a Binary File
- Recipe #3.5: Downloading a Text File
- Recipe #4.1: Scan URL
- Recipe #4.2: Scan for Sites
- Recipe #4.3: Download Binary or Text
- Recipe #4.4: Site Monitor
- Recipe #5.1: Is a URL HTTPS?
- Recipe #5.2: HTTP Authentication
- Recipe #6.1: Extracting Data from a Choice List
- Recipe #6.2: Extracting Data from an HTML List
- Recipe #6.3: Extracting Data from a Table
- Recipe #6.4: Extracting Data from Hyperlinks
- Recipe #6.5: Extracting Images from HTML
- Recipe #6.6: Extracting from Sub-Pages
- Recipe #6.7: Extracting from Partial-Pages
- Recipe #7.1: Using HTTP GET Forms
- Recipe #7.2: Using HTTP POST Forms
- Recipe #7.3: Using Multipart Forms to Upload
- Recipe #8.1: A Cookieless Session

- Recipe #8.2: A Cookie Based Session
- Recipe #9.1: Automatic Choice Lists
- Recipe #9.2: JavaScript Includes
- Recipe #9.3: JavaScript Forms
- Recipe #10.1: A Non-XML Based AJAX Site
- Recipe #10.2: An XML Based AJAX Site
- Recipe #11.1: Scanning for Google Links
- Recipe #11.2: Access a SOAP Server
- Recipe #11.3: A Google Hybrid Bot
- Recipe #12.1: Display an RSS Feed
- Recipe #12.2: Find an RSS Feed
- Recipe #13.1: Find Broken Links
- Recipe #13.2: Downloading HTML and Images
- Recipe #13.3: Spider the World
- Recipe #13.4: Display Spider Statistics

APPENDIX D: SETTING UP YOUR DATABASE

If you are going to use the **SQLWorkloadManager** for the Heaton Research Spider, you will need to create a proper database. Specifically, this database should have the **SPIDER_WORKLOAD** and **SPIDER_HOST** tables. This chapter shows how to create this database on a variety of database servers.

Data Definition Language (DDL) scripts contain the commands necessary to create the tables needed by the spider. DDL varies greatly from database vendor to database vendor. DDL scripts are provided in this chapter for three of the major database vendors. If you wish to use the spider on a database not listed here, you will have to develop your own DDL script based on the tables needed by the spider. Usually, you can just modify one of the scripts here as a starting point.

All of the DDL and configuration files presented in this chapter are contained on the companion download for this book.

DDL for MySQL

MySQL is a free database that you can obtain from the following URL:

`http://www.mysql.com`

To setup a database in MySQL, use the following DDL script in Listing D.1.

Listing D.1: MySQL DDL Script

```
SET NAMES latin1;
SET FOREIGN_KEY_CHECKS = 0;

CREATE TABLE `spider_workload` (
  `workload_id` int(10) unsigned NOT NULL auto_increment,
  `host` int(10) unsigned NOT NULL,
  `url` varchar(2083) NOT NULL default '',
  `status` varchar(1) NOT NULL default '',
  `depth` int(10) unsigned NOT NULL,
  `url_hash` int(11) NOT NULL,
  `source_id` int(11) NOT NULL,
  PRIMARY KEY  (`workload_id`),
  KEY `status` (`status`),
  KEY `url_hash` (`url_hash`),
```

```
    KEY `host` (`host`)
) ENGINE=MyISAM AUTO_INCREMENT=189 DEFAULT CHARSET=latin1;

CREATE TABLE `spider_host` (
  `host_id` int(10) unsigned NOT NULL auto_increment,
  `host` varchar(255) NOT NULL default '',
  `status` varchar(1) NOT NULL default '',
  `urls_done` int(11) NOT NULL,
  `urls_error` int(11) NOT NULL,
  PRIMARY KEY  (`host_id`)
) ENGINE=MyISAM AUTO_INCREMENT=19796 DEFAULT CHARSET=latin1;


SET FOREIGN_KEY_CHECKS = 1;
```

DDL for Microsoft Access

Microsoft Access is a commercial database provided by Microsoft. To use Microsoft Access you can either use the DDL script shown in Listing D.2, or use the **spider.mdb** database that was provided with the companion download.

Listing D.2: Microsoft Access DDL Script

```
CREATE TABLE [spider_host] (
  [host_id] counter  NOT NULL,
  [host] varchar(255) NOT NULL,
  [status] varchar(1) NOT NULL,
  [urls_done] int NOT NULL,
  [urls_error] int NOT NULL,
  PRIMARY KEY  ([host_id]),
  CONSTRAINT  `host` UNIQUE  (`host`)
);

CREATE TABLE [spider_workload] (
  [workload_id] counter NOT NULL,
  [host] integer  NOT NULL,
  [url] varchar(255) NOT NULL,
  [status] varchar(1) NOT NULL,
  [depth] integer NOT NULL,
  [url_hash] integer NOT NULL,
  [source_id] integer NOT NULL,
  PRIMARY KEY  ([workload_id])
);
```

```
create index idx_status on spider_workload (status);
create index idx_url_hash on spider_workload (url_hash);
```

DDL for Oracle

Oracle is a commercial database product. Many companies use oracle. For more information about Oracle you should visit the following URL:

http://www.oracle.com

Oracle also makes a free version of their database, named Oracle Express. This free version allows developers to try the Oracle database, without having to purchase an expensive license. For more information about Oracle Express, visit the following URL:

http://www.oracle.com/technology/products/database/xe/index.html

The DDL script to create the tables on Oracle is shown in Listing D.3.

Listing D.3: Oracle DDL Script

```
-- Create SPIDER_WORKLOAD

CREATE TABLE SPIDER_WORKLOAD
(
  WORKLOAD_ID   INTEGER                         NOT NULL,
  HOST          INTEGER                         NOT NULL,
  URL           VARCHAR2(2083 BYTE)             NOT NULL,
  STATUS        VARCHAR2(1 BYTE)                NOT NULL,
  DEPTH         INTEGER                         NOT NULL,
  URL_HASH      INTEGER                         NOT NULL,
  SOURCE_ID     INTEGER                         NOT NULL
)
LOGGING
NOCOMPRESS
NOCACHE
NOPARALLEL
MONITORING;


CREATE INDEX IDX_STATUS ON SPIDER_WORKLOAD
(STATUS)
LOGGING
NOPARALLEL;
```

```
CREATE INDEX IDX_URL_HASH ON SPIDER_WORKLOAD
(URL_HASH)
LOGGING
NOPARALLEL;


CREATE UNIQUE INDEX PK_WORKLOAD_ID ON SPIDER_WORKLOAD
(WORKLOAD_ID)
LOGGING
NOPARALLEL;


ALTER TABLE SPIDER_WORKLOAD ADD (
  CONSTRAINT PK_WORKLOAD_ID
 PRIMARY KEY
 (WORKLOAD_ID));

-- Create SPIDER_HOST

CREATE TABLE SPIDER_HOST
(
  HOST_ID    INTEGER                     NOT NULL,
  HOST       VARCHAR2(255)               NOT NULL,
  STATUS     VARCHAR2(1 BYTE)            NOT NULL,
  URLS_DONE  INTEGER                     NOT NULL,
  URLS_ERROR INTEGER                     NOT NULL
)
LOGGING
NOCOMPRESS
NOCACHE
NOPARALLEL
MONITORING;


CREATE UNIQUE INDEX PK_HOST_ID ON SPIDER_HOST
(HOST_ID)
LOGGING
NOPARALLEL;


ALTER TABLE SPIDER_HOST ADD (
  CONSTRAINT PK_HOST_ID
 PRIMARY KEY
 (HOST_ID));

-- Create Sequences
```

```
CREATE SEQUENCE spider_workload_seq;
CREATE SEQUENCE spider_host_seq;
```

OLEDB for .NET

There are several different database API's that can be used for database access under .NET. This book uses OLEDB under ADO. It would be relatively easy to adapt to using other ADO wrapped technologies such as ODBC. To access a database you must provide a OLEDB connection string. For example, Listing D.4 shows a **spider.conf** file that uses an OLEDB connection string to access a Microsoft Access Database.

Listing D.4: A Spider.CONF File for OLEDB

```
timeout:    60000
maxDepth:   -1
userAgent:
dbConnectionString: Provider=Microsoft.Jet.OLEDB.4.0;Data
Source=c:\spider.mdb
workloadManager:HeatonResearch.Spider.Workload.SQL.SQLWorkloadMa-
nager
startup:    clear
filter:           HeatonResearch.Spider.Filter.RobotsFilter
```

The line that is specific to OLEDB is the **dbConnectionString**. The following line specifies to use a Microsoft Access Database through OLEDB.

```
Provider=Microsoft.Jet.OLEDB.4.0;Data Source=c:\spider.mdb
```

Other databases can be used. Simply insert the correct connection string for the **dbConnectionString** attribute. Correct, and up to date, connection string information can be found with the documentation for the database you are using.

APPENDIX E: HTTP RESPONSE CODES

There are many different HTTP responses. This appendix lists them. This data was taken from WikiPedia (`http://www.wikipedia.org`).

1xx Informational

Request received, continuing process.

- 100: Continue
- 101: Switching Protocols

2xx Success

The action was successfully received, understood, and accepted.

- 200: OK
- 201: Created
- 202: Accepted
- 203: Non-Authoritative Information
- 204: No Content
- 205: Reset Content
- 206: Partial Content
- 207: Multi-Status

For use with XML-based responses when a number of actions could have been requested; details of the separate statuses are given in the message body.

3xx Redirection

The client must take additional action to complete the request.

- 300: Multiple Choices
- 301: Moved Permanently

This and all future requests should be directed to another URL.

- 302: Found

This is the most popular redirect code, but also an example of industrial practice contradicting the standard. HTTP/1.0 specification (RFC 1945) required the client to perform temporary redirect (the original describing phrase was "Moved Temporarily"), but popular browsers implemented it as a 303 See Other. Therefore, HTTP/1.1 added status codes 303 and 307 to disambiguate between the two behaviors. However, majority of Web applications and frameworks still use the 302 status code as if it were the 303.

- 303: See Other (since HTTP/1.1)

The response to the request can be found under another URL using a GET method.

- 304: Not Modified
- 305: Use Proxy (since HTTP/1.1)

Many HTTP clients (such as Mozilla and Internet Explorer) don't correctly handle responses with this status code.

- 306 is no longer used, but reserved. Was used for 'Switch Proxy'.
- 307: Temporary Redirect (since HTTP/1.1)

In this occasion, the request should be repeated with another URL, but future requests can still be directed to the original URL. In contrast to 303, the original POST request must be repeated with another POST request.

4xx Client Error

The request contains bad syntax or cannot be fulfilled.

- 400: Bad Request
- 401: Unauthorized

Similar to 403/Forbidden, but specifically for use when authentication is possible but has failed or not yet been provided. See basic authentication scheme and digest access authentication.

- 402: Payment Required

The original intention was that this code might be used as part of some form of digital cash/micropayment scheme, but that has never eventuated, and thus this code has never been used.

- 403: Forbidden
- 404: Not Found
- 405: Method Not Allowed
- 406: Not Acceptable
- 407: Proxy Authentication Required
- 408: Request Timeout
- 409: Conflict
- 410: Gone
- 411: Length Required
- 412: Precondition Failed
- 413: Request Entity Too Large
- 414: Request-URL Too Long
- 415: Unsupported Media Type
- 416: Requested Range Not Satisfiable
- 417: Expectation Failed
- 449: Retry With

A Microsoft extension: The request should be retried after doing the appropriate action.

5xx Server Error

The server failed to fulfill an apparently valid request.

- 500: Internal Server Error
- 501: Not Implemented
- 502: Bad Gateway

- 503: Service Unavailable
- 504: Gateway Timeout
- 505: HTTP Version Not Supported
- 509: Bandwidth Limit Exceeded

This status code, while used by many servers, is not an official HTTP status code.

INDEX

A

Address 93-4, 139, 142, 155, 314, 345, 366, 381
AddressFamily.InterNetwork 53, 55, 59
AddSlash 64, 67-8
AddURL 473, 489, 491-4, 512
Advance 207-8, 210, 213-5, 217, 219, 222, 269, 271, 273-4, 276, 290, 292, 297, 299, 302
AdvanceBy 184-5, 197-9
AJAX 74, 305, 309, 317, 336, 339-42, 345-6, 353, 362
  requests 340, 348
AJAX Sites 317, 339-41, 343, 345-7, 349-51, 353-9, 361-3, 365
Alt 40, 45, 105, 111, 231, 313
Amortization schedule 315, 331, 333-5
Ampersand 43, 97, 197-8, 200, 257, 267
Anchor tags 41, 493-4
Apache web server 566
ASCII character codes 191, 197-8
Attribute name 187, 196-7, 203
AttributeName 190, 196
Authentication 98, 128, 153, 158, 160-1, 163, 166-8
Automatic choice lists 309-10, 318-9, 322, 324, 335

B

Binary file 116-8, 120, 124, 131, 143, 145-8, 150, 165, 167
Birth year 382-3, 385-92
Blank
  homepage 75
  line 49, 50, 56, 268
Blocks 95, 120, 314, 388, 463, 471, 486, 530, 568, 576, 579
BODY 40, 45-6, 105, 111, 313-4

Bots
  building 362
  complex 73
  sites welcome 579
  unethical 563
Boundary 260-8, 280-1
  variable 266-7
Br 40, 46, 105, 111, 195, 205, 255, 314, 341, 350
Broken Links Spider 429, 431
Browser 38-9, 41, 48-9, 56-7, 74-8, 86-7, 93, 128-9, 153-5, 256, 287-8, 307-9, 311-2, 342, 395-6
  requests 38
  type 128-9
Browser URL line 258
Built-in web server 71
Button 79, 251, 253-4, 295, 309, 316, 329
  calculate 315-6
  radio 255-6

C

Cache 74, 77, 366, 530-1
CAPTCHAs 564-6, 579
Capture 74, 77, 214, 216, 219-20, 222-3, 253, 271, 273-4, 276-7, 293, 297-8, 302, 332, 334-5
  button 77
Certificate 155-6
Character encoding 197-8
Characters 57, 97-8, 116, 172, 182-3, 185, 191-4, 196-200, 210, 216, 223, 390-1, 482, 488-9, 568
CheckLinks class 429-30
Child elements 406, 410
Choice list 205-6, 209, 211, 309-10, 319, 322
Classes, filter 421, 569

OTHER BOOKS FROM HEATON RESEARCH

Introduction to Neural Networks with Java
by Jeff Heaton
ISBN:0-9773206-0-X

Introduction to Neural Networks with Java teaches the reader to solve a variety of problems using neural networks. The reader is introduced to the open source JOONE neural engine, as well as a simple Optical Character Recognition (OCR) program, the traveling salesman problem and the feedfoward backpropagation neural network.

Build a Computer from Scratch
by Jeff Heaton
ISBN: 0-9773206-2-6

Building a computer is not as hard as you might think. This book shows how to select the best parts and build your very own computer. Knowing how to build your computer saves money and gets you the computer you really want. A computer you build yourself is one that YOU can always upgrade and repair.

Java for the Beginning Programmer
by Jeff Heaton
ISBN: 0-9773206-1-8

If you would like to learn to program in Java but have never attempted programming before, this book takes it from the beginning. This book focuses on the fundamentals of Java programming, such as loops, functions, classes and methods. Emphasis is placed on learning core programming techniques and rather than using an IDE to generate code for you.

To purchase any of these books visit:

http://www.heatonresearch.com/book/

VISIT HTTP://WWW.HEATONRESEARCH.COM

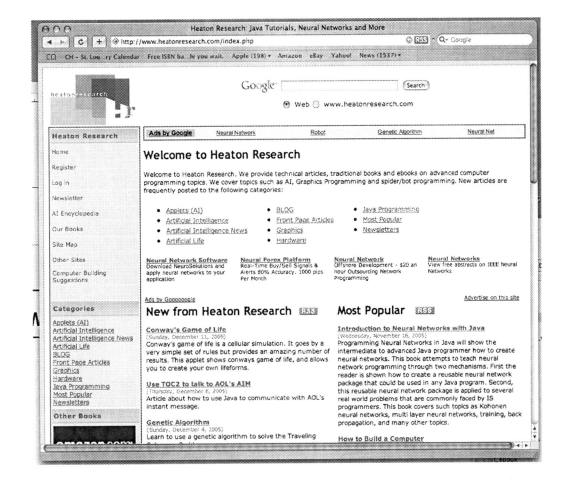

Visit www.HeatonResearch.com for our latest articles and books.

To download the source code to this book visit:

http://www.heatonresearch.com/book/

Printed in the United States
107282LV00005BA/3-4/A